John Chipman Gray

John Chipman Gray

The Harvard Brahmin of Property Law

Gerald Paul Moran
Professor of Law
Florida Coastal School of Law

Carolina Academic Press
Durham, North Carolina

Library of Congress Cataloging-in-Publication Data

Moran, Gerald Paul.
John Chipman Gray : the Harvard Brahmin of property law / Gerald Paul Moran.
p. cm.
Includes bibliographical references and index.
ISBN 978-1-59460-398-3 (alk. paper)
1. Gray, John Chipman, 1839-1915--Biography. 2. Lawyers--Massachusetts--Biography. I. Title.

KF368.G73M67 2010
340.092--dc22
[B]

2010007568

CAROLINA ACADEMIC PRESS
700 Kent Street
Durham, North Carolina 27701
Telephone (919) 489-7486
Fax (919) 493-5668
www.cap-press.com

Printed in the United States of America

For Judith K. Moran

I was fortunate to have a muse who sparked the light in my early years in high school. She was also my high school girlfriend and who, to my delight, became some forty-six years later my wife. It is to her that I dedicate this book with special love and everlasting appreciation.

Contents

Illustrations

Preface

This project started when I was involved with the discussion of whether Ohio should enact a statutory modification to the Rule Against Perpetuities (RAP) for the purpose of allowing the establishment of private trusts to be exempt from the limitations imposed by this ancient rule of law. Recognizing that a number of other states had taken the action for commercial reasons, I was interested in the current function of the rule. Intuitively, it did not appear that there was a current reason for the continuance of the RAP. Yet, to repeal a rule which is so embedded in legal education seemed like a monumental event. A brief review of the legal literature did not provide a current basis for its continuance.

My primary teaching experience at that time was in the area of taxation and my practice involved tax controversies against or as a former representative of the Internal Revenue Service. A comprehensive study of the matter would take an enormous amount of time. Several years later, I retired, as a professor emeritus, from the University of Toledo College of Law and accepted a position with Florida Coastal School of Law. In time, I decided to teach property law and slowly drifted into a comprehensive study of the development of the RAP. It is a complex area of law which calls for extended study. Reading the history of the common law of property, reviewing original cases of importance, and law review articles from the late nineteenth century to the present led me to question the hand of the distinguished Professor John Chipman Gray, as he was the principal marketing agent of the RAP in the United States. He, along with Lord Chancellor Nottingham and Lord Kenyon (as well as others), shaped the contours of the RAP. Gray interpreted the RAP in his famous treatise on the RAP in a very dogmatic and restrictive fashion. Because Gray's treatise on the RAP was, and is, universally accepted, it became obvious that one could not study the RAP as a legal abstraction apart from understanding the life and times of Gray himself.

The more I backed into the study of his life, the more I realized the intrinsic relationship of the man to his RAP. This historical essay is intended to provide that context and also to suggest that there is no present reason for the continued hegemony of Gray's RAP. John Chipman Gray is and continues to be a special scholar. He did so much in his life: soldier in the Civil War, principal participant in the ascension of Harvard Law School in the late nineteenth century, practitioner of the law extraordinaire, founder of one of the major law firms in the United States (Ropes & Gray), founding Editor of *American Law Review*, member of a very distinguished family, and scholar of the first order. As a Brahmin, Gray was trained to be a perfectionist, and certainly fulfilled that mission.

What follows here is an extended essay on the man, John Chipman Gray. The object here is not to exempt private trusts from legal accountability, but to suggest continued utilization of his RAP as achieving that goal constitutes reliance on a custom instilled in legal education for far too long. A rule of law formed when real estate was the foundation of wealth and future interests in dirt were conveyed in kind has little relationship to the availability of a modern complex trust (funded with stocks, bonds, and other intangible assets) that possesses an arsenal of powers exercisable by an active and accountable trustee. I leave it to you to agree or disagree, however, that determination cannot be made without a focus on the hand applying the RAP.

Acknowledgments

I take note of the valuable contributions of the many legal scholars on the common law and express deep respect for their dedicated work in providing a comprehensive narrative of the past. I am fully indebted to their contribution to the goal of attempting to establish a rational framework of the law of property. Although I may personally decry the fiction of the exclusively rational development and/or application of the rules of the common law in the Blackstonian rendition, I would have nothing to address but for the discipline and debt of the massive scholarship produced by the masters of the common law such as Maitland, Pollock, Plucknett, Holdsworth, Baker, Milsom and others of the English sort, as well as numerous American scholars. I owe and express special recognition to the historical scholarship of A. W. Brian Simpson. Also especially important to my study of John Chipman's family was the information provided by Stephen Robert Mitchell's doctorate dissertation (1961) on Horace Jr. Mitchell's dissertation provided important data as it relates to my analysis of the relationship between the two brothers and the enormous impact that the relationship with Horace had on Gray and his scholarship.

The scholarship of Steven A. Siegel on Gray has been also helpful in the development of my thesis although there are differences in our perspective of Gray. Bruce A. Kimball's extensive study on the life and contributions of Christopher Columbus Langdell, the first dean of Harvard Law School, is also noteworthy and particularly relevant.[1] Kimball's scholarship will no doubt secure renewed recognition for the significance of Langdell's contributions to the development of modern legal education. He has "ably rescued Langdell from posterity's condescension."[2] And further, I foremost acknowledge and continue to celebrate the illuminating scholarship, superb insight, and tortuous witticisms of W. Barton Leach whose diligent efforts alone revealed the

1. Bruce A. Kimball, The Inception of Modern Professional Education C.C. Langdell, 1826–1906 (2209).

2. Christopher Tomlins, *Book Review: The Inception of Modern Professional Education*, 59 J. Legal Educ. 657, 662 (2010).

RAP for what it was and remains: an oath of institutional allegiance on the part of the academic community to the mysticism of the legal past.

This extended essay could not have been accomplished without the generous financial summer research grants of Florida Coastal Law School. Dean Peter Goplerud and his administration provided needed resources for employment of several outstanding research assistants. I would particularly note the able assistance of the following past students who have aided me in this endeavor: Lance Neff, JD, Patrick J. Kelly, MD, JD, Catherine Micaud, JD, and Jennifer Shoaf, JD. In addition, I would like to give special appreciation for the editorial and research work of Kyle S[t]ill, JD. Mr. Sill has separately published an article regarding the RAP and its application to commercial transactions; notwithstanding, his contrary conclusion that "the elusive rule against perpetuities will not be going away any time soon."[3] In addition, the assistance of former and present faculty assistants, Holly Bolinger, MaryBeth Evans, and Patricia Maroney, has been invaluable. I further deeply appreciate the editorial assistance and guidance provided by Sondra Greenfield.

I also express deep appreciation for the generous and caring services of the staff of the Florida Coastal School of Law Library and Technology Center, under the leadership of Nickie Singleton, Director, and Martha Smith, Associate Director. In addition, the willingness of Professor Christopher Roederer to read a rough first draft must be more than noted. I equally appreciate the research assistance of the Houghton Library and Harvard Archives of Harvard College and their permission to publish selected portions of materials contained in the correspondence file of Gray as well as letters in the presidential files. My appreciation also extends to the quality of assistance provided by the Harvard Law School Library and the generous services provided by its staff, particularly Lesley Schoenfeld.

Others participants in my life who have added greatly to my sense of exploration include Myrtle Loughney, Professor William H. Osterle (my mentor at the University of Scranton), Donald Keune, Esq., Joseph Patrick Moran (my brother, in whose steps and *direction* I have followed), Nora Kay Zelizer, Ph.D., my special step-children and their progeny, and finally my parents, Evelyn Murray Moran and Joseph Aloysius Moran. Each in different ways has added to my quest for understanding the experience of life.

I must also recognize and express deep appreciation for the willing assistance of Jeffrey B. Gray, Esq., and Roland Gray III, Esq., the great-grandsons of Gray. They openly shared the collected personal and private narrative of

3. Kyle B. Sill, Note, *Is RAP Gone? How* Old Port Cove Holdings, Inc. *Still Leaves RAP Alive in Florida*, 10 Fla. Coastal L. Rev. 491, 504 (2009).

their Gray ancestors. In addition, they provided previously unpublished family pictures of Gray and his wife, Nina. It is not surprising to note Jeffrey and Roland count seven generations of American lawyers in the Gray family dynasty.[4] Nicolas Gray, one of the latest family members of the bar and the great-great-grandson of Gray, made available several memorandums setting forth unique information regarding the careers of John Chipman and Horace Jr.

Finally, Gray was a man of enormous talent and energy and his contribution to the formation of a principled system of property law will be with us forever. Nothing stated herein should be interpreted to the contrary. The spirit of Gray's intelligence and relentless dedication to a legal system by which members of society are held accountable to his form of secular morality will resonate with me and others throughout time. Although Gray's original version of the RAP has been modified, his vision as the Harvard Brahmin on the law of property will be preserved in perpetuity. I hope that this essay will add to his record of exceptional achievement.

---

4. An account of the lawyer tradition of the Gray family was published in the Massachusetts Lawyer Weekly. *See* Dick Dahl, *The Long Gray Line*, 18 Mass. Law. Wkly. 1661, 1666 (May 1991).

John Chipman Gray

Chapter 1

John Chipman Gray and the Rule Against Perpetuity

General Introduction

Although the focus of this extended essay is on the life and times of Gray, the principal mantra of his professional life was the art of deciphering and applying the mystical rule against perpetuities (RAP). As artist Jackson Pollock became recognized for his unique modality of expression, Gray's legal fame is identified by his equally expressive recreation of the RAP. This complex medieval rule of law, born of the English jurists, as interpreted by Gray was the apex and omega of his scholarly achievement. This essay is about his life and the influences on his perception of the function of law in society as gleaned primarily through his definitive work on the RAP.

For those not familiar with the RAP, its present history starts from the original desires of the barons of the thirteenth century to secure relative legal immunity for their estates from the many unknown political and social vicissitudes for the benefit of their descendents under the doctrine of primogeniture. Subsequently, the English jurists of the fifteenth century recognized the devastating economic impact that an estate referred to as a "fee tail" had on the management and productivity of the large manors over time. Under the fee tail conveyance,[1] the barons as owners of large estates conveyed a life estate to their oldest male child and then to the heirs (male) of such child. The net result of such a conveyance was to create a series of life estates, first to the baron's oldest son, then successively to the male line of such eldest son, and then on

1. The mode of conveyance was by a series of successive life estates was authorized by a statute enacted during the reign of Edward I in 1285. The conditional conveyance was keenly sought by the Barons during their ongoing conflicts with the Crown during the thirteenth century. The statute explicitly provided that the intent of the donor shall be observed "so that they to whom the land is given under such condition, *shall have no power to aliene the land so given.*" *See* 13 Edw. I, c. 1 (1285) *De Donis Conditionalabis.*

the failure of male issue of said eldest son, to the next oldest son of the baron, and so forth. This would continue until the entire line of issue failed, which suggests a de facto perpetuity. When and if the line of issue of the donor failed, the estate would return to the donor's heirs by way of reversion (the concept of heirs goes to the broader bloodline and includes others than merely one's issue). Because no one in the sequence of life estate interests had title or power to alienate or mortgage the property, many successors in interest to the fee tail simply drained the profits from the operation of the manor as fast as possible. Each successor tenant-in-tail (the person then entitled to possession of the estate for life) realized he had only one life to live and little incentive to invest in the estate for the benefit of their issue. In three or four generations, this lack of care or investment in the estate frequently resulted in a rundown manor, with a consonant loss of feudal support in the form of revenue or service in kind to or for the benefit of the Crown.

The courts found a way to break this devastating series of life estate conveyances in *Taltarum's Case*[2] by means of a fictional transaction, referred to by A. W. Brian Simpson as a "bizarre procedural fiction, the common recovery."[3] In a sense, this judicial resolution is the initial point of departure in what would eventually become a critical element in the evolution of the RAP, which awaited its formal delivery as a so-called new species of law in 1682 in the *Duke of Norfolk's Case*.[4] From this decision, we have the beginning of the formal invention leading to the final form of the RAP. The rule will eventually require, under Gray's interpretation, that an interest must vest, if at all, within lives in being at the time of creation plus twenty-one years and the period of gestation. Any potential beneficial interests that would not vest within that period would be eliminated as a matter of law. Gray's interpretation became the song of RAP[5] for all law students, up to the present time. Perhaps an unfair interpretation of Gray's rule—should there be any possible way in which an interest might not vest within the prescribed time period; such interest fails upon

2. Taltarum's Case, (1472) Y. B. 12 Edw. IV 19.

3. A. W. B. Simpson, Legal Theory and Legal History: Essays on the Common Law 147 (1987).

4. Duke of Norfolk's Case, (1682) 3 Ch. Cas. 1.

5. The song of RAP according to Professor Gray is as follows: "No interest is good unless it must vest, if at all, not later than twenty-one years after some life in being at the creation of the interests." John Chipman Gray, The Rule Against Perpetuities §201 (2d ed. 1906) (1886). For the three other editions of his major opus, see John Chipman Gray, The Rule Against Perpetuities (1886); John Chipman Gray, The Rule Against Perpetuities (3d ed. 1915) (1886); and John Chipman Gray, The Rule Against Perpetuities (Roland Gray ed., 4th ed. 1942) (1886).

the instant of its attempted creation! Indeed, the RAP became a religion for him and his many subsequent academic supporters, even to this day. The distinguished law professor, George L. Haskins, referred to Gray as "the high priest of the Rule Against Perpetuities."[6] Gray's original version of the RAP is the prism through which all ensuing discussions on the subject matter are considered and/or evaluated. No American law student fails to recall the theme borne of his vision, voice, and dissemination.

Twentieth-Century Perspective on the RAP

Since my first encounter with the RAP in law school, and later in connection with the bar examination, I had little contact with the rule. Years later I became reacquainted with the RAP while serving as a member of a subcommittee of the Estate Planning, Probate, and Trust Section of the Ohio Bar Association, which was created to study and consider the role and function of the RAP in contemporary society. In connection with that project, Craig Frederickson and I completed a very brief analysis of the current necessity for the continuation of the RAP in the age of the extensive use of the modern trusts and published our recommendations.[7] The principal recommendation of the report proposed exempting private trusts from the application of the RAP.[8] Subsequently, this recommendation was adopted after extensive discussion and debate, first by the Estate Planning, Probate, and Trust Section of the Ohio Bar Association and, subsequently, it was favorably recommended for enactment by the delegates of the Ohio Bar Association. Shortly thereafter, the Ohio General Assembly, acting on the recommendation of the Ohio Bar Association and significant political support of the Ohio Banking Association, amended the Ohio Revised Code in 1999. The amended Ohio Revised Code authorized settlors of private trusts to elect out of the application of the RAP so long as the trustee possessed either the power of alienation, or the trustee, or some other person, had the right to terminate such trust.[9]

---

6. George L. Haskins, *Extending the Grasp of the Dead Hand: Reflections on the Origins of the Rule Against Perpetuities*, 126 Univ. Pa. L. Rev. 19, 21 n.7 (1977).

7. *See* Gerald P. Moran & Craig F. Frederickson, *The Rule Against Perpetuity: The Case for the Exemption or Repeal of the Rule*, 6 Prob. L.J. Ohio 10 (1996).

8. A number of other states had previously enacted similar modifications of the RAP by either outright repeal of the rule or rendering it optional.

9. Ohio Rev. Code Ann. §2131.09(B) (West 2009).

The apparent "excesses" impressed on the RAP by Gray led to its revision in the late twentieth century. The American Law Institute (ALI) and the National Conference of Commissioners on Uniform State Laws (NCCUSL), combined with the devastating deconstructive scholarship of W. Barton Leach, revealed the depth of excesses that filled the cup of Gray's RAP. The legal triage of the ALI and others disclosed only that the RAP no longer served a useful purpose in modern society. It had become a mere verbal recitation of benevolent respect that was repeated ad nauseam long after the conflict giving rise to its existence had been effectively eliminated. This is evidenced in that most assets are now held as interests in trust wherein the trustee possesses the right of alienation. The process of revision of the RAP in the twentieth century not only questioned Gray's doctrines on the application of the rule but also, by indirection, the legal integrity and long-standing authority attributed to the RAP. Even worse, the rule itself was recognized by some as an anachronism of excessive complexity and transformed somewhat into an arbitrary rule of a time past. It was only after this process had taken place that the Bar and banking institutions could initiate the process to repeal and/or modify the RAP to carry out their commercial concerns. Some of the dedicated servants of the RAP, attempting to defeat any modification of it, realized the plucking of even one feather might be the beginning of the end of its pursuit at perpetuity.[10] The invention of the period of ninety years did the trick—if ninety years was a proper test for the maximum period in which an interest must vest, why not three hundred sixty years, or even one thousand years. All of this has come to pass. I do not deny that the statutory reforms and conceptual revisions adopted in both England and the United States in the later part of the twentieth century greatly reduced the painful excesses generated by the judiciary and the scholarship of Gray. However, I do question the failure of the participants to focus sufficiently on the relevance or purpose of the RAP. This is particularly true where most future interests that arguably violate the RAP are equitable interests in trusts where the trustee possesses the power of alienation and/or termination. An underlying theme supporting the academic movement to revise the RAP, by adopting the "wait and see" reform, was the recognition that innocent beneficiaries were being denied their rightful interests because of the

---

10. *See, e.g.*, Jesse Dukeminier, *The Uniform Statutory Rule Against Perpetuities: Ninety Years in Limbo*, 34 UCLA L. Rev. 1023 (1987); Lawrence W. Waggoner, *Perpetuity Reform*, 81 Mich. L. Rev. 1718 (1983); Jesse Dukeminier, *Perpetuities: Measuring Years* 85 Colum. L. Rev. 1648 (1985); Lawrence W. Waggoner, *A Perspective of Wait and See*, 85 Colum. L. Rev. 1714 (1985); Lawrence W. Waggoner, *The Uniform Statutory Rule Against Perpetuities: The Rationale of the 90-Year Waiting Period*, 73 Cornell L. Rev. 157 (1988).

application of a dogmatic rule of law born to remedy ancient social conflicts of the English motherland.

The Culture of the Boston Brahmin

Gray was of a generation of highly educated and socially connected patrician families referred to as Boston Brahmins. One of the first uses of the term Brahmin was by Oliver Wendell Holmes Sr., in describing the Brahmin Caste:

> There is nothing in New England corresponding at all to the feudal aristocracies of the Old World. Whether it be owing to the stock from which we were derived, or to the practical workings of our institutions, or to the abrogation of the technical "law of honor," which draws a sharp line between the personally responsible class of "gentlemen" and the unnamed multitude of those who are not expected to risk their lives for an abreaction,—whatever be the cause, we have no aristocracy here as that which grew up out of the military systems of the Middle Ages.
>
> What our people mean by "aristocracy" is merely the richer part of the community, that live in the tallest houses, drive real carriages, (not "kerriages") kid-glove their hands, and French bonnet their ladies' heads, give parties where the persons who call them by the above title are not invited, and have a provokingly way of dressing, walking, talking, and nodding to people, as if they felt entirely at home, and would not be embarrassed in the least, if they met the Governor, or even the President of the United States, face to face. Some of these great folks are well bred, some of them are only purse-proud and assuming—but they form a class, and are named as above in common speech.[11]

Although there is a tendency to overstate the institution of Boston Brahmin, it nevertheless describes an American social class born of prosperity, discipline, education, defined moral values, and continued by the establishment of a traditional pathway primarily for the male progeny to follow. Apart from the importance of cultural values shared in the family community, men and woman of literature, arts, politics, business, and the professions were frequent guests

---

11. Oliver Wendell Holmes Sr., *The Professor's Story*, V ATLANTIC MONTHLY NO. XXVII, 88, Jan. 1860, at 91–92. The senior Holmes followed this apparent first use of the term Boston Brahmin with the publication of a novel the next year. *See* OLIVER WENDELL HOLMES SR., ELSIE VENNER: A ROMANCE OF DESTINY (1861).

of the patrician families. Children were also steeped in religious training, ranging from Congregational, Unitarian, and Episcopal denominations. But such religious exposure was always dusted with a light sprinkling of enlightened skepticism as to sources of creation. Empiricism and pragmatism were emerging forces to challenge the dominant positions of the established religious institutions. The critical point of departure for the Brahmins was the institution of a very demanding sense of personal accountability. Male Brahmins would go to war over slavery on principle, inspired in part by a sense of duty to the community, even though they might have some political and moral distaste about engaging in personal acts of violence to achieve their ends. Not unlike others of the North and the South who served in this bloody conflict, many Brahmins died in Civil War battles at such places as Ball's Bluff, Antietam, and Gettysburg.

The pathway of a young Brahmin generally began with education at the historic Boston Latin School,[12] followed by matriculation at Harvard College,[13] and then, for a lesser number, attendance at Harvard Law School. Gray represents the epitome of this process—he is an ideal representation of a Boston Brahmin. Some number of this class, like Horace Gray Jr., the older half-brother of John Chipman Gray, and Henry Adams, followed the patrician tradition of the young English nobles by either undertaking the Grand Tour and/or engaging in further study at the English or European universities.

This review of Gray's life is not intended to be a definitive biography in a traditional sense, but rather a biographical essay on one of the foremost scholars of Harvard Law School. His work on the interpretation of the RAP and continued hegemony as to its application is a unique achievement in the history of the common law. As I look back at this enterprise, I would assert there is no rule of the common law that is more connected to the person than that which is true of Gray and his RAP.

As a postscript for the benefit of present and future law students, there is a separately prepared explanation in Chapter 11 of the historical antecedent com-

---

12. This famous school of Boston was established in 1635 and flourished as a premier public (exam) school right up to the present time. Its graduates compose very distinguished alumni and are nationally known for their individual and collective achievements concerning both public and private affairs.

13. Harvard College was founded in 1636 by the legislative body of the Massachusetts community. The college received extended support and funding by the community and its leaders throughout its history. Ronald Story's article of some years ago discloses the overall impact of the special support provided to Harvard College by the Boston Brahmin community during the nineteenth century. This close relationship impacted the growth and success of this most prestigious academic institution. *See* Ronald Story, *Harvard and the Boston Brahmins: A Study in Institutional and Class Development*, 8 J. Soc. Hist. 94 (1975).

mon law rules against perpetuities that are an essential part of the process leading to the ultimate synthesis of the modern RAP. Should this ancient rule should have any application to the vesting of a beneficiary's interest in a modern trust? These observations do not proceed from the prevailing rush to the bottom argument offered by some academic scholars of recent times, but rather from the perspective that there is no rational basis why a settlor's trust, in which the trustee possess a power of alienation or termination, should be subject to the grasp of the RAP.

Gray's Philosophical Approach to the Law

Our principal concern here is on the life and times of Gray and its impact on his scholarship; particularly his interpretation of the RAP. It is difficult to assess what particular aspects of Gray's life most directly affected his views on the law. However, there are a number of obvious matters that directly affected his perception and articulation of the rules of law. He was a principal and influential member of the Harvard Law School at a time when a revolutionary movement to study law as science occurred. This radical pedagogical modification thrust the focus of law school study on the case method, while invigorating the classroom experience through the employment of the Socratic dialogue. These two revolutionary factors became the pedagogical norm for most American law schools during the twentieth century.

These radical changes were initially designed by Dean Christopher Columbus Langdell under the guiding influence of President Charles W. Eliot. Justice Felix Frankfurter accurately referred to the faculty of Harvard Law School during this period as the "the days of the Giants." The interaction of the then existing cultural and intellectual ambiance of Harvard Law School are also important factors as they shed light on Gray's classic articulation of the RAP and his promotion of a rather aggressive enforcement of the rule. There is no question that Gray's American condensation of the proposition of the RAP remains the emblematic theme song[14] for every law student of property law since 1886.[15]

14. While touring the library, a distinguished professor of law from another law school, upon being informed that I was engaged in a piece on the RAP, spontaneously offered the Gray theme song: "No interest is good unless...." There is no end to the ritual by which the RAP is ingrained into the law students.

15. Every former law student can recite the formulation of the RAP (*even after two glasses of wine—very impressive*), but few lawyers understand or care what it means in application or why it remains a basic rule of law.

A. W. Brian Simpson explained the nature of Gray's efficient condensation of the RAP.

> No such work ever expressed Langdell's theory of economy of principles more elegantly than Gray's Rule Against Perpetuities (1886). He contrived to reduce the whole body of doctrine, supposedly underlying hundreds of cases, many barely intelligible, to a mere thirty-two words; any cases which were not compatible with his statement of the rule were simply dismissed as wrong. Gray was fascinated with the idea that all perpetuity problems had a discoverable and incontrovertible answer.[16]

J. H. Baker offers provocative guidance to law students with the following words of caution:

> The modern student, like his predecessor of 1831, has to come to terms with the fact that much of the law he learns, perhaps even some of what he is taught axiomatic, will become obsolete in the course of his professional life. The academic discipline of law, therefore, if it is to have any lasting value, cannot confine itself to the mere learning of rules. It must impart some understanding of the rules, and a dynamic sense of legal evolution.[17]

Gray was a principal participant and to some extent both a protagonist and antagonist of the emerging changes adopted during the Langdellian deanship at Harvard Law School. Clearly, Gray was greatly influenced by his personal and professional interactions at the law school, as well as the very forceful reiteration of the formalistic certainty of the common law as proffered by his older half-brother, Horace Jr. (who was not only Chief Justice of the Massachusetts Supreme Judicial Court, but also an Associate Justice of the United States Supreme Court). But it is these two principal interacting and supporting elements that led Gray to speak and write in the language of a precise rule of law; namely deciphering the RAP, with a certain and inexorable correct answer for each problem. Clearly, there are enumerable other factors leading to the construction of an attitude regarding the "strict" enforcement of a principled system of property law. Gray's scholarship on the RAP embraced the thoughtful guidance of a leading eighteenth century expert on future interests, Charles Fearne. Fearne explained the law was not to be decided upon according to the fortuitous whims or discretion of a judge.

---

16. *See* A.W. B. Simpson, Leading Cases in the Common Law, Legal Science and Legal Absurdity 76, 96 (Clarendon Press Oxford 1996) (1995).

17. J. H. Baker, An Introduction to English Legal History V (1971).

> General restrictions in these matters, if universally adhered to with literal strictness, will necessarily involve some apparent absurdities, when applied to the circumstances of certain cases. But to leave it in the breast of a judge to relax or supersede general restrictions and rules, whenever he shall think particular cases not within the reason of them, may perhaps, by some, be thought a more important absurdity, and a matter of greater mischief in its tendency and consequences, than that which is intended to be obviated by it; for this is in fact making the discretion of the judge the only law in such cases. An error our forefathers seem to have been even illiberally studious to keep clear of. For their creed seems to have, what I have read expressed, in so much energy of terms, by a great Judge of these times. *The discretion of a Judge is the law of tyrants; it is casual, and depends upon constitution, temper, and passion. In the best it is sometimes caprice; in the worst it is every vice, folly and passion to which human nature is known.*[18]

Although Gray may not have consciously internalized this advice of Fearne, it was his practice, and it was also particularly true of his brother, to remove any ambiguity in the law, provide correct answers to complex questions, and avoid "public policy" as a basis for any interpretation. A decision was right or wrong; that was and is the law according to Gray. As noted herein, he pilloried New Hampshire Chief Justice Charles Doe for the crafty manner in which he refused to follow the established mandates of the RAP.[19] Yet, it is more than ironic to contrast Gray's draconian enforcement of the RAP with the unquestioned fact that the rule is itself the product of public policy of the English judiciary.

The RAP is so naturally assumed to be perfect and necessary by reason of legal education, mostly of years past, that there is hardly any academic interest regarding an evaluation of its current function or economic impact. Indeed, there never has been an established empirical study of the benefits of the rule, instead we are offered timeless reiterations of academic assertions as to its importance and purposes.[20] The RAP has simply been delivered by *a priori*

---

18. Charles Fearne, An Essay on the Learning of Contingent Remainders and Executory Devises 535 (10th ed. 1844) (emphasis added).

19. *See infra* Chapter 9.

20. The recent law review articles on the competition between the states to provide a more friendly legal environment as it relates to the establishment of trusts is far from a new development. *See generally* Robert H. Sitkoff & Max M. Schanzenbach, *Jurisdictional Competition for Trust Funds: An Empirical Analysis of Perpetuities and Taxes*, 115 Yale L.J. 356 (2005); Stewart E. Sterk, *Jurisdictional Competition to Abolish the Rule Against Perpetuities: RIP For the RAP*, 24 Cardozo L. Rev. 2097 (2003).

indoctrination in law school as sacred legal doctrine.[21] It is that debate on the substantive purpose and function of the RAP that has been obviated by the somewhat exaggerated focus on the economic and political implications of the repeal and its relationship to the generation-skipping-taxes.

The contrast of the person of Gray and his tendency toward mathematical exactitude when juxtaposed with the inherent complexity and contingency of the RAP, not surprisingly, results in a legal prescription that eliminates the slightest touch of ambiguity. As a scholar, law as written by Gray was a perfect science, and anyone who found differently from his formulation of the RAP or his application was wrong. This system of interpretation was thoroughly consistent with the emerging conception of law at Harvard Law School. Morton Horwitz explains the late nineteenth century philosophical approach of Classical Legal Formalism and the role of legal reasoning applied at that time.

> The late nineteenth-century effort to integrate legal doctrines were accompanied by an equally important attempt to create a self-contained system of legal reasoning that would be immune to the charge that it was simply political. As a first approximation, it is accurate to describe this mode of reasoning as "formalistic" or "conceptualistic." It aspired to import into the process of legal reasoning the qualities of certainty and logical inexorability. Deduction from the general principle and analogies among cases and doctrines were often undertaken with a self-confidence that later generations, long since out of touch with the inarticulate premises of the system, could only mistakenly regard as willful and duplicitous.[22]

This approach was clearly a fundamental part of the philosophic environment of Harvard Law School and fits perfectly into Gray's scheme of the RAP. The RAP, under Gray's scholarship, had but one clear and certain answer, and

---

21. *See* Joel C. Dobris, *The Death of the Rule Against Perpetuities, or the RAP Has No Friends—An Essay*, 35 Real Prop., Prob. & Tr. J. 601 (2000).

22. *See* Morton J. Horwitz, The Transformation of American Law 1870–1960: The Crisis of Legal Orthodoxy 16 (1992). For a brief discussion of Florida's attempt to create a tax haven for the wealthy by prohibiting an income and estate tax so as to induce relocation of wealthy residents domiciled in states imposing such taxes during the 1920s, see, for example, Max Oliver Cogburn, *The Credit Allowable Against the Basic Federal Estate Tax for Death Taxes Paid to State Statutes Enacted to Take Advantage Thereof—Constitutional Difficulty and Some Suggested Solutions*, 30 N.C. L. Rev. 123 (1952); E.M. Perkins, *State Action under the Federal Estate Tax Credit Clause*, 13 N.C. L. Rev. 271 (1934); E.M. Perkins, *The Power of Congress to Levy Taxes for Distribution to the States*, 12 N.C. L. Rev. 326 (1933).

anyone who differed from the "master's determination" was wrong. The resulting conception of the RAP also constitutes a new form of legal anthropomorphism. Gray has formulated a rule of law that reflects the intricacies of his unique being. He becomes the American merchant of the alleged perfection of the RAP and its simplistic, dogmatic application.

As a practitioner, Gray was faced with the reality that law was the product of the inventive abilities of the judges as they individually responded to changing factual conditions in the process of applying the relevant legal principles or statutes. Notwithstanding, Gray, as a scholar, reified selected offerings of the court's rationale in specific common law cases, including the infamous *Duke of Norfolk's Case*, into concrete and immutable principles of law from which no further change was necessary or allowed. It is as if under Gray's conceptualization, the law on this particular point had reached its final form of perfection. The RAP was in this sense, and in his specific articulation, the end of law.

This unconditional approach by Gray stands in curious juxtaposition to the fact that the common law was the product of the inventive genius of the English judges. This rigidity of judgment on the part of Gray applied, of course, only where he unconditionally agreed with the judicial determination. As a scholar, he seldom failed to reach a judgment that was not of a conclusive nature. This also applied when he seriously disagreed with the courts, as he did with the judicial enforcement of the spendthrift provision.[23]

Because private practice involves litigation wherein the outcome is seldom certain and frequently contingent, it appears that Gray mostly exorcised the substantial legal experience he derived as a practitioner from his academic scholarship, with the exception of his late philosophical publication in 1908. The written form of law was the ideal and, for Gray, the RAP flowed naturally and flawlessly. This quixotic isolation in the methodology of conceptualizing and describing the law in the formal scholarly sense as completely separate and unconnected from the natural and inherent insights derived from pragmatic comprehension of law in operation, produces or ought to have produced a most conflicted person. Yet, Gray did not reflect that paradox and, not surprisingly, he generated a surreal vision in the perfection of the RAP.

Gray's inability or conscious refusal to allow the merger of the two different processes—the intellectual abstraction of the rhetorical form of law as Gray

---

23. *See* Gerald P. Moran, *A Radical Theory of Jurisprudence: The "Decisionmaker" as the Source of the Law—The Ohio Supreme Court's Adoption of the Spendthrift Trust Doctrine as a Model*, 30 Akron L. Rev. 393, 395–96 (1997); *see also* discussion of the spendthrift provision in Chapter 8, *infra*.

perceived it and his intense and sometime frustrating contingent experience as a lawyer—led to the imposition of his scholarly perception of law almost to the complete denial of his experiences in the actual practice of law. Gray chose understandably, in the context of his time, cultural influences, and personal gestalt, to be consonant with the tenor of other legal treatises. As a result, he wrote upon the law in a relatively dogmatic and doctrinaire fashion. To go against the standard expectations or norms of those he wished to impress and/or secure approval from, including in particular during the early years that of his older half-brother, Horace Jr., was completely unfathomable for Gray. This was not particularly unusual and likely true of other scholars of that time. One would expect to observe some modest aspects, arising from Gray's initial twenty-one years of legal practice, to conflict with his views expressed as a scholar in 1886. It is as if this experience as a practicing lawyer is totally excluded from his life as a scholar. This judgment about the omission of any aspect derived from his years of practice does not fall into the abyss of presentism; namely, the application of present values in judging the past.[24] Rather, it is an attempt to highlight the complete denial of that experience in his writings. The lack of any expression regarding the pragmatic features that reflect his years in the practice of law is unexplainable, except as it reflects the style and mode of scholarly habits of that time. However, Gray did express some of his experiences to a very limited extent in his philosophical effort of 1909.[25]

An unintended consequence of the repeal or modification of the RAP is the possibility that our study of the feudal laws may no longer be a necessary requirement of the first-year course in property in the form and fashion as delivered in the near past.[26] Indeed, some law professors have already revolutionized the focus of their classroom coverage in light of the accelerated modification of property law concepts and the demands of contemporary legal issues.[27] It seems, on reflection, that most of the rules and subtle distinctions of the past property concepts regarding future interests are continued into the present, almost solely, by the prism and application of the RAP. When most future interests today are found in trust instruments, as opposed to deeds and executory devises, the repeal or modification of the RAP may open the door to a

24. *See* Gordon S. Wood, The Purpose of the Past 10 (2009).

25. *See* John Chipman Gray, The Nature and Sources of the Law (1909).

26. *See* Thomas P. Gallanis, *The Future of Future Interests*, 60 Wash. & Lee L. Rev. 513, 549–60 (2003).

27. *See* Ilya Somin, *Should We Teach Law Students the Rule Against Perpetuities?* (Aug. 11, 2007), *available at* The Volokh Conspiracy, http://volokh.com/archives/archive_2007_08_05-2007_08_11.shtml#1186857157.

new form of efficient enlightenment as to the structure of future interests that is no longer dependent on some case decided in the fifteenth or sixteenth century. The formal repeal could be the catalyst to the new establishment of future interests at a far less cost to students and with far more efficient understanding. Indeed, many of the more recent law school casebooks on property are turning from an extended study of future interests to the problems that lawyers of today face in practice. This radical change reflects willingness on the part of the academy to part from the ancient legal distinctions originating from the social and economic conflicts of the late medieval period. Does this discussion by the academic community suggest or imply giving up on the RAP by design? Not necessarily!

Cultural Influences of Gray as Related to the RAP

Gray functioned at the highest level as a law teacher, scholar, and practitioner of the law. It was and remains true that the principal source of his ongoing reputation relates to his scholarly analysis of the RAP in 1886. The theology of the law is largely premised on the belief that the law is rational, consistently applied, and less political. Gray applied his extraordinary scientific interpretation of the RAP in that ambience. This study of Gray and his RAP questions both the scientific assertion of the historic formulaic interpretation of the RAP and explains how the cultural aspects of his life directly impacted his scholarly articulation and formulation of the RAP. It must be recalled that the RAP was a judicial invention developed to mediate pressing social and economic problems relating to certain interests in real property that indefinitely suspended the right of alienation and denied other economic benefits of ownership. Most, if not all, of these future sequential interests were held as in kind, legal life estates in the "dirt."

The English communal problems occurred during the middle and late medieval periods when real estate was the primary medium of wealth. Those problems did not exist in America, as unlimited land was available to the people who migrated here. Moreover, today most assets and real property that are subject to a future interest, are held in a trust in which the trustee possesses the power of sale. This practice of placing property in trust is to be distinguished from earlier types of conveyances where the future interests applied to "in kind" interests in real property, such as certain conveyances in the nature of inter vivos transfers or executory devises. The practice of using trusts as a principal means of conveying a mixture of assets for present and future beneficiaries was emerging in the industrial urban areas of the United States during the same period that Gray was enacting his American version of the RAP through the publication of his classic treatise on perpetuities in 1886.

Gregory S. Alexander focused on the development of the law of trusts during the late nineteenth century and the first two decades of the twentieth century. He explained the process by which trusts were eventually recognized as a separate and distinct legal category.[28] A good portion of this period in which the substantive laws of trusts are established as a discrete category of law occurs during lifetime of Gray. Indeed, Alexander explains that this process was part of the new movement to secure more "rational arrangements" and cites Holmes and Gray, as well as other academics, as being directly involved with this classification reordering.[29] It cannot be doubted that Gray, as a leading practitioner of the law, was a skilled legalist and thoroughly understood the drafting options regarding the uses and functions of private and charitable trusts.

Despite the doctrinal reification and calibration that Gray applied to the RAP and imposed upon the passive American legal community, there is no similar social problem to that which occurred in England simply because future interests might vest outside the time zone of lives in being plus twenty-one years where such property is otherwise directly alienable. Indeed, almost all trust instruments of today provide extensive authority for the trustee to sell and purchase assets as part of its normal fiduciary duty to preserve and increase the value of the corpus.

In this process, Gray converted the RAP into a projection of his personhood, in that it reflected essential characteristics of his apparently stern and demanding character. His view dominated the legal interpretation of the RAP and permanently ensconced the prism by which future American law professors and law students alike were to study and digest his RAP. Jesse Dukeminier and James Krier explained the impact of his scholarship by the following:

> Gray, professor at Harvard from 1869 to 1913, was fabled because he reduced centuries of cases to this one sentence. But there are many complexities hidden in that one sentence. His book became recognized as, *the* authority on the Rule.[30]

In this process, he branded the RAP in a way that considerably reduced an independent evaluation of its purposes as well as the scope of its application,

---

28. *See* Gregory S. Alexander, *The Transformation of Trusts as a Legal Category, 1800–1914*, 5 Law & Hist. Rev. 303 (1987).

29. *Id.* at 308.

30. Jesse Dukeminier & James Krier, Property 302 n.17 (5th ed. 2002).

except for that of a few rare perpetuity scholars of imminent achievement and authority in the academy. In addition, Gray permanently fixed his interpretation of the RAP as a ritualistic aspect of legal education. As law students, we were taught the RAP as an exercise of forced feeding, education by tradition of the past teaching emanating from the authority of the person of Gray. The RAP became an edict of legal education. Gray accomplished this even though the initial creation of the RAP is that of a purely English judicial construct. The renowned scholar of future interests, Lewis Simes, explained the lasting impact of Gray's scholarship of the RAP.

> When John Chipman Gray published the first edition of his treatise on the rule against perpetuities in 1886, the historical method in legal research dominated. This was particularly true of the group of teachers at the Harvard Law School during the deanship of Langdell and Ames. The common law was developed historically from the English cases and was applied and expanded analytically. Most American statutes were thought of almost excrescences; and the true common law was to be found in the written opinion of the English judges. The task of the legal scholar was to rationalize the English historical development. *This was done so ably in Gray's first edition that most subsequent scholars have done little more than follow the pattern he set out. Substantially that is what has been done in this section.*[31]

The focus of this study is on the symbiotic relationship of a man and his rule of law. They are inseparable. To understand the RAP, you must understand Gray. And to understand Gray, you need to understand the RAP. *Le style c'est l'homme.* Some will find this observation to be a hyperbole of extreme proportions. Nevertheless, this biographical essay is offered in support of that thesis.

Symbiotic Relationship of Gray and the RAP

It is not an exaggeration to state that the unique persona of Gray has been transposed into the essential definition and, more importantly, the underlying environmental attitude regarding the manner by which such rule of law is to be applied and aggressively enforced. If there was any theoretical basis by which

---

31. *See* Lewis M. Simes, Handbook of the Law of Future Interests 255–56 (2d ed. 1966) (emphasis added); *see also* comparable observation of Simpson, *supra* note 16 and accompanying text.

the RAP could be violated, Gray would argue the conveyance failed. As noted above, much of the extensive twentieth century scholarship on the RAP has been directly related to eliminating the tautological excesses of Gray's two dominant axioms; that is, the RAP must be remorselessly applied and it functions to defeat the settlor's intent. These elements became the essential core, or DNA, of Gray's RAP.

As a result of the above realization, I became engrossed in understanding the dominant influence that Gray had on the application of the RAP. The underlying purpose of this essay is to challenge the traditional academic support for the relatively unexplored automatic application of the RAP to modern trusts. The principal indictment of the RAP, as it relates to the functional structure of the modern trust, is premised on the basis that such "sacrosanct" rule of law has no substantive purpose in contemporary society, other than to maintain contact with the institutional habits and the customs of past legal traditions. To question the alleged functional objectives of the RAP, it became necessary to address the authoritative interpretation that the distinguished Gray imposed on his rendition of the RAP which, given a choice, he would have renamed the "Rule Against Remoteness."

Moreover, the extensive study of Gray's scholarship on the RAP brought a detailed focus on the cultural aspects of his professional and personal life as they shed light on his professional perspective of this preeminent rule of property law. Gray's authoritative interpretation of the RAP and subsequent brilliant condensation[32] of this complex and mysterious rule of law into a laconic verbal incantation, which allegedly provides scientifically verifiable correct answers, further impelled exploration of the life and times of Gray. The observation of the noted historian Gordon S. Wood that "the problems and issues of the present should be the stimulus for forays into the past,"[33] invites a study of the life and times of Gray.

In the late nineteenth century, when law as science was blossoming at Harvard Law School under the reign of Christopher Columbus Langdell, the scholarship of Gray on the RAP was a cogent example of how law could be reducible to an essential scientific equation. Equally important is the realization that Gray and the RAP existed in a symbiotic relationship.

Out of many different perspectives of the rule, Gray carved his version of a comprehensive rule of law in which the idea of equity was anathema, and its draconian enforcement in a manner comparable to the efficiency of the French

32. See *supra* note 16 for discussion of Gray's condensation of the RAP.

33. Wood, *supra* note 24, at 10.

guillotine was mandatory! If there was any possible way in which a particular conveyance or devise could possibly violate the RAP, Gray would argue that the courts must assume that possibility and rigidly enforce the rule; there was to be no mercy or common sense available to prevent anything but the strictest application of the RAP under his régime. Moreover, the same stringent prohibitions would apply to any possible intervention that just might lessen the pain of its application. Concealed within his interpretation of the RAP was Gray's demand for personal and communal accountability. This perspective further stimulated my study of Gray as it relates to his somewhat disparate functions as a lawyer, teacher, and scholar.

These differing facets of his life do not lead into a naturally integrated conceptual framework. Gray remains somewhat of an enigma; although quite distinctly aware of the consequences of his performance in whatever capacity that he operated. In view of the diversity of his talents, the resonances of his intelligence, to say nothing of his prodigious reading interests, and the scope of his varied experience, Gray is never to be captured by pen. Clearly, he is not reducible to a simple formula of the underlying facets of his life. There is no facile Freudian key that unlocks the man; hence, we are left to theorize from interpretation of his actions and communications from the norms of his time.

Gray was able to achieve the highest level of performance in his professional life, despite the potentially conflicting and differing functions he experienced as lawyer, scholar, and teacher. A lawyer is committed to zealous advocacy in the representation of his or her client, even when this means attempting to modify the scope and application of established legal principles.[34] A scholar conceives the legal régime as having rational coherence and an underlying objective purpose that can be revealed through arduous research and contemplation. And a law teacher attempts to provide guidance on questions of law somewhere between the extremes of both the scholar and the lawyer—nuanced by enlightened judicial decisions, as analyzed through the prism of

34. See the brief and oral argument made by Professor Gray and his son, Roland Gray, in Fitchie v. Brown, 211 U.S. 321 (1908). The mere direction of testator to continue a trust "as long as legally possible" was sufficient to avoid the application of the RAP despite the fact that one of the many named annuitants was a corporation (possibly qualifying as a charitable entity) and not a life in being, as that term applies to only named persons. There was no argument calling for remorseless enforcement of the RAP as recommended by Professor Gray the scholar when acting in the capacity of a lawyer employed to argue for the opposing point of view. The Court sustained Gray's position notwithstanding the decision was arguably at odds with his draconian views as a scholar. This case is, perhaps, the initial prototype of the eventual savings clause provision included in trusts ("as long as legally possible").

his or her unique perspective. Given the evolving view of law at Harvard Law School during the late nineteenth century and the unique influence of Horace Jr., John Chipman selected, followed, and imposed a most formalistic interpretation of the RAP that is rather incongruous with his life as a practicing lawyer, but fully consonant with the idea of law conceived by a scholar as a perfectly integrated system of established legal principles.

The lasting impact of Gray's scholarship on the RAP and his dogmatic, but nevertheless highly scholarly interpretation, brings into focus the enigmatic question of whether and to what extent the personal views and values of Gray are inherently ascribed as constituting the underlying purposes of this most obscure and complex rule of law. Obviously, this inquiry invites a degree of conjecture with respect to the interpretation of his personal and professional life. The suggested answer is in the affirmative.

Although there is extensive academic information regarding Gray, there are modest personal records on the life of Gray. The records of the Gray family available for public inspection in the archives of Harvard University, although meticulously maintained, shed limited light on the personal life of Gray. Some relevant correspondence relating to Gray and his wife can be found in other collections and will be noted throughout. The one exception to the modest records of the Gray family is found in the published correspondence between Gray and John Codman Ropes, his future law partner. These so-called Civil War letters[35] are quite revealing of the judgment and character of the young Gray and his perception of others involved in this historic, bloody conflict. Be assured that aspects of these varied cultural influences on Gray remains a central focus of my study and, to some lesser extent, provide the window to understand his demand for a fierce enforcement of said rule.

Presumably, one should proceed from the philosophical perspective that the law in a presocietal sense does not exist. It is from this natural vacuum or void that law is created (*impregnated*, more precisely) by the interaction of the wisdom and prejudice of those persons ordained to enact, interpret, and apply the rules as concrete statements of communal principles of law. These so-called principles of law are borne by verbal articulations. Subsequently, these authoritative observations are then carefully collated and transposed into written guidelines that are enforced as reflecting the shared values of the community. The written guidelines are formally utilized as the alleged legal basis, albeit possibly more accurately described in part as based upon a fictional founda-

35. *See* John Chipman Gray & John Codman Ropes, War Letters 1862–1865 (Riverside Press 1927).

tion, and authoritatively cited and then liberally applied in the resolution of the principal conflicts arising from the interacting social, political, and economic institutions of a particular time. Another competing narrative for the source of law, which is necessarily parallel to the aforementioned process, remains the methodology wherein the existing norms of society are internalized not only by the community but also by the delegated decision makers. The first of these premises regarding the device of fictions in law relies on the insightful observations of Sir Edward Coke, whereas the second premise is a dutiful collage and acknowledgement to the disparate philosophical theories of Hans Kelsen, Eugen Erlich, and H. L. A. Hart. These internalized propositions are craftily integrated into formal rules by the authority center of the community. The preeminent legal rules are then passed through the generations as sacrosanct shibboleths of wisdom. Thus, every present culture has a past framework that is utilized to construct answers for its present generation. The history of the RAP is an accurate representation of this process. How the RAP survived as a premier rule of property law through the centuries reveals the extent to which the law of the present is institutionally tied to the distant past.

Summary Preamble

This extended essay will provide an historical overview and perspective of Gray's personal and professional life from a study of mostly secondary sources. I will also consider as a critical aspect of this essay the enormous legal impact that Horace Jr., long-time member of the judiciary, had on Gray's unconditional admiration for the perfection of the common law "as he interpreted it." The dominant "professional" relationship that existed between the brothers Gray, and its impact on the scholarship of Gray, has not been fully appreciated before this essay. The imposing nature of Horace Jr. and his professional influence on the early development of brother John Chipman constitutes a major contribution to an understanding of the scholarship of the latter.

Secondly, this essay will consider the influence that the then unfolding radical transition in legal education of Langdellian formalism[36] also had on Gray's

36. See Thomas C. Grey, *Judicial Review and Legal Pragmatism*, 38 Wake Forest L. Rev. 473, 478 (2003), wherein the following definition or explanation of legal formalism is offered:

> Legal formalists emphasize the specifically legal virtues of the clarity, determinacy and coherence of law, and try to sharpen the distinction between legislation and adjudication. Roughly, they can be divided into rule-formalists and concept-

scholarship in connection with his delineation of the purpose, scope, and methodology of the RAP. There is no question that Gray was at the epicenter of the implosion in legal education that occurred at Harvard Law School during his tenure on the faculty. Although he was by profession a practitioner of law, as was true of Langdell, Gray seemingly separated most of the dynamic experience of the practice of law from his more formal academic activities; that is as a scholar and law professor.

Gray's scholarly effort with respect to the RAP created a most draconian principle of law that completely conformed to the emerging construct of the Langdellian law as a science movement. The movement reinforced Gray's personal proclivity to austerity as well as his scholarly tendency to secure accountability of the community by describing rules of law as demanding severe standards of enforcement. This natural progression resulted in a degree of dogmatism on his part. Gray also detested fictitious transgressions from the formal rules of law as he described them. He outdid the English on the appropriate formulation of their own rule of law—quite a professional achievement![37]

The RAP now stands in the twenty-first century at the precipice of extinction, although the remaining loyalist academic supporters of Gray's RAP are far from conceding its formal elimination. This study brings together a rather dissonant and disparate group of issues that directly relates to the impact of Gray's scholarship on the RAP. There is no natural, chronological, or logical organization for the presentation of the interacting factors explaining the symbiotic relationship of Gray and the principal progeny of his academic life—the Americanization of the RAP.

Like life, there is not a perfectly logical structure or combination of events that affect, directly or indirectly, the birth and evolution of this primary rule of law. The RAP is both a dominant fixture of legal education and a fact of the common law. Whether the RAP fulfills the various functions as described by the many academic scribes throughout legal history remains an interesting empirical question that was seldom addressed, particularly during the time of Gray. The legal mind tends to focus on the ascription of purposes and functions in the rendering of the rule, rather than the phenomenological conse-

---

> formalists. The former place more value on determinacy, emphasizing the importance of clear rules and strict interpretation, while the latter emphasize the importance of system and principled coherence throughout the law.

For an earlier defense of legal formalism, see Ernest J. Weinrib, *Legal Formalism: On the Immanent Rationality of Law*, 97 YALE L.J. 949 (1988).

37. *See* C. S., *Limitations of Land to Unborn Generations*, 29 L.Q.R. 304, 304 n.2 (1913) (discussing the impact of Gray's scholarship on the English judiciary).

quences of its application or a determination of who secured the benefit of its rigorous application. This relatively barren intellectual milieu agitated the constant need to conjure the particular purposes of the RAP in the context of the then present norms, as well as to spur the need to rationalize its basis for continuance rather than focus on short and long term empirical results. There is no question that it is much easier to play with the abstract definition of the RAP rather than to ascertain the elusive economic consequences of its enforcement.

In this respect, the alleged scholars of this most secret of all common law axioms find or create a narrative that serves their reading of history. This applies most certainly to a rule such as the RAP, which has been designated as the noblest "sanctum sanctorum of the law." It exists as a product of the English judiciary and was cut from the fabric of the conflict arising under the common law tradition. It, like many of the ancient rules of the common law, was carried by the Crown to the colonial territory and subsequently adopted as part of the legal framework of almost all of the early member-states of the new nation. The legal tenets of the RAP were fully and firmly ratified by and through the delivery of the renowned eminence of Gray and his revered scholarship for another century or so.

Chapter 2

Gray's Cultural Experience and Formulation of the RAP

It is necessary to understand the life and times of Gray as part of the analytical process of his major interpretative work on the RAP. This chapter addresses the personal and professional aspects of Gray. It is asserted here that each person necessarily reflects his or her values in every act of their being; few acts are more potentially prophetic of one's values than that which is revealed in the exercise of scholarly writings offered up as or intended to constitute a rational interpretation or explanation of that which we call the law. It is revealing if one listens to the "form of responses" as separate from content in that most responses disclose a litany of attitudinal conclusions that could hardly be described as the product of rational analysis on given topics such as the death penalty, abortion, or same-sex marriages. Many of the responses take on a preconditioned chain reaction. The educational aspiration is to have one become fully aware of one's preconditioned conclusions and the basis for such a vested framework of thought. Finally, what is the source of each person's formal framework, under what circumstances does that framework change, and why does that change take place, if at all?

Most importantly, how does the search for a framework apply to the analysis of Gray's scholarship? As will be seen, he reflected the formal Brahmin attitude that dominates most of his thought with concerns of accountability, disciplined application of the rule of law, precision in the formal definition of the law, reverential respect for the authority of the decision maker of law (particularly if it is of the English sort), and unlimited acceptance of the correctness of the decision. This is true unless it conflicts with his view of the law. When it comes to enforcing the law, Gray appears to be nearly bereft of empathy, understanding of human nature, or showing the slightest possibility of ever accepting a legitimate excuse.

Is it possible that certain rules of law attract the interests of persons of similar psychological makeup; or is it more likely that the law is a product of persons possessing such psychological makeup? This chapter demonstrates the latter. In an analogous sense, Dukeminier and Krier noted the less than charming personality of Master of the Rolls, Sir Lloyd Kenyon, who was the principal decision maker in the infamous *Jee v. Audley*, 1 Cox 324, 29 Eng. Rep. 1186 (1787). Kenyon was described as follows:

> Kenyon was a narrow-minded judge who openly sneered at equitable doctrines introduced into law by Mansfield. Standing by the ancient technicalities of the law, Kenyon was testy to advocates in his court, blazing into anger when a word or sentence was not in harmony with his sentiments was uttered. It was alleged that Lord Kenyon invariably stiffed waiters by not tipping, not even a half penny.[1]

That Gray was very sociable and charming may have been more a product of his acute awareness of, as well as a conscious and exacting commitment to comply with, the norms of society of the late nineteenth century, as opposed to the expression of some innate personal sensitivity. These characteristics of Gray presumably preceded his life as a scholar and are projected into his principal scholarly books on the RAP and restraints on alienation. Although there is no intent to provide an historical psychoanalysis of Gray, there are numerous tendencies or characteristics of a psychological nature that are more or less confirmed in his published treatises. Another important calibration in understanding the themes and approaches of John Chipman is revealed by his formal and professional relationship to his elder half-brother Horace Jr. The dominant role of Horace Jr. as a judge of many years and his reverential administration of the law, particularly as related to the ancient propositions of the common law, had a major impact on John Chipman's perspective on the law. In this sense, the impact of this relationship on the scholarship and framework of John Chipman with respect to the common law cannot be overstated.

There is a startling congruence in the professional attitudes of the brothers Gray. It starts from the imperial perspective of Horace Jr., and explodes as a finished product in the person of John Chipman. Whereas John Chipman was a refined and charming social being, Horace Jr. was regarded as somewhat boorish or tactless in social interactions.

> [He had] a very high opinion of the dignity of the judicial office, and naturally a great opinion of his own attainments as a lawyer, which were indeed great. He could not endure to listen to a fool, nor could he allow public time to be taken up with arguments of untenable propo-

1. *See* Jesse Dukeminier & James Krier, Property 307 n.21 (5th ed. 2002).

> sitions.... His manners as presiding judge on the bench were regarded by many as harsh, and even offensive.[2]

Chapter 3 further discusses addresses aspects of Horace Jr.'s life and the impact on John Chipman.[3] It must be admitted that the observations of John Chipman are based largely on intuitive interpretations, derived from a description of the facts and circumstances of his life, which are based on a very limited record that is the subject of some speculation.

Although the focus is on the decision maker (judges) as the final arbitrator of the law on a day, there are some situations in which a noted author of a revered legal text or treatise can have a similar major impact on the final articulation of the legal principle that is comparable to the power of a decision maker. John Chipman personally raised this question, although he fully recognized the priority of judges in the determination of legal principles.

> And yet legal treatises, I confidently believe, are destined to play a much more important part in the law than they have hitherto done. I will give but one, though I think the main, reason for this belief, and that is the amount of the law is so enormously increased that its details cannot be known by any one man.[4]

Indeed, the impact of one's scholarship may be so profound that it cements certain questionable assumptions or fictions attendant to the scholar's composition of the rule, as inseparable elements of the rule itself. The or-

---

2. Horace Gray, *Notes*, 36 AMER. L. REV. 886, 887 (1902).

3. There is an anecdote that fully applies here regarding Judge Horace Gray. The story has been told of the following interaction at an oral argument before the Supreme Judicial Court of Massachusetts:

> A venerable lawyer, the Nestor of the Boston bar, addressing the court, announced a legal proposition, and received from Judge Gray, then on the Supreme Bench of Massachusetts, the curt reply: "[t]hat is not the law of Massachusetts, sir." The rejoinder, as promptly made, was, "[i]t was the law of Massachusetts until your Honor spoke."

See 1 GILBERT J. CLARK, LIFE SKETCHES OF EMINENT LAWYERS 350–51 (Fred B. Rothman & Co. 1983). The judge referred to therein was none other than Professor Gray's half-brother Horace Gray. The English have their version of the anecdote. *See* Letter from Viscount James Bryce, to John Chipman Gray, Professor, Harvard Law School (Nov. 1, 1909) (on file with the Houghton Library of the Harvard College, in the John Chipman Gray Correspondence File, BMS Am. 2152 (27)). Apparently, there are many versions of the same story that are attributed to others.

4. J. C. Gray, *Cases and Treatises*, 22 AMER. L. REV. 756, 759–60 (1888).

chestration of the process begins with mixing several separate elements in a rational petri dish that thereafter congeals, by the authority of the author and the quality of his or her work, into the symbiotic unity of oneness; birth of a rule of law, if you will, by rational in vitro fertilization.[5] Generally, all of this does not occur in a vacuum and rests on the interpretation of several interacting cases decided over an extended period of time. For example, the RAP is first, a product of judicial invention as delivered in a series of English decisions and, second, a unique rule of law that is affected through its subsequent reception, interpretation, and modification by the community of scholars who are vested with the authority to effect such changes. There are occasions, however, where the views are first introduced and developed by a legal scholar, and are then followed by the courts' adoption and approval of such principle or concept.

Until such assumptions or fictions are identified as unnecessary accretions by a subsequent higher authority, such as the academy or the judiciary, such matters remain essential components of the formal rule of law that are cited as verities and passed down to future judges, scholars, and cultures. There is, of course, no time set during which the "core" rule of law is to be discovered by a subsequent and future higher authority. A more efficient way of expressing this thought is that the authority of the present always possesses the power to reinterpret the past. However, this may be poor historical methodology. This does not necessarily mean the past has no specific content of an empirical nature, but rather that each interpretation of legal history necessarily adds, modifies, or incorporates the asserted understanding or narrative of the alleged causal connections or purposes. Because the law generally, but in a very subtle manner, conforms to the exercise of political power, or more precisely constitutes the exercise of political power, it imposes a nuanced understanding of the ancient principles of law as they were applied to resolve legal issues of the past. In this sense, the decision maker of the present seldom provides a consistent historical explanation of the past and her interpretation is greatly influenced by her particular cultural perception or framework of the present. There is an inherent ingredient in the legal process that inexorably involves a matter of presentism; the decision maker is always engaged in reformulating (or overruling) decisions of the past to conform to values of the present.

---

5. I refer the reader to my concept of the relationship between the formal and the personal as affecting one's perception and disposition of the legal issues before a decision maker. *See* Gerald P. Moran, *A Radical Theory of Jurisprudence: The "Decisionmaker" as the Source of the Law—The Ohio Supreme Court's Adoption of the Spendthrift Trust Doctrine as a Model*, 30 Akron L. Rev. 462–70 (1997).

Suggesting that one's values or the culture of one's experience are reflected in one's work is not a unique assertion. It is an observation of a sociologic fact that there exists a relationship between one's interpretation of the law with the predisposition of one's personality as a principal influencing factor on one's professional attitude and judgment.[6] A shortcut manner of expressing this concept is that an individual's personal cultural biography impacts on his or her ideology or predisposition: What I see is a product of where I stand—I see what I believe and I believe what I see. Although one is not completely conscious of the source of those factors influencing one's belief, one nevertheless believes it to be true. Truth is not separate from the "who" that I am. It is a principal assertion of this essay that such observation is true of Gray. John T. Noonan Jr., distinguished legal scholar and a judge having senior status on the Ninth Circuit Court of Appeals, expressed the thought so gracefully.

> As I reached what seemed to me the heart of law's dependence on history, however, I became increasingly conscious of the central place of the human person in any account of law. I also became increasingly conscious of the neglect of the person by legal casebooks, legal histories, and treatises of jurisprudence. Only in response of a person to a person, so it seemed to me, did history have significance to law. Neglect of the persons, it appeared, had led to worst sins for which American lawyers were accountable.[7]

At a later point, Noonan adds:

> Little or no attention is given to the persons in whose minds and in whose interaction the rules have lived—to the persons whose difficulties have occasioned the articulation of the rule, to the lawyers who have tried the case, to the judges who have decided it. No key reporting system is keyed to counsel. No encyclopedia of the law is arranged in terms of judges. The prime teaching tools, the casebooks, have been composed to shed light on the life of the rule, not upon parts of the participants in the process. Those in the classic mold, with snippets of appellate opinions arranged to display variations and

---

6. I refer the reader to my concept of the relationship between the formal and the personal as affecting one's perception and disposition of the legal issues before a decision maker. *See* Gerald P. Moran, *A Radical Theory of Jurisprudence: The "Decisionmaker" as the Source of the Law—The Ohio Supreme Court's Adoption of the Spendthrift Trust Doctrine as a Model*, 30 Akron L. Rev. 462–70 (1997).

7. John T. Noonan Jr., Persons and Masks of the Law, at xv (2d ed. 2002).

> contradictions of a principle, carry the indifference to the participants to the maximum.[8]

Noonan is a person of considerable introspection and clearly reveals a passionate desire to be both accurate as well as delicately candid about the life of the law. The legal community needs more of his kind.

To this group of participants who "make" the law, certainly the author of a legal text should be included in those who have a pervasive and profound impact on the ultimate exposition of a principal rule of law. Gray is such an author, and the masks of his alleged scientific and rational methodology need to be considered to ascertain what aspects of his RAP include irrational or unsupported assumptions attached to his less than perfect mathematical assertions. Even Gray recognized that one's political beliefs and institutional culture directly affected the decision maker's interpretation of the law. He noted, for example, that although the judges who gave birth to the spendthrift doctrine were not secret socialists, "they have been influenced ... by that spirit, in short, of paternalism, which is the fundamental essence alike of the spendthrift trusts and of socialism."[9] Thus, the person of John Chipman Gray[10] and his cultural experiences will be reviewed as relevant considerations as to the manner by which they affected his views of the law. Do not expect that this exercise will provide a linear exposition of the legal rule from some understanding of the circumstances of the life of Gray. The Achilles heel of Legal Realism is in exaggerating the legal prophecy potential from some modest understanding of human nature. The complexity of man and woman precludes any precise sci-

---

8. *Id.* at 6. Judge Noonan also stated in the foreword to the 2002 second edition the following:

> Rules are what judges deal and live by. Persons are inextricably part of rules' application. To know the law is to know not its words but its force and power, and to know who will invoke, enforce, and respond to it. The stories in this book are fables of our time. As the old saying has it: the fable is about you.

Id. at xiv.

9. *See* John Chipman Gray, Restraints on the Alienation of Property, at ix (2d ed., Rothman & Co. 1997) (1883). See Chapter 8 for further comments of Gray regarding the egregious implications flowing from the approval of the spendthrift provision by the judiciary.

10. Professor Stephen A. Siegel of DePaul Law School has made Gray a major focus of his scholarship in two significant articles. *See* Stephen A. Siegel, *John Chipman Gray and the Moral Basis of Classical Legal Thought*, 86 Iowa L. Rev. 1513 (2001); Stephen A. Siegel, *John Chipman Gray, Legal Formalism, and the Transformation of Perpetuities Law*, 36 U. Miami L. Rev. 439 (1982). Both of these articles have been very helpful and particular mention must be given to some of the biographical matters contained in the more recent piece.

entific quantification. At best, such consideration provides a significant contextual platform that assists in the evaluation of the extent to which these cultural influences affected Gray and his perception of the law. Considered as such, this information is helpful, but far from conclusive. Notwithstanding, to the extent that the aforementioned cultural factors impacted Gray, it is not surprising that his interpretation of the RAP does not allow for any exception to the disciplined application of the rule of law.

The Gray Family Tree

John Chipman Gray was a member and descendant of a distinguished Massachusetts family. When he considered joining the Union Army during the Civil War as a commissioned officer, Gray secured a letter of recommendation from John Albien Andrews, the then Governor of Massachusetts, for a commission as an aide-de-camp on the staff of Brigadier General Gordon. The letter was sent to the Secretary of War, E. M. Stanton. Governor Andrews' letter stated:

> If my desire will be allowed any influence on the subject, I hope sincerely that the appointment be made, and I commend it to your kindest consideration. Mr. Gray is of a family whose position of service entitle their wishes to much respect; and he himself is a gentleman of high culture and fair military accruements, admirably adapted to such an appointment.[11]

John Chipman's half-brother, Horace Jr.[12] was a member of the bar and eventually appointed to the United States Supreme Court after having served for many years on the Massachusetts Supreme Judicial Court. John Chipman was a descendant of a commercially successful and politically active family. His grandfather, William "Old Billy" Gray (1750–1825) of Salem, was an enormously successful merchant who owned over thirty-eight ships at one time

---

11. *See* Letter, dated September 5, 1862, from John Albien Andrews, Governor, State of Massachusetts, to Secretary of War E. M. Stanton, (on file with the Houghton Library of the Harvard College, in the John Chipman Gray Correspondence File MS Am. 2152, (8), folder ([2] p.).

12. A principal study of the Gray family tree can be found in a doctor of philosophy dissertation on Horace Gray. *See* STEPHEN ROBERT MITCHELL, MR. JUSTICE HORACE GRAY (1961). This dissertation provides a very useful description of the family ancestors and, by indirection, details of the early family environment of Professor Gray; *see also* ROLAND GRAY, JOHN CHIPMAN GRAY MEMOIR 3–4 (1917); EDWARD GRAY, WILLIAM GRAY OF SALEM (1914).

and more than 178 over his lifetime. A number of other merchants who acquired significant wealth through international trading also began their careers in Salem before moving to Boston. William Gray also engaged in extensive foreign commerce, served with distinction in the Revolutionary War, and was active in politics, serving as the Lieutenant Governor of Massachusetts during the period of 1810 to 1812.[13] When William Gray relocated to Boston in 1808, he was considered to be one of the richest persons in the city.[14]

Several decades before moving to Boston, William Gray married Elizabeth Chipman (1756–1823), the daughter of Honorable John Chipman and Elizabeth Brown Chipman of Marblehead. It was a noteworthy event when they married in 1782 that represented the merger of two powerful families. They had ten children, but only six survived into adulthood. Among the well known offspring of William and Elizabeth Gray were Francis Calley Gray (1790–1856),[15] John Chipman Gray (1793–1881), and Horace Gray Sr. (1800–1873). A brochure on the life of Francis Calley Gray indicates the highlights of his life include the collection of diverse art and engravings. He also served on a committee that organized the first art exhibit at the Athenaeum in 1827. In addition, Francis served as a fellow of Harvard College and provided useful guidance regarding the college's financial system.

Because of the practice of naming children after either the father or other ancestors, it is sometimes difficult to identify individuals by name. John Chipman Gray, the focus of our study, was named after his uncle, John Chipman Gray, and signed many of his letters during the Civil War as John Chipman Gray Jr.[16] The uncle, John Chipman Gray, had an equally significant social and financial life in the Boston community as that of his brother, Francis Calley Gray. Family lore of the Gray family expresses the belief that uncle John Chipman Gray may have greatly aided his brother, Horace Sr., during his period of financial stress—which will be discussed in a later chapter.

---

13. The net worth of William Gray's estate was estimated to be $3,000,000 in 1808 when he moved from Salem to Boston. *See* MITCHELL, *supra* note 12, at 7. For a brief and comprehensive review of William Gray's ancestors and descendents, see Gray Family Ancestral Tree (1670–1970), copy provided by Jeffrey Gray and Roland Gray III and on reserve with the author.

14. *See* GUSTAVUS MYERS, HISTORY OF THE SUPREME COURT OF THE UNITED STATES 561 (1968); MITCHELL, *supra* note 12, at 7.

15. See, Friends of Mount Auburn Cemetery (a charitable trust), Person of the Week Francis Calley Gray. See also, a biography of Mr. Francis Calley Gray, MARJORIE B. COHN, FRANCIS CALLEY GRAY AND ART COLLECTING FOR AMERICA (1986).

16. Professor Gray signed his civil war letters as John Chipman Gray Jr., in deference to his namesake, Uncle John Chipman Gray.

All three of the well known children of John and Elizabeth Gray were graduates of Harvard College and very active participants in the Boston renaissance during the early nineteenth century as well as in the explosion of industrial growth as investors and/or managers of various business enterprises. Francis Calley Gray was recognized as a lawyer who worked briefly with Daniel Webster (although he seldom engaged in the practice of law) and an entrepreneur who made diversified investments in numerous business enterprises. He served in the state senate on several occasions. As previously noted, Francis Calley Gray was a noted collector of art. By the time of his death in 1856, he acquired a substantial collection of art. Francis authorized his executor to transfer the collection to Harvard College where it is now housed in the Mongan Center for Prints, Drawings and Photographs at the Fogg Art Museum.[17] In recognition of his many contributions to Harvard College, Francis received an honorary degree from Harvard College in 1841. Obviously, Francis did not find the practice of law necessary financially because of his substantial inheritance from his father and the wise investment he made of such funds.[18] Finally, Francis was recalled in a eulogy given shortly before a meeting of the Massachusetts Historical Society.

> His numerous and generous contributions of time, and of money, and of his own great abilities, in so many ways, to the cause of literature, learning, and science, will form the appropriate theme of those who shall be called to treat him more deliberately hereinafter. I may add only ... that as a man of elegant accomplishments, of vast and varied acquisition, of thorough, exact, and well-digested information, ready ... in public discourse, he has left no superior, and few equals, in this or any other community.[19]

Clearly, Francis was recognized as a major intellectual of his time.

Uncle John Chipman Gray, like brother Francis, was a graduate of Harvard College and a lawyer who was subsequently honored with a doctorate degree

---

17. *See* Mitchell, *supra* note 12, at 8–9 (recalling Francis Calley Gray for finding the original code of laws adopted in 1641 by the Massachusetts Colony; i.e., the "Liberties of the Massachusetts Colony in New England"); *see also* Cohn, *supra* note 15; Judy Jackson & Laura M. Gosman, *Francis Calley Gray America's First Print Connoisseur* (Friends of the Auburn Cemetery 2002) (on reserve with the author).

18. *See* Edward Pessen, Riches, Class, and Power Before the Civil War 54, 158–60, 267 (1973).

19. Comment made by Robert C. Winthrop, Vol. V Proceeding of the Massachusetts Historical Society, Second Series, 311, at 312 (1889–1890). These comments were made on January 9, 1857 and later published as part of the Society's proceedings.

(LL.D.) from Harvard College in 1856.[20] By reason of his substantial inheritance from his father, as well as his fortuitous marriage to Elizabeth Pickering Gardner, the daughter of Samuel P. Gardner,[21] Uncle John enjoyed a life of moderate leisure and civility.[22] The marriage, by and between the children of the established mercantile families of Boston during the early period of the nineteenth century, was like a corporate merger. The family, from this perspective, can be seen as an institutional means to continue the breeding of the elegant elite of the Boston community. It is a natural process of selection and the essential means by which families guaranteed their status of wealth and power for their benefit as well as that of forthcoming generations. This process is a universal experience for most communities, but the manifestation of the unique impact and role of the family as an institution is particularly obvious with the Boston Brahmins. The 1993 study by Betty G. Farrell of the elite families of the Boston community during the nineteenth century verifies this social institution.[23]

John Chipman and Elizabeth Pickering Gray did not have any children. Because of this and other circumstances, such as their substantial inheritances, they were throughout their lives exceedingly financially capable of providing significant assistance to any member of their extended family in need of assistance. This fact gives logical support to the legend of the Gray family that Horace Sr. was financially aided by brother, John Chipman Gray, following his disastrous insolvency.

An interesting fact of the Gray family is the existence of the strong history of lawyers in the Gray family lineage. The present count of lawyers in the Gray family tree reveals seven generations of lawyers. In addition, both the grandfather and father of Horace Jr. and John Chipman married daughters of well-known lawyers. Apart from the seafaring and commercial enterprises, raising young boys to become practicing lawyers was a secret formula for the Gray family.

When William and Elizabeth Chipman Gray relocated from Salem to Boston, William was considered to be one of the richest persons in the city.[24] Horace

---

20. *See* Mitchell, *supra* note 12, at 18.

21. Samuel Gardner was a very successful merchant. *See* Pessen, *supra* note 18, at 113.

22. *See id.* at 159–60. For a list of some of the many positions John Chipman Gray held as an officer and/or member of the Board of Directors, see Betty G. Farrell, Elite Families Class and Power in Nineteenth Century Boston 68, 124 (1993).

23. *See generally* Farrell, *supra* note 22.

24. *See* Myers, *supra* note 14, at 561; Mitchell, *supra* note 12, at 7. There is an anonymously published book in Boston (without the author's name printed therein) that appears to have been written by Thomas L. V. Wilson, The Aristocracy of Boston; Who They Are, and What They Were: Being a History of Business and Businessmen of Boston

Gray Sr. (father of Horace Jr. and John Chipman) was the youngest of the children of William and Elizabeth. Lore has it that when the surviving sons of William came of age, each of them was given a substantial sum. Horace Sr. entered into the family business with his father as a partner.[25] Subsequent to the death of William, the original business enterprise of shipping was successfully continued for some time by Horace Sr. before he decided to diversify most of his investments into the expanding iron works industry. Although Horace Sr. was successful in continuing the family shipping business of his father for some twenty-two years, the decision to convert from his shipping business and invest in the iron works industry eventually proved to be an unqualified economic disaster. Horace Sr. soon found himself caught in a sudden economic downturn which, when combined with what appears to have been poor management of his extensive investments in the iron industry, proved to be financially disastrous.[26]

Trouble in the Financial World of Horace Gray Sr.

The economic failure of his diversified iron manufacturing enterprises forced Horace Sr. to file under the insolvency procedures of Massachusetts in 1847.[27] Although there is never a right time for a family financial disaster, this event had a major impact on young John Chipman and, perhaps, a greater impact on Horace Jr. Nevertheless, this financially embarrassing event strongly in-

---

17–20 (1848). It does appear to have creditable information on the Gray family that is mostly favorable, particularly as it relates to William "Old Billy" Gray.

25. *See* MITCHELL, *supra* note 12, at 21; GRAY, *supra* note 12, at 85.

26. *See* WILSON, *supra* note 24, at 17 (indicating that Horace Sr. had the largest iron works operation in New England, ranging from manufacturing sites located in Maine, Massachusetts, and New York). The numerous reported cases involving litigation set forth *infra* note 33 suggests that the information provided by the Wilson appears to be reasonably reliable.

27. *See* 10 MONTHLY L. REP. 431, 432 (1847). The actual date of the insolvency filing is recorded on November 24, 1847. *See id.* Mitchell made a typographical mistake as it relates to the specific year in which Horace Sr. became insolvent. On page 30 of his study, he notes the date of 1857, but he adds that it was the same year that Horace Jr. started on his grand tour, which was two years after his graduation from Harvard College in 1845. *See* MITCHELL, *supra* note 12, at 30. *But see* Elbridge B. Davis & Harold A. Davis, *Mr. Justice Horace Gray: Some Aspects of His Judicial Career*, 41 A.B.A. J. 421 (1955) (identifying the year of 1848 as being the year of financial difficulty for Horace Sr.).

creased the individual sense of responsibility of the children and certainly stroked the ambition of John Chipman and Horace Jr.[28] This event eliminated the possibility that the children[29] of Horace Sr. would have the choice of living a life of leisure and reflection. The news of their father's financial disaster came to Horace Jr. when he was on the customary grand tour of Europe.[30] This economic catastrophe of the Horace Gray Sr. family was a major social failing of significance and caused, no doubt, a deep sense of embarrassment to a family that was heretofore a well established affluent participant in the Boston community.

That Horace Jr. and John Chipman responded favorably to the financial challenges and social embarrassment that were presented by such a reversal of their father's fortune cannot be questioned. They both subsequently achieved exceptionally distinguished legal careers and social standing of the highest order. They no longer had the discretion to opt for a life with the other three percenters of the Boston community. "Three percenters" is a term describing the group of select beneficiaries who relied on the flow of income from trusts to meet their living standard. John Chipman was eight years old when his father faced bankruptcy and could not at that young age fully appreciate the social consequences to the family. The pain of that reality would slowly become a matter of concern to him as he matured. However, there is no detectable reduction in the social and educational opportunities provided to John Chipman because of his father's insolvency compared to the privileges that were fully available to Horace Jr. One presumes (there is no record on this assumption) that Horace Sr. and his family were provided other economic benefits, perhaps, through the assistance of other members of the Gray and/or the Gardner family. Uncle John Chipman Gray, brother of Horace Sr., was one who presumably provided financial assistance. There is also direct evidence that Francis was involved in the related business enterprises with his brother, Horace Sr.[31] In addition, the wife of Horace Sr., Sarah Gardner Gray, pre-

---

28. John Chipman Gray admitted that such horrific family events had much to do with the subsequent individual successes that were to come to brother Horace and himself. *See* Gray, *supra* note 12, at 4.

29. Horace Gray Sr. (1800–1873) fathered five children with two wives. The children by the first wife, Harriet Upham (1801–1834), were Horace Gray Jr., Elizabeth Chipman Gray, and Harriet Gray. John Chipman Gray and Russell Gray were the progeny of Horace and his second wife, Sarah Russell Gardner. Sarah was the sister of Elizabeth Pickering Gardner, the wife of John Chipman Gray, the brother of Horace Sr.

30. *See* Mitchell, *supra* note 12, at 30.

31. *See* Gray v. Coffin, 63 Mass. (9 Cush.) 192 (Mass. 1852).

sumably was financially well off as a daughter of the enormously wealthy Samuel Pickering Gardner. She could have provided resources after the economic disaster. It is interesting to note that Sarah was also an aunt to the equally wealthy John Lowell "Jack" Gardner who married the infamous Isabella "Belle" Stewart Gardner. Belle is discussed in Chapter 4 as a difficult and demanding client of John Chipman Gray.

Horace Sr. apparently accepted full responsibility for his financial failure and conveyed all of the business assets to a master in chancery for the benefit of the respective creditors.[32] Horace Sr. did not follow careful business practice in operating his diversified iron works businesses. It appears he managed the separate corporate operations in the name Horace Gray and Company, a partnership. By such practice, he did not secure the limited liability which is an essential benefit of utilizing the corporate structure.[33] It is somewhat ironic to note that Horace Jr. was the official court reporter in some of the litigation involving his father's insolvency.[34]

The definitive manner by which Horace Sr. accepted complete responsibility for his financial obligations to other creditors, although he fully exercised all available legal defenses to limit the extent of personal liability, must have resonated with young John Chipman. Indeed, it became by indirection one of the dominant themes of his life as a man and as a scholar. John Chipman's mantra was that man must be accountable for his actions and personal debts! This deep sense of responsibility to one's creditors became a principal theme of young John's experience as he not only accepted but learned from Horace Sr.'s dutiful acceptance of legal and personal responsibility to others occasioned by his business failure. John Chipman passionately reaffirmed this ethical maxim in a second book when he reiterated a simple but comprehensive observation: "If there is one sentiment, therefore, which would appear to be part

32. The legal impact of the conveyance to the creditors by Horace Sr. became the subject of a legal controversy years later when a share of an award for the French spoliation claims were settled. For a full discussion of this event, see *infra* Chapter 3. A general discussion of the Massachusetts insolvency procedures is set forth in the Monthly Law Reporter. *See The Insolvent Law of Massachusetts,* 10 Monthly L. Rep. 33 (1848).

33. As a result, there were a number of law suits attempting to impose personal liability for possible corporate debts. See, for example, Gray v. Coffin, 63 Mass. (9 Cush.) 192 (Mass. 1852); Conro v. Gray, 4 How. Pr. 166 (N.Y. Gen. Term 1852); Catskill Bank v. Gray, 14 Barb. 471, (N.Y. Sup. Ct. 1851); Thomas v. Minot, 76 Mass. (10 Gray) 263 (Mass. 1857); Fisher v Minot, 76 Mass. (10 Gray) 260 (Mass. 1857); Tremlett v. Hooper, 76 Mass. (10 Gray) 254 (Mass. 1857); Herring v. Boston Iron Co., 67 Mass (1 Gray) 1345 (Mass. 1854); Melledge v. Boston Iron Co., 59 Mass. 158 (Mass. 1849).

34. *See* cases cited *supra* note 33.

of all in authority, and particularly of all judges, to fortify, it is the duty of keeping one's promises and paying one' debts."[35]

Most likely, the full implications of his father's failure and public acceptance of his indebtedness festered within John Chipman as he matured into manhood. One could argue that this embarrassing reversal of fortune of the Gray family in 1847 was not to ever be forgotten by John Chipman. More than three decades later it ignited his excoriation of the judiciary for its cavalier and arbitrary enforcement of the spendthrift provisions. The enforcement of such spendthrift provision in a trust allowed the financially secure beneficiaries of a trust to escape paying the lawful claims of their creditors.[36] This was probably the first formal example of the application of law for John Chipman. It is not surprising that he saw securing personal accountability as a major function of the law and an essential ingredient for a safe and secure society. The extended period of years during which the litigation of insolvency issues continued made getting through the social embarrassment more difficult for the entire family. One speculates whether Horace Sr.'s example in facing his creditors, and allegedly without excuses or denial (except where there were substantive questions regarding his personal liability), was indelibly marked on the formative consciousness of a maturing young boy between eight and thirteen years old. As theorized herein, John Chipman was profoundly influenced by this experience and conceptualized the law, in part, as calling for individual responsibility in a manner that allowed for no exceptions. Gray's sense of personal accountability for enforcement of the law became an essential ingredient in the design of his RAP.

There are factors of the Gray family that have not been sufficiently recognized. For example, the Boston community has failed to appropriately recognize the initial contribution of Horace Sr. and others as it relates to the creation of the Boston Public Gardens. As reported by the National Park Service, it was the "first botanical garden in the United States."[37] The details of the original development of the Boston Public Gardens is explained in the nomination form for registration as an Historic Place.

> In 1839 the City granted a group of 17 horticulturalists, headed by Horace Gray, permission to establish a botanic garden on this land. Gray,

35. John Chipman Gray, Restraints on the Alienation of Property, at iii (2d ed. 1895).

36. *See* Chapter 8, *infra*.

37. *See* The Great American Landmarks Adventure, http://www.nps.gov/hps/pad/adventure/bostongard.htm.

> who had a collection of camellias and various varieties of hothouse grapes, envisioned on the site a botanic garden similar to those in European cities. Gray and his group imported an English landscape gardener, John Cadness, to supervise the work of ornamenting the grounds.[38]

The Brighton-Allston Historical Society cites Horace Gray Sr., as the father of the Boston Public Gardens and as "a man who deserves to be better known."[39] One would hope that this omission will at some time be rectified.

Impact of Father's Insolvency on Gray's Articulation of the RAP

We are not privy to how and to what extent the public failure of Gray's father affected him from a jurisprudential point of view. Gray was approximately eight years old when his father filed under the insolvency procedures for the State of Massachusetts. There is no question that Gray's interpretation and application of the RAP follows a super strict and highly unforgiving application to the enforcement of the RAP. Namely, the RAP must be "remorselessly applied," without any exception, and the object of the rule is "to defeat intent." This highly moralistic theme is thoroughly consistent with the possible indelible internalization of one's moral obligation by a sensitive and impressionable young boy. In addition, the process of insolvency continued on for years as is reflected in the extensive litigation history. There must have been an extended period during which the family felt the public awareness or discussion of the insolvency would never die. Gray was, no doubt, greatly affected by his youthful perception of this early traumatic experience with legal accountability.[40] There was no simple escape from the intense social pressures and it would not be too much to expect that Horace Sr. suffered for some period of time with a degree of depression. The existence of financial support from other members of the family would definitely help, but certainly would not eradicate the father's deep and personal sense of failure.

38. National Register of Historic Places Inventory—Nomination Form, Boston Public Garden, *available at* http://pdfhost.focus.nps.gov/docs/NHLS/Text/87000761.pdf, at 3.

39. *See* Dr. William P. Marchione, *Horace Gray: Father of the Boston Public Gardens*, *available at* http://bahistory.org/HoraceGray.html (last visited Feb. 1, 2009).

40. *See* John Chipman Gray, The Rule Against Perpetuities §629 (1886).

Gray, perhaps seeing the cost applied to his father under the legal system, now saw the law as providing certain answers. He opined, with Delphic insight and measured certainty, that the RAP must be enforced as "[i]t is a dangerous thing to make a radical change in a part of the law which is concatenated with almost mathematical certainty."[41] For Gray, there was little to debate when it came to the determination of right or wrong, and the law provided certain guidance in the resolution of that question. Moreover, Gray believed a full measure of punishment must be applied to those who violate the rules. The severity of Gray's moralistic approach to the law imitates the strict accountability that his father faced and accepted. There was no "manly" way other than to face up to the consequences of one's financial debts. That could be accomplished only by way of turning over one's assets to pay to the extent of the net resources. When it came to the interpretation of the law, Gray was caught in a prism of scrupulously enforcing the law. He criticized, some might say severely, any who might favor selective moderation in enforcement of the RAP, whether based on concepts of equity or an open and unconcealed act of mercy.

The standard of accountability ingrained in the Gray family accorded with the established norm of the Boston Brahmins. Paul Goodman, in discussing the values of the Boston elite, offered the following insight:

> The elite entrepreneur was thus not a free agent but a morally responsible person answerable to family and friends as well as to community and conscience. By deviating from expected norms, individuals not only risked censure but also might injure the clan materially and morally. "You should place your standard of action so high," Amos Lawrence advised his brother Abbot, "as to require great vigilance in living up to it." The ideal businessman would risk his property for his honor and for the good of others. Though not legally obligated, J. M. Forbes repaid his father's needy creditors as soon as he had provided a competence for his mother.[42]

Failure to meet that standard would have significant and enduring social consequences for one's family in the in the Boston community.

Thus, John Chipman and Horace Jr. were raised in an environment in which duty was married to one's performance in the conduct of business, whether it

41. *Id.* §871.

42. *See* Paul Goodman, *Ethics and Enterprise: The Values of a Boston Elite, 1800–1860*, 18 Am. Q. 437, 442 (1966).

was in the operation of a trade or the profession of law.[43] Both Horace Jr. and John Chipman most surely desired that their father would always be considered as one who met this standard despite the economic failure of his diverse business enterprises. Each of the brothers entered into a silent contract by which they would double their personal efforts so their individual careers added respect and value to the social reputation of the Horace Gray Sr. family. The Boston community was unusually interconnected by reason of the intermarrying between members of the established Brahmin clans. Score cards indicating the current gain or loss of value for respective families were easily determined. The family rating system was analogous to a daily stock market, and low scores would adversely affect one's marriage potential and job opportunities. These score cards would be shared by and among the then reigning elites through social discourse and, to some extent, be employed to identify one's nexus to positions of social importance.

John Chipman and Horace Jr. were each driven to eliminate the stain of this social and economic catastrophe by securing outstanding achievements in their own professional lives. It is not an overstatement to suggest that their selection of careers in law was, to some extent, a product of their father's failed commercial enterprise. In the case of Horace Jr., there is some testimony as to the relationship between the father's bankruptcy and his subsequent selection of a legal career. Charles Francis Adams, a long-term friend of Horace Jr. for some fifty years, provided the following observation in his eulogy of Horace Jr. before the Massachusetts Historical Society.

> In the very last talk I had with him, on the gallery of his house overlooking the sea about Nahant, a few weeks only before his death, referring to that unformed period (Horace's time at Harvard College between the ages of thirteen and sixteen and the period shortly thereafter) he told me that, in all probability, had Professor Agassiz come to this country two years earlier than he did, he (Gray) would have been a scientific man. At college his inclination had been to natural history; for, outgrowing his strength while a boy,—at the age of twelve he had attained this full height which always thereafter made him noticeable,—he was threatened with pulmonary troubles, and an open-air life, with gun and rod, was prescribed for him. So, for a time, he devoted himself to a study of birds and butterflies, while almost to the close of his life, he was an eager angler. But, shortly after graduation, a change, most fortune for him, was brought about by the busi-

43. *Id.* at 442–43.

> ness failure of his father, of the same name as himself. The senior Horace Gray was, like his son, a man of pronounced characteristics and exceptional ability; but he had the misfortune of being somewhat in advance of his time. Engaged in the development of the then infant iron industries of the country, he, before 1850, projected much which has been successfully carried out only within our own time; and so he shared the fate of many men of force and foresight, who have the mishap of being born too soon—before conditions are ripe for them. The father's bankruptcy changed the whole aspect of the son's future. He had to choose a profession as a means of support, and he turned to law. In doing so, he did but follow what was for him the line of least resistance, instinctively or by chance recognizing his own aptitude. By heredity, he was a lawyer; for, though, so far as I am aware, the Grays had been associated with business and shipping rather than the law. Horace Gray Jr.'s mother was an Upham, and his paternal grandmother a Chipman, the former a name well known at the earlier Massachusetts Bar, and the latter conspicuous in the judicial annals of the Providences.[44]

In the case of John Chipman, we have the specific statement by him indicating that his father's failure had a direct impact on Horace Jr. and him and their drive for success.[45]

Horace Sr.'s obituary in the Boston Globe, although brief, pinpoints the depth of the ongoing concern of the brothers Gray about their father's integrity and honest dealings.

> Mr. Horace Gray, for many years a prominent iron merchant of Boston, died at his residence in this city on Wednesday, at the age of 72. He was the son of the late William Gray, distinguished as one of the foremost merchants of Boston, and carried on for several years his father's interests in the East India Trade. He afterwards went into the iron business, as senior partner of Gray & Co., and continued to engage in trade until twenty years ago, when he retired. *Mr. Gray was a man very well known among business men of this city, who held him in high regard for his integrity and honest dealings.* He leaves a widow and several children, including Judge Gray of the Supreme Court of this state being his son.[46]

---

44. Proceedings from 1903, XVI Massachusetts Historical Society, Charles Francis Adams, President 251, 254–55 (on file with Massachusetts Historical Society).

45. *See* Gray, *supra* note 12, at 4.

46. *Obituary of Horace Gray Sr.*, Boston Globe, Aug. 1, 1873, at A5 (emphasis added).

If this obituary was drafted by the brothers Gray (it clearly sounds in the language and style of both), the mantra of high integrity and honest dealings becomes their dominant and lasting inheritance and the final bequest from their father. John Chipman and Horace Jr. attempted, in many ways, to model their lives in a fashion similar to the idealized virtues attributed to their father. It cannot be questioned that they were equally successful in their very distinguished professional careers, if not excessively so, to the possible detriment of their family life.

Chapter 3

Scholarly Influence of Half-Brother Justice Horace Gray Jr.

Distant in Birth but Identical in Interpretation of the Common Law

The overall affect of Horace Jr.'s significant impact on his younger half-brother, John Chipman, regarding the comprehension and ongoing vitality of the common law has neither been sufficiently recognized nor fully discussed. Stephen Robert Mitchell, a biographer of Horace Jr., identified an aspect of his impact.

> [Justice Horace and John Chipman Gray] were similar to a considerable degree, and it would not be unreasonable to conclude that John Chipman Gray's interests in charitable trusts and the law of real property, for, instance, was fostered, at least in part, by Horace's earlier interest in the same problem.[1]

Because of the circumstances relating to their age differences and dissimilar family experiences, it is a fascinating story to uncover the depth of Horace Jr.'s influence on John Chipman's perspective on the common law. Indeed, to understand the scholarship of John Chipman, a study of his brother's life in the law is essential; a failure to do so constitutes a serious omission. Accordingly, the legal achievements and dispositions of Horace Jr. are addressed from the framework of his extensive career on the state and federal bench and the analytic modality that he employed in arriving at particular decisions. The similarity of legal approach by John Chipman and Horace Jr. with respect to the interpretation of the common law is nothing short of astonishing.

---

1. *See* Stephen Robert Mitchell, Mr. Justice Horace Gray 26–27 (1961).

It should not be presumed that John Chipman and Horace Jr. shared the same family experiences during their early years or that they were emotionally close during the many coterminous years of their personal and professional life. Horace Jr., born March 24, 1828, was the son of Horace Sr. and Harriet Upham Gray.[2] Unfortunately, Harriet Upham Gray died in 1834 of tuberculosis or consumption when Horace Jr. was six years old.[3] Horace Sr. was a successful entrepreneur, recognized philanthropist,[4] and leader of the community. William P. Marchione notes in his discussion on the establishment of the Boston Public Gardens, the significant role played by Horace Sr.

> Horace Gray, the father of the Boston Public Garden, is a somewhat shadowy figure who deserves to be better known. A man of great vision and high public spirit, he was the prime mover and chief financial prop of the early effort to transform the swamp like western fringe of the Boston Common into the park that we today know as the Boston Public Garden.
>
> At the time of his [Horace Gray's] death in 1873, scant notice was taken of his passing in the city's press. His obituary in the Boston Herald, for example, identified him only as a former active merchant and the father of State Supreme Court judge, with no mention of his singular contribution to the beatification of Boston as the founder of the Public Garden.[5]

That public omission as to his role, to some extent, continues right up to the present time.

Three years after Harriet's death, Horace Sr. married Sarah Russell Gardner (July 3, 1837), who bore two children, John Chipman Gray (July 14, 1839) and Russell Gray (November 3, 1850). Thus, Horace Jr. was without a primary maternal caregiver for a period of three years following his mother's death. After his father's remarriage, he had to adjust to his new stepmother as well as contend with his two new much younger half-brothers. Naturally, Sarah Gardner Gray occupied a central position of authority within the newly struc-

---

2. *See* Francis C. Lowell, Horace Gray, Proceedings of the American Academy of Arts and Science 627 (Vol. XXXIX 1904).

3. *See* Mitchell, *supra* note 1, at 25–26, 28; *see also* George F. Hoar, Memoir of Horace Gray Jr., Proceedings of the Massachusetts Historical Society 155–57 (Vol. XVIII 1904). There are other references that Harriet died as a passenger of a shipwreck. *See, e.g.*, Dr. William P. Marchione, *Horace Gray: Father of the Boston Public Garden, available at* http://www.bahistory.org/HoraceGray.html (last visited July. 18, 2009).

4. *See* Mitchell, *supra* note 1, at 26; *see also* Marchione, *supra* note 4.

5. *See* Marchione, *supra* note 3.

tured family and Horace Jr. had to accept the painful loss of his birth mother while learning the ways of his new stepmother. Horace Jr. left home to study at Harvard College at the tender age of thirteen, never returning to live indefinitely in the home.[6] John was two years old and Russell was not even born when Horace Jr. started college.

It could not be an easy childhood pathway for Horace Jr. and, perhaps, not one that he handled well. It also may explain why he left home for college at such a young age. Added to these potential complications were the physical conditions affecting Horace Jr. as a maturing young boy. He was a tall, thin, gangling boy of uncertain health during his early years, who "was threatened with pulmonary troubles" and an open-air life was prescribed for him.[7] He reached his adult height of six-foot-six by the age of thirteen.[8] He clearly stood out among his youthful contemporaries and it would be surprising if he did not, in view of his formidable height, suffer from a degree of self-consciousness that would continue throughout his life. In light of the circumstances of his early years, it would not be unrealistic to believe that Horace Jr. also felt somewhat rejected by family and peers. Without a doubt, he suffered from the absence of consistent maternal care during a critical phase of his maturation.

Charles Francis Adams noted the difficulties that Horace Jr. faced throughout his life and made a brief allusion in his eulogy that poignantly raises a question regarding the level of the social and cultural maturity of his personality, despite the exceptional achievement in his professional life. Adams observed that "there was something at that time very attractive and sympathetic about Horace Gray. A certain brusqueness of manner and roughness of occasional speech which caused him then and later to be criticized by many, were not apparent to me."[9]

Despite John Chipman's emotional and age difference from Horace Jr., he was quick to protect his brother's post-death legal legacy. As evidence of this concern, John Chipman sent two letters to Adams; the first provided advice on selecting several of Horace's constitutional decisions of lasting importance for inclusion in his eulogy, the second severely criticized Adams for his failure to explain in his eulogy the significant contribution that his brother made to the development of constitutional law.[10] The critical letter to Adams provided

6. *See* Mitchell, *supra* note 1, at 26–27.

7. Charles Francis Adams, Proceedings from Massachusetts Historical Society (254) Vol. XVI 1903) [hereinafter Adams Vol. XVI].

8. *See id.*; *see also* Stephen Robert Mitchell, *supra* note 1, at 28.

9. Adams Vol. XVI, *supra* note 7, at 254.

10. John Malcolm Smith, *Mr. Justice Horace Gray of the United States Supreme Court*, 6 S.D. L. Rev. 221, 242 n.91, 243 n.94 (1961) (citing letters September 22, 1902 and October

in part, "Your remarks were not a stump speech nor was the address a bill, but the incongruity was as striking. To those who did understand about the subject, I think you failed to apprehend *les nuances des choises*."[11] There is no question that John Chipman, when prompted by events, had a facile and efficient manner to express his umbrage despite the social standing of the deemed wrongdoer.

Other comments suggest that Horace Jr's personal character was something less than socially charming. "Horace Gray belonged to the class in Boston styling themselves the old aristocracy; he was accused of being obtrusively snobbish; judging from anecdotes related of him, he was no doubt, a thorough snob and a formalist of the most pronounced and provoking type."[12] Yet, others were of a different view, such as Chief Justice Knowlton of the Massachusetts Supreme Judicial Court who described Horace in his eulogy.

> To those of us who knew him in his social relations, a sketch of his life would seem incomplete if it omitted to mention the kindly, cheerful, almost exuberant vivacity of his companionship with his friends. He was a charming host, giving to the privileged guests at his fire side the full measure of his hospitality in generous entertainment and enlivening conservation. The largeness of his nature was bountiful and bestowal, alike in the quiet of his home and the stately environment of the court.[13]

Not surprisingly, Horace Jr. never married until 1889 when he was sixty-one years old. He married Jane Mathews, a woman thirty years younger than he.[14] There may be a pattern of the brothers Gray—John Chipman's wife, Nina, was fifteen years younger than he. Horace Jr.'s wife, Jane, was the

---

17, 1902 between John Chipman Gray and Charles Francis Adams, retained in Justice Gray's papers in the United States Supreme Court). There are also other papers of Justice Gray in the files of the Library of Congress.

11. *Id.* at 243 (emphasis added) (internal quotation marks omitted).

12. Gustavus Myers, History of the Supreme Court of the United States 561 (1968); *see also* Robert Gray, Amy Heard: Letters from the Gilded Age 6, http://www.ee.stanford.edu/~gray/html/amy/amy_5.html (referencing comments of Mrs. Henry Adams stating "Last Sunday Judge Gray to dine. Has not gained in charm of manner in the years since we last met").

13. *See* 182 Mass. 613 (1903), *available at* http://www.massreports.com/memorials/182ma613.htm; Francis R. Jones, *Horace Gray—An Encomium*, 14 The Green Bag 403, 404 (1902) ("No man has ever been more human than he, or had a kinder heart. His ready aid has always been given without sparing to young attorneys.").

14. *See* Mitchell, *supra* note 1, at 231.

daughter of his former colleague on the United States Supreme Court, Associate Justice Stanley Mathews.[15] Mathews died March 22, 1889, a few months prior to their marriage. Horace Jr. attended the memorial service for Mathews in Washington, DC, with other dignitaries of the government including the President and members of the cabinet, Congress, and the Supreme Court.[16]

An instance of unusual of candor and some awkwardness occurred in connection with Horace Jr.'s engagement to Jane. Samuel Williston, serving as a law clerk to Horace Jr., described the following exchange that took place between them.

> One morning Gray approached me with a rather sheepish smile and exhibited a beautiful ring—a sapphire with a diamond on each side of it. He said "you being, if I may say so, in *consimili casu* can perhaps tell me whether this would be likely to please a young lady?" I assured him that the probabilities were great that it would afford pleasure.[17]

Getting married for the first time at an advanced age would be an awkward and highly emotional event for anyone, but even more so for a man of Horace Jr.'s unique character and temperament.

Parallel Pathways on Interpretation of the Common Law

Mitchell possibly understates the depth of the relationship between the brothers as it relates to the common law.

> [The brothers Gray] became fast friends and intellectual companions only after John Chipman entered Harvard College and the Harvard Law School. Horace was then the reporter (1854–1861) of the decisions for the Supreme Judicial Court of Massachusetts. They were never brothers in the usual sense of the term. They saw little of each

15. *See* Elbridge B. Davis & Harold A. Davis, *Mr. Justice Gray: Some Aspects of His Judicial Career,* 41 A.B.A. J. 421, 424 (1955); *see also* John E. Semonche, Oxford Companion to the Supreme Court of the United States 345 (Kermit L. Hall, ed. 1992).

16. See New York Times report of Justice Mathews' funeral, March 26, 1889.

17. Samuel Williston, Life and Law: An Autobiography 97 (Boston Little Brown 1941) (emphasis added).

> other and were unable to share the memories of a childhood together. Their letters were more the exchange of two gentleman scholars interested in the same sort of quiet world than those of brothers. There was evidence in the letters of a great deal of mutual respect, however, and each was constantly soliciting the others' opinion on some unique point of law. Their latter interests were similar to a considerable degree, and it would not be unreasonable to conclude that John Chipman Gray's interest in charitable trusts and the law of real property, for instance, was fostered, at least in part, by Horace's earlier interest in the same problems.[18]

Mitchell was neither fully aware of the commonality of the brothers' view as it related to the perfection of the English common law nor the fixed reverential attitude that John Chipman held with respect to Horace Jr.'s ability to unravel the mysteries of the English common law.

Although John Chipman and Horace Jr. seldom interacted during their early years in the family because of their age disparity, the brothers were fully aware of the achievements of each other and thoroughly proud of the other's professional accomplishments. A comparison of their legal efforts reveals that they both shared an unambiguous commitment to and a religious-like respect for the importance of the common law. From a closer scrutiny of the record regarding the details of the brothers, we see a parallel and similar convergence in regards to their legal approach to, and belief in, the "perfection" of the common law. Their unity in the ascertainment of the common law from their unconditional obeisance, to the authority of the English jurists, could not be more alike. Despite their age differences and emotional separateness, it would not be unreasonable to believe that John Chipman idealized the judicial achievements, social standing, and legal authority of his older brother. Horace Jr. was an eminent legal authority of national prominence, as well as an influential model of overpowering psychological importance to his then maturing younger brother. Nothing was more certain than the well defined jurisprudential methodology of Horace Jr., his unconditional obeisance to the role of precedents of the English authorities, and his professional dedication to the esoteric edicts of the common law.[19]

---

18. Mitchell, *supra* note 1, at 26–27.

19. A 1955 review of Horace Jr.'s judicial aptitude and style by Elbridge and Harold Davis provides, in part, as follows:

> He carried his ideas of historical research into his judicial work and leaned heavily on precedent, his technique in the preparation of a decision being to state the question, bring forward an imposing list of authorities, and at the end sum up

There is limited evidence of the professional relationship between John Chipman and Horace Jr. as adults apart from general correspondence, legal scholarship, and occasional visitations. One event occurred when John Codman Ropes and John Chipman decided to upgrade the location of their law office and move to a more expensive location. In this process, they sought the imprimatur of Horace Jr. on their pending decision. This suggests that Horace Jr. exercised something akin to avuncular authority and that his personal approval of the move had a reassuring impact on the enterprising business partners. This event was described by Albert Boyden, the first historian on the creation and development of the Ropes & Gray law firm: "[T]he choice, after personal inspection, was sanctified by the august approval of no less a personage than Mr. Horace Gray, John's elder brother, already a Justice of the Massachusetts Supreme Judicial Court, hence of judgment infallible."[20] Although emotionally distant, Horace Jr.'s professional experience and business acumen were always available and, when called upon, provided the approval that the fledgling law partners needed.

Another element in the relationship of John Chipman and Horace Jr. relates to their career paths. There is no question that young John Chipman formally mirrored Horace Jr.'s manners in many ways, including the selection of a professional career, choice of educational institutions (Harvard College and Harvard Law School), writing style, and Horace Jr.'s belief that the highest form of legal perfection was always to be found in the opinions of the English judges.

In addition to the mutual concern for the law of real property and charitable trusts,[21] Horace Jr. and John Chipman shared a similar attitude toward explaining the law. It must be admitted that Horace Jr.'s reputation as a judge of

---

> the situation, expressing his opinion in a paragraph or two. Usually he confined himself strictly to the matter at hand, seldom adding anything by way of dicta....

See Davis & Davis, *supra* note 15, at 422; *see also* Semonche, *supra* note 15, at 345–46.

20. It is significant that Horace Jr. was personally requested to approve of the proposed relocation. *See* Albert Boyden, Ropes-Gray 1865–1940, 55 (Privately Printed by Lincoln & Smith Press of Boston 1942).

21. The apex of Horace Jr. as judge can be observed in his work on the law of charitable trusts. *See* Smith, *supra* note 10, at 229 (noting that John Chipman would gladly rest Horace's judicial reputation on his decision in *Jackson v. Phillips*, 96 Mass. (14 Allen) 539 (1867), concerning the establishment of a charitable trusts for the purpose of defeating the institution of slavery and providing relief to fugitive slaves, among other purposes, constituted a public charity and the doctrine of *cy pres* applied to carry out such beneficent directives notwithstanding the subsequent abolition of slavery). *See also* Smith, *supra* note 11, at 229–30.

lasting importance suffered mostly for the period during which he served on the United States Supreme Court. That judicial legacy does not apply to the many years of distinguished service on the Massachusetts Supreme Judicial Court, where his reputation stands in relative high repute. Horace Jr.'s less than distinguished reputation as an Associate Justice of the United States Supreme Court was due, in part, to his professional style of decision writing. According to Ezra A. Thayer, a former law clerk of Horace Jr, he had the "habit of condensing his own statements as severe as his quotations from others were generous, [and this] made it appear as if the larger part of his work was that of marshalling cases."[22] Horace Jr.'s biographer, Stephen Robert Mitchell, adds that "Gray's addiction to historical analyses and collections of cases was the despair of his law clerks."[23]

One observes that John Chipman consciously imitated his brother in the form of his legal scholarship. John Chipman's herald opus on perpetuities is mostly reportage of a series of cases of the English kind in which the matter of an explanatory analysis of the rule and its policy basis are almost completely eliminated. John Chipman believed the true science of the law was to be found in the language that the English judges employed and not on any abstraction of his own making. Indeed, the theme of the Rule Against Perpetuities (no interest is good unless it vest, if at all, not later than twenty-one years after some life in being at the creation of the interests) is the barest minimal text of the rule.

The connectedness of the Gray brothers is further affirmed when one looks at their very similar professional record. Indeed, their styles were similar in that they both focused on the clarification of common law principles as explained and produced by the English authorities in cases of the ancien régimes; notwithstanding, that some of the opinions of such antiquated cases were fraught with inaccuracies and frequently extraordinarily complex. Horace Jr. had an early introduction to the close study of the English authorities by reason of his professional assignment as the official court reporter for the Massachusetts Supreme Judicial Court from 1854 to 1860.[24] In that capacity, he maintained concern for the quality and accuracy of the published opinions of

22. Ezra A. Thayer, Tribute to Horace Gray, Proceedings of the American Academy of Arts and Sciences 321 (June 1904).

23. Mitchell, *supra* note 1, at 117.

24. *See* Office of Reporter of Decisions, Supreme Judicial Court, Massachusetts, Volumes, Gray 1–16, for the period of 1854–1860.

the Massachusetts court. During this time, John Chipman was undergoing the final formal phase of his educational experience at Harvard College, graduating in 1859,[25] and then Harvard Law School, graduating in 1861.[26] He continued his education at Harvard Law School during the fall semester, and received a master's degree in June 1862.[27]

John Chipman was no doubt aware and impressed with the prestigious function that his brother was providing as the official reporter for the Supreme Judicial Court. One wonders whether John Chipman worked for his brother, informally or otherwise, during the period of Horace Jr.'s position as the official court reporter. John Chipman subsequently did work in an editorial capacity for a later reporter of the Supreme Judicial Court, Albert G. Browne.[28] The parallelism of the Gray brothers' legal experiences and unique approach to the law, except that John Chipman was never to become a judge, remains quite remarkable considering their age differences. As to the possibility of a judicial appointment, it should be noted that John Chipman was offered such opportunities, but he refused to accept any appointment. His refusal was due in part to the lack of a satisfying remuneration.[29]

Except for approximately two years, the period between John Chipman's admission to the bar on September 18, 1862[30] and the date of Horace Jr.'s initial appointment to the Supreme Judicial Court of Massachusetts on August 23, 1864, all the formative years of John Chipman's development as a lawyer and law professor occurred during the time that Horace Jr. was serving as a

---

25. *See* Roland Gray, John Chipman Gray, Memoir 4 (Privately Printed 1917).

26. *Id.* at 7. John Chipman attended Harvard Law School for another semester after graduation and he received a master in law degree in January of 1862. *Id.*

27. See written response Roland Gray made on a letter he received from Dean Ezra Ripley Thayer, obviously concerning the preparation of formal remarks regarding Professor Gray's life. Comments of Roland Gray on Letter from Ezra Ripley Thayer, Dean of Harvard Law School, to Roland Gray, Esq., (Mar. 3, 1915) (on file with author).

28. Browne's efforts as editor are found in volumes 100–11 of the Massachusetts reporters. *See* Gray, *supra* note 25, at 37.

29. As to his rejection of the judicial appointment, see Chapter 6. As to concerns of compensation, see J.C. Gray, *Cases and Treatises*, 22 Am. L. Rev. 756, 757 (1888) (discussing the "small salaries and uncertain tenure of the judges ... lessened the attractions of judicial office ... leading lawyers in a State will not accept even the highest judicial positions") and Mark DeWolfe Howe, Oliver Wendell Holmes—The Proving Years 130–31 n.79 (1963) ("It would be a pecuniary sacrifice for Holmes to take the [appointment]." (quoting Judicial Recommendation Letter from John Chipman Gray to Charles C. Beaman, Dept. of State (Nov. 29, 1878))).

30. *See* Gray, *supra* note 25, at 7. During most of this brief period, John Chipman was engaged in the Civil War until he was mustered out in April of 1865.

prestigious member of the bench. Horace Jr. was a prominent member of the bench for approximately thirty-eight years, from the time of his initial appointment to the Supreme Judicial Court in 1864 until his death in 1902.[31] During Horace Jr.'s early years on the bench, he served on the Supreme Judicial Court of Massachusetts, first as an associate justice (1864–1873) and then as chief justice (1873–1881). He was subsequently appointed as the Chief Justice of the Massachusetts Supreme Judicial Court in 1873 upon the death of his predecessor.[32]

Subsequently, Horace Jr. was appointed as an associate justice[33] of the United States Supreme Court and served for the period of 1882 through 1902. Some members of the Bar were initially quite favorably disposed to the appointment. Hampton L. Carson described Horace Jr.

> Uniting to natural ability an unusual and thorough knowledge of law, acquired by careful study and ripened by experience, his accession to a place upon the Supreme Bench of the Union was not only greeted with applause and commendation, but was recognized as a striking feature in a professional career, which resembled, in its steady rise and expansive progression, the promotion of an English lawyer to

---

31. Although he had formally resigned before his death, Justice Gray's resignation was explicitly not to become effective until a successor was appointed. MITCHELL, *supra* note 1, at 306. Moreover, according to Mitchell, Horace died as a sitting member of the United States Supreme Court since President Roosevelt did not appoint a successor until after the death of Horace Jr. on September 15, 1902. *Id.* at 26–27. *But see* SEMONCHE, *supra* note 15, at 346 (reporting that Horace Jr.'s letter of resignation was merely contingent upon the "nomination" of a successor and not upon actual confirmation). Senator Hoar, the principal sponsor of Horace Jr.'s appointment, resolves this slight disparity by explaining that "[o]n the 9th day of July, 1902, he sent his resignation to the President, to take effect *on the appointment and qualification of his successor. So he died in office on September 15, 1902. See* George F. Hoar, *Memoir of Horace Gray*, Vol. XVIII Proceedings of the Massachusetts Historical Society 155, 159 (1904).

32. *See* 3 THE JUSTICES OF THE UNITED STATES SUPREME COURT, THEIR LIVES AND OPINIONS 665, 671 (Leon Friedman & Fred Israel eds., 1997) [hereinafter 3 THE JUSTICES OF THE UNITED STATES SUPREME COURT].

33. As explained in the preface to volume 105 of the U.S. reports: "[t]he Honorable Horace Gray, whose commission as an Associate Justice of this Court bears the date Dec. 20, 1881, took oath of office in open court, Jan. 9, 1882...." 3 THE JUSTICES OF THE UNITED STATES SUPREME COURT, *supra* note 32, at 665, 672. But Gray was formally nominated on December 19, 1881, and confirmed the next day, December 20, 1881, by the vote of fifty-one to five. *See* Davis & Davis, *supra* note 15, at 423. The great-great-grandson of Professor Gray, Nicholas Gray, Esq., provided the author a detailed memorandum on this point of history.

> the most exalted honors. In character as well as leaning, in age and robust vigor, in a majestic presence, he was fit for the work before him. As a presiding Judge he had been strict and punctilious—a trait which, although uncomfortable to the slovens and sluggards of the Bar, had proved an incentive to younger men to acquire technical correctness and precision.[34]

Carson's comments were in the flowery style popular during the latter part of the nineteenth century, but his accurate assessment of Horace Jr.'s commitment to the English authorities as the principal oracles of the law rings true, and the description of his personality are well taken.

Modus Operandi of the Gray Brothers

Marcus Perrin Knowlton, Chief Justice of the Massachusetts Supreme Judicial Court, in a memorial celebrating the life and achievements of Horace Jr. identified the keystone to understanding the philosophical approach of Horace Jr.

> He was accustomed to study expositions of law most eagerly in the opinions of the English judges, which seemed to him to furnish the best standards for the American courts. He was familiar with the personal peculiarities of many of these judges as if they had been fellow workers with him in the same court, and he used their productions in his own judgments with a perfect understanding of their value.[35]

That the brothers subsequently disclosed similar legal traits in regard to legal scholarship suggests that from a technique and style perspective (strong or even perhaps excessive reliance on condensing endless common law cases of the English variety),[36] it is clear that John Chipman was directly affected by the manner and approach employed in his older brother's approach to the law. One might reasonably conclude that young John was equally impressed with the level of judicial power his brother exercised. The major criticism of Horace Jr.'s jurisprudence, according to his friend Charles Francis Adams, was that he

34. 2 Hampton L. Carson, The Supreme Court of the United States: Its History and Its Centennial Celebration 525–26 (1891).

35. *See Proceedings of Horace Gray Jr., Memorial*, 182 Mass. 613, 618–25 (1903) (comments of Chief Justice Knowlton).

36. *Id.*

lacked a "certain philosophical cast of mind" (*punch*)[37] to the resolution of the conflicts of his time that involved new institutional clashes.[38] Adams expressed his opinion of John Chipman's judicial impact by the following:

> If I might venture upon a more detailed estimate, I should add that, in his intellectual *make-up*, while Gray had much logical power and an almost phenomenal memory, which not infrequently asserted mastery over his generalizing faculty—while he had a strong grasp on some principles, which at times he was disposed to carry beyond the limits of what is reasonable—yet he lacked a philosophical cast of mind, which has been the distinguishing feature of all jurists of the very first rank and also that massive practical common-sense which is so prominent a characteristic of great lawyers of another-stamp.[39]

No doubt, these remarks were quite upsetting to John Chipman who was rightfully concerned about preserving the legal legacy of Horace Jr. Stephen Mitchell observed the following about Horace Jr.'s judicial reputation.

> Among the standards for judicial greatness developed by Charles Fairman is "clarity of conceptions," or what Holmes described as the "instinct for the jugular." On this criterion, Gray's score has got to be lower than elsewhere. If a purely legal matter were at issue, Gray had little trouble. But on more complex social and economic questions, Gray was less likely to be incisive. *In cases dealing with perpetuities, for example, Gray had to apply a complicated but certain legal formula to a set of facts, and he did this with deceptive ease.* But Gray never appeared to see the non-legal side of the issues, such as those in the original package or railway tax cases. Gray was not consciously a policy maker. He reduced most of the important social and economic questions to simple legal exercises.... Gray did show flashes of grasping the import of some issues—such as the problems of marine insurance—but, for the most part, he was content to sift things down to the point where they could be settled by precedent.[40]

---

37. *See* ADAMS VOL. XVI, *supra* note 7, at 263.

38. In a separate analysis of Justice Gray's work from the perspective of his outstanding historical skills and knowledge, Professor Robert M. Spector notes that Mr. Adams could never forgive Justice Gray for his rather disappointing decision in *Julliard v. Greeman*, 110 U.S. 421 (1884). *See* Robert M. Spector, *Legal Historian on the United States Supreme Court: Horace Gray Jr., and the Historical Method*, 12 AM. J. LEGAL HIST. 181, 201–02, 209 (1968).

39. *See* ADAMS VOL. XVI, *supra* note 7, 263.

40. MITCHELL, *supra* note 1, at 322–23.

Frances Biddle, a former secretary (now termed *law clerk*) to Justice Holmes, made a similar observation of Horace Jr. as a judge and recalled Holmes' opinion of him:

> An editorial in *The New York Post* suggested that [Holmes] had been more of a "literary feller" than one finds on the bench, and had a strong will to be "brilliant" rather than sound. Doubtless the *Post* felt it was unsound too, although it might not necessarily follow that to be dull was always sound. No one accused his predecessor, Justice Horace Gray, of being brilliant. He combined an enveloping memory with great learning, but somehow; lacked the spark and did not have the "instinct for the jugular" that Choate had attributed to John Quincy Adams. Holmes use to say of Gray that the premise of his opinion and the conclusion stood forth like precipices, with a roaring torrent of precedents between, but he never understood how Gray got across.[41]

Another analysis of the judicial scholarship of Horace Jr. fits within the above-noted description. Mark DeWolfe Howe described the scholarship of Horace Jr.

> Gigantic in frame and commanding in manner, Gray was blessed with a phenomenal memory. Distrustful of literary graces in judicial opinions, he wrote with solid clarity and on many occasions with condensed brevity. Yet, he was plagued by the didactic impulse, and with considerable frequency found irresistible the temptation to display his accumulated store of learning in encyclopedic opinions. A judicial opinion could properly be a monograph in legal history.... By those who see legal history as the sequence of cases in time and logic; he was quite properly conceived to be a legal historian of exceptional competence. There can be no question that he made important contributions to the knowledge of the legal past in a number of judicial opinions and in extrajudicial writings. In cast of mind he was not unlike Chancellor Kent and Mr. Justice Story; learned in the traditional fashion of lawyers, clear-headed after the manner of able judges, he was a man of considerable force and capacity. Yet his most ardent admirers admitted that his intelligence was not philosophical and that his inclination was to write opinions of inordinate length deprived them any semblance of artistry.[42]

---

41. Francis Biddle, Mr. Justice Holmes 102–03 (1942). Obviously, this is a hearsay opinion.

42. Howe, *supra* note 29, at 116–17.

Professor Spector, a more respectful supporter with obvious appreciation for Horace Jr.'s judicial skills from the perspective of his exceptional historical skills, admits:

> Gray's precedent was not *stare decisis*; it was precedent in the sense of keeping with the law in line with the English Common Law, which stood fundamentally for keeping the law well-adjusted to the changing needs of society as judges saw those needs. A precedent in English Common Law is not something that must be followed by a judge because it happened to occur; its only significance as a fact lies in the realization somewhere back in time it occurred because of the demands of society. This is what precedent seemed to mean to Gray, and this is what the Common Law meant to him, and this is what Adams apparently, for all the years of friendship with Gray did not sense. Gray was not a philosophical historian; he was not a political economist; he was not a literary lion. Neither was he a hair-splitter, nor a blaster of new trails through the rocky obstructions of the law. But who is to say that this is what a judge is supposed to be?[43]

Horace Jr. must be respected for his intensive efforts he applied to the development of a rational legal system that is squared with, or takes cognizance of, the norms of the past in dealing with questions of the present. Moreover, a good portion of the legal questions before the bench during the period of his judgeship in the late nineteenth century involved matters of common law such as trusts and estates issues, among other matters. We ought not to blindly criticize him for facing those concerns and attempting to preserve the legal learning of the past, as explained by Justice Felix Frankfurter.

> It is therefore accurate to say that courts [as of 1947] have ceased to be the primary makers of the law in the sense in which they "legislated" the common law. It is certainly true of the Supreme Court that almost every case has a statute at its heart or close to it.[44]

But it is obvious that Horace Jr. was neither comfortable with the range and speed of changing social conditions nor the increasing number of statutes being tested under the constitution.

Yet, there is sufficient similarity to the scholarship and approach exhibited in the work of John Chipman to apply the above quoted observations of Mitchell,

---

43. Spector, *supra* note 38, at 209–10 (emphasis added).

44. *See* Felix Frankfurter, *Some Reflections on the Readings of the Statutes*, 47 COLUM. L. REV. 527, 527 (1947).

Biddle, and Howe concerning Horace Jr. The brothers Gray were extreme legalists, in that the "poison of policy analysis" was eradicated from their individual constructed legal rationale. Public policy arguments were never a problem for the brothers Gray as they are always assured of a correct legal answer on the basis of the application of sound legal principles derived from a thorough and exclusive analysis of the common law.[45] They were also consummate perfectionists in the process of assembling specific rules of law of universal application from the froth of compound and contradictory commentaries of the English authorities as set forth in the common law cases of the ancient régimes. Neither brother suffered from the slightest anxiety of not finding the perfect legal precedent. It is a reasonable proposition to believe that John Chipman, although independent, highly intelligent, and thoroughly self-motivated, closely imitated his brother, whether consciously or not, and formally adopted aspects of Horace Jr.'s approach to the common law.

John Chipman was generally reluctant to publicly disparage the opinions of judges, particularly the English, unless it directly conflicted with his views of the law. Notwithstanding his extensive law practice experience and his personal knowledge of the inherent discretion of judges, John Chipman remained reluctant to criticize judges with one notable exception. Moreover, such action would have severely violated the unwritten covenant that he shared with Horace Jr. These insights, as to the discretion of the decision makers, were not to be disclosed by John Chipman until long after the death of Horace Jr. John Chipman (in his capacity as a member of the Harvard Law School faculty) in a rare burst of publicly expressed anger, bitterly complained in his infamous letter to President Eliot in 1883 that Dean Langdell and Professor Ames are, in fact, substituting their views of the law as the law and fail to recognize that "in law, the opinions of the judges and the lawyers as to what the law is, are the law."[46] This comment was a radical statement for John Chipman at that time and clearly conflicts with the emerging Langdellian tenets in which law was described and delivered as science by the Harvard Law School. Such sponta-

---

45. The law has engaged in inconsistent use of public policy arguments, particularly in the past, to arrive at legal decisions. Judge Burrough noted years ago that: "public policy is a very unruly horse, and once you get astride it you never know where it will carry you. It may lead you from sound law. It is never argued at all but when other points fail." *See* A. H. F. Lefroy, *The Basis of Case-Law*, 22 L.Q.R. 293, 420–22 (1906) (quoting Richardson v. Mellish, 1 Bing. 229, 252 (1824)).

46. See letter of January 3, 1883 to President Eliot from John Chipman Gray objecting to appointing men of limited practical experience to the faculty of Harvard Law School, which is set forth in the text of Chapter 6.

neous, almost fuming, admission on the part of John Chipman would also have been interpreted by Horace Jr. as outright judicial heresy and personally offensive. Horace Jr. believed that the judges found the law and not unlike most of us, what things he believed to be true were, in fact, true for him!

The moderately radical philosophical thoughts about the law as expressed in John Chipman's final book, *The Nature and Sources of the Law*[47] were stored by him as a final bequest for the benefit of future generations and, not surprisingly, delivered after the death of Horace Jr. The views expressed in this philosophical tome, being the last of his three scholarly works, are diametrically opposite to those expressed in his other treatises on perpetuities and restraints on alienation. It is difficult to accept such a radical departure in both content and perspective by the same author. William P. LaPiana accurately discusses the self-evident diametrical contradictions presented by John Chipman's philosophical tome.

> If Gray so wholehearted accepted the notion that law was a construct, dependent on many different factors, including the personal political beliefs of the judges, his scholarship would seem to embody an overwhelming contradiction. After all, he wrote the leading work on an intensely technical area of the law of property, which still bedevils the profession. Gray's treatise on the Rule against Perpetuities is indeed full of rules that are suppose to decide cases even in the face of demonstrable intent of the person who is responsible for the writing being construed "[i]n no part of the law is the reasoning so mathematical in its character." Gray wrote; "[n]one has so small a human element." When the work on perpetuities is considered along with the companion work on restraints on alienation, however, a picture emerges as a consistent thinker.[48]

LaPiana's observations are accurate. The conceptual contrast of the philosophical tome from his treatise on the RAP is so great it is as if John Chipman lived an entire life of extreme monastic restraint and then, upon approaching the end, he found blissful freedom in denying the entire foundation of his life's work. The origin of such philosophical contradictions naturally flows from his life as a lawyer, where inconsistency and uncontrolled chaos in the deliv-

47. *See* John Chipman Gray, The Nature and Sources of the Law (1909).

48. *See* William P. LaPiana, Logic and Experience: The Origin of Modern American Legal Education 15 (1994).

ery of the law is a daily experience. Such final expressions may also be, in part, a final thrust at the enormous compression of the fictions of law that he internalized as a natural cost of choosing a life as a scholar. There must have been many occasions when John Chipman was forced to observe the law in practice in a manner that conflicted with his conceptions of the law as a scholar. In any event, the confessions of a dedicated legal rationalist come far too late in his career for serious reflection, even though portions of his offerings portent to some form of legal realism.[49]

Thus, with the exception of this petition for the admission to the school of legal realism, the consistency of his scholarship remains intact within the prism of brother Horace's commitment to the common law. As previously noted, it is ironic that Mitchell stated, in part, with reference to Horace Jr. "[I]n cases dealing with perpetuities, for example, Gray had to apply a complicated but certain legal formula to a set of legal facts, and he did this with deceptive ease." The modus operandi that the Gray brothers shared reveals an intimacy and commitment to the common law far greater than their more limited biological or social relationship. There is credible evidence to acknowledge that they were indeed identical twins in their approach to the common law. Moreover, John Chipman's legal dependency on his brother's antecedent and unconditional commitment to the common law and the role of precedent is reflected in every aspect of his scholarship on the RAP. Neither would venture far from the English tree of "assumed" legal wisdom.

The touching permanent seal to this intimate legal bond of a most subtle nature between the two socially distant half-brothers can be seen in a modest footnote provided by John Chipman. In his treatise on the RAP, Gray states that it would have been better if the RAP was called the Rule Against Remoteness, referring the reader to a most laconic and remarkable footnote that simply states the following, "This suggestion is due to the late Mr. Justice Gray of the United States Supreme Court."[50] This is quite an amazing reference in that John Chipman's principal scholarly achievement, both as it relates to the purposes of the RAP and recognition of his contribution to the law, is symbolically embodied by the reference to the "Rule of Remoteness." He has by this reference given to Horace Jr. a part of that by which he was recognized as a scholar of unquestioned genius and achievement. This reference, offered in a

49. Justice Holmes had occasion to cite and utilize Gray's philosophical offerings in one of his dissents in 1910. *See* Kuhn v. Fairmont Coal Co., 215 U.S. 349, 370 (1910) (Holmes, J., dissenting).

50. *See* John Chipman Gray, The Rule Against Perpetuities 2 n.2 (3d ed. 1915) (1886).

subtle and laconic fashion, constitutes quite a salient testament from a most taciturn and somewhat distant man.[51] It is from this perspective that a most moving symbolic expression of deep respect seals the brothers Gray together for legal posterity. John Chipman, in the context of this formal and austere man of the law, could deliver no greater commemoration of his brother resting in the bosom of the common law, than this pithy and unemotional footnote. It is, nevertheless, trenchant with the deepest respect of an enduring nature for the guidance and direction that Horace Jr. provided to John Chipman throughout his lifetime. It also reveals more of the man of John Chipman, his personal character, and the significant degree of his personal emotional limitations.

Hence, Horace Jr. was a principal national authority of the law throughout most of John Chipman's career as a law professor and as a lawyer, until Horace's death in 1902. In this sense, John Chipman's legal career was coterminous with Horace Jr.'s speaking on the law as a prestigious national authority while serving either as a judge for the Commonwealth of Massachusetts or as an associate justice of the United States Supreme Court. It is not surprising then that John Chipman, as a fledgling lawyer, would be anything less than immersed in the authority and legal perspective of his brother. They both sang of the perfection of things English, particularly the rules of the common law.

A Case of Financial Inheritance for the Descendants of William Gray

There is a quirky financial episode involving litigation before the United States Supreme Court that directly affected Horace Jr. (as well as his siblings) during the time that he served on the court. A claim of his grandfather, William Gray, against the French government for spoliation of his property (seizure of his vessels and other property) by French cruisers was proscribed by reason of a treaty entered into between the United States and France on September 30, 1800. The litigation generated by this conflict is commonly referred to as the French Spoilations claims and relates to a campaign of the French to seize and confiscate our commercial ships during a time of alleged peace. It took place during the period between the execution of King Louis XVI and the year 1801. As a result of the settlement reached in the Treaty of September 30, 1800, the

51. Another facet that raises some question of John's emotional sensitivity was his moderately apathetic and excessively formal eulogy of John Codman Ropes, his life-long friend and law partner. See *infra* Chapter 5 for a more detailed discussion.

claims of the injured Americans were now to be pursued against the United States. It was not until 1885 that Congress finally enacted a statute that authorized the Court of Claims to hear and try such claims and then to make recommendations to Congress on individual claims arising out of illegal captures, detentions, seizures, condemnations, and confiscations by the French occurring before the Treaty of September 30, 1800. A two-year period of limitation from the date of passage of the Act was provided in which such injured parties could file a claim for recovery in the Court of Claims.[52] This Court of Claims decision is replete with chronological explanations of a unique and fascinating period of our country that deserves further attention by those readers of an historical bent.

In 1891 Congress authorized payment of such claims, not as of right, but as of grace.[53] Horace Gray Sr.—one of five sons and a daughter of William Gray, as well as the father of John Chipman, Horace Jr., and three other children—was an equal residuary legatee of his father's estate along with his four brothers (his sister was excluded as a legatee of the residuary estate but otherwise provided for in the will). Horace Sr. had assigned all of his estate in 1847, by reason of insolvency, to an assignee for the benefit of his creditors under Massachusetts's insolvency law. The question presented was whether the award should go by the will of William Gray to the designated residuary legatees or pass outside of the estate and go directly to the then surviving next of kin as a separate gift to such persons. The Supreme Judicial Court of Massachusetts held that the award should be treated as a residuary bequest under William Gray's will and go to the legal representatives of the residuary legatees (the sons), and the portion going to Horace Sr. should go to his creditors by reason of his prior assignment.[54] For the children of Horace Sr. the decision by the Massachusetts court in *Codman* meant that they would not participate in the substantial financial award.

The Supreme Court of the United States subsequently reversed such holding and held that the terms of the proviso attached to the enacted statute of 1891 authorizing payment controlled the matter of who was entitled to a portion of such award.[55] Chief Justice Fuller, speaking for a unanimous court (excluding Horace Jr. who recused himself from the matter for the reason of a direct economic involvement with the outcome), concluded that "[i]t appears

52. *See* Gray v. United States, 21 Ct. Cl. 340 (1886).
53. *See* Brooks v. Codman, 162 U.S. 439 (1896).
54. *See* Codman v. Brooks, 34 N.E. 689 (Mass. 1893), *rev'd by* 162 U.S. 454 (1896).
55. *See Brooks*, 162 U.S. at 459–60.

to us that Congress intended that the next of kin should be the beneficiaries in every case; that the limitation is express; and that the creditors, legatees, all strangers to the blood, are excluded."[56] The result must have been somewhat awkward for Horace Jr., but nonetheless somewhat financially satisfying for him and John Chipman as well as the other children of Horace Sr.

Judicial Criticism by the Gray Brothers

The Attack of the Dred Scott *Decision*

An interesting facet of Horace Jr. is unusual in that he was willing to publicly confront and severely criticize a decision of the United States Supreme Court. Horace Jr. coauthored with John Lowell a comprehensive legal analysis of the infamous *Dred Scott* decision.[57] Boston was a hotbed of the abolitionists' movement as well as the home to William Lloyd Garrison and others who vehemently protested the institution of slavery. There were numerous incidents in which the Boston community provided protection for African Americans seeking refuge from enforcement of the fugitive slave laws. It is also well known and historically celebrated that the Underground Railroad was operating with full speed in Boston prior to the Civil War. The article did not engage in a discussion of the political causes or potential consequences of the *Dred Scott* decision, but focused solely on a technical legal analysis of the opinion.[58]

> We feel bound to say that the opinion of the Chief Justice is by no means the ablest or soundest of the opinions in this case. It bears marks of great labor, and of anxiety to meet, and, as far as possible to reply to, all objections which might be raised to its conclusions. But in its tone and manner of reasoning, as well as the positions which it assumes, it is unworthy of the reputation of the great magistrate, who for twenty years has maintained the position of the intellectual, as well as the nominal head of the highest tribunal of the country, and to whose grasp of the mind, logical power, keen discrimination, and

56. *Id.* at 460.

57. Dred Scott v. Sandford, 60 U.S. 393 (1856).

58. *See* Horace Gray & John Lowell, *The Case of Dred Scott*, 10 Monthly L. Rep. 10 (1857).

> judicial wisdom, the people have been accustomed to look, with a confidence rarely disappointed, in cases involving great principles of the Constitution of the United States, of the law of nations, and of conflicts between different systems of jurisprudence.[59]

This constitutes a noteworthy stance by Gray and Lowell on a public issue of grave importance and moral implications. Although Gray and Lowell are cited as coauthors, many would agree with the surmise of Robert M. Spector that "a thorough reading of the paper seems to indicate a style and scholarship peculiarly that of Gray."[60] Allegedly President Lincoln was so impressed with this scholarship that he later appointed John Lowell to the federal district court—only a few weeks before Lincoln's assassination. Apart from the question of authorship, the article represents one of the more significant achievements that obviously adds to the reputation of both Horace Jr. and Lowell. It its time, this coauthored article was a very noteworthy strike for the cause of liberty for all. In retrospect, it is disappointing to note that Horace Jr. did not join with Justice Harlan in his eloquent dissent in *Plessy v. Ferguson*.[61]

Chief Justice Doe's Decision Providing Relief from the RAP

John Chipman was more than disturbed by the creative technique employed by Chief Justice Doe to avoid the ultimate sanction of the RAP in the decision of *Edgerly v. Barker*.[62] Doe applied the *cy pres* doctrine to interpret a devise to grandchildren to vest when the youngest reaches forty years of age to mean such bequest vests when the youngest grandchild reaches twenty-one in order to avoid elimination of such bequest by application of the RAP. In so deciding, Doe extensively reviewed the overall objective of the RAP and concluded under the facts of the case and the doctrine of *cy pres* that the testator's general intent trumps the particular intent so that the particular intent cannot be given effect. Accordingly, Doe held the

> [testator's] intent that the grandchildren shall not have the remainder until the youngest arrives at the age of 40 years is modified by his

59. *Id.* at 67.
60. *See* Spector, *supra* note 38, at 181, 190 n.30.
61. Plessy v. Ferguson, 163 U.S. 537, 552 (1896).
62. Edgerly v. Barker, 31 A. 900 (1891).

> intent that they shall have it, and that the will shall take effect as far as possible. *The 40 years are reduced to 21 by his general approximating purpose, which is part of the will.*[63]

John Chipman vehemently criticized the opinion of Doe as if its rationale was comparable to invoking deus ex machina. John Chipman points out the gravamen of his complaint.

> It is true that there is no precedent, which the Court of New Hampshire has to regard as binding, that compels it to follow the rulings elsewhere; but I submit it is a serious thing deliberately to break away from the consensus of the English-speaking world on this subject. True, the matter is not a matter is not one of commercial intercourse, and therefore it is not so important that the law should be uniform upon it; but persons often own land in States other than their own, and it is an evil that the laws governing the settlement and devolution of property should differ.
>
> Again, I am no blind admirer of the Rule Against Perpetuities, but it is a doctrine of purely judicial origin, and it has grown to fit the ordinary dealings of the community. It is, too, a well-established, simple, and clear rule.... The process of adjudication has been a process of clearing and simplification, and the tendency of legislation, so far as it has touched the matter at all, has been to make the rule more stringent.[64]

It is ironic to note that Doe was one of the principal contenders for the appointment to the United States Supreme Court that fell to Horace Jr. in 1881.[65]

The distance between the judicial mind of Doe and the legalistic imperialism of John Chipman Gray, as reflected in their disagreement about the decision in *Edgerly*, is the constant struggle between the need for dogmatic certainty (Gray's view) and the interpretation of rules of law within the ambiance of appropriate concern for exercise of rational discretion in ascertaining the intent of the testator (Doe's jurisprudence). As a biographer of Doe and obviously deeply

---

63. *Id.* at 916 (emphasis added).

64. John Chipman Gray, The Rule Against Perpetuities §§ 869–70 (Roland Gray ed., 4th ed. 1942) (1886).

65. *See* John Phillip Reid, Chief Justice The Judicial World of Charles Doe 370–74 (1967); *see also* Professor Reid's discussion of *Edgerly v. Barker*. *Id.* at 130–31, and the statement that Gray, personally, "had been consulted during the early stages of the litigation" of the case. *Id.* at 324.

appreciative of the unique contributions made by him in the administration of the law, Reid summarizes Gray's criticism of Doe.

> Surely no one suffered greater shock on reading a Doe opinion than did John Chipman Gray when he read *Edgerly v. Barker.* In a blistering, bitter article, calculated to draw blood, he criticized it from every angle and denounced it on every ground. Yet when he came across the question-of-fact argument as it related to giving expression to the testator's intent—the very heart and motivating force of Doe's decision—he dismissed it with the words, "This mode of expression is peculiar to the learned court." In any event, Gray considered it of little importance, and readers, relying on his summary, never got an accurate idea of what the Chief Justice had said. Since the article has been reprinted in every edition of Gray's treatise, most American lawyers have depended on his presentation.[66]

Thus, the difference delivered and blows exchanged, Gray sees the decision of Doe tantamount to a judicial failure of egregious proportions.

John Chipman and Horace Gray Jr., although distant in personal feeling, shared the same view of the role and function of the common law. It was to be preserved for future generations and no judge should decide on a path of public policy that would lessen the importance of the common law.

66. *Id.* at 410.

Chapter 4

The Early Years

Academic Study

John Chipman Gray's early life included traditional study at the Boston Latin School,[1] followed by graduation from Harvard College. Roland Gray succinctly explains his father's education in his privately published memoir.

> Mr. Gray was educated at the Boston Latin School and at Harvard College, from which he graduated in 1859. There is little record left of his school and college days.... Mr. Gray left the Latin School at the end of his third class year, and thus gained a year in entering college. By his own account he did not study very hard in college at any subject except mathematics, in which he was always especially interested. Nevertheless, he obtained fifth in the class. He was a member of the Phi Beta Kappa and of the Hasty Pudding and Porcellian clubs.[2]

John Chipman followed the path of brother Horace Jr. by deciding upon a law career and promptly entered Harvard Law School upon graduation from college. In 1861 John Chipman graduated from the law school and continued his studies there for another semester, receiving a master of laws degree in January 1862.

Intervention of the Civil War

In 1861 the United States was dealing with the beginning of the Civil War. The young men of Massachusetts and other northern states were joining, as a group of friends, into specific local companies from their community. A number of the students and graduates of Harvard College and Law School joined

---

1. *See* Roland Gray, John Chipman Gray, Memoir 4–6 (Privately Printed 1917) [hereinafter Memoir].
2. *Id.*

the Twentieth Regiment of Massachusetts Volunteers. The unique formation of the Twentieth Regiment is noted by Mark De Wolfe, the noted legal historian of Oliver Wendell Holmes Jr.

> The Twentieth differed in significant respects from other of the Massachusetts regiments. It was not, for the most part, organized in the conventional way upon a geographical basis. In the first Massachusetts regiments each company was normally constituted of men enlisted from a single town or community. The Fifteenth, for instance, was a Worcester County regiment with companies of men from Fitchburg, Clinton, Grafton, and other towns of the county. In such organizations pride in the Commonwealth and even devotion to the nation were apt to be subordinate to the consciousness that its officers and men represented a particular locality. The healthy, if somewhat unmilitary, result was a spirit of fraternity among its officers and men. In the Twentieth, on the other hand, there was little attempt to organize companies geographically.[3]

Oliver Wendell Holmes Jr. was one of the Harvard men who joined the Twentieth Regiment. The Regiment as a newly constituted military group was assigned to Colonel William Raymond Lee by Massachusetts Governor, John Albion Andrew, to command the unit on June 27, 1861.[4] Indeed, Howe confirms "that the majority of its officers came from a Harvard background out of the leading families of the Commonwealth."[5] George A. Bruce, a brevet lieutenant colonel, the postwar designated military historian for the Twentieth Regiment, explained the intimate bonding of the Harvard volunteers in this uncertain and dangerous enterprise in a letter dated January 30, 1906.

> The twentieth was one of the most notable regiments in service. It stands fifth on the roll of those that suffered the heaviest losses during the war. It is not unworthy to mention that it was officered largely by young men fresh from Harvard University. For this reason it was popularly known as the Harvard regiment. It was they who gave to it in great measure its character, though associated with them were some others who possessed true military spirit. That they constituted a body

---

3. Mark DeWolfe Howe, Justice Oliver Wendell Holmes: The Shaping Years, 1841–1870, 81 (1957).

4. *See* George A. Bruce, The Twentieth Regiment of Massachusetts Volunteer Infantry 1861–1865, 1 (Houghton, Mifflin & Co. 1906). Holmes, like some of the other men from Harvard University, received a commission as a First Lieutenant in July of 1861. He was assigned to Company A. *Id.* at 11; *see also* Howe, *supra* note 3, at 80.

5. *See* Howe, *supra* note 3, at 82.

> of men of exceptional ability and character is evident from the high rank attained in service by so many.[6]

However, the inevitable concentration of military authority in the cliques of the youthful aristocratic members of the Twentieth Regiment was not always well received throughout the war.[7] In time, these intellectual pragmatists overcame the modest complaints of the few by their daring commitment to battle and equal loss of life and limb. Howe further notes "[t]hat they were well founded did not mean, however, that Harvard group did not serve with extraordinary gallantry and courage."[8]

The Twentieth Regiment was formed in 1861, the year that Gray continued graduate study at the law school. While Gray was studying for his graduate law degree, First Lieutenant Holmes of Company A and his group of Boston compatriots,[9] as members of the Twentieth Regiment, experienced the horrific face of death and severe physical injury in a savage and poorly managed military encounter at Ball's Bluff in late October 1861.[10] This event underscored the importance of experienced military leadership and preparation for the conflict. As an initial battle for the Twentieth Regiment, it was a disaster. The young Holmes received the first of his three serious Civil War injuries at Ball's Bluff shortly after the battle had commenced.[11] It was Holmes' unfortunate experience to be among those selected to be part of a smaller group, ordered by the overly cautious and sometimes reluctant General McClellan, to engage the Confederate flank to provide protection for a larger troop contingent. Holmes' unit was led into a hazardous trap in which they were caught on top of an unprotected bluff overlooking the Potomac River and from which the only possible way of retreat was back across the river. The Confederate forces, securely located in a protected position, were able to apply a torrent of firepower[12] on

---

6. *See* BRUCE, *supra* note 4, at vii.

7. *See* HOWE, *supra* note 3, at 84.

8. *Id.*

9. Among the many volunteers from the Boston area were Henry Ropes (brother of John C. Ropes), Arthur Sedgwick, Francis Winthrop Palfrey, William F. Bartlett, Charles A. Whittier and William L. Putman. *See* BRUCE, *supra* note 4, at 445–519 (roster list of volunteers); *see also* LOUIS MENAND, THE METAPHYSICAL CLUB: A STORY OF IDEAS IN AMERICA 46, 216 (2001).

10. *See* MENAND, *supra* note 9, at 33–38; *see also* ALLAN NEVIS, THE WAR FOR THE UNION, VOLUME ONE: THE IMPROVISED WAR, 1861–1862, 298–99 (1959); JAMES M. MCPHERSON, BATTLE CRY OF FREEDOM 362 (1988).

11. *See* HOWE, *supra* note 3, at 97.

12. See description of the military intensity encountered at Ball's Bluff by Captain Bartlett as republished in *id.* at 96–97.

the brave but youthful members of the Twentieth. As a result of this encounter, many members of the unit were killed or seriously wounded. Holmes' injury (a rifle bullet right above the heart)[13] and his harrowing escape across the Potomac River from capture were never to leave him.[14]

The losses that the Twentieth Regiment incurred throughout the war were very substantial. Bruce reported the total deaths and casualties for the Twentieth Regiment.

> [T]he Twentieth was mustered out, having been in the service four years and ten days, in which time eighteen commissioned officers were killed and thirty-seven wounded, two hundred and sixty-nine enlisted men were killed and six hundred and forty-one wounded. The number lost as prisoners was two hundred and forty-two.[15]

Expressive of Bruce's observation is that on the first day of battle at Gettysburg on July 1, 1863, Lieutenant Henry Ropes, brother of John Codman Ropes, and forty-three of his companions of the Twentieth Volunteer were killed.[16] At the time of the conflict at Gettysburg, Holmes was at home recuperating from his third wound received in the early days of the battle at Chancellorsville in May of 1863 (the actual event occurred just outside of Fredericksburg).

The war had a devastating impact on the young intellectuals of the Boston community. The quiet and seductive poetry of the abstract and philosophical call to action for the notable goals of saving the Union and the freedom of slaves provided an opportunity for the young men to disclose their individual and collective courage and bravery in battle. At first, the call to war for the laudable purposes was enormously energizing to the young intellectuals hungering for meaning and adventure. Subsequently, the experience of battle eliminated the abstraction of the lore of battle and was soon followed by the reality of death, permanent disabilities, lingering trauma, and physical destruction. Holmes Jr., in a letter to his father, noted the observation of a senior officer that "the Twentieth have no poetry in a fight—that is, they don't romanticize the business of war."[17] It would take some time for the veterans of this brutal Civil War, as is true of veterans of other wars, to refocus on the poetry and philosophies of their youth. Holmes Jr. was the exception and quickly turned to po-

---

13. See letter of Holmes to his mother dated Oct. 23, 1861, reporting the details of his wound. Republished in *id.* at 99–100.

14. *See* Menand, *supra* note 9, at 33–38.

15. *See* Bruce, *supra* note 4, at 441.

16. Menand, *supra* note 9, at 46.

17. *Id.* (internal quotation marks omitted).

etry expressing the loss of comrades and friends in battle. And it would not be likely that the post-war philosophy would be perceived as a vision of "divine" perfection. There would be no second springtime for those veterans who were fortunate to return, only a less optimistic confrontation with the realities of economic opportunity and an intuitive experiment with philosophical pragmatism. The post-war development of pragmatism directly related to the people who gathered together in the Metaphysical Club will be addressed later.

The loss of lives suffered by the Twentieth Regiment as well as the other units of Massachusetts caused deep suffering by many families of the Boston community. The existence of one's family pedigree provided no immunity from the indifference of death's calling. On July 3, 1863, Henry Ropes (brother of John Ropes) was killed at the Battle of Gettysburg.[18] John Ropes explained in detail the manner in which his brother was killed in his letter of July 8, 1863.[19] John Ropes further clarified his brother's death in a subsequent letter on July 17, 1863.[20]

Gray's Entry into the Civil War

Following his graduate studies in law and some apprenticeship work, Gray was admitted to the bar on September 18, 1862. Shortly before admission to the bar, Gray sought and secured the recommendation of Governor Andrew in a letter dated September 5, 1862, to the Secretary of War, E. M. Stanton, for an appointment as a commissioned officer.[21] Andrew's letter is quite revealing in terms of the status of the Gray family in the Boston community.

---

18. *See* War Letters 1862–1865: John Chipman Gray *Major, Judge Advocate* and John Codman Ropes *Historian of the War* 141, 149 (Worthington Chauncey Ford ed., 1927) [hereinafter War Letters].

19. *Id.* at 141.

20. *Id.* at 149 ("One of the shells exploded prematurely, and a fragment ... struck Henry in the middle of the back, making a frightful wound, and passed clear through him coming out at his chest in the region of the heart, killing him instantly. Some say that he said 'I am killed.'"). For a more recent history of the Twentieth Regiment see Richard Miller, Harvard's Civil War: The History of the Twentieth Massachusetts Volunteer Infantry (2005).

21. Letter from John Albion Andrew, Governor, Massachusetts, to E. M. Stanton, Secretary of the War, United States of America (Sept. 5, 1862) (on file with the Houghton Library of the Harvard College, in the John Chipman Gray Correspondence File MS Am. 2152 (8)). This is the same Governor Andrew who appointed Horace Gray Jr., at the relative young age of thirty-six, to the Supreme Judicial Court of Massachusetts. *See* Stephen Robert Mitchell, Mr. Justice Horace Gray 54 (1961).

> If my desire will be allowed any influence on the subject, I hope sincerely that the appointment be made, and I commend it to your kindest consideration. Mr. Gray is of a family whose position of service entitled their wishes to much respect; and he himself is a gentleman of high culture and fair military acquirements, admirably adapted to such an appointment.[22]

The greater the elevated social status of a family inevitably provides increased legacies for their offspring. This is true now as it was then. The Gray family had certainly achieved academic, social standing, and had reacquired economic standing of respect and importance in the Commonwealth of Massachusetts. John Chipman Gray was thereby enjoying the ritual benefits of his identity with such family. Admittedly, Gray's academic achievements and his personal character confirmed his entitlement to such a recommendation, but it was his "access" to Governor Andrew that made the difference between him and others comparably qualified.

Although Gray was not considered a radical abolitionist, he was committed to the Union cause. His son Roland explained:

> While Mr. Gray was never an abolitionist, nor an indiscriminate admirer of the Republican party, he was an uncompromising Union man and believed in prosecuting the war with vigor. His fair prospects in his profession, the necessity of standing on his own two feet, and his natural inclination toward intellectual pursuits did not prevent him from volunteering for service in the army. He intended to enter one of the regiments raised in Boston in the spring or summer of 1862, but failed to do so, for some reason not now discoverable. On October 7, 1862, however, he was enrolled as a second lieutenant in the Forty-First Massachusetts Volunteers, to serve for three years.[23]

For reasons unknown, he was unable to carry out his plan of joining one of the units raised in the Boston area in the spring or summer of 1862.[24] One would speculate that he simply attempted to secure the highest commission available for a person of his status, as well as a regiment of his liking. Eventually the recommendation of Governor Andrew had its affect. Gray secured an assignment to the Forty-First Massachusetts Volunteers as a second lieutenant. How-

---

22. Letter from John Albion Andrew, Governor, Massachusetts, to E. M. Stanton, Secretary of the War, United States of America (Sept. 5, 1862) *supra* note 21.

23. *See* Memoir, *supra* note 1, at 7–8.

24. *Id.* at 8–10.

ever, Gray expressed some sarcasm about receiving appointment as merely a second lieutenant in one of his early war letters to John Ropes with the pithy comment: "I have no reason to regret taking a [Second] Lieutenant's place—it makes no difference in my present position and I have rid myself of very distasteful work."[25]

By the time that he was dispatched on October 30, 1862, to Maryland to join the Forty-First Regiment, the new lieutenant was somewhat mystified as the Regiment had embarked on an assignment to New Orleans. Lieutenant Gray was then reassigned to serve General Gordon in the capacity of both secretary and assistant judge advocate.[26] The sudden reassignment to General Gordon also created some degree of confusion, including concern whether he would be able to draw any payment since he was not with his originally assigned regiment.[27]

When Gray left Boston and began his journey into this unknown adventure of the Civil War, he was accompanied on the train ride to Baltimore by a servant of the family referred to in his correspondence as Tom.[28] It was not uncommon for members of elite families to provide a servant to assist their offspring in handling the menial tasks associated with their involvement in the conduct of the war.[29] The first pressing issue for Gray was to find a horse. He shared this experience in his first letter to his mother.

> I have found it impossible to get a horse here and I am going to Washington to-morrow in search of one, that is if I can get over the railroad, as they are very strict about granting papers and I can only get to Washington on the ground that I have not formally reported to the General and am still preparing to do so. If I get a horse in Washington, I shall let Tom ride him up.[30]

As it turned out, Gray was unable to secure a government horse. He ended up buying a private horse for 200 dollars, using his own funds.[31]

---

25. War Letters, *supra* note 18, at 5.

26. *Id.*

27. *Id.* at 3.

28. *Id.* at 2.

29. In moving out with his company on October 30, 1862, Gray noted, in a letter to his sister Elizabeth Gray, that: "The general and myself at the head of the column, the servants behind us (we have seven in all, three white and four black) on the other horses, and the regiments and the wagons trains behind us." *See id.* at 15.

30. *Id.* at 2.

31. *Id.*

Thus, as a member of General Gordon's staff, Gray moved throughout the eastern sections of the country in which the war with the Confederate forces was being waged. The assignment with Gordon carried Gray from Sandy Hook, Maryland, into parts of Northern Virginia, and thence to the southern parts of the Civil War conflict in such areas as Charleston, Hilton Head, Mobile, and Jacksonville. By the end of the war, Gray was somewhat boastful in noting that he had been in at least twenty states.[32]

After serving as an administrative aide to Gordon and traveling throughout various sections of the country, Gray finally secured what he had long sought—an appointment as a judge advocate on the staff of General Foster and promoted to the rank of major.[33] Gray had patiently focused on securing the appointment over an extended period of time and craftily utilized the available influence of his friends and political associates. Not surprisingly, Horace Jr. was very helpful in assisting his brother secure the appointment to the Judge Advocate Corps.[34] The promotion to major was part of the process by which he was appointed to the United States Volunteer General Staff, after having been mustered out of the state regiment. Although the appointment was effective in July of 1864, Gray was not able to join Foster until September of that year.[35] A peculiar aspect of his appointment is that it was not formally approved and sent to him until the war had ended.[36]

Gray served for three years in the Civil War and gave tepid consideration to remaining in the military as a legal advisor after the war assuming that he could retain his rank of major.[37] Except for two military encounters near the end of the war,[38] generally he did not encounter the brunt of battle. Gray was personally engaged in two episodes near the end of the Civil War, one of which involved a considerable loss of life. The more important conflict, from the perspective of loss of life, took place on November 30, 1864 in Grahamville, South Carolina. The second event took place several days later on December 6, 1864 near Coosawhatchie, South Carolina.[39] Gray was principally an aide to Brigadier

32. *See id.* at 401.

33. *See* Memoir, *supra* note 1, at 10.

34. *See* Elbridge B. Davis & Harold A. Davis, *Mr. Justice Horace Gray: Some Aspects of His Judicial Career*, 41 A.B.A. J. 420, 422 (1955).

35. *See* Memoir, *supra* note 1, at 10.

36. *See* War Letters, *supra* note 18, at 482. The formal commission had been signed by President Lincoln, although Gray received it after Lincoln's assassination.

37. *Id.* at 470.

38. *Id.* at 11–12.

39. *See* Memoir, *supra* note 1, at 11.

General Edward E. Potter and assigned to provide dispatches[40] back to Foster who remained on a ship because of a reoccurring injury.

The background to these two separate encounters lies with Union General William Tecumseh Sherman who, in the early part of November of 1864, was concerned that the Confederate forces would concentrate their available resources by using the railroad then operating between Columbia and Charleston.[41] In view of the successful blockade of Confederate ships, the remaining source of supplies was the railroad. Sherman therefore ordered Foster to organize a force to cut the railroad line. Gray was directed to assist Potter by coordinating reports on the battle. By this time, Gray had established his reputation as a highly responsible and thoroughly efficient advisor.

It is not fully clear as to the extent to which Gray was in harm's way, except to the extent he described the experience at Grahamville. In a letter to John Ropes, Gray described the Grahamville episode.

> When the force landed (the troops had debarked from a steamer named Nemala) I accompanied General Potter who was in command, and the fight which ensued was the first time I was ever under musketry fire or indeed any fire of consequence. It is singular that I should have been two years aide-de-camp on the staff of a fighting brigadier without hearing a bullet whistle, and within two months of becoming the legal adviser of a supposed sleeping department, I should be in the midst of a hot fire, for it was brisk work and looked badly for a few minutes.[42]

The adventure at the battle of Grahamville, sometimes referred to as the battle at Honey Hill, was one of the few remaining encounters during the closing period of the Civil War in which the Union forces clearly failed in its objective; to eliminate an important supply route as a necessary step in the forthcoming assault on Savannah. The success of the Confederate forces in South Carolina occurred, in part, because the general of the Georgian troops was authorized to use his group outside of the state. Ironically, the Georgia militia had arrived by train on the specific route intended to be cut just in time to reject the thrust by the Union soldiers.[43]

---

40. *See* War Letters, *supra* note 18, at 447.

41. *See* Noah Andre Trudeau, Southern Storm: Sherman's March to the Sea 298 (1st ed. 2008) [hereinafter Southern Storm].

42. War Letters, *supra* note 18, at 425–29.

43. Noah Andre Trudeau, Like Men of War, Black Troops in the Civil War 1862–1865, 314–33 (1998); *see also* 3 Shelby Foote, The Civil War: A Narrative 653–54 (1974); Southern Storm, *supra* note 41, at 298–301.

The second encounter in which Gray played an important role was referred to as the battle at Coosawhatchie or Tullifinney[44] in which the Union attempted to cut the same railroad line.[45] Although this effort did not meet its full objective, the Union forces were close enough to disrupt utilization of the railroad by cannon bombardment, at least during the day. The loss of life and injury was far less than that which occurred in the conflict at Grahamville.

There were two other notable events in which Gray displayed characteristic bravery. In carrying a dispatch to Sherman through unprotected territory, Gray used his skills and excellent judgment. The extent of the danger was immense. Despite trying and uncertain conditions, he made a sixty-three-mile trip through wilderness and uncharted military territory within twenty hours and only two hours out of the saddle. The one positive, of a personal nature, was that he had a meeting and dinner with Sherman.[46] Another venture in which there was some military hazard occurred when riding on a small boat during the night into Savannah shortly after the Confederate forces had escaped from the city. Stragglers from the Southern troops fired indiscriminately at the boat, causing little damage.

The successful flight of the Confederates from Savannah presents one of the most effective political and unique public relations successes of any military campaign. Having failed to enclose and trap the Confederate military in Savannah, Sherman did not miss a step as he promptly wired the following message to President Lincoln:

> Savannah Ga. Dec. 22, 1864
>
> To his Excellency,
> President Lincoln,
>
> Dear Sir,
> I beg to present you as a Christmas Gift, the City of Savannah with 150 heavy guns and plenty of ammunition; and also about 25,000 bales of Cotton.
>
> W. T. Sherman
> Maj. Gen.[47]

---

44. *See* War Letters, *supra* note 18, at 414–15 (Gray explaining the events at this skirmish in a letter to his mother).

45. *See* Charles C. Jones Jr., The Siege of Savannah in December, 1864, and the Confederate Operations in Georgia: The Third Military District of South Carolina During General Sherman's March From Atlanta to the Sea 92–111 (1875).

46. *See* War Letters, *supra* note 18, at 454–56.

47. *See* Alexander A. Lawrence, Present for Mr. Lincoln 198–205 (1997).

This message avoids, by indirection, the military failure of the Union forces to close the net around the City of Savannah and to trap thousands of the Confederate military defenders led by General William J. Hardee. On December 20, 1865, the Confederate troops loaded their wagons and escaped by night over a pontoon bridge effectively undetected by Sherman's forces. On the following night, Gray watched from Fort Pulaski, located to the east of Savannah, the fiery columns of smoke marking the destruction of the Confederate ship *Savannah* that was trapped in the harbor.

Gray had a number of meetings with Sherman[48] during the campaign to capture Savannah and complete his march to the sea. One of the more memorable meetings occurred the night after the Union capture of Fort McAllister on December 13, 1864.[49] Gray was remembered by Sherman. Ropes reported the recollection of Sherman's referring to Gray as "a very intelligent man, whose name he could not recall."[50]

Except for those encounters, most of Gray's military experience was in the area of administration. This provided him the opportunity of getting lost in the boredom of the less-than-exciting responsibilities of administrative details. Military battle, as noted herein, was never to be a major part of his military resume. There is little information regarding his specific role as Judge Advocate for the Department of the South that indicates the extent to which he used his professional skills as a lawyer. In one letter to his mother, Gray reported that the judge advocate had "taken quite a likening to him" and had asked him after court one day "if [he] would like to be his assistant in the department."[51] Gray refused the position of assistant and successfully held out for a position as judge advocate with the rank of major.

In a letter to John Ropes, dated November 3, 1864, he reported, "[M]y office business occupies me fully four hours a day, not much time you say, but I assure you it is more than most staff officers give to business." However, instead of wasting his exceptional talents during this tedious period of

48. *See* The Harvard Law School Ass'n, The Centennial History of the Harvard Law School, 1817–1917, 202 (1918).

49. *See* War Letters, *supra* note 18, at 425–29; *see also* Memoir, *supra* note 1, at 11–12; Lawrence, *supra* note 48, at 188 (quoting John Chipman's description of General Sherman: "[t]he most American looking man I ever saw, tall and lanky, not very erect, with hair like a thatch, which he rubs up with his hands, a rusty beard trimmed close, a wrinkled face, sharp, prominent red nose, small, bright eyes" and "black felt hat that slouched over his eyes").

50. *See* War Letters, *supra* note 18, at 497.

51. *See id.* at 313 (letter to Gray's Mother dated April 11, 1864).

attending to administrative details, Gray was fully engaged in continuing his academic interests in the study of law by reading extensively on diverse subjects and in different languages, while also maintaining a vigorous and thoughtful correspondence with his friends and family.[52] In short, Gray's legal development was far from being on hold despite being in service during the Civil War. The fulfillment of his yet undefined personal and professional ambition necessarily awaited his post-War adjustment that could take place only after his return to civilian life. Like most veterans returning home after the War, Gray's legal career would be greatly influenced by the opportunities presented by the Boston community.

The above discussion fails to disclose the long arduous process of daily and contingent involvement in a war between citizens. Gray provides the most apt description of his responsibilities as judge advocate in a letter to John Ropes.

> My work is of a miscellaneous character, the mere reviewing of Courts Martial takes but a brief time, but I continually have questions referred to me of a semi-legal character on which General Foster wants my opinion, for example, inquiring into the right of a citizen at Fernandina to pre-empt government land at that place, the right of a U.S. Marshall at Jacksonville to sell a mill used by Government forces, presiding over a board of investigation to decide whether a trader should remain in the Department, the examination of evidence taken in relation to the attack on Fort Johnson in Charleston Harbor in last July, etc., etc. Many questions presented on U.S. statutes, which according to the common mistake of the laity are supposed to be at the end of every lawyer's fingers. And as these Statutes are not always procurable, I often have to act on my idea of what the law ought to be rather than on my knowledge of what it is. Fortunately there is nobody here who can correct me.[53]

Reading the correspondence of the War Letters between Gray and John Ropes gives one a better understanding of the frustrations of the monotonous movement and the uncertainty that all soldiers face every hour of the day. It reveals the voracious and diverse reading habits of Gray as well as the affection that

---

52. Gray described his military life by the following: "[d]uring my army life I have not been lazy, for I can never be comfortable while idle, but my labor has been self-imposed." Memoir, *supra* note 1, at 19. Roland Gray also commented that his father read extensively during the war and his reading focused on Latin, Greek, Italian, French, English literature, theology, history, the natural sciences, military science, and the law. *Id.* at 19.

53. War Letters, *supra* note 18, at 406–07.

he shares with his family and friends. It also reveals discerning judgment regarding the competence of his senior officers.

One should be impressed with the tenacity by which Gray secured the appointment to the position of Judge Advocate of the Department of the South. Gray's description of the life-threatening experience that he faced in the battle at Grahamville (Honey Hill) is very much understated and more accurately described by the historians.[54]

Gray's observations also appear in various books, as the war correspondence is frequently cited for different matters.[55] Another oddity as it relates to the brothers Gray; according to a letter of John Ropes, is that Horace Jr.'s appointment to the Supreme Judicial Court of Massachusetts and Gray's long-sought appointment to the judge advocate corps should become known to Ropes on the same day.[56] The Civil War no doubt had a significant and lasting impact on Gray. He lost many friends due to the killing machine that comes with the assertion of power over another,[57] including Henry Ropes (as discussed above).[58]

There is placed in the hearts of the young under the claim of patriotism, the mystical excitement at facing death for one's country, and challenging the fates. This mystic is part of the lore by which we send our young into battle and sing such songs as "Over There" while praying for their safe return. The moral issues connected to the conflict further inflamed many to break the pernicious chains of slavery. The Civil War took many lives from North and South and permanently dismembered and injured thousands of those who survived. Those unable to serve because of physical limitations frequently felt left out of the excitement. John Ropes, the friend and future law partner of Gray, was unable to serve because of a preexisting physical disability relating to a curvature of the spine.[59] Not surprisingly, John Ropes closely followed the historic bat-

---

54. *See* 3 Foote, *supra* note 43, at 652–53; Southern Storm, *supra* note 41, at 298–300.

55. See for example, Reid Mitchell, The Vacant Chair 104 (1993) wherein Gray is quoted in regards to a graphic criticism of colonel of the Union Army who demands sexual favors of a southern woman, and Alexander A. Lawrence, A Present for Mr. Lincoln 188 (1997) in which Gray is quoted for his artistic description of Sherman shortly after the capture of Fort McAllister.

56. *See* War Letters, *supra* note 18, at 384 (letter dated 25 August 1864).

57. Approximately 500,000 soldiers of the Union and Confederate Armies were killed during the great Civil War. *See generally* United States Department of Veteran Affairs, Fact Sheet: America's Wars, November 2009, http://www1.va.gov/opa/publications/factsheets/fs_americas_wars.pdf; *infra* chapter 5, note 8.

58. *See* Menand, *supra* note 14, at 46.

59. *See* A Memoir of the Life of John Codman Ropes, LL.D. 1, 15 (Privately Published 1900).

tles and it was said of him that "no man known in this country possessed more thoroughly ... the details of the operations of both armies" than him.[60] Gray remarked in his eulogy of John Ropes:

> Had he been an able-bodied man, he would have been foremost to seek a commission, not like many of his contemporaries, merely from a sense of duty, but as seizing the opportunity to gratify his dearest wish and his highest ambition. He would have rejoiced to have ... "Drunk the delight of battle with his peers." But it could not be. He was absolutely debarred. Like Troubridge in the Culloden at the battle of the Nile, he was, in the words of Nelson, compelled to stand idly by, "while his more fortunate companions were in the full tide of happiness."[61]

However, the impact of the war is seldom formally manifested in Gray, except for the extended verbal interchanges about the Civil War expressed between Holmes Jr. and him as they jointly reintegrated into the social community of Boston.[62] One practice that definitely carried into his civilian life was the habit of cursing. Indeed, one might overhear Gray engage in passionate profanity while he was grading law examinations. For law professors everywhere it must be admitted that some things never change!

---

60. *Id.*

61. *Id.* at 56–57.

62. The nature of the experience of death can be seen in a memorial to the deceased of Harvard College on July 21, 1865. The graphic sense of death of the honored heroes removes the celebrated poetry of battle. *See* HARVARD MEMORIAL BIOGRAPHIES vol. 1 (1867). Many of the thirty-nine memorials describe the tragic last minutes of life for these dedicated heroes of the Civil War. For a more recent review of a moving description of the act of dying in the Civil War and the sociology of the process, see DREW GILPIN FAUST, THIS REPUBLIC OF SUFFERING: DEATH AND THE AMERICAN CIVIL WAR (2008).

Chapter 5

Practice of Law and Wedded Bliss

The Mating Season: Readjustment to Civilian Life

Hence it is that the fathers of these men, and ours also, and themselves too, being thus nurtured in all freedom and well-born, have shown before all men deeds many and glorious, in public and in private—deeming it their duty to fight for freedom and the Greeks, even against the Greeks.[1]

Following the bombardment on Fort Sumter by the military forces of the Confederacy on April 12, 1861, and the surrender of the Fort next day, the northern states, as well as their constituent local communities—with rare exception—were fiercely unified in the call for a prompt military response. Abraham Lincoln, as the newly elected president, was unwavering in his iron like resolve to preserve the union.

It is a basic communal norm that individuals as participants of society internalize a deeply seeded sense of obligation to defend and protect country, family, and friends; whether this occurs by volition, imposition, or a combination thereof. The embedded obligatory sense is so overwhelming; it frequently precludes a rational evaluation of the governmental purpose or objective in sending forth a call for military action. As a member of a community and a citizen of a country, each of us is delicately inculcated by the centuries of loyalty oaths given by our ancestors to real and asserted sovereigns. The civilians of each succeeding generation are culturally predisposed (indoctrinated is the unstated word) to accept military assignments of the sovereign, as if it were

1. Plato's Mexnexenus, §9, *reprinted in* Harvard Memorial Biographies ii (Thomas Wentworth Higginson, ed., vol. 1, 1867).

a calling from an oracle most holy. This was particularly true of the young men of the Boston community who were raised in a relatively well educated culture in which duty was the first among many competing virtues.

And so it is not surprising that the young men of Harvard, among the many communities of the North, most enthusiastically volunteered in the Union cause to finally resolve, among other social and political concerns, the moral principle of whether this country could continue on tentative political compromises as a part-slave and a part-free basis. The time for reflection and compromise on a basic moral principle of slavery could no longer be answered by rhetorical devices, craftily designed legislation, or politically drawn lines marking the enforced zones of slavery from those in which freedom was secure for all. The Boston community, as the foremost center of the abolitionists, played a central role on the political movement to permanently eliminate the institution of slavery. The activities of Thomas Wentworth Higginson were typical of a radical Bostonian abolitionist; he engaged in personal communications with John Brown (prior to the attack on Harpers Ferry) and was willing, with others, to assist in developing various plans to instigate political and military confrontation. Higginson was not satisfied with the generally pacifist approach followed by the more moderate members of the movement.[2] After Brown's arrest for the raid at Harpers Ferry in 1859, Higginson remained quite active in his continued support of Brown by trying to raise funds to pay for his legal defense and apparently entering discussions of a drastic plan to secure his release from imprisonment.[3]

The attack on Fort Sumter generated a call for immediate military action and that message reverberated throughout the North. It was well received at the Harvard campus during the late spring of 1861. And who, among the young men, would not delight in participating in the event of their lifetime—challenging death in the abstract, while instantly escaping from the humdrum of one's daily existence? Young men throughout history have been culturally challenged to demonstrate their manhood. Going to war provides the unique opportunity of achieving that instinctual goal. In addition, it is so much more exciting to depart for the unknown as the intensity of one's life during the

2. *See generally* MARY THACHER HIGGINSON, THOMAS WENTWORTH HIGGINSON: THE STORY OF HIS LIFE 190–96 (1914).

3. *Id.* at 195–96. Higginson resigned as a Captain from the 51st Massachusetts Infantry to accept a promotion to the rank of Colonel and to command the First South Carolina Volunteers, which regiment was to be comprised of black men from the South. *See* THOMAS WENTWORTH HIGGINSON, ARMY LIFE IN A BLACK REGIMENT 2–3 (Riverside Press 1900) (1869).

initial phase of mobilization and preparation for battle is felt as if each second is marked forever. The initial gathering of new military groups forming at local fields was a liturgical, emotional, communal event—mothers in tears rightfully fearing the mortal dangers of war contrasted with fathers' presence silently testifying that their sons remained faithful to the sacred family traditions. After modest military training, the new recruits, buoyed with a temporary feeling of invincibility and otherwise emotionally enhanced, were deemed ready to charge into battle. In the similar vein, young Oliver Wendell Holmes Jr., and his compatriots of the Twentieth Volunteer of Massachusetts bravely marched into the indiscriminate volley of death at the debacle known as the battle of Balls Bluff.[4]

Once the battle begins and the call to move forward comes forth, while a comrade to the right or left falls dead, the ability to actually describe the experience of battle remains elusive. Despite the preservation of diaries, the construction of great novels, empirically exacting histories concerning the flow of military conflict, or modern technologies of today that can capture pictures of physical damage as and when occurring, the actual impact of war on the fragility of the human spirit is not measurable by metrics but most aptly communicated by metaphorical descriptions of an artistic nature such as by poem ("In Flanders Fields"), painting (*Guernica*), picture (the young naked girl running from battle in Vietnam), or statue (the Vietnam Veterans Memorial Wall). Holmes Jr. summarized the inherent difficulty of accurately portraying the emotional impact on those engaged in combat or the experience of battle years after the close of the Civil War in a single sentence in 1895: "We have shared the incommunicable experience of war; we have felt, we still feel, the passion of life to its top."[5] And so it has always been.

For the returning soldier who has faced the brunt of battle, coming home frequently requires major adjustments, particularly if home is the symbolic sense of security. There is a dual interactive process involved in that the returning veteran posses a frozen perception of his home while the home is seldom the same as imagined. More importantly, the veteran is no longer the person that he was when he left home. He is a different person. Thus, a suc-

4. Richard F. Miller, Harvard's Civil War: A History of the Twentieth Massachusetts Volunteer Infantry 51–83 (2005).

5. Oliver Wendell Holmes Jr., delivered the speech, The Soldier's Faith, on Memorial Day, May 30, 1895, at a meeting called by the graduating class of Harvard University. For a touching discussion of the immeasurability of war and testimony of the participants in the Civil War, see Drew Gilpin Faust, The Republic of Suffering Death: The American Civil War 209 (2008).

cessful reentry to civilian life requires a reintroduction of sorts in a way that creates a new social environment. Many veterans are unable to make the adjustment and, unfortunately, choose or fall into some form of dissociative lifestyle. This process was more difficult for the defeated soldiers of the Confederacy, as they had to accept the humiliating fact of military defeat as well as the devastating destruction of the general economic infrastructure and possibly their homes. The combination of these results would have a long-term impact on the forthcoming generations of the South. A deeper sense of loss was left for those who had to face the loss of a son, a father, or husband; this required continuing on with life while privately learning how to tolerate the silent never-ending pain.[6]

The number of veterans not returning from the Civil War was truly devastating to families of both the North and the South. The brilliant and thoughtful observation made by General Ulysses S. Grant (immediately following the surrender by General Robert E. Lee at Appomattox Courthouse on April 9, 1865) who, upon hearing the celebratory firing of the cannons by the victors, ordered that the firing cease and said: "The war is over. The rebels are our countrymen again."[7] The total loss of American life (in and outside of battle) incurred during the Civil War of 498,332 persons (including loss of life for both the Union and the Confederacy) exceeds that of any other American war since each death was that of an American.[8] In addition, thousands of the veterans came home with enduring painful infirmities and/or loss of limbs. A concomitant long-term obligation of the community was to care for the sick and those permanently maimed in body and/or spirit.

However, the first matter for the local communities was to provide an appropriate memorial that each of the fallen heroes rightfully deserved. The Harvard community started the process by having a major memorial service for their fallen heroes. The event was scheduled for July 21, 1865 on the Harvard campus. John Codman Ropes alerted Gray to the forthcoming memorial: "You must be here in Commencement week to be at the Commemoration to the soldiers of the College, which will be a great occasion."[9] When it was clear that

---

6. Faust, *supra* note 5, at 170, 266–78.

7. 3 Shelby Foote, The Civil War A Narrative : Red River to Appomattox 951 (1974).

8. United States Department of Veteran Affairs, Fact Sheet: America's Wars, Nov. 2008, http://www1.va.gov/opa/publications/fs_americas_wars.pdf; *see also* Faust *supra* note 5, at 250–65 (clarifying the probable number of deaths exceeded the official report).

9. *See* War Letters 1862–1865: John Chipman Gray *Major, Judge Advocate* and John Codman Ropes *Historian of the War* 496 (Worthington Chauncey Ford ed., 1927) [hereinafter War Letters].

Gray would be mustered out of military service in time to attend, Ropes added in a subsequent letter: "Glad you are bound to come to the Commemoration. I am trying all I know to have wine at the Dinner, but the old fogies are inclined to Cider!"[10]

Holmes Jr. was discharged from the service about a year earlier on July 17, 1864, having completed his three year commitment.[11] He and all of the other veterans, including Gray who had just recently returned from military service, attended the Harvard Commemoration in full military uniform.[12] John Ropes, as a member of the planning committee,[13] also attended in accordance with his plans with Gray. It appears Ropes was successful in securing some alcoholic beverages. A special brew of punch, referred to as "Harvard's 'mystic punch bowls,'" was available immediately after the conclusion of the formal program during a limited social period prior to the dinner.[14] Although ice cold cider was the drink of choice provided free with dinner; alcohol was available for a cash payment—but not at the expense of the Committee. Ropes was partially successful in securing the availability of alcoholic beverages. Woman were not generally invited to the principal dinner on the rationale that some were still in mourning. The women were, however, invited to a separate afternoon lunch.[15]

It was a well planned event and a deeply emotionally moving tribute to the ninety-three deceased warriors of Harvard College (six more deceased would be added to the honor roll after the event);[16] those in attendance must have shared an extraordinary bonding experience not ever to be forgotten. Gray and Holmes Jr., and the other veterans in attendance, also shared a more personal, surrealistic feeling as having bravely faced death and survived apparently intact. In this limited sense, the respective instinctual drive to challenge mortality had been fulfilled. It was also a celebration of seeing and renewing friendships with the other warriors who faced the ultimate and survived—victorious. The juxtaposition of the sadness in honoring the remembrance of your former deceased comrades contrasted with the joyful cognizance of your

---

10. *Id.* at 508.

11. G. Edward White, Justice Oliver Holmes: Law and the Inner Self 65 (1993).

12. Liva Baker, The Justice from Beacon Hill 174 (1991).

13. Hamilton Vaughn Bail, *Harvard's Commemoration Day July 21, 1865*, 15 New Eng. Q. 256, 259 (July 1942) ("[C]lass secretaries were requested to send their addresses to John C. Ropes on behalf of the Committee on invitations.").

14. *Id.* at 267.

15. *Id.*

16. *Id.* at 268.

personal future must have been a difficult experience for the returning veterans. As survivors of a vicious war where loss of life became an expected ritual of each battle, they were now forced into a less romantic and more pragmatic vision of life. They were no longer young men.

The Commemoration was quite special in terms of the liturgical delivery of speeches, poems, prayers, and religious music. So much feeling and meaning were essential elements of the gathering. Hamilton V. Bail described the expansive celebration.

> That Commemoration Day on July 21, 1865, has been called Harvard's greatest occasion—the greatest day the College ever saw—the result in part of the feeling of joy and relief, of thankfulness and rejoicing, with which the end of our Civil War was greeted. Harvard alumni had good reason for jubilation, tinged though it was with sadness, for the College's participation in that ordeal was a large one, and its record was unexcelled.[17]

On each table the names of the fallen were listed. Bail further delineates the entire program and principal participants, including Ralph Waldo Emerson, James Russell Lowell, and Oliver Wendell Holmes Sr., among others. The separate alumni classes of the colleges sat together while the law school (and other graduate schools) was left out as a formal participant.[18] The ceremony ended with a dinner, excluding women for the reason stated above, served at 3:00 p.m. for approximately 1200 guests.[19] An eulogy for each of the deceased students of Harvard College and a description of their fatal incident was subsequently published in three volumes as Harvard Memorial Biographies.

This event was an excellent public celebration regarding the conclusion of the Civil War and provided a natural emotional bridge for the veterans to flow back into civilian life. Although Gray's return was almost simultaneous with the date of the Commemoration, he publicly disclosed little difficulty in reacclimating to civilian life or to starting the new law firm with John Ropes. The professional affairs of Gray were never to be a problem for him; it is less certain whether his social skills regarding the more complex courting competition were equivalent.

---

17. *Id.* at 256; *see also* Miller, *supra* note 4, at 1–7.

18. Bail, *supra* note 13, at 275. The faculty of the law school sent a letter of complaint to the President and Fellows of the Harvard Corporation concerning the fact that all of the graduate schools were "not invited to participate."

19. *Id.* at 262–75.

Spring of 1865: The Dance of Rivalry, Courtship, and Mating

The next phase of Gray's life, apart from starting a new law firm, was finding his spouse of choice. As the professional career came easily, the more challenging issue for him was successfully engaging in the subtleties of courtship competition. Each society has its defined rules for courtship and the social means by which the different genders are allowed to engage in various communal interchanges. The general pattern for informal social interactions, apart from the diverse activities connected to gatherings at church, public events, and private parties, involved the means by which one met members of the other gender having a similar status within the community. The occasion of these planned interactions would be within observation of chaperons. This aspect was certainly part of the early post-Civil War experience for Gray, Holmes Jr., William James, and perhaps, to a lesser extent, Henry James Jr.

For families of a certain social status, the calling upon a family was subject to precise rules during the nineteenth century. This involved first leaving a calling card with the home of the person desired to be visited, followed by waiting until that person reciprocated by leaving a card at your home.[20] In some respects the courtship process was even more formalized for the young persons. In addition, the established expectation regarding the role of young women of the nineteenth century was much encumbered. Lyndall Gordon expressed the parameters: "Well-bred women in that period adopted a frozen manner. It was a sign that you were a lady, a creature of low vitality and virtuous reserve."[21] Social visitation with opposite sexes was not always convenient as the individuals were not always located in the same area. Prior to the invention of the telephone, the principal means of communication was through an exchange of letters; the writing of letters was an art and they became an integral part of the courtship itself.[22] Other than these opportunities for social interaction, it was customary to have extended visits at various locations, particularly when on vacation. For the Brahmin community, that would include gatherings in such places as Newport, Nahant, Martha's Vineyard, Bar Har-

---

20. Arline Boucher Tehan, Henry Adams in Love: The Pursuit of Elizabeth Sherman Cameron 24 (1983); *see also* Robert Gray, Amy Heard: Letters from the Gilded Age 6 (2005).

21. *See* Lyndall Gordon, A Private Life of Henry James: Two Women and His Art 41 (1998).

22. Ellen Rothman, Hands and Hearts 9 (1984).

bor, Maine, and New Hampshire. In addition, the family residences would be open to established friends for parties, diners, tea and talk sessions, and other holiday occasions.

Within two weeks after the Harvard Commemoration, a promising select group of young intellectuals embarked on the courtship competition. Included in this group were Gray, Holmes Jr., William James, and Henry Jr. (perhaps more as an observer of the social process). There is no doubt that Henry Jr. was intensely involved in capturing the details of the social interactions with young women by these three promising intellectuals. The intellectual clique of Gray, Holmes Jr., and William James was notable for its competitive interplay performed before and on behalf of the young ladies of aspiration. The counterpart circle of female companions sought to be impressed included the Temple sisters (Ellen, Katherine, and Mary—all first cousins of William and Henry Jr.), Fanny Dixwell, Clover Hooper, Ellen Hooper, Lizzie Boott, and Sara Sedgwick.

One of the first post-War gatherings took place in August of 1865. Holmes Jr., Gray, and Henry Jr. visited with Mary Temple and her sisters in North Conway, New Hampshire.[23] For Holmes Jr. and Gray meeting Mary was an introduction to one of the most mesmerizing young women of the late nineteenth century. She had beauty, charm, and unusual spirit although not limited to the conventions for a woman of that time. Mary was provocatively direct in conversations with men. No one intimidated her. Henry Jr. captured aspects of her glorious freedom, love of life, beauty, and unfortunate early death. He projected these composites into a number of his fictional characters. Lyndall Gordon observed:

> Mary Temple left behind the mystery of those with promise who die young. An unfinished life cries out for form: this challenge took hold of James with Isabel Archer in *The Portrait of a Lady* (1881), Millie Theale in *The Wings of a Dove* (1902), and in a memoir he published in 1914.[24]

When William returned from his research trip to Brazil with Louis Agassiz in 1865, he went into an active phase of courting.[25] A number of women were particularly attractive to him, including Fanny Dixwell. She later married

---

23. Mark DeWolfe Howe, Justice Oliver Wendell Holmes: The Shaping Years 201 (1957); *see also* Sheldon M. Novick, The Young Master Henry James 121–22, 474–75 n.26 (1996) (opining that Gray did not attend the gathering in 1865, but did so in the next year). For a contrary view, see Gordon, *supra* note 21, at 71 (reporting that Gray attended the 1865 gathering).

24. Gordon, *supra* note 21, at 4.

25. *See* Robert D. Richardson, William James in the Maelstrom of American Modernism 74 (2006).

Holmes Jr. in 1873.[26] William's close first cousins, Mary Temple, Ellie Temple, and Ellie Van Buren visited the James family for an extended stay in 1865.[27] William was given the joyful duty of escorting these young women to parties. The combination of these enjoyable social events led William to admit to a friend that he was "falling in love with every girl he met."[28] Apparently, he was intoxicated with love.

Throughout 1865 to 1869, Mary was adept at simultaneously probing and enticing William at the same time. He had extended philosophical discussions with Mary as she was a frequent guest at the James home in Cambridge. The six Temple children were orphaned by the early deaths of their parents due to tuberculosis. Partly due to this, but also for other reasons, the James family brought them into their social circle. Mary and William's relationship was always complex, intense, and uneven; presumably exacerbated by the fact that they were first cousins. The intensity of William's personal feelings for Mary was troubling to him. He appears to be consistently ambivalent about her; one day a serious admirer and then a day later critical. Mary's death set William free to admit the obvious, he loved her dearly.

Holmes Jr. and Gray were equally entranced with Mary as she treated them as her equals. Although each of the members of the intellectual clique socialized with other women of distinction during the late 1860s; it was their continued interest in Mary that intrigued and challenged them. They were locked in competition for Mary's heart before tuberculosis set upon her. William and Gray, more than Holmes Jr., had long intellectual discussions with her. Holmes Jr. tended to treat women in a more flirtatious manner and his original flair that attracted Mary waned over time—but would return.

In 1868 Mary came down with the same disease that her parents died from, tuberculosis. It would prove to be fatal. During the last two years of her life, Mary reached out for the abstract realization of the normal youthful dreams of romance, marriage, and children. Mary loved life and the excitement it provided. Because of her illness, she turned more than ever to writing as a form of social life while her health was failing. Many of her letters were written to Gray and Henry Jr.

Gray continued to remain a faithful friend to her, but she wanted more from him than it was possible for him to deliver. In a letter to Gray of June 27, 1869, Mary explained that she did not know who he was.[29] Mary was something like

---

26. *Id.* at 142.
27. *Id.* at 74.
28. *Id.*
29. *See* Gordon, *supra* note 21, at 105–06.

the embodiment of Charles Horton Cooley's theory regarding the "looking-glass self,"[30] as she would piercingly reveal what she thought of others, and her view of Gray was particularly upsetting to him. And it should have been, as she described him as having three possible personalities—only one of which was socially desirable. Mary broke the common bond that friends accept. The letter crushed Gray's feelings,[31] it was a direct attack on his self image. Was this a spear of anger Mary projected on the reserved but faithful friend? Or was it an accurate observation that deeply wounded Gray? He could not reinvent himself to the satisfaction of Mary; that was not a choice for him or anyone. The letter of June 27, 1869 was in direct contrast to remarks that Mary had made in an earlier letter of June 3, 1869 to Henry Jr. in which she commented, "There is nothing new to tell you. John Gray and Lizzy Boott were nice as ever—the former rather handsome than ever."[32]

By the summer of 1869, the social competition of the clique continued with others of the Boston community, but there were no engagement offers. William was dating Fanny. Holmes Jr. and Gray, although previously locked into a convoluted competition for Mary, were now withdrawing as suitors as a result of her terminal illness. Nevertheless, Gray was staying faithfully close to Mary as a friend, but found it difficult; perhaps she was taking out the frustrations of losing her life on him.

In retrospect, who of the threesome was of the most interest to Mary prior to the set in of the fatal disease?

> Holmes had been attracted to [Mary]; John Gray was deeply interested—so was William. As Harry said, they all were in love with her, more or less, and they all said so, more or less freely, later. As to whom *she* was in love with, rumor said Gray, Gray said Holmes, and Holmes—who was at that time the closest to William and in the best position to know—said it was William that [Mary] had her eye on, and it was William who was in love with her.[33]

It is doubtful Shakespeare could have prepared a more entangled script for this close group of friends. The unfortunate death of Mary at the age of twenty-four

30. Charles Horton Cooley, Human Nature and the Social Order 179–85 (1902). The looking-glass self is the theory that our self image is a product of our perception as to what other people think of us.

31. *See* Gordon, *supra* note 21, at 106.

32. *See* Novick, *supra* note 23, at 191.

33. *See* Richardson, *supra* note 25, at 97.

in 1870 closed this chapter. Henry Jr. made the ultimate seal of Mary's importance to William and himself.

> Much as this cherished companion's presence among us had represented for William and myself—and it is on *his* behalf I especially speak—her death made a mark that must stand here for a too waiting conclusion. We felt it together as the end of our youth.[34]

Toibin in his fictional novel regarding Henry Jr. has a fascinating answer to the same question.

> Gradually, then, over the days, [Mary] Temple made a choice. She chose subtly and carefully so that no one saw at first that she had done so, but what was not apparent to Gray or Holmes or her sisters became clear to Henry because she wished it to be clear to him. She chose Henry as her friend and confidant, the one she trusted most, could speak to most easily. And she may have chosen Holmes for something, too, because she never ignored him, or shone her light on the others more than on him. But she chose Gray as the one on whom she could have most effect, who most needed her. She paid no attention to his military talk and his gruff, practical comments and his clipped witticisms.[35]

That Gray was deeply touched by Mary is verified by the fact that he retained, presumably secretly, her letters until the final months of his life. Gordon reported the moving nature by which Gray turned over the letters to Alice James.[36] In 1915 Gray said: "I too was never in love with her. I liked better to write to her than to see her. She was the only *just* woman I have ever known. Her friendship is one of the things in my life which I best like to remember."[37]

There is no more revealing or emotional testimony as to Mary's lasting importance to Gray. The clique of the three, excluding Henry Jr., moved on and marriage contracts closed in the forthcoming years; 1873 for Holmes Jr.[38] and 1878 for William.[39]

---

34. Henry James, Notes of a Son and Brother 515 (1914).
35. Colm Toibin, The Master 100 (Paperback ed. Scribner 2005) (2004).
36. Gordon, *supra* note 21, at 349–50.
37. *Id.* at 350.
38. Holmes Jr. married Fannie Dixwell. *See supra* note 26.
39. William married Alice Gibbens. Richardson, *supra* note 25, at 175–76.

Marriage to Anna Lyman Mason: Perfect Spouse, Friend, and Participant in the Gilded Age[40]

There are no letters in the Gray correspondence file of a personal nature relating to the period prior to his marriage to Nina. However, there are several letters concerning the post-War social activities of Holmes Jr., Gray, and William James that are discussed and quoted in several other biographical studies.

Before dealing with the consequences of Gray's acceptance of the full time appointment to the faculty at Harvard Law School, a primary element of his personal life was favorably resolved. He had by this time achieved a position of significance in the Boston community both by birth and personal achievement. It was his good fortune that Anna Sophia Lyman Mason (Nina), a lovely, exceptionally charming, and very intelligent young woman, agreed to marry him. Nina was fifteen years younger than Gray. They were married June 4, 1873, and had two children, Eleanor Lyman and Roland.[41] Nina had a distinguished and proper family ancestry as she was the daughter of Reverend Charles Mason, Rector of Grace Church of Boston, and the granddaughter of Jeremiah Mason, a former Senator of New Hampshire and a leading member of the Bar. Although there is not an extensive formal record regarding her biography, it is clear that Nina possessed a fascinating and intelligent social personality. She was, as was true of Gray, a lifelong and close personal friend of Holmes Jr.[42]

Because Gray was thoroughly committed to fulfilling and excelling in his diverse and demanding professional responsibilities of law professor, practitioner, and eventual treatise writer, one wonders whether he possessed a need, or had the time for, extensive social interaction at home with his family. During the years that he taught at Harvard and practiced law, he was one of the original seven-days-a-week-workers and then some. It is likely that Nina simply made the best of their relationship during the limited time that Gray made available for her and the children. It is possible that Gray expended a good

---

40. Mark Twain and his fellow conspirator, Charles Dudley Warner, authored the novel that gave a name to an era in response to their criticism of the books that their respective wives were then reading. *See* MARK TWAIN & CHARLES DUDLEY WARNER, THE GILDED AGE (Library of America 2002) (1873).

41. *See* ROLAND GRAY, JOHN CHIPMAN GRAY, MEMOIR 23 (Privately Printed 1917) [hereinafter MEMOIR]. Eleanor Lyman subsequently married Henry D. Tutor. *Id.*

42. *See generally* WHITE, *supra* note 11; SHELDON M. NOVICK, HONORABLE JUSTICE: THE LIFE OF OLIVER WENDELL HOLMES (1989).

portion, if not most, of his energy in activities outside of the family. He was very active in law practice, working on most Saturdays and Sundays at his law firm and otherwise engaged in the social activity of participating in the prestigious men's dinner clubs, while conducting a very productive career at the law school and producing at least one of the major legal treatises of his time. In view of these extensive responsibilities and activities, it would not be an inordinate speculation to assume that he was possibly moderately private, reserved, and mostly attempted to recuperate his needed energy while at home.

Nina conducted friendly relationships with others in her community, including men as well as women. It may be that her cordial relationship and extensive correspondence with Holmes Jr. slightly challenged the contours of the social restrictions imposed by the conventions of that time. White stated the following regarding Holmes's social relationship with women:

> Holmes' move to Washington meant his social patterns would also change. In Boston he and Fanny had essentially been recluses, he going out alone periodically to pay social calls on female friends; she going out very infrequently and rarely entertaining at home. In Washington, while Holmes' immersion in social affairs would expand considerably, Holmes' social contacts were more formalized. In the place of conversions with people such as Nina, he began to expand his correspondence friends, especially women.[43]

The envisioned strictures of marriage for women in the nineteenth century is captured most cryptically by then newly wedded Louise Carnegie in a letter dated June 10, 1887 to her mother while on her honeymoon with Andrew Carnegie. She stated, in part:

> Well Mother Mine, we are in the whirl, nothing but a rush and a bang all the while I begin to experience the realities of life now and oh! How I do long for Mother! I am not a bit homesick but I begin to realize how much a man wants and how important it is for a woman not to have any wants or wishes of her own.[44]

---

43. White, *supra* note 11, at 308. White also adds in a footnote following the above quoted statement: "Anita Lyman (Nina) Gray had married Holmes' old friend John Chipman Gray in 1873, and beginning in the 1880s Holmes made it a practice to call on Nina Gray about once a week. His surviving correspondence with her dates from 1887 to 1932." *Id.* at 552 n.43.

44. I would cite first the work of Peter Krass, Carnegie 233 (2002) (quoting Burton J. Hendrick & Daniel Henderson, Louise Whitfield Carnegie: The Life of Mrs. Andrew Carnegie 94 (1950)) for the reference to this classic letter of the nineteenth century and secondarily his source for the letter of Mrs. Carnegie.

Clearly, Nina found time for her own interests and did not relinquish or subordinate all aspects of her life to the interests of her husband. Not unlike most marriage relationships, the nature of her relationship with Gray remains largely a matter of privacy between them, except to the extent one or the other partner has chosen to disclose the nature of their private association by correspondence[45] or otherwise.

Nina had an important and distinguished social position in the community, firstly as an individual in her own right and, secondly, as the wife of Gray. Her beauty was renowned and she was the subject of a commissioned bronze relief portrait in 1904[46] by the world famous nineteenth century sculptor of the so-called Gilded Age,[47] Augustus Saint-Gaudens (1848–1907).[48]

It is revealing that Gray paid a commission of $6,000[49] for the rendition of Nina by Saint-Gaudens. Although the value of Saint-Gaudens's work was unquestionably well established at that time, the amount paid by Gray is, nevertheless, quite a substantial sum in 1904. This purchase alone suggests that Gray was a relatively wealthy person of the professional class, although certainly not in the range of the net worth of the contemporary industrial robber barons of the latter nineteenth century. For comparison purposes, Gray's alleged compensation at Harvard Law School in 1906 was $6,000, plus royalties on his books. Thus, it is likely that his profits from practice of law far exceeded his law school compensation.[50]

---

45. Comprehensive files of the letters of John Chipman Gray were given to Harvard University in 1948 by Roland Gray and Eleanor (Gray) Tutor. The Houghton Library of the Harvard College Library maintains these letters. Having reviewed such correspondence file, I can report that there are no materials contained in such correspondence file of a personal nature written between John Chipman Gray and Nina. Since there must have been some letters between the highly literate couple, it becomes obvious that the family intentionally eliminated such private correspondence from the public record.

46. In a telephone interview August 7, 2003, with Dr. Henry Duffy, curator at the Saint-Gaudens National Historic Site, he reported that the center had retained a smaller bronze relief of Nina that was finished in 1902 and a separate precursor plaster model. All of these separate reliefs are part of the collection at the Saint-Gaudens Historical Site. Since the same sculptor did a bronze relief of Horace Gray in 1901, one wonders whether John Chipman might have also paid for that commission.

47. We can rightly associate the able social critic, philosopher, and writer Mark Twain and his co-author Charles Dudley Warner as the source of that sobriquet. *See* TWAIN & WARNER, *supra* note 40.

48. *See* JOHN H. DRYFHOUT, THE WORKS OF AUGUSTUS SAINT-GAUDENS 252 (1982).

49. *See id.*

50. He had also received an inheritance on the settlement of a shipping claim of his grandfather, William Gray, in connection with the French Spoliations matter. *See* Chapter 3.

Apart from her beauty and charm, Nina was intelligent and literate as well as a published poet.[51] She survived Gray by more than seventeen years and continued to be an important member of the Boston cultural community until her health failed. Nina certainly added to Gray's social standing in many different ways. Her personal story, like so many woman of her generation, can only await a comprehensive biography of her life, not as adjunct of her husband; but rather, from the unique dimensions of her social experiences and purposes as revealed in her life. From Gray's perspective, she was his envisioned perfect spouse of choice, possessing the essential attributes of prestigious social standing while disclosing unique intelligence and charm as well as largely fastened to the well-delineated conventions of their time. Gray, no doubt, recognized how fortunate it was for him to have secured a lifetime partner in her.

The correspondence of the Gray family maintained at the Houghton Library includes letters responding to numerous invitations to gatherings at the family house. One letter suggests a potential romantic interest with Nina from a member of Congress.

> I shall see you in Cambridge at Commencement time. No, my friendship for you cannot die out nor my admiration for you wane. Often have I thoughts for you—often do I think of you. Let me know if you receive this letter and believe me. Yours Very Truly, Franklin Bartlett.[52]

This is not surprising in that most found her to be of noble character, highly intelligent, noticeably creative, and possessed of that rare "gift of imperishable youth."[53]

---

51. *See* ANNA LYMAN GRAY, ALONG THE ROAD (1930); ANNA LYMAN GRAY, THE MAGI BROUGHT FROM FOREIGN PARTS (1918). One letter of the Gray correspondence file includes the following comments regarding her poetry: "[i]t is a great thing to be generous-hearted, and the generosity of your spirit underlies all the thought and all the beauty of these verses." Letter from Morris Carter to Anna Lyman Gray (Dec. 23, 1930) (on file with the Houghton Library of Harvard College, in the John Chipman Gray Correspondence File, Call No. MS Am. 2152, folder ([2]p.)).

52. Letter from Franklin Bartlett to Anna Lyman Gray (Apr. 17, 1894) (on file with the Houghton Library of the Harvard College, in the John Chipman Gray Correspondence File, MS Am. 2152, folder 31).

53. Letter from George Austen Fox to Mrs. Eleanor [Gray] Tudor (Dec. 26, 1832) (Houghton Library of Harvard College, in the John Chipman Gray Correspondence File, Call No. 2152, folder ([4]p.) (45–47)) (regarding the occasion of her mother's death).

Transition from Military Service to Private Practice of Law: Creation of Ropes & Gray

Plans for the practice of law in partnership with John Codman Ropes, his long-time friend, correspondent, and fellow Harvard Law School graduate,[54] were implemented immediately upon Gray's return from the Civil War. In 1865 the law firm of Ropes & Gray was established, which soon became one of the premier law offices of the Boston community. Not surprisingly, the firm of Ropes & Gray still flourishes today.[55] Both of the young men were exceptional in many different ways. Each was highly literate, intellectual, and skilled in a variety of important commercial functions. Ropes became an historian of some renown, writing on, among other matters, the Civil War[56] and the defeat of Napoleon at Waterloo.[57] Ropes and Gray were the founding editors of the law journal, *American Law Review*, and continued in that capacity during the first four volumes (1866–1870).[58] Carl M. Brauer described their activities in the early years of the law firm.

> The young partners [Ropes and Gray] supplemented their incomes by taking outside work, Gray by teaching part-time at Harvard Law School and Ropes by serving as an assistant U.S. Attorney. They were the founding editors of the American Law Review in 1866, for which Little, Brown & Company paid them an annual stipend, out of which they paid contributors ...[59]

---

54. Both men were graduates of Harvard College, Harvard Law School (Class of 1861), and members of Hasty Pudding and Phi Beta Kappa. *See* ALBERT BOYDEN, ROPES-GRAY 1865–1940, 8 (Privately Printed by Lincoln & Smith Press of Boston 1942).

55. *See generally* Ropes & Gray Home Page, http://www.ropesgray.com (providing web access to the still flourishing firm Ropes & Gray). *See also* http://www.ropesgray.com/about/firmoverview/ (describing the firm as a "leading law firm with offices in Boston, New York, Washington, D.C., San Francisco, and conference centers in London and Providence"). It is also indicated that the law firm has over five hundred lawyers. *Id.*

56. *See* JOHN CODMAN ROPES, THE ARMY UNDER POPE (1901).

57. John C. Ropes, *The Campaign of Waterloo,* SCRIBNER'S MAG., vol. 3, issue 4, April 1888, at 387–407.

58. Oliver Wendell Holmes Jr. succeeded them as a co-editor with Arthur Sedgwick and eventually became the sole editor. *See* WHITE, *supra* note 11, at 236.

59. CARL M. BRAUER, ROPES & GRAY 2 (1991); *see also* ARTHUR E. SUTHERLAND, THE LAW AT HARVARD 149 (1967).

Through their involvement in various legal affairs, Ropes and Gray were at the cutting edge of legal developments in the United States and England.[60] Although Joseph Story, James Kent, Simon Greenleaf, George Wythe, Blackstone, and the emerging judicial systems of each of the separate states, as well as other institutions, had laid and delivered the foundation for the successful adoption of the common law, there was a renewed focus in America on things English. A renaissance occurred in the realignment of the perfection of American law from the prism (maze) of the English legal opinions. This development is associated with a number of interacting factors, including an emerging industrialization, a quantitative increase in the number of legal publications (state and federal law reports, English law reports,[61] legal treatises,[62] and related materials), and a noticeable expansion in the administration of law schools by established universities. Also taking place was the emergence of interprofessional, trans-Atlantic communication between the "giants of English legal history" and the American want-to-be scholars seeking the imprimatur from the resident incumbent authorities located in and about the historically well known inns of court—hail Britannica.

Paul D. Carrington labored diligently to establish that a plan of Thomas Jefferson and others was to define a new role for lawyers in the postrevolutionary period in the American civic community that involved a special training and commitment to the law, which was not a derivative of the English model.[63] But the bread that fed the American fledgling lawyer community was the facile doctrines of Blackstone (even if purged of its royalist "sentiments" by St. George Tucker) and the system transplanted was that of the common law.[64]

The law firm of Ropes & Gray, as well as many other legal enterprises located in large urban centers of industrialization, were at the center of these inter-

---

60. The latest English decisions were reported in each volume of the *American Law Review*, along with decisions of the Massachusetts and United States Supreme Court.

61. *See* Frederick Pollock, *English Law Reports*, 37 A.L.R. 684 (1903). Until 1865, there was much confusion as to which of the various English law reports were official. Because of that problem, various legal institutions in England formed the Council of Law Reporting and it appointed Sir Frederick Pollock as the first editor of the Law Reports. *Id.* at 686. This explains in part why the earlier English reports were of less quality than one would expect. Pollock also notes that eighteenth-century judges discredited some of the prior reports. *Id.* at 685.

62. *See* A.W. B. SIMPSON, LEGAL THEORY AND LEGAL HISTORY: ESSAYS ON THE COMMON LAW 273–320 (1987).

63. *See, e.g.*, Paul D. Carrington, *A Tale of Two Lawyers*, 91 NW. U. L. REV. 615 (1997); Paul D. Carrington, *The Revolutionary Idea of University Legal Education*, 31 WM. & MARY L. REV. 527 (1990) [hereinafter Carrington, *Revolutionary Idea*].

64. Carrington, *Revolutionary Idea*, *supra* note 63, at 538.

acting factors and were well prepared to provide needed legal services in exchange for appropriate remuneration. They were also culturally connected to the Brahmin community and provided legal services to a wide variety of the *alliterati* including Henry Adams among others.[65] Henry Adams, a famed intellectual member of the Cambridge and Washington scene as well as a long-time friend of Gray, requested his legal services.

> As I have not succeeded at all in overcoming the feeling that I have no further interest, except as a bystander more or less amused, in the struggles and anxieties of the world; and it is in this frame of mind that I wish for you as trustee, not so much on my account or my wife's—though the selection would have naturally come from both of us—as on account of Ned and his children, whose future is much more on my mind....
>
> As for me, I am going on in the high hopes that sooner or later the future will look natural again. I am surprised to find how easy it is to go on under such circumstances. When one cares for nothing in particular, life becomes almost entertaining. I feel as if I were at a theatre—not a first class, but a New York theatre.
>
> Ever Yours,
> Henry Adams[66]

Gray and Ropes, in their different roles, also contributed to the exploding prosperity of the community, not only as successful practicing lawyers, but also in ways that enhanced the quality of the social, cultural, and economic life of the Boston community. Contributions by Gray included services as a lecturer of law, scholar, and trustee of the Boston Museum of Fine Arts.

One of Gray's more famous clients, and one distinctly different from the typology of his regular client base in Boston, was Mrs. Jack (Belle) Gardner. She is the most unusual and idiosyncratic icon of the Boston society during the latter portion of the nineteenth century. She was born Isabella Stewart in New York and married John Lowell Gardner, grandson of the wealthy Samuel Pick-

---

65. *See* Letter from Henry Adams, Historian-Scholar Extraordinaire, to John Chipman Gray, Professor, Harvard Law School (Jan. 25, 1885) (on file with the Houghton Library of Harvard College, in the John Chipman Gray Correspondence File, MS Am. 2152 (3), folder ([4]p.)) (asking John Chipman to serve as a trustee of a trust established for members of his family). Henry Adams indicates that he (Adams) was suffering from a severe depression. The year of 1885 was to become a devastating time for Mr. Adams as his wife Clover was to commit suicide in December of that same year. *See* PATRICIA O' TOOLE, THE FIVE OF HEARTS; AN INTIMATE PORTRAIT OF HENRY ADAMS AND HIS FRIENDS, 1880–1918, 132–57 (1990).

66. *See* Letter from Henry Adams, *supra* note 65.

ering Gardner. Belle and her husband would inherit significant wealth and they jointly engaged in a social life of a very public nature. John Gardner was a first cousin of John Chipman, and he appointed Gray to be one of the three trustees to supervise a trust, which provided for Belle upon his death.[67]

Belle was never a lady who could easily be satisfied. Louise Hall Tharp notes in her biography of Belle:

> In appointing the three trustees, Jack Gardner had done his best to help his wife after he was gone. He chose George Peabody Gardner, the son of his brother George; Augustus, son of his brother Joseph; and John Chipman Gray, a cousin. Later Augustus, who was also an executor, declined to act as trustee, for no reason given; but his Aunt Belle's temperament may have something to do with it. Gray was a lawyer with a gift with getting along with people almost as difficult as "Aunt Belle." In point of sheer unpredictable eccentricity she probably topped his list of clients, but he was fond of her.[68]

Clearly, Gray had the status, competence, skill, and patience to deal with someone as demanding as Belle.

Following the death of her husband, Belle converted her home into a museum to preserve the expansive collection of art that she and her husband had secured. Having found reasonable rapport and satisfaction with the legal services of Gray, he was naturally the lawyer of choice for Belle. As described by Tharp, Belle desired for many years to provide specific direction for the creation of her museum and every time she rewrote her suggestions, Belle added further restrictions and stipulations until she realized that she needed a lawyer to put all of her rules into some form that no one could change. Gray, her husband's cousin, would be just the man. He had worked with "Cousin Belle" for a good many years now. She told him to make her suggestions eternally binding by putting them into her last will and testament, so this he did in seven long articles. In the seventh article, he really surpassed himself and delighted the client.[69] Although there were subsequent additions to Belle's will after Gray's death, it appears that most of the original restrictions drafted by Gray survived future modifications.

Cleary, Gray was a natural lawyer for the wealthy members of the Boston community and, particularly, for a difficult person to deal with, like Belle

---

67. *See* Louise Hall Tharp, Mrs. Jack: A Biography of Isabella Stewart Gardner 215 (1968).

68. *Id.*

69. *See id.* at 312.

Gardner. He had the disciplined skill of listening as well as the institutional habit of internalizing his personal values and opinions so as not to interfere with the concerns of the client while always maintaining their confidences. Added to this mixture was his reputation as an exceptional lawyer who consistently provided quality legal service to the Bostonian community. Gray in his quiet manner had the refined "gift of getting along," even with those possessing the extreme eccentricities of Belle Gardner.[70]

The further ambitions of Gray were soon to be delineated by the manner in which he responded to an offer to join the faculty of the Harvard Law School as a full-time member in 1875. He had by this time charted a successful career as a diligent lawyer, legal editor, and lecturer on the law at Harvard Law School. The opportunity to teach on a full-time basis raised the question that only he could answer: that is, would his current commitments, particularly to the practice of law, allow sufficient time for him to take on such additional responsibilities? After some negotiations, Gray answered in the affirmative, subject to certain conditions regarding the nature and extent as to the continuation of his private practice. These matters were explicitly addressed as part of the essential details attached to his acceptance of the appointment.

Addendum: The Establishment of Judicial Law Clerks

The economic expansion of the United States in the latter portion of the nineteenth century as an emerging industrial world power led to a tremendous increase in the amount of litigation, and resulted in a greatly increased demand for legal services by individuals, corporations, and other institutions.[71] Robert Bloom, Deputy Administrative Assistant to the Justices of the Supreme Judicial Court, explained the unique factors regarding the explosion of litigation, which led in part to the development of the institutional use of law clerks

70. *Id.* at 215. Gray was also asked by her to serve as a member of the Board of Trustees of the Museum. Professor Gray died in 1915, which was several years prior to the death of Mrs. Jack. She executed her final will on the 9th day of May in 1921, and a codicil thereto on the 17th day of January, 1924. There has been recent litigation before the Supreme Judicial Court concerning the excessive restrictions imposed in the will. *See* Docket No. SJ 2008-0532, The Isabella Stewart Gardner Museum, Inc. v. Coakley (Filed Dec. 5, 2008 Mass. Supreme Judicial Court). The court authorized the implementation of the requested renovations notwithstanding the detailed restrictions set forth in the will. *See id.*

71. *See* Brauer, *supra* note 59, at 3–4.

by judges and the formative role that John Chipman and Horace Jr. played in this development.

> Horace Gray instituted the practice of using law clerks due to the rising appellate caseloads. About the time Gray became an Associate Justice of the Supreme Judicial Court, appellate courts in the United States were hit with a tidal wave of cases. Among the reasons for this phenomenon were the industrial revolution, the spread of railroads, rapid development in corporate and tort law, and the population growth. In 1873, partly in response to the rising appellate caseload, the Legislature increased the number of Supreme Judicial Court justices to seven and in this same year, Gray was named Chief Justice.
>
> Gray assumed a greatly increased workload. Not only was he writing almost twenty-five percent of the court's opinions, but also he was presiding over trials (torts, divorce, contract, and capital crimes) that were still part of the Supreme Judicial Court's jurisdiction. The new Chief Justice needed help. In 1875, he turned to his half brother, John Chipman Gray, a professor at Harvard, to recommend a recently graduated and highly ranked Harvard Law School student to fill a new one-year position that Gray called "secretary" and we now identify as "law clerk." One of the first of Gray's new law clerks was none other than Louis D. Brandeis. As it appears that the new position was not publicly funded, it is most likely that Gray paid his law clerks out of his own pocket.
>
> Horace Gray was the first judge of the United States Supreme Court to use law clerks. When he joined the United States Supreme Court, in 1882, Justice Gray continued the practice, which eventually spread to other courts throughout the country.[72]

---

72. Robert Bloom, Deputy Administrative Assistant to the Supreme Judicial Court Justices, *The Origin of the Supreme Judicial Court Law Clerk System*, http://sjclawclerks.socialaw.com/history.htm (last visited July 6, 2009); *see also* KARL LLEWELLYN, THE COMMON LAW TRADITION: DECIDING APPEALS 321–22 (1960); THE OXFORD COMPANION TO THE SUPREME COURT OF THE UNITED STATES 345 (Kermit L. Hall et al. eds., 1992) (affirming Horace Jr.'s role in the foundation of the institution of law clerks and John Chipman's role in assisting his brother).

Chapter 6

Harvard Law School Years

Eliot: Guiding Innovator of the Academic Law School

The leadership skills and commitment of Charles William Eliot, president of Harvard College,[1] were particularly crucial in defining the academic future of the law school and its conceptual function within the university community. Eliot's contributions to the law school have been recognized by several legal historians, but not universally recognized by the law school community. Without his selection of Christopher Columbus Langdell as dean of the law school and his ongoing personal support of the scientific nature of law, the history of the study of law in the United States might have been considerably different. LaPiana accurately notes the role of Eliot in the revolutionary modifications in the delivery of legal education.

> Langdell is almost universally regarded as the guiding force in the transformation. It was Eliot, however, who hired Langdell in circumstances that help reveal his plans for the school and explain many differences the school confronted in fulfilling those plans. Eliot guided the internal transformation of the school in conformity with his views of a properly rigorous academic environment, mediating conflict among the faculty and playing a major role in selecting its members. Eliot even had an important part in establishing Langdell's most remembered contribution—the case method of teaching law.

1. President Eliot was elected as the new president on March 12, 1869. He promptly responded to a succinct, but critical, report regarding the conditions of the law school submitted by the Visiting Committee in late 1869. The first result was in the subsequent resignation of Professor Parsons as the Dane Professor. *See* 2 Charles Warren, History of The Harvard Law School 355–59.

> Eliot was a major actor in the reform of the Harvard Law School from within.[2]

The shared contributions of Eliot and Langdell were so successful that they inevitably lead to the establishment of look-alike law schools, mostly operating under the wings of traditional universities, the enthronement of the teacher-scholar as the center of legal learning, the employment of the case method, and an idiosyncratic utilization of the so-called Socratic dialogue that was as diverse in operation as there were personalities involved in the universe of law school teaching. Yet presidents of universities, as the principal supervisors and mediators of faculty matters,[3] are called upon to respond to both the legitimate complaints of the faculties as well as those of questionable importance that are submitted by the more unique and eccentric members of the faculty. When, as can be expected in any community of academics, one or more members of the faculty is not satisfied with the dean, the faculty turns to the president of the university for "instantaneous" resolution of their complaint.

Eliot's contribution to Harvard Law School was more important than a sponsorship of Langdell as he actively engaged in faculty selections, responded to operational problems, and was at least a co-architect in the conceptual design of the academically reformed law school.[4]

---

2. William P. LaPiana, Logic and Experience: The Origin of Modern American Legal Education 7 (1994).

3. Other examples of the importance of a president's involvement in law school matters where politics may be getting out of hand due to the demands of the "Young Turks" or "Entrenched Old Guard" are part of the lore of the law school community. *See, e.g.*, Laura Kalman, Legal Realism at Yale 1927–1960, 58–62 (1986); *see also* Alpheus Thomas Mason, Harlan Fisk Stone Pillar of Law 131–40 (1956) (quoting former dean and later Chief Justice of the United States Supreme Court, Harlan Fiske Stone: "Long tenure as the head of any institution tends to emphasize [the dean's] faults and minimize his strong points, and in that situation a change is good for both the individual and the institution").

4. Franklin Fessenden described the effective working relationship between President Eliot and Dean Langdell and how other law schools requested their assistance with respect to implementing the Harvard model of legal education. *See* Franklin G. Fessenden, *The Rebirth of Harvard Law School*, 33 Harv. L. Rev. 493, 516 (1920); *see also* Charles W. Eliot, *Langdell and the Law School*, 33 Harv. L. Rev. 518 (1920). The recent and excellently researched series of articles by Bruce A. Kimball regarding the problematic quality of the prior scholarship on the life and times of Dean Langdell suggests that reliance on such distorted scholarship must be done somewhat skeptically. *See* Bruce A. Kimball, *Young Christopher Langdell, 1826–1854: The Formation of an Educational Reformer*, 52 J. Legal Educ. 189, 227 (2002).

Gray's Appointment to the Law School Faculty

The next phase of Gray's professional career[5] provides a comprehensive context in which to review whether being a successful lawyer and a part-time lecturer of law was sufficiently satisfying to him. Gray had taught at Harvard University Law School on a part-time basis as a lecturer since 1870, having received his initial appointment as a lecturer December 24, 1869. The date of his appointment is important only as it relates to the academic question of who joined the faculty in any capacity first—Langdell or Gray.[6] Gray continued as a lecturer[7] until receiving the offer as a full-time appointment professor as the first[8] Story Professor of Law on March 18, 1875.[9] This faculty offer was contingent on the express understanding that he would surrender his practice of law. Gray's son, Roland,[10] asserted that his father delayed acceptance of the initial offer as a full-time professor because of his persistent refusal to give up his practice of law.[11] Roland related the contractual perspectives of Harvard Law School and Gray.

---

5. Interestingly, Justice Oliver Wendell Holmes Jr., maintained a close relationship with both Nina and John Chipman Gray throughout his life. *See generally* G. Edward White, Justice Oliver Wendell Holmes—Law and the Inner Self (1993).

6. Roland Gray was quite explicit and adamant in stating that his father preceded Dean Langdell. "Professor Gray began to teach at the Law School before Dean Langdell came to it, and he had the longest service of any teacher there." Roland Gray, John Chipman Gray, Memoir 29 (Privately Printed 1917) [hereinafter Gray Memoir]. Sutherland asserts the "technical" priority of Gray's appointment over Langdell by the following: "Gray was appointed a lecturer on December 24, 1869; thirteen days later Langdell (January 6, 1870) became the Dane Professor of Law." Arthur E. Sutherland, The Law at Harvard 166, 234 n.7 (1967). However, there is some disagreement as to the date of Gray's appointment; Roland asserts that the critical date was December 4th, but Charles Warren agrees with the same date of December 24, 1869 as specified by Sutherland. *See* Gray Memoir, *supra* note 6, at 21; *see* 2 Warren, *supra* note 1, at 363. In any event, whichever of these dates is correct, Gray's initial appointment at Harvard Law School is technically before that of Langdell. In this very limited sense, Gray was the last of the pre-Langdell law professors.

7. He was subsequently reappointed as a lecturer for the years 1871, 1872, and 1873. *See* The Harvard Law School Ass'n, The Centennial History of the Harvard Law School, 1817–1917, at 206 (1918).

8. *Id.*

9. *See* Gray Memoir, *supra* note 6, at 21.

10. Roland Gray was a graduate of Harvard Law School, an excellent law student, a law clerk for Uncle Horace at the United States Supreme Court, and he practiced with his father in the firm of Ropes & Gray.

11. *See* Gray Memoir, *supra* note 6, at 21, 29. Sutherland also notes "Gray continued to practice law actively for the rest of his life, the only professor since 1870 to do so." Sutherland, *supra* note 6, at 190 n.37.

> But President Eliot and Dean Langdell doubted whether practicing and teaching could be successfully combined. Mr. Gray would have been made a professor earlier than he was if he had been willing to give up his practice. He refused the appointment offered with that condition, because he believed that he would be a better teacher for doing so; and finally he was made a professor on his own terms.[12]

Gray believed that continued practice would make him a better teacher and possibly a more grounded scholar.[13] His belief was not speculation; he had been teaching on a part-time basis as a lecturer and understood the contribution to teaching that practice provided.

It would also be more financially rewarding for Gray to continue both careers than to depend solely on academic compensation and any potential increases as determined in the discretion of the administration. It seems inappropriate to discuss one's personal compensation and how that might have affected certain life choices. Such a discussion violates an unstated norm of the law school community. Nevertheless, it can be argued that Gray's private law practice involved a greater time commitment on his part than the formal record discloses and that economic security was and always remained an important value for him.[14] It is interesting to consider why Gray would turn down a possible appointment to the bench. Roland Gray suggests the rejection of a judicial appointment by his father was "chiefly because of his devotion to the Law School and his purpose to write on topics which attracted his interests."[15] Gray's adamant refusal to give up his practice of law to teach at Harvard Law School means that he was not willing to look to the compensation from the Law School as his sole source of income. In short, Gray was never unconditionally dedicated to the Law School from the inception of his full-time appointment in 1875. However, those of the Harvard Law School community were distinctly of the contrary opinion.[16] In his eulogy of Gray, Dean Ezra Ripley Thayer quoted a portion of a letter that Gray wrote to a friend shortly before his death relating to his

---

12. Gray Memoir, *supra* note 6, at 29.

13. *Id.*

14. For evidence of his concern for economic security, see *infra* note 17 and accompanying text. *See also supra* Chapter 3, note 29.

15. *Id.*

16. See *infra* note 28 for Dean Thayer's views of Gray's commitment to the Law School.

goals as a scholar and the limitations imposed thereon by reason of his concern for economic security.

> Some fifty years ago I was determined that I would write two things: first, write a book on the Rule against Perpetuities, which would be a model text-book; and secondly, write something on analytical jurisprudence; and I have had these objects in mind ever since. Of course, the cares of the world and the deceitfulness of riches and the lust of other things have choked the "word," but they have not entirely destroyed it. I may say that I have pursued at eve what I pursued at morn.[17]

This is a revealing personal statement by Gray. He admits by indirection that the acquisition of financial resources constituted an essential element of his life and that this drive was a somewhat divisive factor that limited his scholarship, and possibly reflects the reason for his later refusal of a judicial appointment.

It is also possible that the judicial arena presented an excessive conflict for a person whose opinions of the law, as a law professor, were so perfect and otherwise unassailable in the classroom; that is, his opinion of the law was never subject to reversal by a higher authority or lacked the support of a majority of the court. One wonders, despite his many years of practice, whether the possibility of contentious conflict with others of equal status would create unacceptable stress for him. Certainly, he had incurred some legal disappointments in practice; no one wins all the time.

The law school "industry" had serious concerns about the activities of the faculty regarding other commercial affairs. Some members of law school faculties consult on private matters, others engage in arbitration or mediation, whereas some engage in private practice. There are arrangements in which the time commitments are diligently limited and other situations where that is not true. Unlike medical school, where practice is recognized as enhancing the skills of a faculty member, law schools are constantly concerned about the potential abuse. Nevertheless, as a part-time lecturer, Gray found the demands of the combination of the two careers obviously exciting, acceptable, and challenging.

During these contractual negotiations, Dean Langdell, acting under the tutelage of President Charles W. Eliot, was leading the law school into what

17. Ezra Ripley Thayer, *John Chipman Gray*, 28 Harv. L. Rev. 539, 540 (1915).

became the golden age[18] of scientific legal analysis: the case method.[19] Not surprisingly, Langdell was antagonistic to Gray's maintaining a dual career of teaching and the practice of law. Such an arrangement was completely antithetical to the law school design of Langdell. Admittedly, the old way of teaching law presented serious deficiencies of a troubling concern to the new dean of the law school, and to Eliot. Adding to the concerns of Eliot and Langdell was the fact that the principal full-time professors (Parker, Parsons, and Washburn) of the past administration were practitioners of law.[20] Because radical pedagogic innovation was the motivating factor for these two determined administrators, the appointment of Gray and his demand to continue in his private practice like the law teachers of the recent past was quite problematic. Perhaps, the deciding factor in Gray's favor was that he had the obvious potential to become an outstanding legal scholar and that his teaching record was a known positive commodity.

The quality of legal education at Harvard Law School, according to Lewis D. Brandeis, was not suffering from a complete lack of direction[21] during the preceding years. Nevertheless, Stephen Robert Mitchell describes the uncertain quality of legal education at Harvard Law School when Horace Jr. attended in 1848 as follows:

> The Harvard Law School, in [Horace] Gray's youth, was still largely bound to the old traditions. Students sat at the feet of great men who had been great judges and great advocates. Story and Parker and Parsons and Greenleaf fought again the battles of the courthouse and passed on to new generations of students the taut thrills of victories witnessed and shared. (The sweetest sound in the world, save a woman's "Yes," said the old Parsons to his classes, was the sound of the jury foreman announcing: "We hold for the plaintiff.") The young men ar-

18. It may be that the customary story of law as science from the perspective of Dean Langdell understates the role and influence that President Eliot had on the entire graduate program of Harvard University, including the law school. Eliot was appointed President of Harvard University in 1869 and he personally selected Langdell as part of his mission to focus on science as the backbone of higher education. Echoes of this possibility are implied or raised by Menand. *See* LOUIS MENAND, THE METAPHYSICAL CLUB: A STORY OF IDEAS IN AMERICA 341 (2001).

19. See generally *infra* note 26 and accompanying text for discussion of the radical changes effected in legal education.

20. *See* WHITE, *supra* note 5, at 91.

21. This does not mean that these leaders were deficient; as Brandeis noted each had achieved a measured sense of success in publication and/or in lecturing on the law. *See* Louis D. Brandeis, *The Harvard Law School*, 1 GREEN BAG 10, 16–17 (1889).

> gued cases at the law clubs and at the Moot Court, over which distinguished judges presided. They breathed nothing but a legal atmosphere. Yet in all their legal education the reasoning power was concerned with, and developed by, the consideration with general legal principles, and adjudged cases played a comparatively small and secondary part. All of this changed during Gray's career. The case method of study, which was to become standard, had its beginnings with Gray and his fellow students at the Harvard Law School. Their faith in the efficacy of the new method of study was more than justified, and although he and his friends were brought up and educated under the old system, they were among the best examples of the new.[22]

Legal pedagogy was not very systematized until the appointment of Langdell in 1870. The deans of any of our great present day law schools would probably have been justifiably shocked had they inspected the facilities at Cambridge and analyzed them in terms of their experience. Such a dean would have found it a modest educational institution. Here was a school without examination either for admission or for a degree. Here were three faculty members giving only ten lectures a week to 115 students, of whom fifty-three per cent had no college degree. Here he would have found a curriculum without rational sequence of subjects, and a decaying and inadequate library. The three principal law professors[23] (Joel Parker, Theophilus Parsons Jr.,[24] and Emory Washburn) of the 1860s did not, as a rule, impose any significant demands on the students (for example, there were no tests and classes were offered on a purely lecture basis).

An unsigned article, attributed to Oliver Wendell Holmes Jr., set forth the following description of the quality of legal education at Harvard.

> For a long time the conditions of the Harvard Law School has almost been a disgrace to the Commonwealth of Massachusetts. We say "almost a disgrace" because, undoubtedly, some of its courses of lectures have been good, and no law school of which this can be said is hope-

22. Stephen Robert Mitchell, Mr. Justice Horace Gray 33–34 (1961).

23. For an apt description of the less than exciting teaching skills of the triumvirate of Parsons, Parker, and Washburn, see Kimball, *supra* note 4, at 227.

24. He was the son of the famed Theophilus Parsons, former Chief Justice of the Massachusetts Supreme Judicial Court, of whom it was said that the senior Parsons was "The Awfullest Parsons." Adieu to Professor Carrington and Charles Warren. *See* Paul D. Carrington, *The Revolutionary Idea of University Legal Education*, 31 Wm. & Mary L. Rev. 527, 569 n.341 (1990); *see also* 2 Warren, *supra* note 1, at 124.

> lessly bad. Still, a school, which undertook to confer degrees without any preliminary examination whatever, was doing something every year to injure the profession throughout the country, and to discourage real students. So long as the possession of a degree signified nothing except a residence for a certain period of time in Cambridge or Boston, it was without value.[25]

In view of this situation, Eliot and Langdell were committed to an agenda that would effect a major pedagogical change in the operation of the law school and increase its academic connectedness to the broader academic community of Harvard College. This revolution in legal education would forever change the locust of legal education from the office of the lawyers and judges to the University controlled Law School. Laura Kalman identified the dramatic change in the locus for delivery of legal education.

> During the nineteenth century, an aspiring lawyer usually entered the profession by apprenticing himself to an established lawyer, and those who did attend lectures and read the treatises law schools required perceived them as secondary to the apprentice experience. Langdell transferred the study of law from the office to the University.[26]

In addition, the revolutionary modification also created and installed the full-time academic law teacher as principal interpreter of the new science of the law.

Clearly, the stubborn response of Gray directly conflicted with the then emerging radical pedagogical paradigm at the Harvard Law School. Notwithstanding the institutional pressures for consistent treatment of the faculty and Langdell's demands, Gray held firm for what he believed was appropriate and secured permission to practice on a limited basis before accepting a full-time appointment to the faculty as the Story Professor of Law. The successful negotiations[27] provided Gray exactly what he desired, but placed him directly in

---

25. *Summary of Events*, 5 Am. L. Rev. 177 (1870–1871). According to Professor White, Oliver Wendell Holmes wrote this editorial piece while he was serving as editor of the *American Law Review*. *See* White, *supra* note 5, at 91.

26. Laura Kalman, Legal Realism at Yale 1927–1960, at 11 (1986).

27. In the history of the American law schools, we seldom have an accurate report on negotiations of law professors or of the individual career as actually experienced at particular legal institutions. We have for the most part a closed in society except for the traditional rumors that abound in any community. *See* Alfred S. Konesfsky & John Henry Schlegel, *Mirror, Mirror on the Wall: Histories of American Law Schools*, 95 Harv. L. Rev. 833 (1982). One can find some pieces or hints of "truth" in the normal retirement "eulogies" of faculty members that are published in the law reviews or alumni journals. However, Albert Sacks

opposition to the jurisdictional dictates of Langdell—not a good way to start a new full-time career. Nevertheless, most of the Harvard faculty were of the view that Gray's complete commitment to the law school was unquestioned. Dean Thayer noted:

> Although he continued to practise [sic] while he taught (a thing made possible by what he described as his "very peculiar and very fortunate" relations with his partners, and his not less fortunate and peculiar mental gifts and methods of work), he always put the law school first, and more than once thought of giving up practice for the same reasons which led him to decline the highest judicial office.[28]

Eliot's offer to Gray, apart from the issue of private practice, included the provision that he be appointed the Story Professor of Law at the compensation of $4,500 per annum.[29] The exact terms with regards to the right to engage in a limited practice of law remain unknown.[30] Samuel Williston expressed the view that Gray was generally present four days a week at the law school.

> When not teaching, most of the professors were withdrawn in the library stack, where students in those days did not much venture. Gray, however, sat at a large table in an alcove opening out of the student's reading-room. This fact and his friendly and helpful ways made him much resorted to by the students. Though he was actively engaged in practice in Boston, he generally spent four days of each week at the school. Much of the time while he was there I suppose he was working on business of his office. His partners doubtless enabled him to specialize his own work, so that much of it could be done in Cambridge.[31]

Albert Boyden, the first historian of the law firm of Ropes & Gray, saw matters somewhat differently. He was of the view that Gray: "was at the law school

---

reminds us that eulogies, according to Dr. Johnson, "... are not given under oath." *See* Albert Sacks, *Remembering Austin Scott,* 33 HARV. L. SCH. BULL. 27, 28 (Fall 1981).

28. Thayer, *supra* note 17, at 543.

29. *See* ALBERT BOYDEN, ROPES-GRAY 1865–1940, at 82 (Privately Printed by Lincoln & Smith Press of Boston 1942) ("Gray's law school compensation was to increase to $5,000 by 1889 and then later to $7,500.").

30. I do not have a copy of his original appointment contract setting forth the conditions regarding his practice of law with Harvard University, nor am I certain one can be found in the available records.

31. Samuel Williston, *John Chipman Gray*, 28 HARV. L. REV. 544, 545 (1915).

at least two days a week."[32] The amount of time that Gray engaged in practice during his years on the Harvard Law School faculty remains uncertain, and is largely a matter of speculation. One assumes that in the later years, Gray applied greater attention to the practice of law than he did during the earlier years of his service at Harvard. It is also likely that the perspective or opinion of some members of the faculty differed considerably from each other and also possibly from Gray's personal assessment as to the extent of his involvement in practice. The faculty differences of attitude or judgment with respect to a particular faculty member's attendance relates in part to law school politics as opposed to such faculty member's actual involvement with outside economic opportunities. This issue perennially exists in most law schools and is frequently the source of intense institutional conflict and personal antagonism among the faculty.

Although seldom noted, Roland Gray admitted that his father not only practiced law throughout his entire academic career, but he was also the "head of the firm"[33] until his death in 1915. As it turned out, Gray's assessment of the positive pedagogical benefits from private practice, to say nothing of the compensation potential from the dual careers, was correct in that it forced him, reluctantly, to deal with the indeterminacy of law. Despite the experience in practice dealing with the indeterminacy of the law, Gray's scholarship, apart from his philosophical piece, seldom ever reflected uncertainty about conceptual doctrines of the common law. A former law partner of Gray and then Justice of the Massachusetts Supreme Judicial Court, William Caleb Loring, expressed the belief that Gray continued in practice because he truly believed that "he would be a better teacher of the law."[34] Loring and other members of the Boston Bar concurred in that assessment.

> [Gray's capacity] for voluminous occupations is apt to go with a loose fiber, or, one might say a somewhat coarse grain, but Gray was delicate, accurate, and fined grain. Like his entire race, he was keenly observing without showing it, seeming to see from the sides of his eyes like a woman. And none of his remarkable qualities and capacities remained isolated or futile, but they all united to give character to the stream of his thought. It will be seen that I am trying to describe a master, one who was listened to with equal respect by clients, by courts, and by all students of the law, and at the same time an extraordinary and delightful man,

32. *See* BOYDEN, *supra* note 29, at 74.

33. *See* GRAY MEMOIR, *supra* note 6, at 21.

34. *Id.* at 126 (citing comments Justice Loring made at the Proceedings of the Boston Bar before the Supreme Judicial Court on October 23, 1915).

> whose conversation gave equal pleasure to specialists and men of the world.[35]

Gray was a new breed of scholar-teacher-practitioner, which is a subtle but important pedagogical deviation from the original design of Langdell.[36]

However, in the practice of law, Gray did not charge excessive fees, and on occasion, any fee. Carl Brauer, a later historian of the law firm of Ropes & Gray, stated "Gray's indifference to such mundane matters as billing were apparently compensated by Ropes' vigilance."[37] Ropes happily remarked, "[I]f a man comes into my office *and takes off his hat* ... I can send him a bill for any talk that takes place."[38] Gray took over the reins of the law firm after Ropes' death in 1899. Roland Gray was an associate of the firm at that time and made partner in 1902.

John Chipman possessed a sophisticated and defined perspective regarding the role of law in society and expressed the belief that scholarship raised man's search for human justice. He saw Law, properly considered, as constituting the essential standard that guaranteed the maximum security for society. However, the law, if it is to realize such a goal, requires constant and diligent protection by each generation of well-educated judges and lawyers, as well as "law professors," that have an understanding of the complexities or chaos of the practice. This is about as philosophical as Gray would get regarding the law. He saw Law, properly considered, as a pragmatic force for the good of the community when administered by an appropriately learned judge. Law's principal function was to make members of society responsible for their actions. Gray was not aware of the degree to which he necessarily imputed his highly personal, perhaps ritualistic, and certainly inflexible philosophical approach regarding the law into his actual determinations of the precise dictates or principles of the common law.

Law as Science: Langdellian Innovation under Eliot's Supervision

The change in teaching methodology (the Socratic dialogue and case method) also occurs simultaneously with legal education becoming a part of a tradi-

---

35. *Id.* at 50.

36. There is always some number of the faculty of urban law schools who engage in the practice of law, whether under the label of "consulting" on specific legal matters, by direct participation as a "partner," or that of an "of counsel" relationship with an established law firm.

37. *See* Carl M. Brauer, Ropes & Gray 3 (1991).

38. *Id.*

tional academic institution of higher learning. One can ask whether the movement of law training to university centers under the alleged scientific modality of Langdell was the essential fiction necessary to allow law schools to participate (make claims on university resources) like other colleges of the university. As such, the emerging university law schools secured economic protection. First, for the principal economic benefit of the faculty, and second, for the opportunity for the successful monopolization of legal education as a separate specialized industry through to the latter part of the twentieth century. That university supported legal education as envisioned by Langdell dominates the field of legal education is not to be questioned. In this regard, LaPiana succinctly notes the consequences:

> Perhaps most important, Langdell's and Eliot's new model school claimed to provide the one only true method for training future members of the profession. A system of apprenticeship dominated by active members of the profession gave way to academic training dominated by active members of the profession—full time teachers of the law.[39]

The next phase of Gray's academic career relates to his entanglement with a transformative change in the form and delivery of legal education at the Harvard Law School. In Gray, we observe the radical[40] transition in the history of the American legal education system. He is the quintessential medium in which to observe the revolutionary changes that occurred in the delivery of legal education by a university connected law school. Most of these radical changes initiated during the latter part of the nineteenth century, matured in the twentieth century, and continue to dominate in the twenty-first century, despite excessive claims of and some actual major innovations with respect to skills training.

The first major modification can be seen both in the style of teaching law that was encountered in the classroom and, equally important, in the identity and prior legal experience of the law professor—from one who had extensive

39. LaPiana, *supra* note 2, at 7.

40. Although Gray reluctantly acquiesced in the movement to adopt the case method, he certainly was not an active supporter of the Socratic methodology that is normally associated with the case method. Furthermore, I am far more skeptical of his complete commitment to the case method and the Socratic methodology than the role assigned to him by others, including his contemporaries and legal historians. There is no question that he initially was rather critical of the change in teaching methods along with Professor James Bradley Thayer. *See id.* at 15.

prior legal practice experience as a judge or practitioner to one that may have had very limited practice experience other than that of clerking for a judge.

This change in the nature and prior experience of the law professor (apart from coterminous demise of learning the law from a practicing attorney by one apprenticing in such lawyer's office[41] as a precondition to admission to the bar) was somewhat revolutionary from the customary lecturing by practitioners (lawyers and judges) to a bored, laid-back group of indifferent students.[42] The law students were now "theoretically" confronted with a unique classroom confrontation, sometimes of an invigorating and/or intimidating nature,[43] that was the result of the implementation of the so-called Socratic interactive classroom exchange concerning real cases.[44] Law schools, after the spread of the "Langdellian metamorphosis"[45] occurred, would no longer be centers for the passive taking of notes by students who suffered from a permanent case of ennui,[46] a condition further exacerbated by an active social life which was then otherwise unchallenged by reason of the absence of final examinations. Under this new régime, law students would be directly challenged in the classroom and had to be prepared,[47] in theory, for a rapid series of separate hypothetical legal questions arising from the unique patterns of real cases

---

41. The life and education of Justice Joseph Story presents a representative narrative of the basic legal education and training by way of apprenticing for young men after the Revolutionary War. *See* William W. Story, The Life and Letters of Joseph Story (Law Book Exchange, Ltd. 2000) (1851). Story had a most remarkable career. He, along with the writings of James Kent, provided much of the "intellectual" foundation for American private law. *See* A. W. B. Simpson, Biographical Dictionary of the Common Law 491–93 (1984). George Wythe was of course the first American law professor connected with higher education. He was appointed as a professor of law at the College of William and Mary and served in that capacity during the period of 1779 to 1791. For a comprehensive biography of his life, see Robert B. Kirtland, George Wythe: Lawyer, Revolutionary, Judge (1986).

42. Are not law students by definition bored and somewhat laid back despite the eloquence and charm of the law teacher?

43. Does this description reflect your experience of legal education or that of the present law students?

44. For a review of Langdell's early years, see generally Kimball, *supra* note 4.

45. A detailed, varied, balanced, and learned analysis of the impact of President Eliot and Dean Langdell on the Harvard Law School can be found in Professor LaPiana's book. *See generally* LaPiana, *supra* note 2.

46. Not all the benefits of our high tech society and its utilization in the classroom are positive.

47. The ideal is seldom fully realized after the first year of law school; second and third year law students frequently learn just enough to make a response in class that reflects some effort at preparation.

that were now set forth in casebooks. Without question, the theory of this innovation was largely of Langdell's making, but its application was found in the teaching brilliance of two youthful and energetic law professors, James Barr Ames[48] and William A. Keener.[49]

Contrast to contemporary times, where a teacher is frequently confronted by a class of law students who spend most of their time capturing the highlights of the classroom discussion behind turned on laptop computers and not enough time "thinking." What we actually experience as a student and how it is described remains one part reality and two parts fiction, whether it is a description of a class in the late nineteenth century or the early twenty-first century.

Normally, we hear of the outstanding academic success of Ames who spent his entire professional life (1877–1909) at Harvard Law School and became dean before declining health necessitated his sudden resignation. There is no question that his success was a direct product of his enormous talents and prodigious pedagogical efforts. As noted by Arthur E. Sutherland, it was Ames who was the academic engine by which the ideal of the case method and the Socratic dialogue were first so carefully blended.

> Langdell, backed by Eliot in 1873, chose Ames as assistant professor. Ames was as great an innovator as Langdell. He was the new sort of teacher; a man comparatively young, whose professional accomplishments all were to be in writing, teaching, and in an educational administration, with no preliminary experience in practice or on the bench. Ames was Langdell's disciple; he used Langdell's method better than Langdell himself.[50]

The distinguished legal historian Charles Warren describes Ames as the person "who adopted heart and soul Langdell's Case System."[51]

---

48. *See* The Harvard Law School Ass'n, *supra* note 7, at 175–89.

49. *See id.* at 222–23. The Centennial History of the Harvard Law School explained the difference between Ames and Keener:

> Upon Justice Holmes' resignation in 1883, William A. Keener was appointed assistant professor, and subsequently Story Professor. Keener was a teaching genius. Not a scholar, nor well-loved like his colleagues, he had a most remarkable ability to instruct by the Socratic method. His method differed greatly from Ames'. Ames led; he drove. Ames aimed to persuade; Keener aimed to convince, even against the will. His favorite form of argument was the *reductio ad absurdam*; and he had wonderful skill in detecting imperfect reasoning.

Id. at 40–41.

50. Sutherland, *supra* note 6, at 164.

51. 2 Warren, *supra* note 1, at 363 n.1.

It appears that William Keener[52] was foremost among the faculty in the use of the new pedagogy in that he was a most naturally gifted teacher in the use of the Socratic dialogue. Ames was the first to effectively administer the new style of Socratic teaching in that he was appointed to the faculty in 1873, whereas Keener joined the faculty ten years later in 1883. Thus, Ames effectively carried the burden in demonstrating the pedagogical utility of the Socratic dialogue because his mentor, Langdell, was somewhat challenged in applying his theory of pedagogy in the classroom.

Notwithstanding Ames' contribution, it was generally recognized that Keener possessed the unique combination of skills and personality to fully deliver the spirit of the Socratic dialogue in the classroom. There is far less recognition regarding the importance of the role that Keener played with respect to the Socratic dialogue and the support he gave to the Langdell modality of teaching law. Keener came to the teaching of law with four years of private practice experience. He, however, was a zealous supporter of the scientific approach of Langdell and directly confronted those who might question the importance and the utility of this exciting new system of legal education. It was soon obvious to the Harvard law faculty that Keener was different and more confrontational with law students, particularly the first-year recruits. As noted in The Centennial History of Harvard Law School:

> Keener was a natural teacher. He was, perhaps, at his best with first-years men, who began by hating him, presently admired him grudgingly, and by the middle of the year swore by him. He had a remarkable power of forcing even the dullest to see a point or follow a train of reasoning by sheer weight of argument. He was a persistent and relentless cross-examiner, catching up everything the student said and compelling him to justify it, ruthlessly exposing all fallacies, drag-

---

52. Keener also defended the new form of teaching in two separate articles. *See* William A. Keener, *The Inductive Method in Legal Education*, 28 Am. L. Rev. 709 (1894); William A. Keener, *Methods of Legal Education*, 1 Yale L.J. 143 (1893). *Compare* J. C. Gray, *Cases and Treatises*, 22 Am. L. Rev. 756, 761 (1888) wherein Gray formally expressed positive views as to the use of the case method:

> The best material for legal education would undoubtedly be real cases, and the fact that a student in a lawyer's office has real cases to deal with, is some compensation, though very inadequate one, for the unsystematic instruction and the consequent waste of time, which is usually the lot of students in an office. But as students cannot have a series of real cases following in orderly sequence to be decided solely for their edification, the next best thing is to give them an orderly sequence of cases that have been decided.

> ging the student out of all bypaths of argument, and making him tread the straight and narrow path of dialectic whether he would or not. No student of his who in the first month ventured to support his argument by the statement that a certain court had so held in a certain case will ever forget the retort: "But suppose the court had held the other way?"[53]

Keener enjoyed his well-deserved reputation as the most outstanding teacher on the Harvard Law School faculty, although he was neither generally well liked by some members of the faculty nor considered a scholar.[54]

One doubts that Keener suffered from an excess of humility. He served on the faculty at the Harvard Law School from 1883 until 1890 when he suddenly departed to join the faculty of the Columbia Law School.[55] Two reasons for Keener's departure were that he was not included in a salary increase for full professors of law, as well as the timely receipt of an offer from Columbia Law School President Seth Low[56] that included more compensation.[57] LaPiana notes that Keener brought his robust and confrontational style of the Socratic dialogue in connection with utilization of the case study to Columbia Law School where he was fondly known by his students as "the red-bearded son of a bitch."[58]

Many of the legendary teaching greats and academic luminaries of Harvard Law School followed these first two leaders of the new style of pedagogy. Three such outstanding successors to Ames and Keener, law professors Joseph H. Beale, Samuel Williston, and Austin Wakefield Scott. They must be included among the second wave of Langdellian philosophical acolytes.[59] Gray, of course, had developed his own personal teaching style some time before the successful acceptance of the Langdellian revolution. Although Gray published six volumes of casebooks on property that were used in his course on property law,

---

53. THE HARVARD LAW SCHOOL ASS'N, *supra* note 7, at 222.

54. *See id.* at 41.

55. *See* LAPIANA, *supra* note 2, at 19–20, 94. Dean Roscoe Pound, reflecting on his year (1889) as a student at Harvard, expressed his positive views with respect to the teaching skills of Keener, Scott, Williston, and Ames. *See* Arthur E. Sutherland Jr., *One Man In His Time*, 78 HARV. L. REV. 7, 11 (1964); *see also* STAFF OF THE FOUNDATION FOR RESEARCH IN LEGAL HISTORY UNDER THE DIRECTION OF JULIUS GOBEL JR., A HISTORY OF THE SCHOOL OF LAW COLUMBIA UNIVERSITY 135–86 (1955).

56. *See* LAPIANA, *supra* note 2, at 19–20, 94.

57. According to LaPiana, the reason why Keener left was solely due to the compensation matter, citing a letter from him to the President and Fellows of Harvard College. *Id.* at 94 n.92.

58. *Id.* at 27.

59. *See, e.g.*, Sutherland, *supra* note 55, at 11 (observations of Pound).

and expressed formal support for the case method[60] innovation of Langdell, he paradoxically remained fixed to his original style of lecture and thoughtful reflection.[61]

Nevertheless, there is a tendency to associate the case method with the Socratic teaching style; however, the case method of study can be adopted without using the Socratic dialectic. Because Gray adopted and produced six casebooks on real property there is no proof that he changed his personal teaching style to employ, aggressively or otherwise, the interactive Socratic exchange to challenge or befuddle his students. In short, there is no significant evidence that Gray ever changed his teaching style to accommodate the Socratic dialogue. It was neither his personal style nor suited to his personality. The subject of his teaching style is further developed in a subsequent section of this chapter.

Relation of Case Method to Socratic Dialogue

In Justice Felix Frankfurter's remarks concerning the life of Williston and his experience at Harvard Law School, he noted:

> Of course, I could not say anything about Professor Williston without talking about Harvard Law School. In the history of institutions devoted to the scientific investigation of problems in any particular field of human concern, especially those of law, and also training practitioners in the various endeavors in which lawyers are called upon to serve, there probably is not another school that had as many members of its Faculty of the caliber of Williston as was true of Harvard Law School of his day. Among his colleagues were Christopher Columbus Langdell, James B. Ames, John Chipman Gray, Roscoe Pound, James Bradley Thayer, Jeremiah Smith, Joseph H. Beale, Austin W. Scott, and with each of these he served a long stretch. Historians have always denominated this period of the School's life as the "days of the giants."[62]

---

60. *See* LaPiana, *supra* note 2, at 102–03; *see also* J. C. Gray, *Methods of Legal Education: IV*, 1 Yale L.J. 159 (1892). Gray also published six case books on matters relating to real property.

61. Sutherland Jr., *supra* note 55, at 11–12; *see* LaPiana, *supra* note 2, at 25 n.91 (describing Gray's original views regarding teaching style as expressed in his letter, dated June 9, 1870, to Eliot). See also Pound's description of the teaching style of Gray, *infra* note 74 and accompanying text.

62. Felix Frankfurter, *Samuel Williston: An Inadequate Tribute to A Beloved Teacher*, 76 Harv. L. Rev. 1321 (1963).

Frankfurter's observation refers to the well-known story called the "Harvard Narrative" of doing legal education. The case method of Langdell, as delivered through the technique of the so-called Socratic dialogue, effectively dominated the mainframe of the American legal educational experience through most of the last century. The Langdellian hegemony as to the preferred method of legal pedagogy reigned supreme and the law school industry as a result remained for decades institutionally resistant to any modification from this teaching paradigm. The concept of law, according to Langdell, included the express belief that law was knowable in a similar manner as other scientific inquiries, and that it requires that the basic doctrines or principles of law be mastered through study of the relevant cases wherein these essential legal principles are embodied.[63] Teaching law under a scientific[64] methodology equates with the similar systems applied by the other constituent colleges of a university. By portraying the scientific method as an essential aspect of legal education, it justifies a law school's membership as a vital component of an academic community. This was much to the satisfaction and design of Eliot, who was by profession a man of science.[65] Under such philosophical conception, the training of lawyers now requires an academic institution because the subject matter of law is not unlike the discovery, definition, and application of scientific principles, which are applied in other areas of academic study. In this sense, the study of law becomes the principal, if not the exclusive, domain of academic institutions, and the apprenticeship system quickly fades from the process of training new lawyers. Accordingly, the academic model thereby eventually eliminates the competing apprenticeship system wherein law was taught by judges and practitioners on a part-time basis in skill training centers, whether such location was in the classroom or in a law office.

In commenting on the recommended period of legal study in law school from two to three years, the editors of the 1895 *Yale Law Journal* accurately identified the importance of academic control over the delivery of legal education by the following:

---

63. *See* Christopher Columbus Langdell, Selection of Cases on the Law of Contracts preface (1871); see also discussion of James Willard Hurst, The Growth of American Law 262–63 (1950).

64. Even the great Holmes originally gave support and expression to the thought that the law was somehow quantifiable in a scientific sense before becoming a judge. Professor White noted the following in his biography of Holmes when reporting a speech that then Chief Judge Holmes gave before the Bar Association of Boston on March 7, 1900, after having served for more than twenty years on the Supreme Judicial Court of Massachusetts. *See* White, *supra* note 1, at 253–54.

65. *See* LaPiana, *supra* note 2, at 7–8.

> The added year of law study falls in very aptly within this tendency. A man who means work may look at a law school course in just two ways—as a sort of manual training school which will carry him through to the bar in the fewest months, or as a period of thoughtful theoretical study which will give him a deep foundation. Fortunately our schools at Yale and Harvard are making the latter ideal a success which is wholly impossible in a city like New York.[66]

Thus, the university community becomes the standard for the development of legal education for the future.

Although the principal mechanism for the English delivery of legal education was through the diverse freestanding Inns of Court, the interaction of the Inns and its relationship to the judiciary and admission to the bar, created a university-like community of an informal and undefined nature.[67]

The success of the Harvard legal education system in the nineteenth century was complete in all respects. As a direct result of such reorientation in the study of law at Harvard Law School, the principal mechanism to acquire a legal education in the United States promptly shifts from that of apprenticeship relationships with a judge and/or a lawyer during the eighteenth and nineteenth centuries, to that of a law student attending a law school as a part of a traditionally established institution of higher learning. There was much celebration of the academic achievement, and direct proof of the economic success was evidenced by the substantial increase in the number of students who thereafter sought admission and were willing to pay the applicable tuition at Harvard Law School. The number of law students attending Harvard Law School after Langdell's appointment dropped from 136 in 1870–71 to 113 in 1872–73.[68] As Franklin G. Fessenden, one of the seven original law students in Langdell's first-year class at Harvard, reported:

> Mention has been made of the fears that the School would be ruined financially. It was said that [Langdell] had no practical administrative

---

66. *Editorials*, 5 Yale L.J. 143 (1895).

67. Professor Simpson provides an excellent and efficient summary of the early development of legal education in England and expresses the view that the cluster of the various Inns of Court located in a particular center of London as amounting to the establishment of a university of sorts although not connected to a traditional university such as Oxford or Cambridge. *See* 2 A.W.B. Simpson, English Common Law, The New Palgrave Dictionary of Economics and the Law 57, 63 (1998).

68. Franklin G. Fessenden, *The Rebirth of Harvard Law School*, 33 Harv. L. Rev. 493, 515 (1919–1920).

> sense, that he was a mere theorist. During the early years of his services these fears seemed justified. The income fell off. As has been said before, there was an insistent desire that there should be an increase in numbers and income. We need not go over in detail the financial story. It is enough to say that in 1870, when he began, the funds were small in amount, and that in 1895, when he retired, the total was $360,000 invested and a cash surplus of $25,000. Excellence has received its reward.[69]

When Langdell retired in 1895, there were 413 students.[70] This constituted more than a threefold increase in the number of students from the low point reached in the academic year 1872–73. The increase in the number of students and the receipt of greatly increased tuition was proof that the Langdellian system of legal education was successful. It is no surprise that nonprofit academic institutions are equally dependent and desirous of profits from operations.

The metamorphosis for the delivery of legal education as it relates to the Langdellian hypothesis of law as science and the formative character of the teacher swiftly became the dominant system for the delivery of legal education during the latter part of the nineteenth century. Indeed, it blossomed into the overwhelming choice for the delivery of legal education in the United States during the twentieth century. There is no last word on legal education, as the incessant drive for the development of new perspectives or technologies is always in process and the study of law does not exist in isolation, it remains directly affected by other pressures for social change.

The Invention of the Academic Lawyer

Before Langdell, and his successful experiment with Ames, there was no career opportunity or job description for an exclusively academic lawyer. This experiment gave birth to the career of the purely academic lawyer. The invention of the academic lawyer is more important to the modality of the modern law school as an institution than is the recognition given to the employment of the Langdellian innovations; namely, the Socratic dialectic as a means to ascertain the scientific rules of law and the simultaneous development of the casebook. Viewed in this context, exclusive focus on the aforementioned pedagogic innovations conceals the more serious revolutionary change in the type

---

69. *Id.* at 515–16.
70. *Id.* at 515.

of persons who will "own and operate" the centers of legal education. This radical departure in the paradigm is mostly excluded from consideration. This change in the background of the new teacher of law was an explicit goal of Langdell despite the fact that he had extensive private practice experience.[71] Langdell, regarding the desired law teacher, stated:

> I wish to emphasize the fact that a teacher of law should be a person who accompanies his pupils on a road which is new to them, but with which he is well acquainted from having often traveled it before. What qualifies a person, therefore, to teach law is not experience in the work of a lawyers' office, not experience in dealing with men, not experience in the trial or argument of causes—not experience, in short, in using law but experience in learning law; not the experience of the Roman advocate or of the Roman praetor, still less of the Roman procurator, but the experience of the jurisconsult.[72]

In this objective, Langdell was immensely successful.

In this respect, Gray did not meet the description of an academic teacher that Langdell sought. This difference set the stage for personal conflict that ultimately came to pass. Gray represents that rare breed of practitioner-teacher-scholar. His teaching style reflected the traditional style of earlier law school teaching technique: that is, lecturing on the certain topics as well as reflecting on one's legal thoughts and sharing relevant experiences confronted in practice.[73] Pound described Gray's teaching in response to Sutherland's questions.

> Gray was a master of [property]. Gray was an outstanding influence with me. I think I owe a great deal to him.

---

71. In The Centennial History of the Harvard Law School 1817–1917, Gray was referred to as "a scholarly lawyer." The Harvard Law School Ass'n, *supra* note 7, at 206. This is a refreshing description of the difference from a pure academic lawyer: i.e., a law professor who has little practice experience and, most likely, little or no interest in such activity from that of a practitioner who reveals interests in both practice and scholarship.

72. James Willard Hurst, The Growth of American Law 263 (1950).

73. For example, during Justice George Sutherland's legal education at the University of Michigan Law School, the former judge and constitutional scholar, Thomas McIntyre Cooley, and the then equally eminent Chief Justice of the Michigan Supreme Court, James Valentine Campbell, among others, lectured to him. The weekly system of legal education at Michigan at that time was comprised of ten lectures a week and some moot court training for the students. *See* Joel Francis Paschal, Mr. Justice Sutherland: A Man Against the State 16, 20 (1951). Judges were a main element of most of the regular legal educational systems until the consequences of the Langdellian revolution became the catalyst for a radical change in the identity of "who" was to be the teacher.

> How did Mr. Gray teach? Did he use the dialectic process? ... Well, Gray would sometimes think out loud in class. He would ask questions occasionally; he might get into a discussion; but he knew the law of real property inside out. He was a learned scholar, a great scholar. I owe a great deal to him. He would do curious things.... That was Gray; he was very abrupt in his speech. I remember in class one day in first-year property—Gray would every once in awhile go off on some medieval matter that hadn't been of any consequence even as late as Coke—one morning he put something that depended on a case way back in the thirteenth century, on some queer question of tenure; and then he turned to the man in the front row and said "What do you think of that?" Well, the man floundered; so Gray then tackled another, and he went along and then finally tackled me. I had been thinking about it hard. I gave him an answer. He looked at me in astonishment; he would pull his beard, this way, "Hmm, Hmm." "Well," he said, "That's mighty ingenious but it isn't so!" Then he quit and went on to something else. He was a great teacher after all.[74]

Pound's observation of the teaching style of Gray creates the image of an expert on the law of property who most likely was not one to confront or challenge the student in the classroom, and who enjoyed asking rhetorical questions that were trenchant for further review and reflection by students outside of the class.

Although the legal community of the past celebrated the case method and the Socratic dialogue as identifying the ultimate rule of law and its (problematic) relationship to the scientifically correct answers on the "Bar Exam," the academic community obviously seldom ever reflects positively on the early heritage of the practitioner-teacher, frequently a judge, as constituting a particularly important and historic part in the history of legal education. The primary focus of legal education after the full impact of the Langdellian legal revolution occurred is the conjured version of the newly created, purely academic, career of teacher-scholar as fictionalized in the iconic movie "The Paper Chase." Eliot spoke eloquently of this institutional innovation at a celebration marking Langdell's twenty-five years of service.

> Professor Langdell early advocated the appointment, as teachers of law, of young men who had no experience whatsoever in the active profes-

74. Sutherland Jr., *supra* note 55, at 11–12; *see also* LaPiana, *supra* note 2, at 25 n.91 (describing Professor Gray's original views regarding teaching style as expressed in his letter, dated June 9, 1870, to President Eliot).

> sion. What a venture was that, gentlemen; what bold advice for the head of the School to give! This School had never done it; no School had ever done it; it was absolutely a new departure for our country in the teaching of law. I remember very well how reluctantly the Corporation and the Board of Overseers consented to the first experiment on this point, namely, the appointment for a limited term of five years of Assistant Professor James Barr Ames (prolonged applause). You may well applaud now, gentlemen, when the success of that experiment has been absolutely assured; but what was the courage which first suggested the experiment? Now that experiment, too, has not only been extended in our own Law School with perfect success but it has been adopted by various other law schools throughout the country. And what does this mean? What is to be the ultimate outcome of this courageous venture? In due course, and that is no long term of years, there will be produced in this country a body of men learned in the law who have never been on the bench or at the Bar, but who nevertheless hold positions of great weight and influence as teachers of the law, as expounders, systematizers, and historians. This, I venture to predict, is *one of the most far reaching changes in the organization of the profession that has ever been made in our country.*[75]

Faculty Conflict and Gray's Plea to Eliot

It is interesting to contrast Gray's initial attitude with respect to the methodology designed by Langdell and delivered most effectively by Ames, the principal faculty ally of Langdell. During life on a faculty, there are occasions where matters of principle are viewed, so desperately important that the normal mores of social propriety are not sufficient to restrain one's behavior. On such occasions, the tensions arising from the differing concerns may cause each of the interacting participants to attain the exaggerated level of open and hostile nonsense. It is frequently referred to as academic regression and to some extent is inevitable in situations wherein competing faculty members of excessive self-importance are forced to coexist over extended periods of time. It matters not that such unexpressed feelings have heretofore been percolating for some time, so long as the feelings are carefully suppressed from public disclo-

75. Report of President Eliot's speech *in* 2 WARREN, *supra* note 1, at 389 (emphasis added).

sure. This situation can seed institutional dissention among the faculty as well as lead to the establishment of separate faculty cliques to the enduring frustration of a dean. Indeed, decanal resignation sometimes is mistakenly offered as the only mechanism to renew the spirit of faculty cooperation.

The occasion of Gray's outburst took place in January of 1883. The academic issues affecting the faculty during the fall semester of 1882 were simmering and reached the volatile point with the sudden and frustrating departure of Holmes in December 1882. The background to this event is cogently relevant. Holmes' reputation as a scholar of the common law was well-established and confirmed by the publication of his infamous book of the common law.[76] Yet, Langdell had valid and personal reasons to question the commitment of Holmes to the newly defined educational mission of the law school. Holmes had criticized the new approach to the study of law at Harvard Law School in a note published in 1870.[77] Subsequently, he was critical of Langdell's casebook and also ascribed to the dean, in an unsigned review of his casebook, the sobriquet of being "the greatest living legal theologian."[78] Holmes, however, did laud the dean in a separate commencement address.[79]

There were extensive efforts on the part of "some members" of the faculty to secure the appointment of Holmes. Noteworthy, neither Langdell nor Ames was interested in securing an endowment to fund the compensation conditions set forth by Holmes. However, James Bradley Thayer took it upon himself to secure the needed funds to secure the endowment.[80] The subsequent and unexpected departure of Holmes to accept an appointment to the Massachusetts Supreme Judicial Court was a rather startling turn of events to say the least. Holmes' departure left an opening in the faculty that needed to be filled. It was of no import to the faculty that the reason for Holmes' departure was because of the availability of a judicial appointment that he desperately sought and immediately accepted after teaching for only the fall semester. This was a very painful conclusion to a long and drawn out effort to secure a position for the talented Holmes. White reviews the dynamics of this frustrating effort that caused some deep irritation on the part of the law school faculty and administration alike, particularly as it relates to Holmes' acceptance of the

76. Oliver Wendell Holmes Jr., The Common Law (1991) (1881).

77. *See Summary of Events*, 5 Am. L. Rev. 177 (1870).

78. *See Book Notices*, 14 Am. L. Rev. 233, 234 (1880).

79. White, *supra* note 1, at 197 (reporting that Dean Langdell was lauded extensively for his contributions to the law school by Holmes in a commencement address in 1880).

80. *See id.* at 200–01 (discussing the events surrounding the offering of a contract to Holmes).

judicial appointment before any prior notification to administrators of Harvard University.[81]

The suppressed conflict[82] that was festering between Langdell and Ames on one side of the faculty against Thayer and Gray became quite evident during this fiasco with Holmes. However, Eliot was the power behind every major decision at the law school and the hiring matter was also a crucial issue for him.[83] Langdell and Ames were the principal means by which Eliot achieved his goal of converting the law school to an academic venture of a scientific nature. Yet, the immediate need for employment of another faculty member following the sudden departure of Holmes was obvious to all of them. Eliot promptly made a faculty appointment offer, presumably after private consultation with Langdell, to William A. Keener, a lawyer of modest legal experience. This offer was made shortly after the resignation of Holmes and without prior notice to the other members of the faculty. Eliot and Langdell conveyed the offer of a faculty appointment to Keener on December 28, 1882. Keener promptly accepted the appointment.[84]

It is most likely that the appointment was made and then announced to Thayer and Gray at a faculty meeting held on the night of January 2, 1883. This announcement quickly brought the pot to the boiling point. After having tentatively secured the appointment of another practitioner in the form of Holmes, Thayer and Gray were now facing the probable loss of voting power on faculty issues to the extent Eliot would not otherwise intervene in their favor, assuming that Keener would likely join with the Langdell-Ames camp.

This is the background leading to Gray's passionate and highly critical letter sent to Eliot on January 3, 1883.[85] Gray most vehemently objected to the practice of appointing lawyers to the faculty of modest legal experience and directly criticized the methodologies of Langdell and his prodigy Ames.[86] By

---

81. *See id.* at 200–09.

82. *See* LaPiana, *supra* note 2, at 18 (referring to the conflict over the honors program at Harvard Law School in 1878 between the two defined cliques of the faculty; namely Langdell and Ames vs. Thayer and Gray).

83. *Id.*

84. *Id.*

85. LaPiana focuses on this letter to establish the differences in the faculty views and clarifies that the initial offer to Keener was subsequently withdrawn. *See id.* at 18–19. Siegel focuses on the same letter to establish the principal philosophical differences between Langdell and Gray. *See* Stephen A. Siegel, *John Chipman Gray and the Moral Basis of Classical Legal Thought*, 86 Iowa L. Rev. 1533 (2001).

86. Letter from John Chipman Gray, Professor, Harvard Law School, to Charles W. Eliot, President, Harvard College (Jan. 3, 1883) (on file with Harvard University Archives, Box 71, Folder 1883 (G-L)).

far, Gray's letter is the most revealing emotional outburst by this esteemed professor of law. Never before or afterwards did Gray communicate in writing such an unprotected or candid expression of frustration. It may be that Gray maintained a marginally composed facade during the meeting on the night of January 2, 1883, but the matter festered overnight resulting in the missive sent to Eliot. The letter includes a number of criticisms of importance.

> Dear Mr. Eliot:
> 40 State Street
> January 3, 1883
>
> I want to say what I could not say last night. I said that the profession generally believed that students of the law should be taught (not by great men) but by men who had considerable practical experience; that to choose an inexperienced assistant professor would be considered either a confession of pecuniary and inimical weakness, which would be most injurious, or a resolution to train men by teachers without experience in affairs; that the school had gone against the opinion of the profession in requiring admission examinations and in extending the courses for three years, and we have suffered severely in numbers in consequence; and that we cannot now afford to go against professional opinion on this point, on which lawyers are much more unanimous than on others, and if anything is to be done it should not be done until we have recovered from the effect of our other changes. This I think, if the profession is wrong.
>
> But I now want to say that the profession is right. The school has suffered from applying rules true in other matters to the law. I can quite believe that in an industrial school a man of small experience may often be a better teacher than one of much larger practice. The truths of natural science and the best means of applying them are independent of opinion.
>
> Such a force will have such an effect, whether the man who applies it thinks it will or not, that is, the opinion of practicing chemists and engineers are not the object of study in a scientific school, but the fact of chemistry and science are what ought to be studied.
>
> *But in law the opinions of judges and lawyers as to what the law is, are the law.* And it is in any true sense of the word, as unscientific to turn from them, as Mr. Langdell does, with contempt because they are "low and unscientific," as for a scientific man to decline to take cognizance of oxygen or gravitation because it was low and unscientific. Whether they be low or not, they are the basis of legal science.

It is the tendency of every professor of law to substitute his views of what the law ought to be for that which actually obtains. I have constantly to be on the guard against it. The greater a man's force and enthusiasm the greater the danger. Langdell's intellectual arrogance and contempt is astounding. I may forgive it in him or Ames, but in an ordinary man it would be detestable.

The idols of the cave, which a school bred lawyer, is sure to substitute for the fact, may be much better material for gymnastics than the facts themselves and may call forth more enthusiasm in the pupils, but a school where the majority of the professors shun and despise the contact with actual facts, has got the seeds of ruin in it and will go and ought to go to the devil. The very excellence its methods will send it there all the faster.

As the faculty has been constituted, you have been able to save us from several follies. I dread to see a majority of the faculty made up of professors whose opinions and trainings will [more or less?] tend to divorce the school from the facts which the students have to meet in the world.

Excuse my damnable iteration. I have the matter very much at heart.

Yours very truly,
John C. Gray
Hon. C. W. Eliot[87]

This is a most remarkable outburst by Gray.[88] He was not the only person to question the appointment of Keener. Ephraim Gurney, dean of the college faculty, also filed a vociferous objection to the employment of Keener. At this point in Gray's academic career, he is fighting for a faculty of experienced lawyers and is obviously engaged in a comprehensive disagreement with all or most of what Langdell and, more importantly, Eliot are committed to—namely, a transfor-

---

87. *Id.* (emphasis added)

88. *See* Letter from Ephraim Gurney, Dean of Faculty, Harvard College, to Charles W. Eliot, President, Harvard College (on file with Harvard—Presidential Papers, Box 71, folder 1883 G-L); *see also* LaPiana, *supra* note 2, at 18 (attempting to unravel the scrawl and clarifying Gurney's concern about the appointment of Keener and the administration of the law school by Langdell). The opening portion of the letter has a phrase that is quite popular in academia. Gurney opened by stating: "I am sorry to say I could not sleep last night as well as usual, and as I lay awake I found my mind revolving about the Law School problem and what you said about it in the part of the report that you read to me." Sutherland made a comprehensive interpretation of Gurney's letter. *See* Sutherland, *supra* note 6, at 187–90.

mation in the delivery of legal education. Gray's candid admission that "the opinions of judges and lawyers as to what the law is, are the law" stands directly in opposition to the structure of his two principal treatises on the law wherein the law is somewhat frozen in place and beyond modification by the hand of a judge. Recall, Chief Justice Doe crafted a creative application of the doctrine of *cy pres* to avoid the failure of a bequest in a trust because of a violation of the RAP. This subjected Doe to severe criticism by Gray under the view that the "existing law" as designed by predecessor jurists must be vigorously applied to the facts.[89] There is no room in Gray's world for judicial discretion.

The assertion that the law is the product of judges is diametrically opposite to the entire construct of Gray's scholarship on the RAP and restraints on alienation. Such a proposition of law is offered by Gray three years before the completion of his treatise on perpetuities and made in the same year that his book on restraints on alienation was published. Ironically, when Gray was exercised by a legal decision that failed to measure up to his opinion of the "law," it was entirely appropriate for him to professionally and personally excoriate the judge.[90] In his first book on restraints on alienation, Gray vehemently decries the judges for their enforcement of the spendthrift provision in a trust instrument. Consistency is not a necessary condition for a lawyer; but it is for a scholar! Gray was both. He lived in both worlds. Yet, Gray's philosophical propositions of the law were neatly packaged and quite separate from his traditional legal scholarship. In Gray's world of practice, law is the product of what judges say. In the scholarship arena, a jurist has no independent voice and the preexisting law must be rigorously applied as it exists. This dilemma is never resolved by him. It reflects the difference of his life as a scholar and that of a practitioner of the law; the dual elements are never synthesized.

After excoriating Langdell for treating law as a science separate from the views of the judge, the style of Gray's scholarship is largely in the asserted scientific modality of Langdell. Moreover, Gray reveals an unconditional commitment to the interpretation of the "common law" as he sees it and, not surprisingly, his personal abstraction of the legal principles is most "exacting." Langdell should have fully enjoyed the scholarship of Gray, but in view of their ongoing personal antagonism it is likely that he failed to see they were more alike in respect

89. See his personal denunciation of Chief Justice Doe's decision at John C. Gray, *General and Particular Intent in Connection with the Rule Against Perpetuities*, 9 HARV. L. REV. 242 (1895). The editors of the *Harvard Law Review* noted in the same volume the passing of Chief Justice Doe and provided a very complementary observation of his contributions to the development of the law. *Id.* at 534–35.

90. *Id.*

to their scholarly view of the law. Notwithstanding their personal conflict, both were practitioners of the law. The conflict between them may have been caused by their unique personalities rather than their collective or individual views of the law. As practitioners of the law, both had experienced the natural chaos of practice and witnessed the contingent determination of the law in specific cases. Neither could be the ideologue as conjured up by traditional scholarship.[91] Gray made several remarks that judges were the source of law in his epic work on the RAP. For example, Gray questioned Charles Sweet on a point of law by the following: "Mr. Sweet, surely, cannot be suspected of holding to the vulgar error that judges cannot make the law"; and further stated that the RAP is "not a statute, it is judge-made law, and there seems no reason why, as cases arise, the judges should not define the scope of the law that they have made."[92] But such observations are far from the dominant mode of his scholarship. Law as science was the dominant form and style of his scholarship.

Apart from Gray's later philosophical offerings in *The Nature and Sources of the Law*, there are few occasions when Gray "the lawyer" comes out of his law office and candidly shares the realities of his practice in his scholarship. The outburst of Gray set forth in his letter to Eliot remains the foremost exception. This is one of those rare events in which Gray cites the decisionmaker as the source of law.

These remarks constitute remarkable admissions by Gray and support, to some limited sense, his later attempts in discussing jurisprudential questions in his last book, *The Nature and Sources of the Law*. The admissions made in the letter are reflective of Gray's experience as a lawyer that was, for the most part, intentionally suppressed in the form of his scholarship on the RAP as well as in his opus on restraints on alienation. Gray's major opus on the RAP was written on the analysis of the specific details of decided English cases and assumes the ex cathedra perfection of the common law judicial pronouncements. There is little explanation with respect to the underlying bases of the decisions in his treatise on the RAP. Moreover, Gray presents the law of the RAP in the nature of a conclusion that represents a summary of rules that have reached a final product of legal precision akin to a scientific revelation. It is

91. For a renewed perspective of Dean Langdell, see BRUCE A. KIMBALL, THE INCEPTION OF MODERN PROFESSIONAL EDUCATION: C.C. LANGDELL, 1826–1906 (2009), and Bruce A. Kimball, *The Langdell Problem: Historicizing the Century of Historiography, 1906–2000s*, 22 LAW & HIST. REV. 277 (2004).

92. JOHN CHIPMAN GRAY, THE RULE AGAINST PERPETUITIES §§296, 298, 326–27 (Roland Gray ed., 4th ed. 1942) (1886); *see id.* §728 (Gray stating very precisely that: "The Rule against Perpetuities is judge made law").

not an easy book to read, although its impact on the legal community was enormous on both sides of the Atlantic. He reduced, or more appropriately eliminated, the role of public policy (at least to the barest minimum) even though the RAP is purely a product of judge-made law. In many respects, the form of Gray's discourse on the RAP was in the scientific language as envisioned by his academic protagonist, Langdell! Gray constructed a RAP that was to be impregnable from modification and mathematically applied by judges in a most remorseless fashion as if they were martinets.

Contradictions abound, mostly because Gray's suppressed anger bubbled out of control and found expression in the letter to Eliot. There, briefly, came the person of Gray, socially emancipated by extreme frustration. Roland noted that his father had a temper; however, it was seldom available for public observation. For that moment, Gray lost his self-imposed social constraints that were otherwise perfectly internalized by this most private Brahmin.

He would not return to these admissions (law viewed as a product of the opinions of the judges) in public until he made, what could be called a deathbed conversion. As a result, Gray is frequently cited as some ill-defined precursor to legal realism by reason of his lecture given at Columbia Law School in 1908,[93] which was subsequently published in 1909 as *The Nature and Sources of the Law.*[94]

Gray's ironic philosophical contortion is understandable as a reflection of his many years in the practice of law. This form of legal philosophy comes by way of acquired skepticism, frequently flying under the more acceptable term of pragmatism that is founded in the empirical realities of the practice of law. Most likely, Gray did not believe that such radical description of the law could be publicly disseminated without incurring the potential wrath of the legal community of the late nineteenth century. He was then immersed in a law school that was engaged in the commitment to some form of classical formalism; that is, the process whereby the essential legal principles would be established and logically applied on a consistent basis. In conducting the scientific search for the essential legal principles, the law school was attempting to model itself as a community engaged in a search for the scientific determination of the prescribed rules of law. It is not likely that Gray, whose proclivity was one of avoiding personal confrontation, was ready to confront these deeply held conventions and customs that are reflected in his scholarship on the RAP and restraints on alienation. Yet, this is not to suggest or infer he was an unconditional

---

93. *See* John Chipman Gray, The Nature and Sources of the Law vii (2d ed., Beacon Press 1963) (1909).

94. *Id.*

ideologue of classical formalism. Gray simply chose to mimic the style and assumptions of that dominating system in almost all of his formal scholarship on property issues. He internalized a belief that the law of the past must be "preserved." Thus he appears more a preservationist of law past than a strict ideologue of classical formalism. This does not involve a contradiction of legal philosophy; it explains his modus operandi as a scholar.

Gray was aware of these issues and was equally concerned about the loss of the virtues protected by the legal system. He made mostly conscious choices about self-definition, conventions, and the various norms of his time. He was not imprisoned by the normative expectations of others. However, Gray was not one by personality to make startlingly new observations on or about the law. Gray gingerly laid out his unconventional thoughts with appropriate conditions and sagacity in his philosophical tome. Although some do not believe Gray went far enough to be recognized as a philosophic innovator of the law for the reasons discussed *infra*,[95] he was keenly interested in what the "establishment" thought of his philosophical work.[96] The number of persons who provided positive feedback on his philosophical tome included Frederick Pollock,[97] William A. Taft,[98] T. Cyprian Williams,[99] and Viscount James Bryce[100] who was then serving at the British Embassy.

---

95. See discussion in text, Chapter 7.

96. *Id.*

97. *See* Letter from Sir Frederick Pollock, to John Chipman Gray, Professor, Harvard Law School (Oct. 23, 1909) (on file with the Houghton Library of the Harvard College, in the John Chipman Gray Correspondence File, BMS Am. 2152 (135–36)) (acknowledging receipt of his lectures at Columbia University Law School and informing Gray that: "our Court of Appeals has before it the question of whether the so-called rule of double possibilities applies to equitable remainders, and you no doubt will be freely cited").

98. *See* Letter from William H. Taft, President, The United States of America, to John Chipman Gray, Professor, Harvard Law School (Oct. 10, 1910) (on file with Houghton Library of the Harvard College, in the John Chipman Gray Correspondence File, BMS Am. 2152 (157)) (commenting on the receipt of his book *The Nature and Sources of the Law*).

99. *See* Letter from T. Cyprian Williams to John Chipman Gray (Nov. 20, 1909) (on file with Houghton Library of the Harvard College, in the John Chipman Gray Correspondence File, BMS Am. 2152 (157)).

100. Letter from Viscount James Bryce, to John Chipman Gray, Professor, Harvard Law School (Nov. 1, 1909) (on file with the Houghton Library of the Harvard College, in the John Chipman Gray Correspondence File, BMS Am. 2152 (27)) (acknowledging receipt of his philosophic tome and relaying the following story: "You may remember the story of the judge who interrupted counsel and said 'Mr. So and So, that is not the law' and counsel's reply 'It was the law until your lordship spoke'").

Gray and University Relations

With respect to law school issues at the administrative level, Gray was more intensely involved and personally challenged by the emerging issues confronting the law school during the decade of the 1880s. It was in this decade that Gray's academic standing as an outstanding scholar was achieved by the publication of his two major treatises. Now the next step in the development of the law school was to be determined by critical faculty hiring decisions and the quality of the administrative skills of Langdell and his successors. These were important concerns for Gray. He forthrightly communicated his views on a variety of relevant issues to Eliot.[101] One would have to say that although Gray won many battles, perhaps more in private practice than he did at the law school, Eliot maintained an abiding commitment to the goals and objectives of Langdell. Gray eventually adjusted to these realities and was forced to accept that his concerns and influence, although important and always heard, were seldom acted upon by Eliot. It may be assumed that Eliot's appointment of Ames as the successor dean to Langdell in 1895 provided a definitive statement about the future direction of the law school and that such decision foreclosed any possible thoughts of more serious influence with respect to the administration and future direction of the law school by Gray. It is noteworthy that Harvard University conferred a well deserved honorary degree on Gray in the year of 1895, along with Holmes Jr., Frederick Pollock, and others. Eliot was a superb politician when it came to overseeing the development of the law school, and the conferrence of these honorary degrees, especially as it relates to Gray, may have been to procure Gray's continuing commitment to the administration of the law school under Ames. Quite possibly, these changes in the administration of the law school additionally enhanced and further cemented Gray's commitment to the practice of law.

There is a peculiar letter sent years later, dated April 7, 1909, from Eliot to Gray chastising him for his "lack of reverence and that respect for ceremonial observances" attendant to his indifferent failure to respond to a possible appointment as ambassador to England.

> Dear Mr. Gray,
> Your sentiments concerning the ambassadorship seem to me to lack reverence and respect for the ceremonial and social observances which are to be expected of a conservative lawyer and Episcopalian.

---

101. *See, e.g.*, LaPiana, *supra* note 2, at 18–19 (discussing Gray's letter and the principal concerns of Gray).

Am I right in inferring from your remarks of April 3 that you would not care to go to England yourself as the American ambassador?

Sincerely yours,
Charles W. Eliot[102]

It is not known whether Eliot had authority to tender such an offer on behalf of President William Howard Taft. However, the implication of this letter may have been a disguised invitation for Gray to consider leaving the faculty by the mechanism of the potential appointment to the ambassadorship. Presidents of universities are fairly ingenious in their Machiavellian means by which they "reward" the voices of opposition and/or the discontented tenured faculty.

It is noteworthy that the renowned history of Harvard Law School by Charles Warren published in 1907 did not highlight the contributions of Gray or the impact of his efforts on the success of the law school. Perhaps, the histories of law school successes or failures are seen through an analysis of a dean's ability to provide leadership while dealing somewhat effectively with the contending constituent forces of the administration at the university level and the idiosyncratic complaints of the faculty. In this sense, the contributions of a specific professor seldom stand out or are of significant interest to historians, in comparison to those which are attributed to a dean (whether real or fictitious).

Gray Teaching Style Unaffected by Case Method and Socratic Dialogue

With respect to his teaching style and the adoption of the case method, Professor Gray was as unique in this endeavor as in other parts of his career. One might speculate that his teaching style, as a lecturer of law, was well developed before accepting his full-time appointment. By that time, Gray had been teaching on a part-time basis for approximately four and one-half years as a lecturer at Harvard Law School.[103] Langdell accepted decanal responsibility for

102. Letter from Charles W. Eliot, President, Harvard University, to John Chipman Gray, Professor, Harvard Law School (Apr. 7, 1909) (on file with the Houghton Library of the Harvard College, in the John Chipman Gray Correspondence File, call number MS AM 5152, (40)).

103. It may be that Gray taught for three and a half years before receiving his full-time appointment as the Story Professor of Law on March 18, 1875; the secondary information on this point creates a degree of uncertainty in that he was appointed as a lecturer in 1869 and that appointment was renewed in 1871, 1872, and 1873. However, one assumes that

the administration of the law school in 1870 and was fully committed to the case method well before Gray received a permanent faculty appointment as the Story Professor of Law.[104]

Yet, Gray's teaching style was described as follows:

> His method of teaching was always thorough and interesting, but it was not always the same. He had been educated in the old days of the lecture system, and began by following that system, with modifications of his own. Even after Langdell and Ames had made the case system a success, Gray long continued his own method, not requiring students to state and discuss cases, but announcing a list of cases to be read as a preparation for each lecture, and then giving a lecture of artistic form, with a beginning, middle, and end, but with occasional questioning. These lectures were models of exposition; and a peculiarly skillful passage was the introductory paragraph in which, beginning with the words "The last time," Gray summarized the results of the preceding lecture in such a way as to give an appropriate introduction to the work of the day, but spoke so rapidly that his words could not be taken down as a substitute for the full lecture.[105]

Gray candidly expressed his view of the range of teaching styles with respect to the case system.

> I have used the expression "case system," but I do not like it, for it suggests a hide-bound and stereotyped method of instruction. Nothing could be further from the truth. No scheme of teaching affords greater scope for individuality. To Professor Langdell goes the credit at in-

---

he also taught from 1874 to March of 1875 when the permanent offer was made and accepted. *See* Thayer, *supra* note 17, at 540.

104. Indeed, Dean Langdell's infamous casebook on Contracts published in 1871 initiated a fundamental change in the focus of legal study. It was to follow the theory articulated in the preface:

> Law, considered as science, consists of certain principles or doctrines. To have such a mastery of these as to be able to apply them with constant facility and certainty to the ever tangled skein of human affairs is what constitutes a true lawyer; hence to acquire that mastery should be the business of every earnest student of law....

C.C. Langdell, A Selection on the Law of Contracts (1871).

105. The Harvard Law School Ass'n, *supra* note 7, at 210–11.

troducing the method at Cambridge, *but styles of teaching of the different professors are as unlike as possible. We agree only in making cases, not text-books, the basis of instruction.*[106]

It is a fair assumption that although Gray gave formal affirmation to the use of the case system, he did not employ the many other technologies included in the general teaching approach of Langdell, particularly the Socratic method as delivered by Ames and Keener. Despite the innovations as initiated by Langdell, Gray's teaching style was and remained more akin to that of the past. But he was a master of property law. Recall the specific testimony of Pound, quoted above, describing Gray in the classroom. Admittedly, Gray was reluctant to publicly reject the teaching technology of Langdell and others of the faculty, and was personally resistant to a modification of his teaching. Gray was profoundly certain of his knowledge of property law and completely confident of his teaching. He would bend, but alas never change.

In short, Gray was well aware of the new teaching model[107] and must have made some accommodation to the new program by the time of his full-time appointment. Formally, most of the evidence clearly supports the view that Gray did, in fact, eventually publicly support the pedagogical use of the "Case Method."[108] Recall the idea of the Langdellian case method, itself, did not find instantaneous acceptance at Harvard Law School by the students[109] or the faculty. It took a number of years before there was universal support by all or

---

106. Gray, *supra* note 52, at 762 (emphasis added).

107. As Moorfield Story stated: "He began to teach by lecturing, but gradually became converted to more modern methods.... He treated his pupils as fellow-students, working with him on an equal footing to learn the truth." Remarks of Moorfield Story at Bar proceeding honoring John Chipman Gray, *in* Gray Memoir, *supra* note 6, at 101.

108. For a less than enthusiastic endorsement of the case method of legal education in 1893, see Emlin McClain, *The Uses of Cases in Teaching Law*, 3 Yale L.J. 17 (1893). Albert Boyden, author of the first history on the evolution of the law firm, notes the early attitude of Gray with respect to the case method by quoting a letter written by Gray to John Codman Ropes, dated January 7, 1865. In the letter, Gray commented: "[t]he thought of Leading Cases was a most happy idea on the part of Smith. I know of no way so excellent for the *learning* of the law." Boyden, *supra* note 29, at 25.

109. Dean James Barr Ames noted that the original handful of students studying under Dean Langdell and using his casebook were referred to, somewhat disparagingly, as "Langdell's freshman." *See* James Barr Ames, *Professor Langdell—His Services to Legal Education*, 20 Harv. L. Rev. 12, 13 (1906). Others have referred to the original group as "Kit's Freshman." *See, e.g.*, Kimball, *supra* note 91, at 283.

most of the participants for that innovation.[110] So, Gray's initial timid reluctance to accept the case method was not particularly unusual. Indeed, according to Wambaugh, the use of the case method "in 1870 appeared to many persons, and indeed to most, impractical and unscientific."[111]

Gray normally began class in his early years with a summary of the last class. Joseph H. Beale, a former student and subsequent colleague, described Gray's teaching style.

> In those days, when Austin Hall was still very new, Gray had not yet accepted the study of cases as the basis of instruction. He gave out weekly a list of authorities to be consulted, and then in class lectured to us with a clearness, precision, and perfection of form that was all his own. His mind was well adapted to teaching law in this way: his sense of form and proportion, his skill in exposition, his certainty of using the right word, made even Foremedon in Reverter and the Statute of Uses as interesting as Ashwell's case or the "last clear chance". During the first ten minutes of a lecture he was in the habit of giving a summary of the preceding lecture, and these summaries were far from the least instructive parts of his lectures. It is hard to see how his method of instruction could have been improved by the use of a casebook, though he himself was already coming to believe that the use of a casebook was the only satisfactory method of study from the student's point of view. A few years later he prepared his own series of books, and became one of the most vigorous and effective defenders of Langdell's system of instruction.[112]

Gray had the amazing consistency of finishing each semester at precisely the same page[113] whether relying on his notes as in the past, or using a casebook.[114] This exactitude suggests that he did not open the classroom discus-

---

110. *See* Eugene Wambaugh, *Professor Langdell—A View of His Career*, 20 Harv. L. Rev. 1, 3 (1906).

111. *Id.* at 2.

112. *See* Joseph H. Beale, *John Chipman Gray*, 28 Harv. L. Rev. 548 (1915).

113. Joseph H. Beale noted that the precision of Gray's teaching could be found in the fact that one mark in his casebook served to mark the stopping place for each lecture and this casebook had been used for fifteen years. Beale also found this to be true with respect to a course he taught in conflicts: "He lectured for two years in the early seventies on the Conflicts of Law. The manuscript of his lectures, written in his hand writing and tied with a blue ribbon, marked at the end of each day's work, and the marks for two years were the same." *Id.* at 549.

114. *Id.*

sion to a Socratic[115] dialogue with the students.[116] Obviously, a teaching habit and style, like a golf swing, once established is not easily modified. Cleary, his teaching habit and style as a lecturer was well established before his full-time appointment to the faculty in 1875. In the early phase of his part-time teaching, Gray expressed his view directly to Eliot. As LaPiana reports:

> After his first term as a lecturer, John Chipman Gray wrote to Eliot that his experience in the classroom had convinced him that lectures were the best means of teaching beginning students. Like Washburn's ideal lecture, Gray's would restate and illustrate principles the students would already have encountered in their reading.[117]

Gray continued to follow a time schedule associated with a lecturing system, but also slightly adjusted his original system to focus on cases. As part of that modification, he eventually prepared his own series of casebooks.[118] The first edition focused extensively on English cases. Gray noted in the preface of the casebook:

> Further, the reading of these cases, it should be remembered, is intended to be accompanied by oral instruction, and therefore they are without the comments which would, on so difficult a subject, be desirable if the cases were meant for solitary study.
>
> A special difficulty in dealing with the law of property, and particularly of real property, is to determine how much to dwell on parts of the law which have become partially obsolete. No two persons would probably decide this question in exactly the same way. I have endeavored to bear in mind, on the other hand, that a real knowledge of the law as it is, requires a knowledge of the law as it has been; and on the

115. Even the great Holmes, in the brief time he taught at Harvard Law School, attempted to engage in a Socratic dialogue with the students. *See* White, *supra* note 1, at 532 n.12.

116. See comments of Professor Beale, to the effect that Langdell "as a result of failing sight, he never used the Socratic method in his teaching." *See* Joseph H. Beale Jr., *Professor Langdell—His Later Teaching Days*, 20 Harv. L. Rev. 9 (1907).

117. LaPiana, *supra* note 2, at 25.

118. It is interesting to observe that the first volume of Professor Gray's six volume set casebook is entitled *Select Cases and Other Authorities on the Law of Property*, and included numerous quotations from Bracton, Williams on Real Property, Blackstone Commentaries, Littleton and others. Ironically, Professor Gray apparently followed the organization of Emory Washburn's textbook on property that was published in 1860. *See* Lawrence M. Friedman, History of the American Law 632 (1985).

> other, that I am working for men who are preparing themselves to be lawyers, and not merely students of legal history.[119]

In addition, Gray is formally on record as saying that "the method of study by cases is the best form of legal education that has yet been discovered,"[120] and others have attested to his support and advocacy of the case method.[121] But the record falls far short of establishing that Gray's eventual enthusiastic acceptance of the case method necessarily establishes that he actually employed a Socratic dialogue or open-ended interaction[122] with his students. Nor is it likely that he called on students to find the "scientific" principles of the common law, although he published several casebooks on property. More likely, Gray orally laid out what the law was for his students and utilized his casebooks in support of his analysis of the law.[123] Beale noted the following regarding Gray's impact on students: "probably his most striking characteristic as a lawyer and teacher of law was the authority by which he spoke. It never occurred to any of his students that there could be a doubt about his conclusions."[124]

Accordingly, some would argue that Gray fits within the general Langdellian concept that law was a science[125] and taught law from that jurisprudential premise.[126] Indeed, his style and modality of lecturing were well established and clearly explained in the preface to his casebook.[127] What most likely hap-

---

119. 1 John Chipman Gray, Select Cases and Other Authorities on the Law of Property vii–viiii (2d ed. 1905).

120. Gray, *supra* note 52, at 763.

121. See remarks of Professor Samuel Williston at the Proceedings of the Boston Bar regarding the effect that Gray's reputation stood the law school in good stead as he advocated the adoption of the new methods of Langdell to the Bar. Republished in Gray Memoir, *supra* note 6, at 115.

122. Dean Pound's testimony, as previously set forth, about his class recollection of Gray suggests that he was meticulous in his presentation, precise in his description of the legal principles, and extraordinarily clear in his delivery. Gray was, no doubt, the type of teacher who had the assurance of his legal knowledge and the experience of practice to be certain that which he spoke as the law was, in fact, the law.

123. Seigel cites the outstanding scholarship of LaPiana for the proposition that Gray utilized the Socratic methodology. *See* Siegel, *supra* note 85, at 1532 n.132; *see also* LaPiana, *supra* note 2, at 25–26, 101–03.

124. Gray Memoir, *supra* note 6, at 74.

125. Louis D. Brandeis explained the Langdellian scientific philosophy rather well. *See* Brandeis, *supra* note 21, at 19.

126. *See* Siegel, *supra* note 85, at 1530 n.114.

127. 1 Gray, *supra* note 119.

pened is that he gave formal support to the "Harvard Narrative" of doing legal education while conducting his classes in the same ancient fashion of lecturing on the correct "scientific" rules of property law as he saw them.[128] Gray's casebook[129] contains an express statement of guidance regarding his view of teaching the law with the use of the casebook: he explicitly stated, "Furthermore, the reading of the cases is intended to be accompanied by oral instruction."[130] Most certainly, his lecturing did not come in the form of questions.

It is most likely Gray did not have the patience or the interest to play the legal hide-and-seek game in the classroom. He was the recognized quintessential expert on the law of property, both by reputation of students of the law and by achievement in practice of law. The legendary story is, according to the students: "if you want to know what the law used to be, ask Langdell; if you want to know what it will be, ask Beale; if you want to know what it should be, ask Ames; but if you want to know what the law *is*, ask Gray."[131]

Gray's objective was to train law students to grasp his knowledge of the law for use in practice; it was not to inspire or train legal theoreticians or historians for the ages. Indeed, Roland Gray notes that his father "disliked the-

128. I have secured a printed copy of Gray's lectures referred to as Volume III: "Acquisition of Real Estate," and Volume IV: "Acquisition of Property on Death of the Former Owner." There is no date of publication or publisher noted in the small printed book. This printed copy of the lectures appears to be the notes of Gray's class taken by his students and then printed with comments of the master contained therein. The cases are discussed in detail with pointed observations from Gray. The context of the discussion of the cases and the specific guidance offered by the alleged comments of Gray do not reveal anything close to a Socratic interaction with the students. Without further understanding or information regarding these printed lectures, I hesitate to place much reliance on them.

129. In Louis D. Brandeis' article on Harvard Law School published in 1889, he set forth the law school's curriculum which provides notice that while a textbook on property was required for Gray's first year course on property, there was no such similar requirement for his second year course on property. *See* Brandeis, *supra* note 21, at 18–19. This could mean that Gray used the same casebook for both property courses or that he had not yet prepared a new book for the second course by that time. The record is uncertain. The course of instruction notice for the year 1888–1889 also indicates that in addition to no textbook for his second year course on property, there were no required textbooks for Gray's courses on Jurisdiction and Practice of United States Courts, Wills and Administration, or in his course on Law of Persons. *Id.* Gray's six volumes of property casebooks were produced during the period of 1888–1892. *See* Boyden, *supra* note 29, at 147.

130. See *supra* note 119 for cite to the entire preface.

131. *See* Boyden, *supra* note 29, at 153. Even though the story may be apocryphal, it still reflects on the student perception of Gray and to that extent is insightful. For the New York version of this anecdote, see David W. Peck, Decisions at Law 260 (1961).

ories of pedagogy; in matters of education he declared himself an empiric."[132] As quoted below, Gray frankly admits that the use of the casebook at Cambridge did not imply uniformity or agreement with respect to teaching style.[133] His succinct words on styles of teaching, previously quoted, deserve to be reiterated:

> I have used the expression "case system," but I do not like it, for it suggests a hide-bound and stereotyped mode of instruction. Nothing could be further from the truth. No scheme of teaching affords a greater scope of individuality. To Professor Langdell belongs the credit of introducing the method at Cambridge, but the styles of teaching of the different professors are as unlike as possible. We agree only in making cases, not textbooks, the basis of instruction.[134]

This would appear to imply, if not rising to an outright admission, that the master of property law did not employ the Socratic dialogue. Eugene Wambaugh, a colleague, explained Gray's teaching style and utilization of the casebook.

> Gray's own use of the case system in the classroom resulted neither in mere comments by the instructor nor mere discussion by the class; but it resulted in an attractive and useful combination. His charm was found in his clearness, thoroughness, common sense, homeliness, and willingness to confess ignorance and to ponder upon novel suggestions. When he leaned back and slowly thought aloud, he gave a lesson in thoroughness and humility which may not have been the least valuable part of the mark left by him on his students.[135]

Finally, it does not appear that Gray was a performer of great classroom fame or charm; although he was knowledgeable, respectful, and slightly demanding. Intimidation of students, if it occurred at all, was merely a by-product of his well-known standards for excellence, comprehensive understanding of the law, and the clearly defined expectations that he imposed on his students.

Gray was deliberate, precise, thorough, and comprehensive. In reference to style, he spoke quietly with absolute authority. No one could challenge him

---

132. Gray Memoir, *supra* note 6, at 30. Does this mean Gray preferred not to engage in theoretical questions in the classroom and instead focused on problems of practice, or that each teacher has an institutional practice that suits them, thank you?

133. *See* Gray, *supra* note 52, at 762.

134. *Id.*

135. Gray Memoir, *supra* note 6, at 80–81.

or his expertise on questions of property law. He was the center of that which was the law of property in the United States. The radical changes in legal pedagogy developed at Harvard Law School in regards to the use of the Socratic dialogue were mostly demonstrated by Ames and Keener and to a much lesser extent by Langdell. During his early years of teaching,[136] Gray maintained his fixed sea legs in the classroom and continued teaching in the same way[137] as in the past, although giving formal support to the Langdellian Revolution. Professor Gray was not a man for all seasons. He was the perfect model of that which was right for the law as he saw it; a distinguished, intelligent, competent lawyer and scholar of the law. He was, if anything, completely confident in his own perfection and the exactitude of the common law as he saw it. To the extent that law was now taught at Harvard Law School as scientifically quantifiable, this environment fully complemented his personal and professional judgment regarding the perfection of the law as a system of coordinated rules.[138] Not surprising, Gray was also very stubborn, even possibly bordering on a touch of arrogance that was mostly concealed by his quiet and reserved manner. In addition, Gray picked up a habit of swearing "in a most satisfying way."[139] This habit was most likely a consequence of his days in the army.[140] He was not generally confrontational except when someone crossed or violated his unstated personally internalized sense of righteousness. And like most of mankind, he also had a temper, but it was seldom manifested in public.

Consistency in thought or act is not the hallmark of a legal system. The primary role of the legal process is to mediate conflict and provide a rationale for the resolution. Scientific certainty has little to do with the law; it is determined to be the law for that day only. We seldom, if ever, sustain transcendent propositions of law that are consistently determined as a fact and are enforced for the indefinite future except for glorious legal abstractions such as inherent rights of man.

---

136. The conclusion of Professor Kimball is that Dean Langdell used the so-called Socratic method, at least, during the early years of his teaching career. *See* Kimball, *supra* note 4, at 68–69.

137. See *supra* note 113 for Beale's description of Gray's teaching system.

138. Professor Siegel, in an impressive scholarly manner, delineates a significant and subtle philosophical difference of Professor Gray from the more rigid, classical, scientifically oriented philosophy of Dean Langdell in his second study. *See generally* Siegel, *supra* note 85. The principal basis for the difference is due to the more extensive practical knowledge that Gray acquired in his fifty years of private practice of law.

139. Joseph H. Beale, *Langdell, Gray, Thayer, and Ames—Their Contributions to the Study and Teaching of Law*, 8 N.Y.U. L.Q. 385, 388 (1930–1931).

140. *Id.*

Gray and Student Relations

With respect to Gray's professional relationship with students and his personal experiences on the law school faculty, the following brief observations are noteworthy. A feeling that all law teachers can freely identify with is that Gray "detested reading examination books" and it appeared that he frequently had many such exams to read.[141] Gray was personally supportive of students, their academic achievements, and frequently assisted them in securing further employment opportunities. He, for example, provided a letter of introduction in 1911 for the very academically talented upstart, Felix Frankfurter, to Holmes Jr.[142] Equally important is the supportive role that Gray played in connection with his half-brother, Horace Jr. Jointly they established the institution of law clerks and their employment by judges. In addition, they initiated the faculty practice of recommending recent law graduates of exceptional academic achievement as law clerks.[143] Where would the courts be today if it were not for the institution of law clerks? This was an important innovation, and perhaps most of the honor and recognition for this institution should be accorded to Horace Jr. However, Gray personally selected all of the secretaries (law clerks) of Holmes Jr. from the third year students of Harvard Law School from the date of Holmes' appointment in 1902 until Gray's retirement in 1913.[144] Finally, the law firm of Ropes & Gray was a frequent source of employment opportunities for recent graduates of the Harvard Law School. Boyden, historian of Ropes & Gray, 1865–1940, noted:

> Of the thirty-six men who have been made partners, all but two were graduates of Harvard Law School, and the proportion among the as-

---

141. *Id.* at 388–89.

142. *See* LIVA BAKER, FELIX FRANKFURTER 36 (1969). Years later, Holmes Jr. gladly recalled the letter of introduction that Gray had sent him about the promise of Felix Frankfurter. *See* ROBERT M. MENNEL & CHRISTINE L. COMPSTON, HOLMES AND FRANKFURTER: THEIR CORRESPONDENCE 1912–1934, at 63–64 (1996). When Frankfurter was on the Harvard Law School faculty, he provided law clerks to Holmes Jr. *See* HELEN SHIRLEY THOMAS, FELIX FRANKFURTER 10 (1960). It is noteworthy that Baker also indicates that during the period when Felix was matriculating at Harvard Law School he provided legal research assistance to Gray in connection with one of Gray's books. *See* BAKER, *supra* note 142, at 15. Frankfurter actually selected Holmes Jr.'s law clerks, apparently sight unseen by the Justice, from the graduates of Harvard Law School for a period of years beginning in 1915. *See* MENNEL & COMPSTON, *supra* note 142, at xvi.

143. *See* DAVID M. O'BRIEN, STORM CENTER 130–31 (2005).

144. *See* FRANCIS BIDDLE, MR. JUSTICE HOLMES 12 (1942) (noting Frankfurter succeeded Gray in the tasks of assigning secretaries to Holmes Jr.).

> sociate-lawyers has almost been as large. To a considerable degree this was due to Mr. Gray's thirty-eight years of Professorship there, which brought under his eye those youths whose law school careers showed promise for the future.[145]

These efforts on the part of Gray reflect a natural student-centered approach by him occurring a century or more before such theme became the signature trademark for many of the contemporary law schools.

145. Boyden, *supra* note 29, at 129.

John Chipman Gray, Story Professor of Law (1875–1883), Royall Professor of Law (1883–1913), Harvard Law School.

The young Miss Nina Lyman Mason.

Horace Gray Jr., Associate Justice of the United States Supreme Court.

John Codman Ropes (circa 1870),
co-founder of the prestigious law firm, Ropes & Gray.

John Chipman Gray upon graduating Harvard College, 1859.

Oliver Wendell Holmes Jr. upon graduating Harvard College, 1861.

Mary (Minnie or Minny) Temple, age 16, with her hair cut short (1861).

Mary Temple, age 24 (1869), one year before her death.

Harvard Law School Faculty, 1901: (top row, left to right) John Chipman Gray, Joseph Brannan, Jeremiah Smith, Samuel Williston, Eugene Wambaugh, Dean (Emeritus) Christopher Columbus Langdell; (bottom row, left to right) Jens Iverson Westengard, Joseph Henry Beale, Edward Henry Strobel, James Bradley Thayer, Dean James Barr Ames.

Christopher Columbus Langdell, Dean (1870–1895), Harvard Law School.

James Barr Ames, Dean (1895–1910) Harvard Law School.

James Bradley Thayer (circa 1885), Royall Professor of Law (1874–1883), Weld Professor of Law (1883–1902), Harvard Law School.

William Albert Keener, Assistant Professor of Law (1883–1888), Story Professor of Law (1888–1890), Harvard Law School.

Albert Martin Kales, Visiting Professor (1916–1917), Harvard Law School.

Maj. John Chipman Gray (pictured here as Lt.), Civil War (served 1862–1865).

Nina Lyman Gray.

Mrs. Nina Lyman Gray (1922), the widow of John Chipman Gray since his death in 1915.

Chapter 7

Gray as Philosopher in the Age of Classical Formalism

Each profession seeks methods by which the systems and theories of the past are categorized so that scholars of the present can analyze the strengths and weaknesses of such tentative (but accepted) sobriquets. The ascription of classical formalism to the theory of law during the nineteenth century is a perfect example of this process.

> But what *is* formalism, and what is so bad about it? Even a cursory look at the literature reveals scant agreement on what it is for decisions in law, or perspectives on law, to be formalistic, except that whatever formalism is, it is not good. Few judges or scholars would describe themselves as formalists, for a congratulatory use of the word "formal" seems almost a linguistic error. Indeed, the pejorative connotations of the word "formalism," in concert with the lack of agreement on the word's descriptive content, make it tempting to conclude that "formalist" is the adjective used describe any judicial decision, style of legal thinking, or legal theory with which the user of the term disagrees.[1]

Gray as Legal Philosopher

Gray practiced continuously from 1865 to 1915, this includes two years after a serious illness required his retirement from teaching in 1913. He derived, from his many years of practice, a vast amount of practical understanding from his observation of law in operation. This experience must be distinguished from law as conceived and taught at Harvard Law School under the hegemony of Dean Langdell[2] and his successor disciples. More importantly, the

---

1. Frederick Schauer, *Formalism*, 97 Yale L.J. 509, 509–10 (1988) (footnote omitted).

2. Some relatively recent scholarship of importance has questioned the appropriateness of classical formalism being attributed to Dean Langdell. *See, e.g.*, Bruce A. Kimball, *Langdell*

iconoclastic and erratic aspects of resolving complex issues in the practice of law could never escape Gray's keen observation of the intricate means by which seasoned lawyers bend the law and/or create the facts that serve the interest of their clients. Would not the dynamic legal experience faced by him over the many years of practice completely preclude the acceptance of an unconditional belief in the conceptualization of law as science; or, of a legal system that theoretically posits or assumes law as consistently influencing the outcome of conflicts to be based solely on the exercise of imminent rationality?[3] Langdell had also practiced law for some sixteen years prior to being appointed to the faculty at Harvard Law School—would he not also be similarly aware of the implications of and about the law derived from practice in a manner similar to that of Gray? That question relates to whether Langdell was truly a principal supporter of the formalistic approach to law, or to the so-called science of the law as referred to in the preface of his casebook on contracts, *Selection of Cases on the Law of Contracts* (1871).

Certainly, Horace Gray Jr. was fully engaged in the historical search for the answers within the scientific framework of the common law; positing that there is a preexisting answer to be found in the common law. His judicial career was one in which he found the core legal principles in the precedential decisions of the past; most of which were those of the English jurists. Horace Jr. represents the epitome of this approach to law and highlights the perception that judges find the law rather than create the law. And he was a principal mentor to John Chipman.

When addressing the ways of the past and categorizing the then dominant philosophical system, it is habitual that legal historians and philosophers engage in two diametrically opposed patterns: the first approach tends to greatly overstate enduring benefits of their earlier institutions of thought, whereas the second approach oversimplifies the thesis of earlier thought and promptly implodes the inherent weakness of such philosophic offerings. Another most enjoyable enterprise is in rescuing previously deconstructed institutions of thought by asserting the previous oversimplification erroneously interpreted the actual meaning and content of the prior theory. A related derivative practice magically occurs through the process of an historical revision of a designated sym-

---

on Contracts and Legal Reasoning: Correcting the Holmesian Caricature, 25 LAW & HIST. REV. 345 (2007); Bruce A. Kimball, *The Langdell Problem: Historicizing the Century of Historiography*, 22 LAW & HIST. REV. 335 (2004).

3. *See generally* Ernest J. Weinrib, *Legal Formalism: On the Immanent Rationality of Law*, 97 YALE L.J. 949 (1988) (defending law as other than merely political as argued by the proponents of Critical Legal Studies).

bolic proponent of a particular philosophical movement through a *more* detailed analysis of his or her life. This results in a radical recharacterization to the extent that such person is now deemed profoundly opposed to, or more nuanced than, such system of thought.

Endless scholarly debates are waged about the underlying sociological realities of a prior time; the process is further complicated by describing the past in a way that conforms to aspects of the preferred contemporary thought. This interpretive process of the past is aided in part by the subtle retroactive attributions of present thought. The result is manufactured cohesion of ideas that do not necessarily fit together and the invention of new terminology to capture the nuanced approaches to the past. In short, prior descriptions or understandings of the past are always changing through the hands of the present. Somewhere there is an actual reality regarding the past, but it is exceedingly difficult to capture through the political eye of the present.

Oliver Wendell Holmes Jr. was one of the first to publicly question the philosophical constructs of Langdell. Holmes hurled critical comments[4] regarding the alleged perfection of the Platoesque conception of law as developed and applied at Harvard Law School. In an unsigned review of the second edition of Langdell's casebook on contracts, Holmes Jr. made notable comments that were quite caustic:

> Mr. Langdell's ideal in the law, the end of all his striving, is the *elegantia juris*, or *logical* integrity of the system as system. He is, perhaps, the greatest living legal theologian. But as a theologian he is less concerned with his postulates than to show that the conclusions from them hang together.[5]

Holmes Jr. added to the review a memorable aphorism: "The life of the law has not been logic, it has been experience."[6] Yet, Holmes Jr. had close connections with some members of the faculty (Thayer and Gray) and, indeed, secured a somewhat controversial appointment to the faculty only a brief time after the review of Langdell's book. Then Holmes Jr. promptly resigned from the faculty to accept a judicial appointment after teaching for only one semester. This action was not well received as Thayer invested substantial time in securing an endowment to support Holmes Jr.'s appointment. Yet, a few

4. Unsigned review by Oliver Wendell Holmes Jr., *A Selection of Cases on the Law of Contracts, with a Summary of the Topics Covered by the Cases by C.C. Langdell*, 14 AM. L. REV. 233 (1880).

5. *Id.*

6. *Id.*

years later Holmes Jr. spoke favorably of the Langdell system on the occasion of the two-hundred fiftieth anniversary of the founding of Harvard College. Holmes Jr. noted the significant contributions of Langdell.

> During the short time that I had the honour of teaching in the school, it fell to me, among other things, to instruct the first-year men in torts. With some misgivings I plunged a class of beginners straight into Mr. Ames' collection of cases, and we begin to discuss them together in Mr. Langdell's method. The result was better than I even hoped it would be. After a week or two, when the first confusing novelty was over, I found that my class examined the questions proposed with an accuracy of view which they never could have learned from text-books, and which often exceeded that to be found in the text-books. I, at least, if no one else, gained a good deal from our daily encounters.[7]

It was not politically or socially possible for Holmes Jr. to consistently attack the scientific conception of law and, for whatever reason, he, paradoxically, extolled the study of law as espoused by Langdell. Gray was equally ambivalent as Holmes Jr. to the gospel according to Langdell. But how and in what manner did Gray respond to the views of his colleagues on the faculty of the Harvard Law School?

Harvard Law School and Its Scientific Modality

During the emergence of the scientific approach to law at Harvard Law School, there was no contemporaneous categorical reference to a jurisprudential school designated as constituting classical formalism. The apt title of classical formalism was attributed, *ex post facto*, to the Langdellian era some decades later, by the proponents of legal realism.[8] The principal question is whether Gray can be, as some claim, considered an incipient or founding mem-

---

7. Oliver Wendell Holmes Jr., Speech at the Quarter-Millennial Celebration of Harvard College (Nov. 5, 1886), *in* 3 L.Q.R. 118, 122 (1887).

8. William L. Twining, Karl Llewellyn and the Realist Movement 7, 10–11 (1973). Karl Llewellyn provided his analysis from the perspective of the Grand Style and the Formal Style. *Id.* at 210–14.

ber of the so-called school of legal realism that became the center of controversy during the 1920s and 1930s.

Some things are certain. In the later part of the nineteenth century, there was a period of academic study in which the focus of legal study was to scientifically identify the essential principles of law; it was initiated during the twenty-five year tenure of Langdell at Harvard Law School.[9] These legal principles, according to Langdell, were to be found in the raw material of cases and extracted by induction and summarized into general principles of the law. From these fundamental legal doctrines, specific rules of law would be excised and deductively applied to resolve future legal conflict. Law, using scientific theory, was autonomous and answers were predictable. This was the heart of the so-called Langdellian approach to the study of law.

Langdell was pleased to explain the context of the law school and its connection to Harvard College by the following:

> To accomplish [the true interests of legal education], so far as they depended upon the law school, it was indispensable to establish at least two things—that law is a science, and that all the available materials of that science are contained in printed books. If law be not a science, a university will consult its own dignity in declining to teach it. If it be not a science, it is a species of handicraft, and may best be learned by serving an apprenticeship to one who practices it. If it be a science, it will scarcely be disputed that it is one of the greatest and most difficult of sciences, and that it needs all the light that the most enlightened seat of learning can throw upon it.[10]

Another critical element of Langdell's academic responsibility, as revealed and confirmed by the above quote, was the necessity of transforming the law school so that it would look, feel, and operate in a manner comparable to other academic parts of the Harvard community. Accordingly, the law school had to quickly assume the appearance of the scientific enterprise, and, on this point, Eliot would accept nothing less. Langdell's creative invention in redesigning the mode of operation at the law school exceeded the contractual expectation imposed on him by Eliot. Moreover, this rationalization universally justified the logical connection of law schools to rightfully partake as constituent mem-

---

9. *See generally* C.C. Langdell, *Teaching Law as Science*, Address Before the Harvard Law School Association on the Occasion of the Two Hundred and Fiftieth Anniversary of Harvard College, *in* 21 Am. L. Rev. 123, 123 (1887).

10. *Id.*

bers of university communities and, thus, the apprenticeship process by which one became a lawyer in the nineteenth century eventually evaporated. The law school thereinafter was seen as a natural and essential component of most major universities.

Langdell's theory of law as science was most artistically delivered in the classroom by James Barr Ames and William A. Keener.[11] The second wave of Langdellians—Joseph Henry Beale and Samuel Williston—carried on the so-called scientific tradition in teaching and scholarship in the twentieth century to its apex and possibly to an excess. Roscoe Pound accurately tabbed the academic eras of Harvard Law School.

> Four important periods may be recognized in the history of Harvard Law School: the Story-Greenleaf period of nineteen years from 1829 to 1848; the Parsons-Parker-Washburn period of twenty-one years from 1848 to 1869; the Langdell-Ames period of thirty-nine years from 1870–1909; and the Williston-Beale, or, as I have called it after the manner of Lewis Carroll, the "Bweasliston period," of twenty-nine years from 1910 to 1938.[12]

Beale and Williston, as the designated successors to the Langdell-Ames era, were major leaders in academia during the early part of the twentieth century. Both were dedicated to preserving and enforcing the philosophical ideas attributed to Langdell and Ames.[13] Indeed, Beale willingly accepted a two-year appointment in 1902 to serve as the first dean of a law school at the University of Chicago with the primary objective of seeding the legal methodologies as developed by Langdell at Harvard Law School.[14] Ames willingly delegated Beale, subject to certain conditions, to carry out this assignment.[15]

Gray was on the faculty during the entire Langdell-Ames period and retired, because of health reasons, during the early Williston-Beale period. He accepted, perhaps somewhat reluctantly and passively, the realities of teaching with a faculty that by and large considered the training of law students under the umbrella of scientific instruction in the classroom as the ultimate form of pedagogy. Despite the emergence of new theories of jurisprudence that questioned unremitting reliance on a self-contained structure of preexisting legal

11. *See supra* Chapter Five.

12. Roscoe Pound, *Joseph Henry Beale*, 56 Harv. L. Rev. 695 (1943).

13. *See* Twining, *supra* note 8, at 6–7.

14. *See* Edward Rubin, *What's Wrong with Langdell's Method, and What to do About It*, 60 Vand. L. Rev. 609, 616–17 (2007).

15. *Id.*

principles, such as sociological jurisprudence,[16] the dominant theory of law was seldom challenged by the academic community and greatly increased the respect and authority of Harvard Law School. This pedagogic methodology (casebook and Socratic dialogue), and philosophy (subsequently baptized as classical formalism) considered together seized and imposed a lasting hegemony over the American legal education community for more than a century to follow.[17] A totalitarian régime attempting to prescribe restrictive course content for its law schools could not have secured greater compliance than that which occurred by choice of the American law school community; surprisingly, all of this took place in a country known for its freedom of expression.

This philosophical aspect, although originally much admired, was eventually the subject of intense criticism.[18] Gray was there at the creation of this so-called energetic modality of teaching law and understood the importance of securing a principled legal system that was consistently applied. He could not avoid being affected by the environment and the philosophical proselytizing by some of his colleagues. During the period the revolution in the teaching of law took place at Harvard Law School, Gray was personally interactive with a variety of highly intelligent, visionary personalities who were fully engaged in designing new descriptions of an intellectual nature regarding radical changes then taking place in society. Included in this intellectual milieu with Gray were Oliver Wendell Holmes Jr., Henry Adams, William James, Henry James Jr., Chauncey Wright, Moorfield Storey, and Charles Sanders Pierce, among others. This emerging intellectual community was set to reinterpret the social forces in a somewhat radical fashion while challenging the conventions of the nineteenth century. Initially, they secured some academic acceptance of their new philo-

---

16. By 1908 Dean Pound was beginning to envision law as serving the ends of society. *See* Roscoe Pound, *Mechanical Jurisprudence*, 8 Colum. L. Rev. 605 (1908) [hereinafter Pound, *Mechanical*]; Roscoe Pound, *The Need for Sociological Jurisprudence*, 19 Green Bag 607 (1907); Roscoe Pound, *Do We Need a Philosophy of Law*, 5 Colum. L. Rev. 339 (1905).

17. Edward Rubin, *What's Wrong with Langdell's Method, and What to Do about It*, 60 Vand. L. Rev. 609, 613 (2007). Professor Rubin notes the following:

> Nearly one hundred years have passed since 1914, of course, and we still rely on Langdell's substantive innovations.... One can understand that law schools in the early decades of the twentieth century, having just adopted the Harvard model as a thrilling innovation in legal education, would be reluctant to admit that it had-fallen out of date and would be institutionally incapable of taking another broad revision of their teaching program. *But how can we explain the continued survival of a professional training program that is so obsolete, so discontinuous with the profession that it allegedly prepares its students to enter?*

Id. (emphasis added).

18. *See generally* Schauer, *supra* note 1.

sophical propositions; but in the main, these persons were far more important for the twentieth century influence they brought to the academic community. In short, this iconic group was an important bridge from the philosophical thought of the past to the imponderables of the twentieth century.

Gray, although personally involved in the interaction, continued to disclose a moderately passive nature with this energetic, ambitious community of intellectuals. Moorfield Storey, despite having a friendship with Gray over a forty-year period and attending monthly meetings, recalls that Gray, while listening closely to the interaction at the meetings, "he himself said little."[19] Yet, Gray was fully conversant with the new visions of his intellectual associates.[20]

Gray lived in two competing intellectual descriptions of society and of men and women; first, with his colleagues at the law school, and second, with his iconic intellectual friends off campus. In addition, Gray as a lawyer was directly involved in offering legal services to the Brahmin community and understood that making social enemies would possible have a deleterious impact on his law business. William C. Loring, a longtime friend of Gray, noted the technique by which Gray avoided revealing his own views: "Did you ever meet [Gray] when the conversation [with him] did not turn on matters which interested you and when the discussion was not from your point of view rather than his?"[21] Gray was consistently cautious in social exchanges. Gray generally conducted relationships of a business and personal nature in a manner that skillfully avoided conflict by restraining spontaneity and protecting feelings or ideas of his own; despite the fact that he had, on occasion, an explosive temper.

How was Gray to resolve these conflicting intellectual forces—the Platoesque conceptualism in vogue at the law school, the inherent experiences as derivates from the practice of law, and the changing views of society emanating from his energetic intellectual friends and associates? He did not resolve them, and he never committed consistently to a particular philosophical approach. Gray's tome on jurisprudence[22] is implicitly offered by him as a means to deny that whatever his ex cathedra interpretation of the RAP represents, he was not unconditionally committed to what was eventually referred to as classical for-

---

19. Roland Gray, John Chipman Gray, Memoir 103 (Privately Printed 1917) [hereinafter Gray Memoir].

20. *See generally* John Patrick Diggins, The Promise of Pragmatism: Modernism and the Crisis of Knowledge and Authority (1994); Louis Menand, The Metaphysical Club: A Story of Ideas in America (2001).

21. Gray Memoir, *supra* note 19, at 130.

22. It should also be noted that Gray published a modest article on jurisprudence. *See* John C. Gray, *Some Definitions and Questions in Jurisprudence*, 6 Harv. L. Rev. 21 (1892).

malism. This is a difficult, if not impossible, argument for Gray to make as his book on perpetuities is the epitome of classical formalism.

Impact of Law Practice on Gray's Philosophy

Then there was the issue of the practice of law and its impact on Gray and his philosophy. Could his late philosophical publication reflect aspects of Gray's angst foisted upon him by incorporating verities derived from his extended legal practice with an ethereal composition of legal philosophy? There is a possible admission as to this inherent conflict when Gray explained the period over which his philosophical ideas distilled in *The Nature and Sources of the Law*.

> Some fifty years ago I came across a copy of Austin's "Province of Jurisprudence Determined," ... and since then, although my work has been mainly on other lines, the subject has seldom been for long wholly out of my mind. I put my ideas into substantially their present shape a dozen years ago; I have held them in abeyance more than the prescribed nine years.[23]

Although the practice of law was a dominant factor throughout Gray's life, one can neither quantify the amount or degree of its influence on his philosophical thought. But, there is no question it constituted a basic reality that was part of his daily experience. Also, the visual and tangible results derived from the practice of law were never theoretical and always in direct contrast to the abstractions and prophecies incurred in the life of an academic.

In addition to Gray, others saw and understood the importance of the practice of law as supportive of success as an academic teacher. Albert M. Kales, former law student of Gray, fostered a unique relationship with his former teacher. Kales became both an antagonist of Gray's scholarship concerning the RAP and, yet, a professed protagonist of Gray's successful achievement in teaching and scholarship. Kales desired to be Gray-like as he became a scholar of future interests (authoring casebooks and treatises on the subject), a distinguished practitioner, and also a law teacher. Kales taught at Northwestern Law School and other law schools, in addition to having taught at Harvard for one academic year. Gray and Kales argued on a series of subtle points of property law in a number of published law review articles as well as in extended per-

23. *See* John Chipman Gray, The Nature and Sources of the Law vii (2d ed., Beacon 1963) (1909) (footnote omitted) [hereinafter Nature and Sources].

sonal correspondence.[24] Kales asserted that the practice of law was an essential ingredient for the success of any academic teacher.

> [Handling appeals for other lawyers by teachers] would not only produce a substantial income and confer standing at the bar among lawyers and judges, but it would make the difference between a somewhat colorless academic teacher and one who knew the problems that were vital and could assume to speak with some authority. Contests with able counsel and the effort to persuade judges of ability and long experience on the bench regarding the very problems taken up in the class-room, would furnish a training for teaching which, in the writer's opinion, could not be excelled.[25]

Unfortunately, when Kales sought permission to practice on a limited basis while teaching at Harvard Law School, it was not granted by the recently appointed dean, Roscoe Pound, nor supported by the second wave of Langdellians.[26] Thus, Kales' modest condition for a limited appellate practice precluded his acceptance of a permanent appointment to the faculty at Harvard. But Kales and Gray recognized the underlying reality flowing from the practice of law (time, place, contingencies, status of the claimants and lawyers, ideology and personhood of the decisionmaker, impact of the existing norms of the community, the influence of economic and political factors, as well as other related social factors), directly conflicts with the academic tendency to conceptualize the diverse interacting forces as emanating under some semblance of pseudoscientific law. Description of these factors as constituting an essential element in the formation of the law was not in favor and was suppressed, *sub silento*, by the voice of the reigning authorities of the legal establishment. In juxtaposition to the asserted theoretical resolution of conflict as a perfect exercise of rationality, practitioners recognize that there is at least an equivalent portion of art applied in the molding of a favorable legal result as there is a scientific exposition of the legal principles. Gray and his antagonistic disciple Kales, although experts on the complex and intricate nature of future interests that frequently invites mathematical analysis, were aware of the degree to which other factors influence the ultimate determination of the law. Kales, for example, vehemently pointed out the significant differing decisions of various jurisdic-

---

24. See *infra* Chapter 9 for a critical review of their professional differences.

25. Albert M. Kales, Estates, Future Interests and Illegal Conditions and Restraints in Illinois vii–viii (1920).

26. *See* Albert Martin Kales, Correspondence on the Rule Against Perpetuities, 1904–1913: Finding Aid (Feb. 2006), http://oasis.lib.harvard.edu/oasis/deliver/~law00184.

tions concerning similar property issues. He asserted, therefore, that lawyers need to study the laws and decisions of particular jurisdictions. Accordingly, Kales authored a treatise solely on the laws and cases in the State of Illinois in contrast to Gray's treatise on the RAP in which he provided authoritative guidance for all jurisdictions. Unlike Gray, Kales accepted that there were no consistent answers on questions of future interests.

Others noted the importance of continuing the practice of law as a positive facet in Gray's success as a teacher. Loring addressed the issue directly.

> Ordinarily the practising lawyer is not a good teacher of law and the teacher of law is not a good practising lawyer. But for Mr. Gray the decision was a wise one. He was the better teacher for being in active practice; he was the better lawyer from the learning which came from teaching law.[27]

As to his approach to scholarship, Gray was, in the matter of the RAP and to a much lesser extent restraints on alienation, committed to a system of universal correct answers. In his philosophical tome, Gray expresses, hints, or suggests the diametrically opposite view. Typical of Gray's radical philosophical difference is his observation:

> It has been sometimes said that Law is composed of two parts,—legislative law and judge-made law,—but in truth, all the Law is judge-made law. The shape in which a statute is imposed upon the community as a guide for conduct is that statute as interpreted by the courts. The courts put life into the dead words of the statute. To quote again from Bishop Hoadly; a sentence which before I have given: "Nay, whoever hath an *absolute authority* to *interpret* any written or spoken laws, it is *he* who is truly the *Law-giver* to all intends and purposes, and not the first person who first wrote or spoken them."[28]

This quote is a most contrary observation on the part of Gray particularly from the perspective of his scientific conclusions set forth in his substantive treatise on the law of perpetuity. The observation is, however, consonant with Gray's emotional outburst set forth in his letter of 1883 to Eliot (what the judges say is, in fact, the law)[29] voicing complaints about the criticism heaped on judges by Langdell and Ames. These realities as to the inherent contingency of the

---

27. Gray Memoir, *supra* note 19, at 126.

28. Nature and Sources, *supra* note 23, at 125. Note also that Gray was to reiterate this now famous quote from Bishop Hoadly in other portions of his book.

29. See *supra* Chapter 6 for the contents of the letter.

law and the dominant role and function of decision makers were always known to Gray in his role as a practitioner; unfortunately, seldom shared in his substantive scholarship. In this respect, Gray was engaged in a direct contradiction.

Gray as an Incipient Legal Realist

Gray submits an application to be considered a charter member of the class of the so-called school of legal realism on the basis of *The Nature and Sources of the Law*. The application necessarily presents the question as to the definition of legal realism; and whether it constitutes a separate brand of legal philosophy is an ageless query.[30] Mostly we observe the past through the terminology or prisms created in the models cast by prior scholars; some of whom have less distance and greater propinquity with the past. Legal realism, either as a term of art or as a philosophy of law, had not fully matured during Gray's tenure on the faculty.

Legal realism was to some extent a political movement of confrontation as well as a passionate rejection (in the 1920s and 1930s) of the inductive or deductive scientific conception of law. The scientific conception law as posited by Langdell, and supported under the watchful eye of Eliot, was a matter of intense debate on and off the Cambridge campus during the early part of the twentieth century. The overwhelming success of the Langdellian philosophic theory and pedagogic innovations in legal education during the later part of the nineteenth century is beyond question. But its success led to the stagnation of contemporary thought, prevented further development, and thereby it became a victim of its domination. The overwhelming success of the scientific philosophy inevitably led to a call for its rejection. Pound, in leading the law school community from a fixation on law as science more than a hundred years ago, succinctly observed: "Legal systems have their periods in which science degenerates, in which system decays into technicality, in which a scientific jurisprudence becomes a mechanical jurisprudence."[31]

The principal benefit of the domination of scientific thought was the creation of legal realism; a new pragmatic perspective on or about the law re-

---

30. Pound focused on this question and it lead to the infamous exchange between him and Professor Llewellyn which, no doubt, permanently separated sociological jurisprudence from legal realism in America. *See* Roscoe Pound, *The Call for Realist Jurisprudence*, 44 Harv. L. Rev. 697 (1931); Karl Llewellyn, *Some Realism About Realism—Responding to Dean Pound*, 44 Harv. L. Rev. 1222 (1931); *see also* Twining, *supra* note 8, at 70–83.

31. *See* Pound, Mechanical, *supra* note 16, at 607.

flecting, in part, the mixture of expansive thoughts and empirical information then exploding from other social, psychological, and economic systems. Legal realism was an attempt to bring facets of human experience (political, emotional, and economical) into the process of understanding the role and function of law in society and, most importantly, controlling law's impact on society. Pound first raised important questions, influenced by continental philosophers of the law, Rudolf von Jhering and others, about the social purpose of law from the perspective of its actual impact.[32] Pound held that law could be a means (active social engineering), rather than an end in itself, to improve conditions.

Pound's encounter in the 1930s with leading realist philosophers, Karl Llewellyn and Jerome Frank, was possibly inevitable but quickly became personal and acidic.[33] Some scholars do not believe that the conflict between them involved serious difference over substantive approaches to law and reflects the ambitions of the participants.[34] These developments took place in the decades following Gray's death. In what sense are they relevant to the question of whether Gray was an incipient realist?

Although Gray necessarily wrote in the code of the law, language, and concepts of his time at Harvard Law School (as we do today, assuming there is an agreed-upon text), there is infrequently a word or thought expressed by Gray in which he identifies a philosophic problem from the many ambiguous decisions and scholarship offerings of the English authorities in either of his two classic, dogmatic treatises. Gray offered some shibboleths in *The Nature and Sources of the Law*, but the observations were never fully integrated into any portions of his traditional scholarship. He saved these thoughts or nuggets of reality of the law for public disclosure at the end of his serious days of scholarship. That philosophic book was a direct product of his lectures sponsored by the Carpentier Foundation[35] that he delivered at Columbia Law School in 1908.

As a scholar of substantive law over the many years, Gray's focus was the simple determination of the absolute correct rule of law, and although it may be filled with tentative and enduring legal fictions, that was the consistent methodology of his scholarship. There was little room for ambiguity in his vision of

---

32. Roscoe Pound, *Fifty Years of Jurisprudence*, 51 Harv. L. Rev. 777, 777 (1938) (citing Roscoe Pound, *The Scope and Purpose of Sociological Jurisprudence*, 25 Harv. L. Rev. 140, 166–68 (1911)).

33. *See, e.g.*, George C. Christie & Patrick H. Martin, Jurisprudence 761–75 (2008).

34. *See id.*

35. Nature and Sources, *supra* note 23, at vii.

the law, despite the implications of the experience in the practice of law for some fifty years. All that Gray passed on is his uncertain, penultimate perambulations set forth in his philosophic tome. The early perceptions of the law imposed on Gray, a thoroughly diligent, intellectual lawyer, influenced as he was by the power and majesty of Justice Horace Gray Jr., significantly limited both his articulation and publication of insightful observations derived from his experience as a practicing lawyer. Added to these limitations on John Chipman's philosophic vision were the existing and dominant influences of the Langdellian implosion of law as science. These combined factors prevented a legacy on or about the law of a unique nature, rich in detail, minimal in abstractions, descriptive of the role of the human process, and finally of a lasting and trenchant vision of the underlying reality disclosing the inherent inventiveness of judicial resolutions. If this had occurred, Gray would have been a charter member of the school of legal realism.

Categorizing Gray's Philosophical Offerings

A significant number of scholars have addressed the question as to whether Gray is a significant precursor to the school of legal realism; some of their views are briefly discussed below.

The most thoughtful discussion of Gray's philosophic orientation is by Stephen A. Siegel who has made Gray a major focus of his scholarship.[36] In Siegel's second article, he crafts the critical question as to which philosophical school applies to Gray by the following: "At present, a scholarly opinion is divided over whether John Chipman Gray was a paradigmatic classical scholar or whether he had escaped those confines to become a progenitor of legal realism."[37] After a considered and extended analysis of Gray's writings as well as comparison with others of his scholarly community, and aspects of his social interactions, Siegel reaches the following conclusion:

> Gray's jurisprudence was a blend of classical and post-classical elements. Gray, it is fair to say, took classical orthodoxy to the verge of

---

36. Stephen A. Siegel, *John Chipman Gray, Legal Formalism and the Transformation of Perpetuities Law*, 36 U. Miami L. Rev. 439 (1982) [hereinafter Siegel, *Legal Formalism*]; Stephen A. Siegel, *John Chipman Gray and the Moral Basis of Classical Legal Thought*, 86 Iowa L. Rev. 1513 (2001) [hereinafter Siegel, *Classical Thought*].

37. Siegel, *Classical Thought*, *supra* note 36, at 1529.

> modernism. But, in the end, Gray sufficiently cabined his modernism with a host of pre-modern assumptions so that, ultimately, his legal philosophy stayed within the classical fold. As a result, his doctrinal treatises, which exemplify his jurisprudence, are masterpieces of classical legal culture.[38]

In short, Gray was unable to fully bring his personal experience as a lawyer or his exposure to emerging consideration of pragmatism as a means to escape or overcome the defining normative conventions and other influences of his time. In this failure, he is not alone. As a result, there is an irresolvable conflict in his role as a philosopher in which he attempts to take steps out of the normative conventions of his time, as well as the methodology applied principally in his ultratraditional treatise on the RAP.

Nevertheless, a number of scholars, such as Morton Horwitz, would include Gray as one of the incipient legal realists who criticized Classical Legal Thought.[39] Jerome Frank, a dedicated legal realist and fact skeptic of the first order, was most impressed with Gray's philosophical offerings and cites him quite favorably in some respects in his books.[40] Indeed, the Bishop Hoadley quote proffered by Gray[41] (whoever interprets the law is the source of the law) is included in two of Frank's books. However, Frank raises serious questions as to Gray's qualification for membership because "Gray ... failed to follow his own thesis to its logical conclusion and ... believed that a court makes new law only when it evolves a new rule of decision."[42] In addition, William Seal Carpenter was somewhat impressed with Gray's thoughtful criticism of Austin in discussing the identity of the sovereign.[43]

---

38. *Id.* at 1596.

39. *See* Morton Horwitz, The Transformation of American Law 1870–1960, at 182, 314 n.88 (1992) ("Just as Holmes was an acknowledged inspiration for the new jurisprudence, so too [was] John Chipman Gray.").

40. *See* Jerome Frank, Law and the Modern Man (Coward-McCann 1970) (1930) [hereinafter Modern Man]; Jerome Frank, Courts on Trial: Myth and Reality in American Justice (Atheneum 1963) (1949).

41. *See infra*, Chapter 7, Interpretive Analysis of Gray's Philosophy, for entire quote of Bishop Hoadley.

42. Modern Man, *supra* note 40, at 285 n.3. Other scholars have delved into Gray's focus on the Bishop Hoadley comment and the implications flowing therefrom. *See* Michael Steven Green, *Legal Realism as Theory of Law*, 46 Wm. & Mary L. Rev. 1915, 1988–93 (2005).

43. William Seal Carpenter, Foundations of Modern Jurisprudence 14, 17 (1958).

William L. Twining, a major and important historian of Llewellyn and the realist movement, has also considered Gray's philosophical offerings as it relates to the issue on realism. His conclusion is quite profound on the question.

> [T]here is little in the book that is either original or profound. Its chief virtues are its lucidity and its homely common sense which help to make it unusually readable for a treatise on legal philosophy. Philosophically it is rather naïve, the work of a learned man of affairs who wandered belatedly into the realms of abstract analysis.... In fact Gray's ideas presented no serious threat to the Langdellian orthodoxy.... Gray could be said to have taken a step away from Austin and Langdell in the direction of realism. But in his teaching he was, if anything, pre-Langdellian, he was an outstanding but essentially orthodox legal scholar and as a theorist he went less far than Holmes.[44]

Of course, Llewellyn did not include Gray as a legal realist in his reply to Pound.[45] However, Llewellyn did make references to Gray in other articles.

A more recent review of legal realism by Michael Steven Green reinterprets the infamous Hoadley quote,[46] utilized by Gray to suggest that judges are the source of the law, as erroneously taking the finality of a judgment as equating to the conclusion that whatever the judge says is the law.[47] Green observes that "the law is not (always) what courts say it is" and that "[t]he realists were therefore wrong to derive the decision theory from the principle of judicial finality."[48] As such, the elliptical phrases portending of a major departure from the traditional jurisprudential thesis as expressed therein by Gray ought not to be taken seriously.[49] One can fully appreciate Gray's attempt to reflect portions of his experience in practice, but it appears it was an attempt to speak the language of Zeus by one who was either hesitant to fully disclose or intentionally refrained from doing so. Indeed, Gray personally expressed a negative view of himself as a philosopher of the law. When discussing his philosophical tome

---

44. Twining, *supra* note 8, at 21–22.

45. *See* Llewellyn, *supra* note 30, at 1226 n.18.

46. *See infra*, Interpretive Analysis of Gray's Philosophy, for entire quote of Bishop Hoadley.

47. *See* Green, *supra* note 42, at 1988–93.

48. *Id.* at 1993.

49. Professor Green also clarifies explicitly the reason why Frank did not consider Gray a realist. *Id.* at 1990–91.

in a letter to Frederick Pollock, he wrote that he was one "on whom the clothes of an analytical jurist do not fit well."[50]

Gray's Treatises on the Law

So far, there has been little direct discussion of Gray's philosophical effort as explained in *The Nature and Sources of the Law*.[51] Gray's steps into the philosophy of the law are probably more important for the reluctant attempt to expound some cryptoform of legal realism than for what he actually stated about the legal process. His legal attitude is essentially a rare, perhaps contradictory, mixture of pragmatist, practitioner, and academic dogmatist of the first order. Idiomatic of Gray is his belief that his personal knowledge of the law was, in fact, the law. Gray's treatise, *The Rule Against Perpetuities,* was an ex cathedra, dogmatic interpretation (assertion) of the common law cases that is fully anchored in the ambience of the law as science movement associated with the reign of Langdell.[52]

Gray's other treatise, *Restraints on the Alienation of Property*, was not completely within the scientific modality of Langdellian thought, as the subject matter of the study precluded the invention or articulation of an overarching principle of law. It was by the nature of the many fact sensitive cases concerning differing degrees of restraints that rendered it impossible to synthesize them under the umbrella of one rule. Gray does set forth a series of principle rules at the end of his book as a summary of the decided cases. In the insightful words of Pound, it was not possible to achieve a scientific synthesis of the differing limitations involved in the fact sensitive cases. The various restraints on alienation were imposed by differing conditions and limitations. As such, there is a discussion of various decisions reflecting the subtleties and calling for a weighing of the overall impact of the same on the right of alienation. Gray observed the objective of this modest treatise.

---

50. *See* Frederick Pollock, *Comments*, 31 L.Q.R. 341 (1915). But see Charles Sweet, *John Chipman Gray* (ob. Feb. 25, 1915) 31 L.Q.R. 338, 340 (1915) for favorable comments by the acerbic Charles "The" Sweet on Gray's tome *The Nature and Sources of the Law* ("To see Gray at his best we must turn ... to his essay on *The Nature and Sources of the Law*.").

51. Nature and Sources, *supra* note 23.

52. Professor Thomas C. Grey clarifies the philosophical perspective of the Langdellian regime in an analysis of the rise and fall of the then dominant legal thought, otherwise referred to in his article as a "classical orthodox system of thought." *See* Thomas C. Grey, *Langdell's Orthodoxy*, 45 Pitt. L. Rev. 1, 5 (1983).

> It is the purpose of this essay to consider how far such restraints can be lawfully imposed; in other words, with what limitations, if any, does the law say, "It is against public policy to allow restraints to be put upon transfers which public policy does not forbid."[53]

Admittedly, Gray possessed an encyclopedic knowledge of the law of his time, particularly as it related to the common law of real property, and a confident belief in the perfection of his analysis of the *law*. The domination of the well defined legal and social culture of the Brahmin community, combined with his well recognized intellectual talents and/or presumption as to the perfection of his analysis of ambiguous case law, precluded Gray from adequately confronting the contradictions or ambiguities that otherwise existed in or about the determination of the law. He, nevertheless, assumed that his interpretations of complex common law principles of law were properly decipherable by a person of his unique precision. Gray seldom approached the law with open-ended questions; he unconditionally provided answers—the law! There is an ingredient indigenous to teachers of the law, similar to that of judges: what they believe to be the law (or ought to be the law) is the law in their classroom.[54] This habit of thought emanating from the act of teaching sometimes feeds back into one's scholarship.

Although Gray was academically orientated and possessed a comprehensive knowledge of diverse issues of his time, a philosophical calling did not naturally apply to him. Although he was encyclopedic in his comprehension of the law, Gray was not philosophical by nature or, perhaps, by choice—he did not wish to reveal his thoughts. Gray appears to have been very deliberate in all of his communications and consciously avoided proffering ideas that were not generally accepted by his contemporary scholars or friends. He enjoyed the privacy of ascertaining the limitations of others without sacrificing his own concealed insecurity. The insecurity is part intentional, as a lawyer engaged in practice does not want to offend his or her clients by their own personal views. Although Gray was very interactive with the intellectuals of his community, seldom did he focus on his beliefs, but rather had the technique of converting most conversations to the interests of the other person. Finally, Mary Temple

53. *See* John Chipman Gray, Restraints on the Alienation of Property 2 (2d ed. 1895). According to Beale, this is the book that was allegedly written because Gray had lost a case. *See* Gray Memoir, *supra* note 19, at 74.

54. Years ago the principal janitor of my law school, John, upon confronting several of us students upon our leaving the library and noting our not so concealed smug "attitude" stated: "for every decision in those law books up there, one lawyer won and the other lost. You are not so smart."

challenged Gray to reveal his inner-self and this angered him, because it is possible he did not have the facility to share his inner-feelings. A combination of these factors gives rise to what is described herein as a concealed insecurity by an otherwise highly intelligent Brahmin. This conscious adjustment in habit of conducting affairs was much to his personal satisfaction and financial reward.

As briefly discussed above, the communication constraints applied as well to Gray in his social life. Storey, one of Gray's life-long acquaintances, provided a very apt and accurate description of the manners and ways of him:

> He had decided opinions and was always willing to state them, but was not concerned that others should adopt them. He espoused no cause, but was a scholar interested in observing and studying the world and feeling no obligation to take part in its conflicts. He was more at home in the library than in the arena. His true role was that of the student, the teacher, and counselor, and he was guided wisely in choosing the work of his life.[55]

It is as if Gray was there for the principal cultural and educational interaction of the Cambridge community, but his unique perspective is either missing or not recorded. Most likely, private interactive thoughts of a controversial nature were not recorded as such radical thoughts could have an adverse impact on his growing law business or conflict with the established beliefs of his colleagues. But more importantly, in the person of Gray, we have the quintessential "orthodox" gentlemen. He never revealed the slightest departure from the existing norms of his time, either in deed or in word, with the exception of his extreme frustration about the hiring of relatively inexperienced law professors. He was a willing prisoner of his time, as is true of most of us in the present.

Interpretive Analysis of Gray's Philosophy

Several scholars have treated Gray's observations in *The Nature and Sources of the Law* as a serious and important philosophical contribution. However, these scholars fail to establish the case that he was an important philosopher of law. Perhaps it was expected for a man of his position, background, and achievement to participate in this higher form of legal conceptualization. And,

---

55. Moorfield Storey, Memorial of John Chipman Gray at the Proceedings of the Boston Bar and the Supreme Judicial Court of Massachusetts (October 23, 1915), *reprinted in* GRAY MEMOIR, *supra* note 19, at 95, 103.

when given the invitation, Gray could not resist. He was driven at some level to confront and compare the realities of law in operation which he experienced in the daily practice of law with the transcendental nature of law. There was to be no escape from this as he was constrained by his legalistic style of some thirty-five years that dominated the main focus of his two major treatises on the RAP and restraints on alienation.

In view of this entrenched legalistic style of communicating the law, the comparison of abstract law with his experience as a lawyer presented a conceptual dilemma that Gray could not resolve. In short, he failed to reach any meaningful description or resolution of these two different forces. Nor would Gray publish his philosophical efforts before the death of his brother, Horace Jr., who was an ever present forceful influence on the formative views of Gray regarding the common law. It cannot be denied that Horace Jr., was both an intimidating brother and zealous advocate of the perfection of the common law. What has been attributed by some to Horace Jr. could equally apply to John Chipman.

> His life has been the studious, secluded life of a scholar, immersed in and satisfied by his great subject. Yet his long and great career has brought him a profound knowledge of men and of affairs. Although his life has been spent in rendering decisions, no man ever had less pride of opinion. When pleased with his work as embodied within a decision of the Court, he has been glad, not because it redounded to his own credit, but to the credit of the law. In truth, he had been a high priest of scientific jurisprudence. He has felt that praise and merit were due not to him but to the science whose oracle he was.[56]

With these institutional and personal restraints, it is not surprising that the temerity Gray applied in his philosophical treatise would not have the impact of his other scholarship efforts. Gray's delivery of legal philosophy is, with all due respect, very disappointing. He discusses issues by reviewing traditional theories of law by looking at theories of others. This provides a mechanism to discuss the problems without a commitment. For example, he states:

> A *third* theory of the Law remains to be considered. That theory is to this effect. The rules followed by the courts in deciding questions are not the expression of the State's commands, nor are they the expression of the common consciousness of the people, but although what the judges rule is the Law, it is putting the cart before the horse to say

56. Francis R. Jones, *Horace Gray: An Encomium*, 14 Green Bag 403, 405 (1902).

> that the Law is what the judges rule. The Law, indeed, is identical with the rules laid down by judges because they are the Law, they are not the Law because they are laid down by the judges, or, as the late Mr. James C. Carter[57] puts it, the judges are the discovers, not the creators, of the Law. And this is the way that judges are apt to speak of their functions.[58]

To say that Gray was not by nature philosophical does not mean that he had little to say of lasting import, but rather that his description of the legal process from a philosophical viewpoint adds little to the comprehension of such a legal system.

Some statements on the part of Gray that support the perspective that judges are a source of the law or make the law may sound to be, and are, within the realm of what became the philosophical school of legal realism. The more trenchant and provocative observations of Gray are almost sound bites for the school of legal realism.

> *The Limits of Judicial Power.* Thus far we have seen that Law is made up of the rules for decision which the courts lay down; that all such rules are law; that rules for conduct which the courts do not apply are not the Law; the fact that the Courts apply the rules is what makes them the law; there is not a mysterious entity "The Law" apart from these rules; and that judges are rather the creators than the discovers of the law.[59]
>
> The courts put life into the dead words of a statute. To quote again from Bishop Hoadly, a sentence which I have before given: "Nay, whoever hath an *absolute authority* to *interpret* any written or spoken laws, it is *he* who is truly the *Law-giver* to all intents and purposes, and not the person who first wrote or spoke them."[60]

However, most of the philosophical aspirations of Gray are entirely discordant and in direct conflict with his living credo as forcefully reiterated in his major

57. Mr. James C. Carter, a distinguished practitioner and a graduate of Harvard Law School, was considered by Brandeis and others as a significant leader of the New York Bar. Louis D. Brandeis, *The Harvard Law School*, 1 Green Bag 10, 22 (1889).

58. Nature and Sources, *supra* note 23, at 93. This aphorism or maxim sounds much like an offering of Sir Coke: "*Judex bonus nihil ex arbitro suo faciat, nec propositione domesticate voluntatis, sed juxta leges et jura pronunciet.*" (A good judge does nothing of his own judgment, or from the dictate of private will; but he will pronounce according to law and justice.) 7 Co. 27.

59. Nature and Sources, *supra* note 23, at 121.

60. *Id.* at 125.

works and career. Indeed, Justice Frankfurter was moved many years later to impose constraints on Gray's frequent quotation of Bishop Hoadly by noting, "[B]y admitting that there is some substance to the good Bishop's statement, one does not subscribe to the notion that they [judges] are law-givers in any but a very qualified sense."[61]

As a practitioner who engaged in significant appellate litigation, Gray understood that judges had significant discretion when resolving a legal issue. As a treatise writer of major significance, he knew it was important for him to accurately and precisely lay out the essential contours of the applicable legal principles. As a scholar of the common law, Gray was forced to admit the obvious fact that the common law was an invention of the English jurists.

As an academic, he thoroughly enjoyed the unlimited power of clarifying the law and pointing out the deficiencies of decisions that failed to reflect his views. In the classroom, the law professor's judgment of the law equals, or perhaps exceeds, the authority of the United States Supreme Court and the only similarity between both institutions is that there is no appeal from either. In his blistering letter to President Eliot on January 3, 1883, Gray chided law professors for their lack of respect for the judiciary and then stated: "It is the tendency of every professor of law to substitute his views of what the law ought to be for that which actually obtains. I have constantly to be on guard against it."[62] Conversely, Gray spoke as if he were the last correct word on the precise rule of law. He seldom accepted uncertainty or ambiguity in the law. The one reported exception occurred when he was confronted by a novel question in the classroom.[63] His training and personal vision always assumed or acted as if there was only one correct answer for the ages. And, not surprising, it was his answer!

Caught between these restrictive parameters, Gray had to reluctantly describe the legal system in a way that provided some precognitive reluctant admission of legal realism but without seriously criticizing the traditional narratives that the law was, in part, largely found or discovered by the judges. This is not an easy logical line for anyone to walk, but for Gray, he cautiously waggled between the two diametrically opposite sides of legal philosophy. It was about all he could do. In short, it was simply impossible for him to go far from the

61. Felix Frankfurter, *Some Reflections on the Reading of Statutes*, 47 COLUM. L. REV. 527, 533 (1947).

62. Letter from John Chipman Gray, Professor, Harvard Law School, to Charles W. Eliot, President, Harvard College (Jan. 3, 1883) (on file with Harvard University Archives, Box 71, Folder 1883 (G-L)).

63. See Chapter 6 for comments of Pound regarding a classroom interaction with Gray.

normative philosophical descriptions of the law. For Gray to go further would be tantamount to a formal act of heresy. Despite his knowledge acquired from his many years as a practitioner and the recognition that "law in action" defied any description that suggested it was certain and predictable, Gray's exposure to and immersion in the school of "law as science," as well as the entire discipline expressed in his scholarship, trumped the reality that courts did in fact exercise considerable discretion in making its determination of the law.

There is an aspect of Gray's philosophical effort that relates to who he was and what he may have been trying to articulate. His selection of Hoadley and other comments regarding the matter of judges either finding or creating the law could be interpreted by indirection. Gray would not like to be personally quoted as saying something that would have constituted a form of heresy from the perspective of his culture. But it was acceptable for him to use someone else to say what he himself could not say. Thus, the act of selecting Hoadley possibly represents more of Gray's beliefs than most of us realize. This would be a perfect Grayism—utilizing another person to say something he believes in without, of course, being responsible for the statement itself. From this perspective, Gray was challenging the reigning philosophical forces at Harvard. If that be true, Gray should be included a crypto-realist. But, as Gray did not provide his personal analysis of the law with respect to this, he loses as being an early proponent of legal realism.

In conclusion, for Gray to speak differently on the philosophical aspects of law without the attachment of opaque conditions or circular reasoning remained wholly beyond his reach. Legal philosophy was not his métier.

Resolution of Gray's Philosophical Analysis

It is not surprising to see Gray's attempt to bring together the diverse experiences with the law in the final years of his life. He must have felt some degree of isolation during the final decade of his career on the faculty of Harvard Law School. He had seen the comprehensive changes that took place: the appointment of Ames as Langdell's successor; the empowerment of a second generation of Langdellian disciples; and the deaths of his brother, Horace Jr., his long-time law partner, Ropes, and his closest colleague on the faculty, Thayer. These and other factors must have disengaged him from the dominant culture of the Harvard Law School community. Thus, Gray's philosophical attempt in the 1908 Columbia Law School lectures reveals a man struggling to explain the empirical details of his conscious experience as a practitioner of law in the philosophical law-language of his time and suggests an anguished and modest separation from the dominant orthodoxy of his time: classical formalism. Assuming that the terminology applicable to a particular manner or description of a defined philosophical movement has a precise and consistent definition, it cannot be denied that Gray, the scholar and teacher, was one who cautiously followed that mode of expression for over forty years (1865–1908). Llewellyn described the Formal Style of law:

> The Formal Style is of peculiar interest to us because it set the picture against which all modern thinking has played—call it, as of the last eighty or ninety years, "the orthodox ideology." That picture is clean and clear: the rules of law are to decide cases; policy is for the legislature, not for the courts, and so is change even in pure common law. Opinions run in the deductive form with an air or expression of single-line inevitability. "Principle" is a generalization producing order which can and should be used to prune away those "anomalous" cases or rules which do not fit, such cases or rules have no function except, in places where the supposed "principle" does not work well, to accomplish sense—but sense is no official concern of a formal-style court.
>
> Langdell's dazzling contract-construct is the American archetype of such a set of principles....[64]

It is not surprising in view of the description of the Formal Style that Llewellyn does not include Gray as a legal realist although Twinning quite favorably considers Gray to have had a positive influence on the development of legal realism.[65]

During this period, he wrote of and about the law as if he were dealing with scientific certitude. He was in form and style a quintessential representative of the school of classical formalism. That was his life's work. To the extent his philosophical offering was at odds with the dominant thrust of his scholarly production, the question then becomes one of evaluating the overall impact of his scholarship. Here again, the overwhelming impact must be given to his classical treatises on the RAP and the matter of restraints on alienation. Gray could have been the founding member of the school of legal realism as a natural derivative of his many years in the practice of law. However provocative some of his comments may have been in 1908, they do not eliminate his life-

---

64. Karl Llewellyn, The Common Law Tradition: Deciding Appeals 38 (1960).

65. *See* Llewellyn, *supra* note 30, at 20 ("[Gray was a] down-to-earth, undoctrinaire individualist, a master of the magisterial lecture, and more obviously a man of affairs than most of his colleagues, Gray went his own way at Harvard and was only converted very late to 'the case system.'").

long unconditional obeisance to the dominant theme of explaining the law in accordance with the constructs of classical formalism, nor establish that he was a legal philosopher of consequence. Interestingly, although his philosophical offerings are of limited value, Gray's shocking thrusts are of such a nature that he has and will continue to be cited and studied by many jurisprudential scholars.

The American age of so-called classical formalism of the late nineteenth century necessarily embedded a series of values and policies that impacted most law professors, especially the new breed of teacher-scholars. Gray, like his brother Horace Jr., treated law as if it was a neutral and balanced system, having no preexisting preferences. For Gray, the law was to be consistently applied in a fashion that just happened to comply with a sense of secular morality "as he saw it." The law, therefore, was not simply obligatory by the authority of the community, but also morally beneficial. He, as a classic Brahmin of his times, carried a well-defined and personal sense of duty and obligation into his construct of the law. He studiously avoided the question of the ultimate source of law and was willing to treat law as if it were connected to a fictitious skyhook. And to this assumption, Gray zealously applied his exceptional analytical talents to the preservation of rules of law and also to defend and maintain the fiction of consistency, regularity, and fairness. This was his secular and moral religion, as well as his failing limitation as it relates to a philosophical perspective.

Chapter 8

Consideration of *Restraints on the Alienation of Property* and the Spendthrift Provision

Gray's Separation of the RAP and Restraints on Alienation

Apart from his limited entry into the philosophy of law previously discussed, Gray's principal scholarship interest took him into two related areas: direct restraints on the alienation of property and study of the RAP. A main theme of the two books was the determination that there are "two separate and distinct objectives" regarding these ancient common law concepts. He wrote the two books on substantive property law on his judgment that they were unrelated: *Restraints on the Alienation of Property*[1] (*Restraints*) and *The Rule Against Perpetuities* (*Perpetuities*).[2] However, the two books essentially represent a common theme that can be considered as two separate roads leading to the importance of the liberty of alienation as developed under the common law, despite Gray's tenaciously held view that the doctrines have different functions.

Gray is completely clear about the functional differences of the two common law concerns and succinctly explains that in the introduction to the first edition of *Perpetuities*.

---

1. John Chipman Gray, Restraints on the Alienation of Property (2d ed., Rothman & Co. 1997) (1883) [hereinafter Restraints].

2. John Chipman Gray, The Rule Against Perpetuities (Roland Gray ed., Little, Brown & Co. 4th ed. 1942) (1886) [hereinafter Perpetuities]. There are four editions of Gray's book on perpetuities. The first edition was published in 1886, the second edition in 1906, the third edition in 1915, and the fourth edition was published under the editorship of his son, Roland Gray, in 1942.

> The ambiguity in the meaning of the terms [restraints and perpetuities], which is perhaps the chief reproach of our law, has worked great harm with the matters here considered. The Rule against Perpetuities should have been called the Rule against Remoteness. It is aimed at the control of future interests; it has nothing to do, save incidentally, with present interests. But its name is a constant temptation to treat it as aimed against restraints on the alienation of present interests. Hence frequent lapses into error, from which the courts have recovered themselves slowly and painfully; and hence also statutes, like those of New York, whose interpretation has cost, and will cost, a subsidy. If this book has any merit, it is in the more or less successful attempt to free the subject from this source of confusion and mistake.
>
> In many legal discussions there is in the last resort, nothing to say but that one judge or writer thinks one way, and another writer or judge thinks another way. There is no exact standard to which appeal can be made. In questions of remoteness this is not so; there is for them a definite recognized rule: if a decision agrees with it, it is right; if it does not agree with it, it is wrong. In no part of the law is the reasoning so mathematical in its character; none has so small a human element.
>
> A degree of dogmatism, therefore, may be permitted here which would be unbecoming in other branches of the law. If the answer to a problem does not square with the multiplication table one may call it wrong, although it be the work of Sir Isaac Newton; and so if a decision conflicts with the Rule against Perpetuities, one may call it wrong, however learned and able the court that has pronounced it.[3]

Gray adds:

> When I began to collect the authorities, I did not clearly apprehend that the Rule against Perpetuities had no direct connection with the restraints on alienation, and I intended to devote a chapter to these restraints; but as I went on I saw that such a chapter would be out of place, and therefore concluded to treat the subject in a separate essay.[4]

3. *Id.* at x–xi (footnotes omitted).

4. *Id.* at xi n.3.

In this absolute sense, Gray was committed to the separateness of the related issues and converted the RAP into a straight algebraic formulation by which the results of decisions could now be scientifically verifiable. In short, there was no discretion left to the courts as a result of his draconian mathematical formulation of the RAP. Answers forever after were either correct or erroneous by reason of a remorseless application of this medieval rule.[5] From a limited perspective, Gray was the creator and enforcer of the RAP, although it was admittedly an original invention of the English jurists. For many scholars and jurists, Gray's encryption constitutes the genius of his contribution to a consistent and systemic resolution of perpetuity issues.

Gray's Attack on the Enforceability of the Spendthrift Provision

A spendthrift provision included in a trust instrument prohibits a beneficiary from assigning or otherwise encumbering his or her interests and prohibits the right of a creditor to attach the same. The courts in most states have recognized the right of a grantor to impose conditions of this nature on establishment of an interest in trust so that the beneficiary enjoys the financial security while avoiding the payment of most of his creditors.[6]

Gray's first book, *Restraints*, represents, in part, his personal response to the decision handed down by the United States Supreme Court in *Nichols v. Eaton*.[7] The preface to the first edition of *Restraints* reveals why he undertook this scholarly project. Gray stated:

> How far the law will allow a man to enjoy rights in property which he cannot transfer, and which his creditors cannot take for their debts, is a question becoming more and more frequent in this country. In 1876 I shared the surprise, common to many lawyers, at the opinion of the Supreme Court of the United States in the case of *Nichols v. Eaton*, 91 U.S. 716, containing, as it did, much that was contrary to what, both

5. This precision in the law calling for a logical application of the rule according to Gray sounds and looks a lot like the mechanical jurisprudence that Dean Pound suggests would necessarily lead to decay. Roscoe Pound, *Mechanical Jurisprudence*, 8 COLUM. L. REV. 605, 612 (1908).

6. *See* JESSE DUKEMINIER, ROBERT H. SITKOFF & JAMES LINDGREN, WILLS, TRUSTS, AND ESTATES 614–16 (8th ed. 2009).

7. Nichols v. Eaton, 91 U.S. 716 (1876).

> in teaching and practice, I had hitherto supposed to be settled law. Upon investigation, I became convinced that the questions raised by that opinion could be satisfactorily solved only by studying as a whole the history and present condition of the law governing restraints on the transfer of property, both voluntary and involuntary; and I determined that I would at some time collect the authorities for that purpose. The present essay is the result of this determination, the carrying out of which has been delayed by other engagements until now. Begun for my own enlightenment, I publish it as the first attempt, so far as I know, to deal systematically with the whole of a legal doctrine, whose development is, I venture to think, in danger of being marred by too exclusive an attention to particular aspects.[8]

Gray's comments above disclose that his roles as teacher and practitioner are encountered, not surprisingly, as a singular experience. It is clear that he believed the proposition of law offered by the *Nichols* decision was wrong!

Gray's extreme irritation concerning the judicial approval of the spendthrift provision is not the voice of a waffling equivocator, but rather the voice of one who intends to establish, by the publication of the first edition of *Restraints*, that the decision was wrong.[9] Justice Frankfurter stated when discussing techniques of statutory interpretation that "it makes a great deal of difference whether you start with an answer or a problem."[10] In this case, Gray arrives with a contrary opinion that he intends to substitute as the law and thereby eliminate the legal implications of the *dicta* in *Nichols*.

Gray's first edition of *Restraints* is a direct product of that clearly stated goal. How painful it was to him when the Massachusetts Supreme Judicial Court decided to follow the *Nichols* decision in *Broadway National Bank v. Adams*.[11] Unfortunately, Horace Jr. was no longer on the Massachusetts bench when *Broadway National Bank* was decided, nor was he serving on the United States Supreme Court when it rendered the prior decision in *Nichols*. Nevertheless, one can easily envision the pain Gray endured, personally and as a scholar, when his home team, the Massachusetts Supreme Judicial Court, rendered its critical decision in 1882 of *Broadway National Bank* enforcing the spendthrift provision.

---

8. Restraints, *supra* note 1, at xiii.

9. *See* Roland Gray, John Chipman Gray, Memoir 74 (Privately Printed 1917).

10. Felix Frankfurter, *Some Reflections on the Reading of Statutes*, 47 Colum. L. Rev. 527, 529 (1947).

11. Broadway Nat'l Bank v. Adams, 133 Mass. 170 (1882).

Ironically, in contrast to Gray's passionate antagonism to the judicial approval of the spendthrift provision, the indomitable master of property and estate law actually utilized a spendthrift provision in his own personal testamentary trust![12] Of course, he utilized this provision only after it was established as enforceable under the law.

Footnote to Legal History

Would the Massachusetts Supreme Judicial Court have decided differently in *Broadway National Bank* if Chief Justice Horace Gray Jr. had remained on the court? This is an important question as Horace Jr. was on the Massachusetts Supreme Judicial Court when oral arguments were first held in *Broadway National Bank* in November of 1881. Because Horace Jr. had been appointed to the United States Supreme Court on December 18, 1881, and confirmed the next day, he was no longer on the Massachusetts bench when the case was reargued in March 1882. If he had not been appointed to the United States Supreme Court, the intriguing question is whether *Broadway National Bank* would have been decided differently. Beyond doubt, the judicial record of Horace Jr. reveals that he consistently, if not exclusively, relied on English precedents. There was no such authority on the part of the English jurists recognizing the enforcement of a spendthrift provision.[13] Thus, it is highly unlikely that Horace Jr. would approve of a legal technique that had no direct English ancestry. Hypothetically, he would neither have concurred with the court's decision, nor would he have allowed, if possible, the other members of the court to arrive at that conclusion. During his time on the Massachusetts court, Horace Jr. was a dominant force and his influence on the law weighed heavily on his

---

12. *See* Will and Codicil of John Chipman Gray (approved in the Probate Court for Suffolk County on March 11, 1915) (partial copy on file with author). The copy was graciously provided by Jeffrey B. Gray, Esq., great-grandson of John Chipman. A provision created trusts under section 12 of the Will and required that: "[t]wo-fifths of said residue I give to my son and the said Perkins and their heirs, in trust to pay the net income to my wife to use it for her benefit, *without power of anticipation on her part or liability for her debts*, during her life." *Id.* (emphasis added).

13. The English utilized other techniques to accomplish the similar function such as the creation of a discretionary trust or a so-called protective trust. *See* Davis J. Hayton, Hayton and Marshall Commentaries and Cases on the Law of Trusts and Equitable Remedies 281 (11th ed. 2001) ("It has long been established that, whilst a condition or a proviso for forfeiture of an interest on bankruptcy or attempted alienation is void, a determinable limitation of an interest to last until bankruptcy or attempted alienation is valid.").

peers. He was with the majority in most cases and seldom filed written dissents as Horace Jr. believed dissents "weakened the prestige of the Court."[14] This is some indication, albeit far from proof, that he controlled the outcomes of most litigation before the Massachusetts Supreme Judicial Court during the period that he served as Chief Justice.

It is intriguing to ask why *Broadway National Bank* was reargued after Horace Jr. left[15] to accept an appointment to the United States Supreme Court.[16] One can speculate whether Horace Jr. would have allowed the establishment of a doctrine of law that had no legal parentage under the English common law or whether there might have been a tentative agreement by the members of the court prior to his departure to deny the recognition of such a spendthrift doctrine. In addition, as a logical derivative to the aforementioned and as extended speculation, whether Horace Jr. shared any aspect of these possible details with his brother. It is almost certain, if not certain, that Horace Jr. would never share intimate discussions of members of the court in conference, as that would violate his high standards of judicial conduct. However, he could have expressed his personal displeasure with respect to the published decision in a manner that suggested that the reargument and final decision were not to his liking without disclosing any confidential aspects of the court's operations. Such potential additional information, if any such data was shared between the brothers Gray, would have increased the intensity of academic eruption on the part of John Chipman as well as partially explain the personal intensity that he showered on the court's jurisprudence in that case.

Pain of the Judicial Invention of the Spendthrift Doctrine

The crushing decision upholding the spendthrift provision came down shortly before Gray, as a fledgling scholar, completed his first legal treatise on the subject matter of restraints.[17] It must have been a truly sad day for this de-

---

14. Robert M. Spector, *Legal Historian on the United States Supreme Court: Horace Gray Jr., and the Historical Method*, 12 AM. J. LEGAL HIST. 181, 185 (1968).

15. *Broadway Nat'l Bank*, 133 Mass. at 175 ("[T]he case was argued at the bar in November of 1881 and then reargued in March of 1882.").

16. Nicholas Gray, the great-great grandson of John Chipman, shared a private research memorandum of his clarifying the speed at which Justice Gray received Senate approval of his appointment to the United States Supreme Court.

17. See the last paragraph of the preface to the first edition, wherein he stated "I should add, that the book was substantially written before the publication of the decision of the Supreme

termined man of legal science and a devotee of the perfection of the common law when this decision was rendered. When Gray published a second edition of *Restraints* in 1895, it was manifest that a majority of the other state courts had, by and large, *enacted* a judicially created[18] immunity from payment of one's debts for the exclusive benefit of a relatively small clique of designated wealthy beneficiaries.

Obviously, trusts providing such immunity were created and funded by the aristocratic families of the American society: that is, the patrician families who obviously had acquired assets well in excess of their present and future living needs.[19] Adding to this discomforting legal result from the perspective of Gray was the fact that the spendthrift doctrine was uniquely a prodigy of the American judiciary. It was delivered without the imprimatur or nexus of a formal legal lineage by, to, or from the English authorities. In short, the doctrine was not otherwise grounded in the English common law.[20]

The doctrine was uniquely born of the values consonant with the emerging Gilded Age in that it conferred privilege and protection exclusively for the benefit of the property class; however possibly to the detriment of a commercial enterprise. Gray was not constitutionally able to accept this radical departure from certain basic norms or his personal moral values. Gray's family and the other Brahmins conformed to the norms of society. These values were fully internalized in Gray, and as he stated with respect to the moral duty to pay one's debts: "If there is one sentiment, therefore, which it would seem to be the part of all in authority, and particularly of all judges, to fortify, it is the duty of keeping one's promises and paying one's debts."[21]

The morally responsible action taken by Horace Gray Sr. to voluntarily convey his net assets to his creditors upon his insolvency in 1847, was quite embarrassing and caused a lasting social stain on the Gray family name. In light of that experience, John Chipman would never favor a legal technique by which

---

Judicial Court of Massachusetts in *Broadway Bank v. Adams*, 133 Mass. 170," Restraints, *supra* note 1, at xiv.

18. Lawrence M. Friedman, *The Dynastic Trust*, 73 Yale L.J. 547, 572–86 (1964); Gerald P. Moran, *A Radical Theory of Jurisprudence: The "Decisionmaker" as the Source of the Law—The Ohio Supreme Court's Adoption of the Spendthrift Trust Doctrine as a Model*, 30 Akron L. Rev. 462–70 (1997).

19. Not all state courts reached the same result and some states took a long time before approving of the spendthrift provision. *See, e.g.*, Scott v. Bank One Trust Co., 577 N.E.2d 1077 (Ohio 1991), *rev'g* Sherrow v. Brookover, 189 N.E.2d 90 (Ohio 1963).

20. *See Broadway Nat'l Bank*, 133 Mass. at 172; *see also* Pac. Nat'l Bank v. Windram, 133 Mass. 175 (1882).

21. Restraints, *supra* note 1, at iii.

one could have access to financial security while avoiding payment of one's debts. Such legal opportunity from the viewpoint of John Chipman was simply morally reprehensible.

The preface to the second edition of *Restraints* is filled with revelations of his worst fears.[22] Gray's fears ran the gamut of tortured concern for the immediate impact that *Nichols v. Eaton* would have on moral norms of society and the corrosive impact of judicial approbation of a technique by which certain recognized and accepted basic norms of our society would be violated: that is, that every person is bound to keep his or her promises and obligated to pay his or her debts.[23] He succinctly explained the legal and moral implications of this decision.

> And yet I cannot recant. Doubtless I may exaggerate the importance of the matter; but, so far as it goes, I still believe, as I said in the first edition, that the old doctrine was a wholesome one, fit to produce a manly race, based on sound morality and wise philosophy; and that the new doctrine is contrary thereto.[24]

Clearly, Gray was a man of honor and any legal technique by which a person, particularly a profligate, might escape from his or her legal responsibility was simply abhorrent to him. Recall the apocryphal student story referred to in Chapter 12 in which Gray ambivalently decided not to allow a student suffering from an excess of enjoyment to return to his dorm because he had not returned before midnight, despite the temporary disability of the student. The moral of the story is that Gray's sense of accountability trumped his sense of justice. It is not unusual for students to psychically intuit the persona of their teacher through shared fictitious stories. This narrative seems particularly apt of Gray.

Law as the Source of Secular Morality for Gray

The preface to the second edition of *Restraints* contains an aggressive attack on the integrity of the judiciary by one who did not publicly generally display such feelings. Gray had railed against criticism of judges by his faculty adversaries, Langdell and Ames. But when he was of a contrary view to a particular decision—like the enforcement of a spendthrift provision—Gray was

22. *See id.* at v.
23. *Id.* at iii.
24. *Id.* at v.

willing to speculate on nonlegal factors affecting a decision. Indeed, it was not beyond Gray to conjure judges' personal political philosophy as a major influence of a decision.

> Of course, it would be absurd to say that the learned judges who have aided in the introduction of spendthrift trusts have been secret socialists; but it is none the less true, I believe, that they have been influenced, unconsciously it may well be, by those ideas which the experience of the last few years has shown to have been fermenting in the minds of the community; by that spirit, in short, of paternalism, which is the fundamental essence alike of spendthrift trusts and of socialism.[25]

Gray also identified as a major concern the attack on the freedom of contract. Perhaps, and unfortunately for one who tends to be slightly obsequious, the preface reveals Gray's sacred paean to the responsible enforcement of contracts and its importance to the preservation of society.

> There is a strong and increasing feeling, and a feeling which has already led to many practical results, that a main object of law is not to secure liberty of contract, but to restrain it, in the interest, or supposed interest, of the weaker, or supposed weaker, against the stronger, or supposed stronger, portion of the community. Hence, for instance, laws enacted or contemplated for eight hours' labor, for weekly payments of wages by corporations, for "compulsory arbitration," &c., that is, laws intended to take away from certain classes of the community, for their supposed good, their liberty of action and their power of contract; in other words, attempts to bring society back to

---

25. *Id.* at ix. We should not forget that during the disturbances and rapid changes in our society of that time, Horace Jr. was serving as Associate Justice of the United States Supreme Court and he was far from voting against the interests of the property class in many instances. In addition, Roland Gray, the son of John Chipman, served as a law clerk to Uncle Horace in 1898. *See* Albert Boyden, Ropes-Gray 1865–1940 (Privately Printed by Lincoln & Smith Press of Boston 1942). In view of the family connections, it would be not unrealistic to presume that John Chipman was both fully cognizant and mostly in consort with the dominant values and economic theories of his class. Certainly, he discloses no known disagreement with such values or the then tendency of the Supreme Court to affirm decisions that were generally favorable to the property class. Accordingly, John Chipman viewed the enforcement of the spendthrift provision as a serious aberration in that its enforcement violated the sacred freedom of contract. It constituted in his mind an egregious and unforgivable legal misadventure.

> an organization founded on status and not upon contract. To a frame of mind and a state of public sentiment like this, spendthrift trusts are most congenial. If we are all to be cared for, and have our wants supplied, without regard to our mental and moral failings, in this socialistic Utopia, there is little reason why in the mean time, while waiting for that day, a father should not do for his son what the state is then to do for us all.[26]

Gray is not being retroactively criticized for aberrational political or legal views of the ancien régime. He was simply reflecting the dominant legal and social milieu of the nineteenth century for one of his class. As noted above, freedom of contract was considered a sacrosanct legal value and reigned supreme in the minds of many of those of the dominant economic class.[27] Accordingly, the entrenched attitudes or norms would not be exorcised by one's appointment to the bench; indeed, such attitudes or norms were frequently found embedded in the legal principles as articulated and applied by some of the judges.

The Supreme Court, during the late nineteenth and early part of the twentieth century, initially denied enforcement of a wide variety of state legislative enactments intended to provide for general relief and welfare of the community under the substantive due process clause as a violation of the liberty of contract. A perfect illustration of this historical legal process can be seen in the case of *Coppage v. Kansas*.[28] The Court in *Coppage* struck down as unconstitutional a statute that precluded an employer from requiring employees to agree, as a condition of employment, not to join a union. As explained by Justice Pitney in *Coppage*:

> Neither the doctrine nor the application of [freedom of contract] is novel; we will endeavor to re-state some of the grounds upon which it rests. The principle is fundamental and vital. Included in the right of personal liberty and the right of private property—partaking of the nature of each—is the right to make contracts for the acquisition

26. Restraints, *supra* note 1, at ix.

27. *See, e.g.*, Lochner v. New York, 198 U.S. 45 (1905) (holding a New York state law limiting the maximum number of hours that a baker could work unconstitutional as the law constituted an interference with the liberty of contract). In his dissent, Justice Holmes noted that the 14th Amendment "does not enact Mr. Herbert Spencer's Social Statics." *Id.* at 75 (Holmes, J., dissenting).

28. Coppage v. Kansas, 236 U.S. 1 (1914).

> of property. Chief among such contracts is that of personal employment, by which labor and other services are exchanged for money or other forms of property. If this right be struck down or arbitrarily interfered with, there is a substantial impairment of liberty in the long-established constitutional sense. The right is as essential to laborer as to the capitalist, to the poor as to the rich; for the vast majority of persons have no other honest way to begin to acquire property, save by working for money.[29]

Justice Holmes was quite aware of the judicial arbitrariness of imputing economic theory as the "Constitution is not intended to embody a particular economic theory, whether of paternalism and the organic relation of the citizen to the state or of *laissez faire*."[30] In time, his message was eventually received by the Court and can be seen in the opinion of *Nebbia v. New York*,[31] wherein the Court stated "that though the court may hold views inconsistent with the wisdom of the [state enacted] law, it may not be annulled unless palpably in excess of legislative power."[32]

However, Gray's concerns as to the role and function of the state remain as cogent to the contemporary debates of today as they were to the debates of the past. We still question how far the government should provide a guarantee to some form of lifetime security. Obviously, the more extensive the government undertakes social commitments of a comprehensive nature necessarily imposes greater tax costs on some individuals, reallocates private property, and decreases the important communal norm of self-reliance. Added to the disparity between the different groups is the salient factor that law was originally drawn as a measure to protect and preserve the assets of the few. These concerns were culturally inbred, intellectually rationalized, and defended by Gray and others of his social class. It is, however, important to note that Gray objected to the spendthrift provision in the instance where it protected a member of his class. It is especially noteworthy that Gray acted on the legal and moral principle, not on the identification of the beneficiary of the rule.

The preface to the second edition of *Restraints* captures the times and, more importantly, the personal temperament of Gray, the man, as no other pub-

---

29. *Id.* at 14.

30. *Lochner*, 198 U.S. at 75 (Holmes, J., dissenting); *see* 2 LAWRENCE H. TRIBE, AMERICAN CONSTITUTIONAL LAW 560–86 (1988).

31. Nebbia v. New York, 291 U.S. 502 (1934).

32. *Id.* at 516.

lished writing of his comes close to revealing. It is simply the most direct and spirited revelation of Gray that he allowed to be disseminated for public consumption. As he stated: "I have written other things, for one motive or another, but this essay wrote itself. While I was musing the fire burned. *Vae mihi si non evangelizavero* [woe to me if I do not preach the gospel]."[33] His passion, anger, and frustration pour forth. There is not the slightest degree of measured restraint that one ordinarily expects of and from Gray. His cultivated erudite caution so painstakingly preserved in most of his scholarship was simply overtaken by this "plainly egregious" judicially invented edict by which a person could evade the rightful claims of his creditors.

Considering the judicially manufactured creditor exemption for the exclusive benefit of the "three percenters" of the Boston community, Gray no doubt deeply recalled the enduring family embarrassment resulting from his father's insolvency. His family faced their responsibility at great social cost; should not others equally pay the piper? He and Horace Jr. accepted their plight and each of them became self-made professional successes. Without such legal accountability of the person, how is the morality of society to be preserved and maintained? These were very troubling questions for Gray as he saw the law as the ultimate secular source of morality. *Enforcement of the law was his mantra!*

Joseph Henry Beale passed on the story, perhaps apocryphal, that Gray wrote *Restraints* because he lost a case on point and intended to prove that the Supreme Court's *dicta* in *Nichols* was wrong; thereby rectifying an egregious legal error.[34] If there is any truth to that story, one can appreciate the depth of his personal angst and professional sense of failure. *Query*: whether the complaint of Gray is derivative mostly of the scholarly element of his character or from the frustration and irritation of a practicing lawyer who loses a case, as well as the belief that it affects a massive departure from the important norm that one should pay his debts. This question is asked here in a rhetorical sense in that there are not two separate dimensions to Gray's character; he existed as a singular person (teacher-practitioner-scholar) with interacting internalized values about the role and function of law. In discussing the *Nichols* case, he stated, "I shared the surprise, common to many lawyers, at the opinion of the Supreme Court of the United States in the case of *Nichols v. Eaton*, 91 U.S. 716, containing,

33. RESTRAINTS, *supra* note 1, at iv (citing 1 *Corinthians* 9:16–17). It is a truism to observe here that Gray was one who saw the law as providing definitive guidance that required strict enforcement.

34. *See* GRAY, *supra* note 9, at 74.

as it did, much that was contrary to what, *both in teaching and practice*, I had hitherto supposed to be settled law."[35] The experience of Gray as teacher and lawyer is identical.

Indeed, Gray was moved to note the unity of his character in his obviously intended vindictive response. He was a personal and legal moralist regarding the function of law in society![36] Gray used scholarship as a means to clarify the law from his perspective of the social needs of the community "as he saw it." Law, when applying Gray's thesis, requires that individuals fulfill their duty and meet their moral responsibilities. The divergent and arbitrary catch in regards to Gray's jurisprudence is that such duties and moral responsibilities were those of his preordained selection.

It may be that Gray was more interactive in legal literature than he was in personal relationships. He appears to have enjoyed the experience of engaging in battle in the controlled environment of scholarly publication, where he found a considerable degree of national respect, peer recognition, and, most certainly, personal approbation.

He was an advocate as well as a scholar. However, there may exist an inherent conflict between the tensions flowing from one's role as a practicing lawyer (as an advocate of a client's interest) and that as a scholar, particularly when one is employed to provide legal representation on a issue that one has previously taken an adverse position in published scholarship.[37] Opponents in litigation could cite Gray's scholarship in support of their position and that would be a problem for Gray the practitioner-lawyer. In this sense, he may unknowingly have been less of an advocate and more of a teacher-scholar acting as a jurisconsult[38] not of the Roman Empire, but of the common law. This is not a criticism of Gray, but it does describe his institutional experience of

35. *Id.* at xiii.

36. Roland Gray noted, in referring to *Restraints*, that "[Gray] had always an ethical purpose in writing his books—to make law a better instrument, to remove defects (as he phrased it) which 'lessen its value as a guide to conduct.'" GRAY, *supra* note 9, at 34.

37. John Chipman ran into this problem on at least two separate occasions. *See* Fitchie v. Brown, 211 U.S. 321, 326 (1908); *see also* W. Barton Leach, *Powers of Sale in Trustees and the Rule Against Perpetuities*, 47 HARV. L. REV. 948, 950 (1934).

38. John Maxcy Zane, perhaps an underrated historian, explained the function of the jurisconsult:

> The jurisconsults, therefore, applied themselves to find the underlying principle that would make a general rule and at the same time be consonant with right. These general rules of the jurisconsults applied by taking a particular case and making a particular analysis of it so as to bring it under a general rule of law by means of analogy, extending the rule on the grounds of utility and social ex-

providing correct legal answers to his primary constituents; namely, clients, students, and other legal authorities.

Gray, when on the public stage, was a model citizen of importance in the Boston Brahmin community. Not only could Gray have qualified as a character portrayed in a story or novel of Henry James, in that he presented the appearance of the more noble elements and accouterments of that which would have been expected of a professional man of his stature; he was, in fact, portrayed in various stories of James.[39] Gray became, not surprisingly, the personification of what he was—the wise, "institutional" Brahmin of the nineteenth century.[40]

> pediency. This is the method of judges today, proceeding on the analogies of prior established rules as shown in published decisions.

John Maxcy Zane, The Story of the Law 163 (The Liberty Fund, Inc. 1998) (1927).

39. *See* Sheldon M. Novick, The Young Master Henry James 125–26, 133, 141 (1996).

40. Gray was harmoniously synthesized with his Brahmin DNA, unlike some, like Thomas Lamont. It was said of Lamont, "He was so successful at playing the aristocrat that he passed for the genuine article." Ron Chernow, The House of Morgan; An American Banking Dynasty and the Rise of Modern Finance 220 (Grove Press 2001) (1990). Cary Grant allegedly said it more succinctly in describing his screen persona: "I pretended to be somebody I wanted to be, finally I became that person. Or he became me."

Chapter 9

Gray and His Contemporary Critics

Gray's treatise on the Rule Against Perpetuities (RAP) was a work of major academic proportions at the time of its publication in 1886 and for many decades thereafter. The book was received as the principal authority on the matter of perpetuities by the academy and the judiciary. The result of his scholarly effort reveals the discovery of a perfect rule of law (the "scientific inner core") that is logically derived from his examination of the holdings of hundreds of English cases[1] as well as selective reliance on the teachings of two other treatises by English authorities on the same subject matter. This was, and remains even today, a masterful accomplishment. His succinct remarks on the matter of perpetuities became the unchallenged American gospel for the academy with rare exception. As a result, Gray secured noted academic disciples who actively disseminated and passionately defended his doctrine on the RAP over the twentieth century.

The purpose of this discussion is to ascertain who, among his contemporaries, expressed disagreement with Gray's legal edicts on the RAP, and the manner by which he responded to those critics. As a participant in the Civil War, Major Gray was by training a warrior of the quiet type—a warrior of the written word whose sword was his pen.

Sir Howard Warburton Elphinstone

One of the early reviews of Gray's book, *The Rule Against Perpetuities* (*Perpetuities*), published in 1886, received a favorable analysis from a leading English authority, Sir Howard W. Elphinstone.[2] However, Elphinstone questioned

1. *See* A. W. Brian Simpson, Leading Cases in the Common Law, Legal Science and Legal Absurdity 76, 96 (Clarendon Press Oxford 1996) (1995).

2. *See* H.W.E., *Review of The Rule Against Perpetuities*, 2 L.Q.R. 394 (1886).

Gray's position that a determinable fee could not be created after the promulgation of the *Statute of Quia Emptores* in 1290. The increased authorization under the Statute for a transferee to alienate without prior permission of the transferor was interpreted by Gray as eliminating the possibility that any condition or collateral limitation could be imposed on a conveyance. Thus, a violation of the condition would not divest the transferee's interests in the fee.

In most simple terms, a determinable fee, under the common law, is a conveyance of a fee to a transferee that includes a certain condition or collateral limitation which requires that the fee interest instantly revert to the transferor upon the violation of the stated condition. If, contrary to Gray's position, the imposition of the condition creates an enforceable determinable fee despite the enactment of *Quia Emptores*, then upon the violation of the stated condition the property held by the transferee would instantly revert back to the said transferor.

Gray interacted skillfully in responding by combing his two critics, Elphinstone and H. W. Challis (discussed below), who while disagreeing with him on the enforceability of a determinable fee are equally at odds with each other.[3] A typical condition or limitation creating a determinable fee would be a conveyance by Jones of Blackacre to Tinkerpaw *so long as alcohol is never sold on such property*. Should alcohol ever be sold on such property at any time in the future, no matter when, Blackacre instantly reverts to Jones. Jones' interest, prior to the violation, is a possibility of reverter. If Jones was deceased at the time of violation, then the named devisees of Jones will take, and if no valid will, such real property descends to his heirs. When the condition is for the exclusive benefit of the transferor, as in this example, there is no time limit during which such imposed condition remains enforceable. The interest lasts, theoretically, for the indefinite future. It is this type of conveyance and condition which Gray asserts was eliminated by *Quia Emptores.*

Elphinstone, a well known conveyancer of the English legal community, wrote several articles concerning property during the late nineteenth and early twentieth centuries. He also co-authored a later edition of a treatise on the law of property.[4] Elphinstone opened the debate on the determinable fee issue in his original review of Gray's book. Gray was of the opinion that such interest (a determinable fee) could not be created under the common law after the en-

---

3. *See* John Chipman Gray, The Rule Against Perpetuities 712 (Roland Gray ed., 4th ed. 1942) (1886) [hereinafter Perpetuities].

4. Howard W. Elphinstone & Frederick T. Maw, The Modern Law of Real Property (5th ed. Sweet & Maxwell 1906) (reviewed in 22 L.Q.R. 320, 332–33 (1906)).

actment of *Quia Emptores*. Elphinstone argued that the transferee, by reason of the Statute, is made subservient to the overlord of the transferor and now holds directly of said overlord. Sir Howard asserted that the overlord, not the original transferor, now enjoys the interest, referred to as a possibility of reverter, created by reason of the condition imposed on the original conveyance. Thus, Elphinstone argued that *Quia Emptores* merely shifted, as opposed to completely eliminated the interest, the beneficiary from the transferor to the overlord of the transferor.

It is obvious that Gray was not a person psychologically suited to leave the last word to a critic.[5] Gray responded quite promptly to the modest criticism of Elphinstone.[6] But this issue potentially threatens, albeit very indirectly, a major aspect of Gray's construction of the RAP. It was immediately clear to him that if such a determinable fee interest was valid and the possibility of reverter existed in the transferor or his or her heirs (or in the overlord of the transferor as Elphinstone erroneously suggested), would violate the RAP in the same way as would a gift over, on the same condition, to a designated successor third party. Clearly, such a shifting executory interest (causing the fee to shift from the original transferee to a successor third party) would not necessarily vest within the prescribed period of the RAP and, thus, such interest would fail.

This application of the RAP to a possibility of reverter does not have the same result when applied to a shifting executory interest. The identical condition reveals diametrically opposite results. This is due to the fact that a possibility of reverter is always deemed vested whereas the shifting executory interest remains contingent and does not vest until the event occurs. Because the RAP focuses exclusively on the date of vesting *in interest*, the possibility of reverter is *never* subject to failure under the RAP whereas a shifting executory interest is always subject to the RAP. This inconsistency in the treatment of the identical condition, depending on whether it is attached to the transferor or the transferee side of the equation, relates more to the failure of the English jurists to establish a conceptually logical basis for the RAP and Gray's pliant acquiescence.

Obviously, the prospective interests of a *stranger*, the original transferee or an alternative beneficiary of executory interests, were always historically more

5. Gray, perhaps in jest, identifies the signer of the article, H.W.E., as Sir Howard Warburton Elphinstone, as the proper name of the person who published a somewhat critical review of his book. *See* PERPETUITIES, *supra* note 3, at 712.

6. *See* J.C. Gray, *Determinable Fees*, 3 L.Q.R. 399 (1887).

suspect than the so-called *retained* interests of the transferor under the common law. As to the *retained* interests of the transferor, all are deemed vested in interest even though vesting in possession is delayed until and when a violation of the condition occurs.

Thus, the distinction of vesting in interest, as opposed to vesting in possession, becomes a weak reed on which to rationalize the radical differences in the result for what are in substance the identical future interests from the perspective of time. This inconsistent treatment of a possibility of reverter and a shifting executory interest, based on the identical condition, is very troubling if one believes the law should reflect equivalent outcomes for similar interests subject to the same condition.

This inconsistency largely destroys the principal thesis of Gray's scholarship with reference to the assertion that the RAP should have been called the Rule Against Remoteness; particularly, if one sees the critical concept of vesting in possession as distinguished from vesting in interest as the pivotal distinction for purposes of the RAP. The absence of a logical distinction reveals that the alleged difference of the rule is completely historic, lacks substance, and appears highly fictional! Indeed, this egregious inconsistency destroys the integrity of the RAP.

Gray recognized this incongruity between a possibility of reverter and an executory interest both in the initial position taken in his law review response[7] to Elphinstone and later in his revised comments, which are included as Appendix E in *Perpetuities.*[8] It is expressly noted by Gray that remote limitations are universally "disapproved at the present day" but that "[t]here is an alleged exception in the case of possibilities of reverter" and "[i]t is practicable to give a reasonable construction to *Quia Emptores* which will do away with the supposed objectionable exception."[9] Thus, Gray's position that *Quia Emptores* ef-

---

7. Professor Gray states that if a conveyance of a building is made by A to B so long as used for a dwelling, a subsequent suit by the Crown when B uses the building for a shop would fail:

> I should say it could not [be enforced], because (1) since the Statute *Quia Emptores* there can be no possibility of reverter; (2) if there could be [a possibility of reverter], the one which it is here attempted to create is too remote. But what would be the answer of those who deny these propositions?

Id. at 402. The reference of Gray to a suit by the Crown is on the premise of Sir Howard's criticism that such retained interest of the grantor would be attributed to the grantor's lord after *Quia Emptores.* Gray's response is that such interests fail on the basis of remoteness apart from the question of who has such interests; i.e., the grantor or the grantor's lord.

8. *See* PERPETUITIES, *supra* note 3, at 716.

9. *Id.*

fectively eliminates the existence of a possibility of reverter also neatly eradicates the conceptual inconsistency that otherwise exists between the treatment of those very comparable interests. In short, a shifting excutory interest is void unless it vests in interest (frequently the same date on which it vests in possession) within the period prescribed by the RAP, whereas a possibility of reverter is not otherwise limited or affected by the RAP. The possibility of reverter is always deemed vested in interest and thus completely immune to the bite of the RAP. Other authorities have similarly recognized the incongruity of not applying the RAP to the possibility of reverter.[10]

In view of that importance and the desperate need to create the appearance of consistency in the perfect rule of law, Gray clairvoyantly identifies his dilemma.[11] Because Gray asserted that the possibility of reverter could not be enforced after the enactment of *Quia Emptores*, the issue of treating all interests of the transferor, including the possibility of reverter, as vested was not needed to justify the diametrically opposite results. Thus, under an assumed hypothetical transfer of Blackacre by Jones to Tinkerpaw *so long as no alcohol is ever sold on the property, and if such sale of alcohol occurs, then to Smith*, the shifting executory interest of Smith fails. It fails for the obvious reason that it will not necessarily vest in interest within the period of the RAP. However, the same conveyance and condition, without a gift over to Smith, would instantly revert back to Jones. Gray judiciously danced around this unsolvable dilemma that renders his maxim—the rule is one of remoteness in vesting—as lacking a rational basis. In short, his asserted "rule again remoteness in vesting" is simply another fiction of the law lacking of logical *consistency*. Since a possibility of reverter existed under the common law and was treated as a vested interest, Gray's infamous "rule of remoteness" is simply a product of historic mythology and survives only by the authority of courts, supported and disseminated by the unique scholarship of Gray, and cemented into the core of the common law.

Thus, the keystone to the RAP became that of vesting in interest as opposed to the more rational test of vesting in possession. Because of this inconsistency, many states have enacted laws restricting the maximum period during which a possibility of reverter is enforceable. What is magnificent about the common law is the moderately unrestricted elasticity and/or authority to reinterpret its past doctrines in ways that meet the perceptions and standards of the persons

10. *See* J.H. C. Morris & W. Barton Leach, The Rule Against Perpetuities 209–18 (2d ed. 1962) [hereinafter Morris & Leach]; Charles Harpum (Robert Megarry & William Wade), The Law of Real Property 337–38 (6th ed. 2000).

11. *See supra* note 7 and accompanying text.

in power. And no one would seriously challenge that Gray was such a man in power.

H. W. Challis

Another English scholar of significance, H. W. Challis, focused directly on the same issue as discussed in the exchange between Gray and Elphinstone.[12] Noting that Gray relied, in part, on a treatise of Sanders[13] for the proposition that *Quia Emptores* had eliminated the determinable fee, Challis stated:

> That a cardinal result of the Statute of *Quia Emptores* should be left to be discovered by Sanders in the nineteenth century seems to me, I confess, what Chillingworth calls "extremely improbable and even cousin-german to impossible." That Lord Coke, Plowden, Croke, Sir Henry Finch, Lord Nottingham, the author of the 'Touchstone,' Serjeant Maynard, Vaughn, Treby, Powell, Lord Hardwicke, Preston, Fearne, Butler, Watkins ... should have passed their lives in intimate familiarity with the Statute, without anyone of them lighting or stumbling upon what, if it were true, would be a fairly obvious truth, is not a hypothesis to be accepted, unless no other rational explanation of the language of the Statute can be found.[14]

Unlike the erroneous theory of Elphinstone that the possibility of reverter was reassigned to the overlord of the transferor, Challis saw such an interest as one retained by the transferor and not otherwise affected by *Quia Emptores.* Challis' major contribution to the debate regarding the existence of a determinable fee was to clarify that *Quia Emptores* applied only to a conveyance in which the grantor made a conveyance of his entire interest (fee simple absolute) to another. This was a point of law that Gray was not to win,[15] as well as one that was impossible for him to concede.[16] The failure to concede this point of law

12. *See* H.W. Challis, *Determinable Fees*, 3 L.Q.R. 403 (1887).

13. *See* Francis W. Sanders, An Essay on Uses and Trusts 208 (5th ed. 1824). See also Gray's statement: "Mr. Sanders was the first author to distinctly recognize, or at any rate to state, that the Statute *Quia Emptores* put an end to determinable fees." *See* Perpetuities, *supra* note 3, at 34.

14. Challis, *supra* note 12, at 403 (footnote omitted).

15. *See* Lewis M. Simes & Allan F. Smith, The Law of Future Interests §283 (1956); William R. Vance, *Rights of Reverter and the Statue of Quia Emptores*, 36 Yale L.J. 593 (1927).

16. *See infra* note 17 for specific concession by Roland Gray.

is completely understandable in view of its impact on the logical construction of his alleged rule of remoteness in vesting. Gray personally was never able to concede any aspect of this technical debate regarding the impact of *Quia Emptores*, and the reluctant concession was eventually proffered by his son, Roland Gray, in the 1942, fourth edition of *Perpetuities*.[17]

Charles Sweet

Another formidable scholar and a sometime critic of Gray's scholarship was Charles Sweet. He is referred to as Charles "The Sweet" because he provided a caustic review of the third edition of *Perpetuities*,[18] published in 1915 shortly after Gray's death. The review constituted a partial eulogy of Gray and his life as a scholar. Sweet's review reveals a man whose natural temperament is very critical, quite personal, and definitely sarcastic. Indeed, in the first sentence of the article, The Sweet acerbically notes most English lawyers refer to Gray as "a one-book" man.[19] He then offers extended observation regarding Gray's intellect.

> And yet the doctrine of perpetuity and remoteness is not a subject which was calculated to bring out the best side of Gray's intellect. It is full of anomalies and absurdities, most of which are due to historical accidents, although some, as Gray himself points out, arose from the inability to grasp the true nature of the doctrine of remoteness which our judges showed at a critical stage in its development. Such a subject cannot, one would think, have appealed to Gray's intellect, which had high scholarly and scientific qualities. And he had the defects of his qualities.... Gray had a feeling akin to compassion; to his clear logical intellect such a state of mind was almost inconceivable. In his attempt to construct a symmetrical and scientific Rule Against Perpetuities, Gray felt hampered by the numerous doctrines which our judges from time to time invented in order to preserve the free alienation of land, and so far as they were inconsistent with his own

17. "In previous editions of this work, it was argued that determinable fees were likewise impossible in most American jurisdictions. *In the present edition, however, it is conceded that such estates can be created in America.*" PERPETUITIES, *supra* note 3, at 721 (emphasis added).

18. *See* Charles Sweet, *John Chipman Gray* (ob. *Feb. 25, 1915*), 31 L.Q.R. 338 (1915).

19. *Id.*

> rule he disregarded them. He saw the wood, but failed to see all the trees.... But in their systematic treatises on the English law of real property, American lawyers seem to treat it as if it were a collection of rules drawn up by one legislator at one time, and therefore capable of being classified under leading principles.[20]

Apart from the appropriateness of such a cryptic review included as a partial eulogy and devaluation of a major scholar's contribution, there are aspects of Sweet's observations regarding Gray's mode of intellectual operation that are somewhat astute and insightful, despite the passing of almost a century. Sweet had many disagreements with Gray's positions, but a further discussion of the details of those differences would not appreciably add to the succinct and comprehensive critical conclusion stated above. It must also be noted that Sweet conceded, albeit reluctantly, the depth and influence that Gray's perpetuity scholarship had on the English jurists.[21] In addition, Sweet was very impressed with Gray's philosophical treatise, "the charm of its literary style, and the acuteness of [Gray's] reasoning."[22] Sweet was not receptive to the views of others and was especially assertive as to the perfection of his legal judgments. It was like Gray debating Gray—neither man showed the slightest uncertainty as to his convictions.

Sir Frederick Pollock, long-term editor of the *Law Quarterly Review*, judiciously decided to insert a brief, but clearly more favorable and expressive, comment on the same page immediately following the critical review by Sweet. Pollock offered personal and sensitive expressions of concern and respect for Gray and his scholarship.

> A most learned and most unaffected scholar, he resembled in this quality of magnanimous simplicity a beloved master of an earlier generation in a different branch, the late Prof. Cowell of Cambridge. I

---

20. *Id.* at 338–39.

21. Sweet also observed the impact of Gray's scholarship on the first page of his article immediately preceding the extensive quote set forth above:

> [Gray's treatise] has the proud distinction of having influenced the decisions of our Courts.... [O]n the question of whether a legal contingent remainder can be void for remoteness ... our judges have followed his lead, in blissful ignorance of the fact that most English real property lawyers of the last two generations, from Fearne down towards, thought differently. Gray's opinion that an unrestricted condition of re-entry is void for remoteness has also been adopted by some of our judges.

Id. at 338.

22. *Id.* at 340.

> highly agree with Mr. Sweet's high estimate of The Nature and Sources of the Law: Gray made new and excellent points, for example, on the well-worn topic of Sovereignty. His own estimate of that work was diffident; in writing to me he called it "the work of a man who may be at home in discussing the differences between Sanders and Preston or between my friends Cyprian Williams and Charles Sweet, but on whom the clothes of an analytical jurist do not fit very well." But in that opinion he will not be followed.[23]

Pollock was acting, no doubt, as a responsible editor of the *Law Quarterly Review* and also addressing the loss of a personal friend[24] and American scholar of importance, in addition to providing a level of professional equilibrium and respect for a fallen comrade. The critical attitude of Sweet, expressed above, was most likely fostered and developed as the two scholars heatedly debated[25] the meaning and implication of the famous decision of *Whitby v. Mitchell.*[26]

A number of scholars have debated the legal basis of the court's ruling in that case and have struggled to ascertain if the opinion correctly expressed the law at that time. One can line up the experts and jurists during the late nineteenth and early twentieth centuries on either side of the tennis net. Ironically, there was an interesting disagreement between a father and son, most likely occurring after the father's death. T. Cyprian Williams, among other scholars, vehemently disagreed with the court's decision in *Whitby* and strongly supported the position of Gray.[27] This reveals an iconic conflict between T. Cyprian Williams and his father, Joshua Williams, a principal authority that the court relied upon in *Whitby*.[28] Joshua authored thirteen editions of his treatise, be-

---

23. *Id.* at 341 (comments of Sir Frederick Pollock).

24. Pollock, Holmes, and Gray were awarded honorary degrees from Harvard in 1895.

25. *See* Charles Sweet, *Perpetuities*, 15 L.Q.R. 71, 84 (1899) [hereinafter Sweet, *Perpetuities*]; John Chipman Gray, Whitby v. Mitchell *Once More*, 29 L.Q.R. 26 (1913), *reprinted in* app'x K of PERPETUITIES, *supra* note 3, at 800 ("The reason given for the alleged rule is that the law will not allow a possibility on a possibility. Mr. Sweet rejects this reason emphatically, I say with contempt."); Charles Sweet, *The Rule in* Whitby v. Mitchell, 12 COLUM. L. REV. 199 (1912) [hereinafter Sweet, *The Rule*].

26. Whitby v. Mitchell, (1890) 42 Ch.D. 494.

27. T. Cyprian Williams, *Contingent Remainders and the Rule Against Perpetuities—A Criticism of the Case of* Whitby v. Mitchell, 14 L.Q.R. 234 (1898).

28. JOSHUA WILLIAMS, PRINCIPLES OF THE LAW OF REAL PROPERTY 380, 624–25, app'x E (T. Cyprian Williams ed., 17th ed. Sweet & Maxwell 1892) [hereinafter LAW OF REAL PROPERTY].

fore Cyprian took over as the editor of the book and was himself recognized as an important scholar on the law of conveyancing.

The essential holding of *Whitby* was based upon an ancient rule providing a legal life estate to an unborn child with a remainder to an unborn child of such child was void ab initio.[29] Part of the confusion as to the validity of this seldom recognized rule of double possibilities was derived from the often quoted observation of the master logician of the common law, Sir Edward Coke, who stated "*potentia est duplex, remota et propinqua.*" This observation was converted into the shorthand rule prohibiting "double possibilities" and was a condensed version of what was commonly referred to as the rule prohibiting the creation of an unbarrable estate. An unbarrable estate could be accomplished by a conveyance of an estate to two or more successive persons that were unknown and unborn at the time of the conveyance and whose interests were contingent by definition. For example, a conveyance of Blackacre to the first child of Edward for life (Edward has no child at the time) and then the remainder interest to the first child of the unborn child of Edward.

The confusion between the reference to the rule of "double possibilities" and the creation of an unbarrable estate was a constant thorn in the English jurisprudence and frequently the subject of extended debate. Indeed, Lord Nottingham was moved to deny the rule of double possibilities in *dicta* almost two hundred years prior to the decision in *Whitby* in his much celebrated decision in the *Duke of Norfolk's Case*.[30] This denial suggests that the confusion of double possibilities was long lasting and, perhaps, a shared product of study derived from the Inns of Court wherein students were, like today, prone to seek security in designing simplified formulas to resolve complex legal issues. This proposition also became a standard theme for those engaged in the practice of conveyancing. As Joshua Williams explained, "[Double possibilities] came to be generally defined in a sort of working rule adopted by conveyancers and quoted by judges.... The reason assigned for [the rule], however, was not always the same.... This rule gained authority from general use."[31] From the milieu of conveyancing practice, a standard rule of law evolved as a maxim.

Gray's position rested on the view that the RAP was the exclusive rule by which a future contingent interest (whether a contingent remainder or an executory interest) would either fail or be enforced at law. It was insisted by Gray

29. *Whitby*, 42 Ch.D. 494 ("For that proposition I do not want any higher authority than that of the late Joshua Williams, who was certainly one of the best real property lawyers that existed in my lifetime.").

30. The Duke of Norfolk's Case, (1682) 3 Ch.Cas. 1, 29.

31. Law of Real Property, *supra* note 28, at 380 (footnotes omitted).

"that no such rule [double possibilities] had been formulated before the Rule against Perpetuities."[32] Indeed, he had previously stated that the rule prohibiting an estate for life to an unborn person followed by a remainder to the child of that unborn person was "a non-existent rule based on an exploded theory."[33] For Gray, the RAP was the exclusive means by which to eliminate interests tending to a perpetuity (remote vesting); the attempted resurrection of an uncertain and unfounded rule should be permanently purged. Gray was neither exposed to the practice of conveyancing nor was he exposed to the maxims of practice. He relied exclusively on decided cases for his position.

Sweet made it a habit to attack[34] Gray's views on the issue of whether there was an "*ancient rule against perpetuities*"[35] (i.e., essentially the creation of endless limitations for life in favor of succeeding generations that effected an unbarrable estate).[36]

> Mr. J. C. Gray is a courageous heretic. He denies the existence of a rule which, so far as English lawyers are concerned, is pretty firmly established by the decisions of two judges of first instance ... and six appellate judges.... The existence of the rule is also supported by the authority of Lord Northington, Lord Keyon, Lord Ellenborough, Lord St. Leonards, Mr. Fearne, the Real Property Commissioners, Mr. Preston, Mr. Charles Butler, Mr. Burton, Mr. Joshua Williams, Mr. Leake, and Mr. Challis. They are all wrong, according to Mr. Gray.[37]

Sweet continued in a footnote:

> [T]he fact that Mr. Gray holds heretical views on an important question of English real property law does not seem to be generally known, for the tendency of our judges is to regard him as orthodox, if not infallible.[38]

Sweet's position that there were earlier common law rules against perpetuities and that such rules voided hybrid conveyances attempting to effect the

32. Gray, *supra* note 25, at 27.

33. Perpetuities, *supra* note 3, at 321 (the quote appeared in the first edition of the book at page 209).

34. *See* Sweet, *supra* note 18; *see also* Charles Sweet, *The Monstrous Regiment of the Rule Against Perpetuities*, 18 Jurid. Rev. 132 (1906).

35. Sweet, *The Rule*, *supra* note 25, at 390.

36. *Id.* at 392 n.6.

37. C. S., *Limitations of Land to Unborn Generations*, 29 L.Q.R. 304, 304 (1913).

38. *Id.* at 304 n.2 (emphasis added).

creation of successive unbarrable life estates is most likely valid. In the view of preeminent English historians of the common law, like Sir William Holdsworth[39] and A. W. B. Simpson,[40] it could not be questioned that prior common law rules regarding conveyances tending to a perpetuity existed and were enforced by the courts. However, these rules were considerably different both in form and in time than the subsequent judicial invention of the modern RAP. Sweet sustains this proposition concerning the prior rules through a good portion of his scholarship.

> Mr. Gray ... den[ies] that there is any rule of the common law forbidding the limitation of remainders for life to successive generations; Mr. Gray contends that the rule is simply an instance of the modern Rule against Perpetuities. But in arriving at this conclusion Mr. Gray seems to me to have overlooked these passages in *Chudleigh's* case and Sheppard's Touchstone, which clearly show that the rule against the limitation of successive life estates to unborn generations existed at common law before the Statute of Uses, and cannot by any stretch of the imagination be said to be derived from the modern Rule against Perpetuities.[41]

On the point of the rule of double possibilities, Gray was accurate and correct that there was no case other than *Whitby* that specifically relied on such a doctrine to reach a decision.[42] The attitude of Sweet was not entirely negative with respect to Gray; there are notable instances in which he favorably cites Gray.[43]

Unlike many debates with respect to the validity of legal rules where the answer is seldom or never conclusively resolved, the weight of the then contemporary English authorities appears to support[44] the position of Sweet, assuming

39. *See* 7 Sir William Holdsworth, A History of English Law 197–214 (5th Impression 2003) (1925).

40. *See* A.W.B. Simpson, A History of the Land Law 210–12 (2d ed. 1986).

41. Sweet, *Perpetuities*, *supra* note 25, at 84.

42. Judge Kay, the principal jurist in *Whitby*, relied on the modern RAP in a subsequent comparable case. *See In re* Frost, (1890) 43 Ch.D. 246, 252–54.

43. For example, Mr. Sweet said the following about Gray a few years after his death: "Mr. Gray was perhaps a little impatient in dealing with anomalies arising from historical causes, but on such a question as the validity of 'trusts' without a beneficiary, his clear logical mind made him a useful guide, and we might do worse than follow him." Charles Sweet, *Restraints on Alienation II*, 33 L.Q.R. 342, 362 (1917).

44. See 35 Halsbury's Laws of England §§903, 485 (4th ed. 1981) for the position that the rule of *Whitby* accords with that as articulated by Sweet.

the conveyance is analogized as another more complicated contrivance to create another form of an unbarrable estate.

It should be noted that the Commonwealth of Massachusetts enacted a statute indicating that the matter of a possibility on a possibility was to be subject to the modern RAP,[45] thus supporting its favorite son, Gray. It is also noteworthy to point out that the English included a specific provision in the Property Act of 1925 repealing the rule of *Whitby*.[46] However, one would not ordinarily expect Parliament to enact a provision to invalidate the rule of *Whitby* unless it was the opinion and belief that such rule remained a valid statement of the law. Conversely, one could equally argue that such enactment constitutes an affirmation that there was no such common law rule, or if there was, it should not continue. The common law mind allows for the creative difference of opinion; indeed, it begets the ability to have support for almost any position.

Judge Jabez Fox

The late nineteenth and early twentieth century American critics of Gray's scholarship were considerably less confrontational as well as less persuasive than their English counterparts. Two principal exceptions were Jabez Fox[47] and Albert Martin Kales. Kales is by far the more important of the two. Fox expressed contrary views on only one occasion, whereas Kales was a scholar of standing on future interests. But it should be noted that Fox was not short of academic standing, as he was not only a judge but also a law professor at Boston University Law School.[48]

Fox objected to Gray's principal thesis that the rule should have been known as the Rule Against Remoteness rather than the Rule Against Perpetuities. Fox not only disagreed with Gray's nuanced application of the Rule Against Remoteness, but also with his concomitant proposition that alienability was merely an incident of the RAP rather than its object. Fox's article relied on a string of citations to express statements made by courts in a number of opin-

45. MASS. GEN. LAWS ch. 184, §3 (2009). This language has not changed since 1916. *See* Charles Sweet, *Contingent Remainders and Other Possibilities*, 27 YALE L.J. 977, 979 (1918). This enactment is somewhat like a paean to Gray.

46. Law of Real Property Act, 15 & 16 Geo. 5 1925, c. 20. §161 (Eng.).

47. *See* Jabez Fox, *The Criticism of Cases*, 6 HARV. L. REV. 195 (1892).

48. *See* David J. Seipp, *125th Anniversary Essay of Holmes's Path*, 77 B.U. L. REV. 515, 551 (1997).

ions. Somewhat surprising is the fact that among the cases cited by Fox is the much-debated *Whitby*. In Gray's response we find the paternalistic admonition that one should carefully distinguish the *dicta* from the *ratio decidenti* and that, by implication, the critic Fox had failed miserably in this respect.[49] Gray's discussion of the cases as well subsequent appellate reversal in two instances strongly suggests that Fox's scholarship is lacking.[50] Gray caustically noted that Fox's inability to understand the courts' rulings was akin to treating "rulings of the Court as mutterings of a Balaam's ass, absolutely true, but not presupposing any conscious intelligence in the creatures from whom they proceed."[51] Fox made the grave error of not including a complete quotation of Associate Justice Horace Gray Jr.'s opinion in the Massachusetts case of *Odell v. Odell*.[52] The omitted portion is exactly the signature statement of law (assuming one follows Gray's unique interpretation of such language) in support of Gray's enduring legal maxim.[53]

The quote as set forth by Fox is: "[T]he reason of the rule is, that to allow a contingent estate to vest at a more remote period would tend to create a perpetuity by making the estate inalienable."[54] Gray added the continued quotation omitted by Fox: "... for the title of the first taker would not be perfect, and until the happening of the contingency it could not be ascertained who was entitled, and the estate could not be alienated, even, as had been said, if all mankind should join in the conveyance."[55]

Gray's mantra consistently separated the matter of direct restraints on alienation from and distinct of the RAP.[56] Gregory S. Alexander clarified Gray's mantra.

> Gray divided all of the law of restraints on alienation into two categories, direct and indirect restraints (which involve what property lawyers now call "remotely vesting future interests"). The latter was the province of the Rule Against Perpetuities, while the former dealt

49. *See* John Chipman Gray, *Remoteness of Charitable Gifts*, 7 Harv. L. Rev. 406 (1894).

50. *Id.*

51. *Id.*

52. Odell v. Odell, 92 Mass. (10 Allen) 1, 5 (Mass. 1865).

53. *See* Gray, *supra* note 49, at 410.

54. Fox, *supra* note 47, at 196 (quoting *Odell*, 92 Mass. at 4).

55. Gray, *supra* note 49, at 411(quoting *Odell*, 92 Mass. at 4).

56. Professor Alexander explains to the uninitiated the legal problem of the RAP and the matter of remoteness of future interests in the same example that Professor Gray uses to sustain the separate function of the RAP. Gregory S. Alexander, Commodity & Propriety: Competing Visions of Property in American Thought 1776–1970, at 449 n.40 (1997).

> with restrictions that a previous owner placed on the power of subsequent owners to transfer property interests. It was this aspect of the law of restraints on alienation that was the locus of the most important conflict regarding the relationship between the alienability policy and the social vision of protectionism.[57]

Freedom of alienation can be a problem under both approaches. Gray's assertion as to the essential differentiation between the two is central to his position on the RAP. He desperately needed to create a mutually exclusive function for these two related concerns of the common law. This alleged differentiation constituted a necessary fiction and practical precondition to the establishment of his remoteness dogma. This differentiation is the formative as well as the centerpiece on which Gray's asserted function of the RAP depends.

> The judges, from the earliest of times, have been opposed to perpetuities. I do not know that any one has thoroughly investigated the cause, but the fact, I suppose, is undeniable.
>
> A perpetuity could arise in two ways, *first*, by taking from the owner the power to alienate property; *secondly*, by allowing interests to be created *in futuro*. In the beginning these ideas were confounded; gradually they were differentiated; the *first* gave rise to the Rule forbidding restraints on alienation, the *second* to the Rule against Perpetuities.
>
> When this differentiation occurred, it was inevitable that a further question should arise. Is the second rule merely a form of the first? Is a remote future interest objectionable only because for too long a period there may be no one who can give a good title; or is it objectionable also because the policy of the law does not allow interests so uncertain in value to hamper a present ownership? Under many circumstances, whichever principle was applied, the judgment would be the same; but, finally, cases arose which required a decision of this question, and in them it was held that the second rule was more than merely a form of the first, and that interests, although alienable, might yet be bad for remoteness; or, in other words, that the validity or nonvalidity of an interest did not depend solely on whether the alienability of the property was affected, but on whether the interest was upon a remote condition.[58]

57. *Id.* at 287–88. But Gray's formal and stringent separation of the problem of alienation as confronted either by direct or indirect restraints is neither necessary nor required.

58. Gray, *supra* note 49, at 409–10.

It now became clear to Gray that the phrase "even if all mankind should join in the conveyance" meant that the right of alienation exists, and thus the only reason for invalidating the conveyance rested solely on the matter of remoteness. That is not the only interpretation that one could reasonably apply to such phrase. It could mean, among other considerations, that even though fiduciaries could be appointed to represent the unborn classes or uncertain contingent beneficiaries so that a sale could proceed, the extent of the encumbrance that such future interests imposed on the possibility of a sale was so great as to negate the pragmatic likelihood that alienation of the property could ever take place. Thus, it is logical that the second rule is a derivative form of the first and depends on the degree of impracticability of alienation. Admittedly, we are searching for the mind of the medievalist jurists as they minted the legal structure, and reasonable speculation on either side cannot be satisfactorily validated. But alienation is the dominant concern throughout the historic development of property law during the entire late medieval period.

Returning to Gray's conflict with Fox, the omitted portion of the quote from *Odell* clearly meant a victory for Gray as to the ultimate function of the RAP; i.e., alienation or remoteness.[59] This conclusion is premised upon the view that *Odell* is the ultimate resource to resolve this ageless question. Yet, there is no question that Gray's answer became *the* answer for the legal establishment both in America and in England.[60]

Interestingly, in the same article, Fox attacked the scholarship of another icon of the common law, Oliver Wendell Holmes Jr. Fox disagreed with Holmes Jr.'s assertion regarding the legal basis for the imposition of liability on the master for the torts of the servant committed in the course of the master's business.[61] That Fox was both a judge and a law professor gave him standing and personal fortitude to confront and disagree with the two renowned masters of the common law.

---

59. Since Horace Jr. was the author of the opinion in *Odell*, one wonders whether the brothers Gray discussed this decision extensively at some later point, and further whether it is possible that the idea of "remoteness" was born through such interaction on this case. It might also explain John Chipman's recognition of Horace Jr. as the actual creator of the "rule of remoteness." *See* PERPETUITIES *supra* note 3, at 4 n.2. It must be noted that John Chipman also relied on William David Lewis' treatise on perpetuities as Lewis used the term remoteness of limitations extensively throughout his book. *See* WILLIAM DAVID LEWIS, A PRACTICAL TREATISE ON THE LAW OF PERPETUITIES OR REMOTENESS IN LIMITATIONS OF ESTATES (1843).

60. 7 HOLDSWORTH, *supra* note 39, at 215–16 ("Professor Gray is preeminently the historian of the modern rule against perpetuity.").

61. *See* Fox, *supra* note 47, at 197–200.

Albert Martin Kales

Gray's interaction with Albert Martin Kales is of a different quality. First and perhaps foremost, Kales was a graduate of Harvard Law School, class of 1899,[62] and after graduation he became an academic scholar. He was a student of Gray's[63] and apparently structured, whether intentionally or not, a good portion of his academic career on many of the same issues that became the principal focus of Gray's scholarship, and in particular, the entire matter of future interests.[64] Perhaps Kales was greatly influenced by Gray as a teacher and scholar during his period as a student at the Cambridge Law School.[65] Yet, it is equally conceivable that Kales was disappointed in the limitations or arbitrariness that frequently resulted in the denial of the grantor's desires because of the stringent application of the technical rules as proffered by Gray; this is particularly true of Kales as he matured as a scholar. In addition, the humanizations of principal authority figures, like Gray, may be a lifetime process; i.e., the slow process by which one reduces the personal perception of power of early authority figures.

Kales possessed great analytical skills and, equally important, the discipline to apply those skills. Kales displayed eclectic scholarly interests without any reduction in productivity;[66] he was exceptionally prolific. Also, he maintained active correspondence with Gray over a long period regarding the matter of future interests.[67] However, there may have been little personal friendship be-

---

62. *See* THE HARVARD LAW SCHOOL ASS'N, THE CENTENNIAL HISTORY OF THE HARVARD LAW SCHOOL 1817–1917, at 388 (1918) [hereinafter CENTENNIAL HISTORY] (listing Kales as a law graduate and a law professor).

63. See Albert Martin Kales, *The Next Step in the Evolution of the Case-Book*, 21 HARV. L. REV. 92, 100 (1907) wherein he refers to being a student in Gray's class. Professor Leach noted the personal relationship between Gray and Kales by the following comment: "Albert Kales was a student, if not a disciple, of Gray and like him was no mean hand at rationalization...." W. Barton Leach, *The Rule Against Perpetuities and Gifts to Classes*, 51 HARV. L. REV. 1329, 1350 (1938).

64. Is it possible that Kales did some research for Gray while a student at Harvard Law School? Since Roland Gray had graduated in 1898, a class prior to that of Kales in 1899, it is also possible that these two students had some interaction during law school.

65. During the late nineteenth century, the Harvard Law School was frequently referred to as the Cambridge Law School.

66. See, for example, Kales' engaging analytical destruction of the traditional distinctions between vested and contingent remainders. Albert Martin Kales, *A Modern Dialogue Between Doctor and Student on the Distinction Between Vested and Contingent Remainders*, 24 L.Q.R. 301 (1908).

67. Indeed, they had significant correspondence over a decade, which is maintained at the Harvard Law School. *See* CENTENNIAL HISTORY, *supra* note 62, at 221.

tween the two, particularly from Gray's side. Their interchange was, perhaps, more analogous to an intellectual fight with Kales challenging the master Gray. Occasionally, a teacher is "benefited" with the presence of a student of the law who is exceptionally talented and tends to engage in a convoluted form of internecine warfare during regular classroom discussions. This type of interaction is seldom productive or educational.

Obviously, one cannot assert that the above describes Kales' behavior as a student in Gray's class, but there is no doubt that his postgraduate confrontation with Gray and the existing enigmas of the law of property are consistent with this possibility. Recall, Gray was in the final years of a great academic career, whereas Kales was filled with the energy and ambition attendant to the process of building a new career. The synergy between the two set up a sort of cat and mouse game. While Kales would chew on the cheese of Gray's scholarship, Gray would seldom pounce publicly on Kales' concerns.[68] By not responding, Gray assumed and/or desired that Kales would move on to other subjects. Yet, it is equally likely that at this time Gray's dual career of an academic who was also fully engaged in the practice of law did not allow sufficient time for dealing with such consuming and constraining scholastic entanglements.

Kales' achievements as a scholar and his iconoclastic tendencies were well known by the faculty of Harvard Law School. Indeed, he provocatively quibbled with two of their verboten signature propositions that had become intimately associated with the quality of legal education as delivered by the renowned law school at Cambridge. First, Kales challenged the idea of a national casebook[69] as being the final product in the evolution of legal education because, as he noted, each jurisdiction of the respective states necessarily added its own unique legal twist to the existing common law doctrines.[70] Kales' scholarship was leading him to the recognition of the emergence of an American jurisprudence on common law issues that did not necessarily require or involve a definitive reliance on matters Hail Britannica. It is interesting to note his criticism of the national case-

---

68. Included in the history of Harvard Law School are references to Gray's correspondence with Kales that are cited as part of Gray's scholarly record.

69. Kales, *supra* note 63. Because Kales was directly attacking the casebook mantra of the Harvard Law School, he vehemently emphasized that he was speaking only for himself. *See id.* at 92 n.1 ("The views expressed [herein] must not be taken as representing those of any other member of the faculty of which [Kales] is a member, much less as being the foundation of any action by the school in the scope and subject-matter of its teaching.").

70. In this respect, he published a treatise on future interests for the State of Illinois. *See* Albert M. Kales, Estates, Future Interests and Illegal Conditions and Restraints in Illinois (1920) [hereinafter Kales, Future Interests].

book questions whether the principles of real property emanating, for example, from Gray's casebook can fully apprize a new lawyer of the law of future interests in the State of Illinois. Kales succinctly answers the question: "If this experience and experiment are worth anything, I have no hesitation in declaring that it is high time we ceased pretending that the mastery of Gray's Cases on the subjects of future interests is a quick asset in Illinois."[71] Kales is far short of calling for the development of an American jurisprudence that supplants or eliminates the English version of the common law, but he implicitly recognizes the vast number of cases arising in the various states arriving at positions that are not necessarily consonant with the dictates of the English authorities. Also, each of the respective states was starting to judicially modify, as well as codify, unique aspects of the common law as reflecting its emerging norms.

Kales' discussion about the changes from 1870 to 1907, particularly the number of reported decisions of the various jurisdictions, suggests that each separate state jurisdiction was in the process of attaining its own mature legal system.

> There was at that time, perhaps more nearly than at any time since, what may have been called a body of American law, *i.e.*, rules of the common law which all the states together adopted, and all alike were apt to follow, but which no one state had wholly applied in the reported cases. Those conditions dictated the present character of the Harvard Law School case-book. That they have gone by for many states needs no demonstration. That they are rapidly disappearing for other states every decade will testify. With the passing of these conditions must pass the Harvard Law School case-book in its present form.[72]

He further clarified his thesis in a latter portion of the same article:

> [T]he law is the body of rules which are enforced in [each of the respective states'] jurisdiction, and the original sources of that law are not to be found in the English reports, or in the reports of other states, or even in the mixture which the present Harvard Law School case-book contains. They are to be found in the reports of the given jurisdiction just as truly and just as clearly as the sources of what Professor Langdell in 1871 called the common law were to be found for the most part in the English cases. The reports in each of such jurisdictions have be-

71. Kales, *supra* note 63, at 104.

72. *Id.* at 106 (footnote omitted).

> come the principal, and for a very large body of rules the only, original sources of the law of that jurisdiction.[73]

Kales also attacked the pristine establishment of the academic scholars in control of the law school who did not also engage in some limited form of law practice.[74] He was very careful to exclude from the description of desirable legal practice for the academic scholar responsibility that involved actual client care. Because the *Harvard Law Review* published both of his relatively provocative articles, it was only natural that some members of the Harvard faculty found that an immediate response was obligatory. In separate addenda to both of these articles, Ezra Ripley Thayer[75] and Eugene Wambaugh[76] politely defended the institutional stance of the law school. The Harvard Law Review appears to have adopted a peculiar institutional attack on Kales. On at least three separate occasions, the Review provided esteemed professors of the law school the opportunity of instantly criticizing Kales by addendums published to his articles.[77]

Kales' article regarding the next step in the evolution of the casebook was sufficiently provocative in that it exasperated some of the academic leaders of legal education, who promptly organized a panel[78] on the topic to provide needed institutional assurance that the final step in casebook technology had been reached.

Kales also applied his brand of objective analysis to various aspects of Gray's scholarship on future interests. Without stating the obvious, Kales possessed

---

73. *Id.* at 113 (emphasis removed).

74. Albert Martin Kales, *Should the Law Teacher Practice Law?* 25 Harv. L. Rev. 253 (1911).

75. *Id.* at 269–73 (note of Ezra Ripley Thayer).

76. *See* Kales, *supra* note 63, at 118–19 (brief note of Eugene Wambaugh).

77. *See supra* notes 75, 76; *infra* note 87.

78. Professor Steve Sheppard explains, in an excellent article, the critical response of the academy to Kales' criticism:

> Langdell's disciples did not enthusiastically greet these transformations. A 1907 panel of the Association of American Law Schools fired the first salvos responding to Kales's [sic] article of that same year. Penn dean William Draper Lewis, Columbia dean George Kirchway, and Harvard dean James Barr Ames all attacked the idea that law schools should provide "knowledge" rather than the "power of legal reasoning."

Steve Sheppard, *Casebooks, Commentaries, and Curmudgeons: An Introductory History of Law in the Lecture Hall*, 82 Iowa L. Rev. 547, 617 (1997). In addition to the deans named by Professor Sheppard, the following other persons also participated on the panel: John D. Lawson, William E. Waltz, Ernest G. Lorenzen, George H. Fall, Hollis R. Bailey, Albert H. Walker, and Albert M. Kales. *See* 31 A.B.A. Proc. 1012 (1907); Centennial History, *supra* note 62, at 371.

the institutional ingredients as it related to intellect and discipline, although unintentionally, to threaten or raise the ire of Gray both personally and professionally. Gray was the reigning authority, fully vested in the sinecure position as the American master of future interests. Perhaps Kales' academic thrusts were also a convoluted mechanism by which he sought the master's approval for his innovations and proposed solutions to some of the future interest quagmires and/or enigmas. The framework of their relationship did not naturally make for a likely close friendship. The extended academic correspondence between the two of them was so significant that it is treated as part of Gray's scholarship record.[79]

The public disagreement between Gray and Kales was mostly of a professional nature; seldom was it consistently personal or contentious. As noted, Kales was a prolific scholar[80] who addressed an eclectic category of legal issues.[81] Kales brought substance to the understanding of future interests, naturally rejected formalistic answers, and identified certain issues which he believed that Gray had not fully answered.[82] Kales' principal disagreement with Gray throughout their professional interactions was a rejection of Gray's determination of an interest based solely on the formal structural language of the conveyance rather than on the intent of the grantor. Kales focused more on the overall personal intent of the grantor and questioned Gray's so-called robotic interpretive technique, which strove for legal consistency at the expense of any concern for the determination of the grantor's intent. Gray treasured consistency in rules of law, whereas Kales sought satisfaction in the enforcement of the grantor's wishes. Kales explains how his thinking differs from Gray's.

> [T]he learned author [Gray] seems to fall away from his own premises. In § 104 he puts the case of a gift "to A for life, remainder to B

79. *See* Centennial History, *supra* note 62, at 202.

80. A partial listing of Kales' extensive scholarship is set forth in *id.* at 307–10.

81. Among the many legal publications Kales addressed the following issues: (1) Kales, *supra* note 63 (questioning the evolution of the national casebook and suggesting that casebooks should be tailored according to the law of each particular state); (2) Kales, *supra* note 74 (questioning whether law teachers should be excluded from practicing law while teaching, but specifically limiting teachers' involvement with client care); (3) Kales, Future Interests, *supra* note 70 (exploring future interest law in the State of Illinois); (4) *Contingent Future Interests After a Particular Estate of Freehold*, 21 L.Q.R. 118 (1905); *Vested And Contingent Remainders*, 8 Colum. L. Rev. 245 (1908); *Several Problems of Gray's Rule Against Perpetuities, Second Edition*, 20 Harv. L. Rev. 192 (1906) [hereinafter *Several Problems*].

82. *See Several Problems*, *supra* note 81.

> and his heirs, but if B dies before the termination of the particular estate, then to C and his heirs." Of course the remainder to B is, by his definition, vested, though actually subject to a condition precedent to its taking effect in possession.... Yet in § 105 the learned author intimates that "if the law looked on vested and contingent interests with an impartial eye, it would seem that such remainders should be held contingent.... But the preference of the law for vested interests has prevented this view being adopted." This is confusing. If he means that from the modern point of view the remainder ought to be held contingent, he is correct; but his original hypothesis is that the distinction between vested and contingent remainders is not a rational one from the purely modern point of view. The statement that the preference of the law for vested interests makes it vested, implies that it is held vested as the illogical relaxation of a general rule by which it would be contingent; whereas the fact is that the result is according to the general rule of law (doubtless of feudal origin), and is no doubt entirely consistent with the principles and reasoning upon which that rule was founded,—whatever they may be.[83]

Kales looks at the substance of B's plight as requiring that B must in fact survive A to take, and not on the sequential formal arrangement of the terms of conveyance; whereas Gray follows a mechanical interpretation and disregards the substance of the language utilized as well as the fact that B's interest is, in reality, subject to a condition precedent. In this analysis, Gray is following traditional analysis of the common law. But the perspective of Gray increases the likelihood of following a consistent legal path for the interpretation of conveyances. In this sense, certainty and consistency are achieved, but obviously at the expense of the alleged grantor's subjective intent. This philosophical difference between the two carries throughout their scholarship. For example, Gray fixates on the goal of certitude by consistently applying established legal rules; whereas Kales remains frustrated by the illogical nature of such a legal system, particularly when such rigid application of rules defeats the alleged unambiguous intent of the grantor. Kales searches for a rational legal system and asserts that the rules as applied by Gray are frequently a product of historic accidents; i.e., freezing some portions of the opinions of common law judges as if they created transcendent principles of law rather than provided temporary solutions or rationalizations to complex social problems.

---

83. *Id.* at 192–93.

Gray formally responded in print on only two occasions to Kales' issues. The first response[84] of Gray occurred when Kales questioned the application of the RAP to a class gift by way of a devise to the grandchildren of A, a living person, to be paid to them at age twenty-five. This simple fact pattern has been a point of contention for scholars throughout the history of the RAP. Under the problem presented by Gray in section 121(b)[85] of his second edition, A has one child living at the time of the testator's death. Kales questioned how this devise to the grandchildren can be invalid as to the living grandchild, whereas Gray indicated that unless the devise was divided into two separate bequests (a devise to those living at A's death and a second gift to those born after A's death), the entire gift is void. According to Kales, such bequest is good to the grandchildren who are living at the death of A, and it fails with respect to the other grandchildren who are born subsequent to A's death. Kales intuitively approached what became the rule of convenience as a technique to avoid the RAP, but without any firm commitment to such rule or its application.[86] It appears that Gray did not wish to engage Kales on this issue or enter into a dialogue with Kales on the possibility that the devise constitutes two separate gifts. As Gray explained:

> The first part of Mr. Kales's [sic] article is devoted to demolishing a "conceivable" adversary who is supposed to say that the devise consists of two gifts. There is somewhere in the books—I believe it is in the Kentucky reports—a case where a judge, irritated past endurance by the stupidity of the plaintiff, exclaims, "And what has this blooming geranium of a plaintiff have to say?" The appellation is a trifle vague, but it somehow fits this "conceivable" gentleman. He is a foeman quite unworthy of Mr. Kales's [sic] skillful rapier. I certainly shall not come to his assistance. Let him be anathema.
>
> The true view is, of course that there is a single gift with qualification, modification, or proviso attached.[87]

---

84. Albert Martin Kales, *Vested Gifts to a Class and the Rule Against Perpetuities*, 19 Harv. L. Rev. 598, 604 (1906) (note of John C. Gray). Some years later, Kales expressed the rule of class gifts as actually adopted and without additional comment in his 1920 treatise on the law of future interests in Illinois. *See* Kales, Future Interests, *supra* note 70, at 774–75.

85. *See* Perpetuities, *supra* note 3, at 605–07 (previously cited as section 121(b) in the second edition).

86. Indeed, Gray cites Kales' suggestion as the source of his criticism of *Kevern v. Williams*, (1832) 5 Sim. 171, a case noted for extending the doctrine of *Andrews v. Partington* to grandchildren. *See* Perpetuities, *supra* note 3, at 606 n.5. *Cf.* Morris & Leach, *supra* note 10, at 121.

87. Gray responded in an addendum to Kales' article. *See* Kales, *supra* note 84, at 604.

After this biting comment, Gray responded and agreed that there existed a serious question, but then he chose not to take a position on the proposed solution of Kales. As Gray cryptically stated, "It seems a troublesome and difficult question. I feel no present call to enter upon it."[88] Gray was clearly committed to one answer on the application of the RAP to class gifts. He was a strong advocate for the enforcement of the class gift rule: if one member of a class might violate the perpetuity period the entire gift fails, even to those members who otherwise comply with such period.[89] Gray's response to the solution proffered by Kales does not appear to be one of respect or admiration for Kales. Yet, Gray reluctantly and indirectly acknowledges Kales as a worthy challenger who possesses a "skillful rapier" and cites him as pointing out the problem.

The Gray and Kales Dialogue

The next academic interchange[90] between Gray and Kales reveals a more respectful attitude on the part of Gray toward Kales. And, this later response probably constituted the last law review article that Gray published as he retired from Harvard Law School abruptly in February of 1913 after suffering a "sharp illness" earlier that year.[91] His scholarship activities might have continued, presumably at a much reduced capacity for two more years inasmuch as the third edition of *Perpetuities* was published in 1915, the year of his death.[92] Notwithstanding the possibility that stress and time may have taken their toll on Gray, the energy and creative talents that he demonstrated for over forty years or more, as well as his enormous commitment to quality scholarship and the logical presentation of his arguments, remain of highest quality and unique authority (despite one's disagreement). This last published law review article subsequently became Appendix L in *Perpetuities*.[93]

The last issue over which the two academic masters of future interests formally debated related to the validity of a general power of appointment exer-

88. *Id.* at 605.

89. *See* PERPETUITIES, *supra* note 3, at 394.

90. *See* Albert Martin Kales, *General Powers and the Rule Against Perpetuities*, 26 HARV. L. REV. 64 (1912).

91. *See* CENTENNIAL HISTORY, *supra* note 62, at 213.

92. Professor Gray died on February 25, 1915, slightly more than two years after his resignation from the faculty.

93. *See* Kales, *supra* note 90; *see also* PERPETUITIES, *supra* note 3, at 809–22; John Chipman Gray, *General Testamentary Powers and the Rule Against Perpetuities*, 26 HARV. L. REV. 720 (1913).

cisable solely by will. The question presented was: whether, in respect to a solely testamentary power, for purposes of the RAP, the vesting period starts with the date of the donor's creation of the power or at the date of its exercise by the donee. There is a direct and uncomplicated disagreement on this issue by these two masters of future interests.[94] Gray eventually expressed personal friendship and appreciation of Kales' work on future interests.

> My learned friend, Professor Kales, in an article which he kindly communicated to me, and has now published in this Review.... Mr. Kales's [sic] suggestions on the law deserve so much respect, and to me personally have been so often valuable, that I am moved to say a word or two why I cannot adopt them in this matter.[95]

There is no question that both agreed that where the donee has the power to exercise, either by deed or by will, the time is measured from the date of execution of such power. This agreement is based on the fact that the donee could take such property for her own benefit at any time; thus, having an equivalent fee interest. However, with a power exercisable solely by will, Gray asserted that the time is measured from the date of the creation of said power. Gray explained the difference is due to the critical fact that in the instance of a testamentary power, the donee does not have a personal right to enjoy property during his or her lifetime. Gray amplified:

> But a man cannot, in the eye of the law, be at the same time alive and dead. So long as he is alive, the condition necessary for the exercise of the power is not fulfilled, and after he is dead he cannot be an appointee. And this is not only so as a metaphysical necessity. When a donee is given a general power by deed on his marriage, the creator of the power means to give the nominal donee on his marriage the absolute interest in the property; he does not mean to delegate his own right to make a limitation. But when he gives a testamentary power, he distinctly means that the donee shall have only a delegated authority; he does not mean at any time, or on the performance of any condition, to make a gift to the donee himself.[96]

Thus, the testamentary power is to be tested for the RAP vesting purposes from the date of its creation. Kales disagreed with Gray's position[97] that the date of

94. *See* Kales, *supra* note 90; Gray, *supra* note 93.

95. Gray, *supra* note 93, at 720 (footnote omitted).

96. *Id.* at 722.

97. *See* PERPETUITIES, *supra* note 3, at 513–16, 515 n.2.

the creation of a testamentary power is critical for vesting purposes of the RAP.[98] Mere possession of a testamentary power pragmatically denies the donee the option of direct personal enjoyment of the assets. However, that is not true of a general power exercisable *inter vivos* by deed or other written instrument. In the latter circumstance, the donee possesses the right at any time to take such assets for her personal enjoyment. For Gray, this was the principal distinction by which the former was most likely invalid and the latter most likely valid for purposes of measuring the vesting time for the RAP. Each of them had some judicial support for their respective positions.[99]

Kales attempted to show the similarity of the interests of a donee of a testamentary power with that of an owner of property at death by the following analysis:

> What, then, is there that an owner of property can do in the way of disposing of his property at the moment of his death which the donee of a general power to appoint by will cannot accomplish? Nothing! *Ergo*, the donee of a general power to appoint by will, if that power be valid in its inception, is, at the moment when he may exercise the power, practically the owner.[100]

Shortly after these articles were published, Kales received support in another article by J. L. Thorndike.[101]

This disagreement regarding the application of the RAP to a testamentary power of appointment has been resolved in America largely in favor of Gray's analysis.[102] Indeed, one authority noted the resolution of this issue was due, in

---

98. *See* Kales, *supra* note 90, at 69.

99. *See* Rous v. Jackson, (1885) 29 Ch.D. 521, 527; *Re* Powell's Trusts, (1869) 39 L.J. Ch. 188. Although *Rous v. Jackson* overruled *Re Powell's Trusts,* Gray's continued support of *Powell's Trusts* and his influence on American jurisprudence of future interests resulted in his views being adopted as the majority position. For a discussion of the rule in England, see Gould, *General Testamentary Pores and the Rule Against Perpetuities*, 58 L.Q.R. 400 (1942).

100. *See* Kales, *supra* note 90, at 67.

101. J.L. Thorndike, *General Powers and Perpetuities*, 27 Harv. L. Rev. 705, 709 (1914).

102. *See* Wayne R. Bettner, *The Rule Against Perpetuities As Applied To Powers Of Appointment*, 27 Va. L. Rev. 149 (1940); 3 Herbert T. Tiffany & Basil Jones, Tiffany Real Property §713 (2009) (1939). Although the rule is different in England, Gray's analysis represents the overwhelming view in America. *See also* 6 American Law of Property §24.34 (1952). Notwithstanding, it is interesting to note that the assets subject to an exercised testamentary general power of appointment are largely subject to the claims of the creditors of the donee in America. *See* 2 Simes & Smith, The Law of Future Interests §945 (2003); *accord* Drye v. United States, 528 U.S. 49 (1999). It is appropriate to recall that remarkable wisdom of the genius of one Ralph Waldo Emerson, who thrust upon the mortal condition of man that hum-

part, to "... the special deference [the courts paid] to the views of Professor Gray, [which] ... prevented any independent judgment on the part of the court."[103] Game, set, and match for Gray; but the victory is, in some respects, by default because some of the judicial decisions were greatly influenced by Gray's scholarship and the fact that he was recognized as the reigning authority in the matter of the application of the RAP.[104]

The English and Irish courts have long followed the rule that the validity of the execution of a testamentary general power of appointment is viewed from the date of execution or appointment rather than the date of creation because of the precedent of *Rous v. Jackson*.[105] Morris and Leach have closely analyzed that case and have identified what they believe to have been a serious misinterpretation of the principal authority relied upon by the court in *Rous*.[106] There are only two instances[107] noted herein in which Gray vigorously rejected a proposition of the English case law, and such rejections were always to sharpen the cutting edge of the RAP.

Kales stands out as an unusual scholar on future interests and always remained a dedicated student of Gray as a person and scholar. In the second edition of Kales' book on future interests, he not only dedicated the book to the Master Gray, but added, "He was the better teacher for being in active practice; he was the better lawyer from the learning which came from teaching law."[108] For fourteen years (1902–1916), Kales taught at Northwestern Law School before accepting an appointment to Harvard Law School where he taught for only one year (1916–1917). Unfortunately, Kales rejected an offer for a permanent position as the law school administration refused to allow him to engage in a limited appellate practice.[109]

---

bling, intemperate, but nevertheless accurate, observation regarding "consistency as being the hobgoblin of little minds." That proposition was never to be a problem for the judiciary.

103. Bettner, *supra* note 102, at 175.

104. *See* MORRIS & LEACH, *supra* note 10, at 147 ("The present authors believe that the sounder view is that of Gray and the American courts which have followed him.").

105. Rous v. Jackson, (1885) 29 Ch.D. 521.

106. *See* MORRIS & LEACH, *supra* note 10, at 148–49.

107. *See* Whitby v. Mitchell, (1889) 42 Ch.D. 494; *Rous*, 29 Ch.D. 521.

108. KALES, FUTURE INTERESTS, *supra* note 70, at iii.

109. Kales was a natural successor to Gray, but in view of his idiosyncrasies, found it necessary to refuse the offer as Harvard would not grant permission for him to carry a personal case load of six appellate cases a year. This was critical to Kales as he believed practice made for a better teacher and scholar. He died in 1922 of typhoid fever. *See* Albert Martin Kales, Correspondence on The Rule Against Perpetuities, 1904–1913: Finding Aid, Harvard Law School Library, http://oasis.lib.harvard.edu/oasis/deliver/~law00184 (last visited Oct. 25, 2009).

Clearly, Kales was not of a quotidian nature and he may have been possessed, with good reason, with an excess of his academic importance. Kales had a diverse legal career as an academician, practitioner, and scholar—much like his ideal mentor and sometime antagonist Gray. That Kales was of the finest intellect was not to be questioned, but whether his personality was of the kind with which one would choose to professionally cohabit, either as a long time colleague on the faculty at Harvard Law School or as a personal friend, is a separate question upon which the record at this point in time is far too sparse for one to speculate. Kales then decided, perhaps somewhat abruptly, to return to private practice in Chicago.[110]

> Mr. Kales has for many years filled an unusual position of service to Harvard Law School, by subjecting its theories of law and law teaching to continuous and beneficial criticism. For years he carried on with John Chipman Gray a correspondence about future interests, now in the possession of the library, out of which came several articles on both sides. Professor Kales' attack on the non-practicing academician and the national case-book have rallied members of the Faculty to the defense of these well-tested traditions. Whether teaching in Cambridge or regrettably absent *in partibus infedelium* he has always put Harvard Law School on its mettle.[111]

Although Kales made significant contributions to the clarification of future interests and many other aspects of the law, it is somewhat surprising that he is, perhaps, most remembered for the design of the judicial merit selection plan along with Roscoe Pound and John H. Wigmore.[112]

The essential difference between Professor Gray and Kales relates to different choices each made with respect to the interpretation of legal instruments.

110. He argued at least one tax case before the Supreme Court shortly before his death in 1922. *See* Merchants' Loan & Trust Co. v. Smietanka, 255 U.S. 509 (1921).

111. Centennial History, *supra* note 62, at 221–22. Like so many personal elements in the history of faculty life, the underlying story revealing the principal reasons for what appears to be an impetuous departure remain sealed in the minds of those members of the faculty now deceased. Admittedly, he was by personal proclivity an agitator-provocateur in the true sense of the word. Since this description of Kales was written during the period that he had served on the faculty, the description may be trenchant with hidden meaning. *See id.* ("... he has always put Harvard Law School on its mettle.").

112. *See, e.g.*, Peter D. Webster, *Selection and Retention of Judges*, 23 Fla. St. U. L. Rev. 1, 23–24 (1995); Michael R. Belknap, *From Pound to Harley: The Founding of AJS*, 72 Judicature 78, 84–85 (1988); Jeffrey D. Jackson, *The Selection of Judges in Kansas: A Comparison of Systems*, 69 J. Kan. B. Ass'n 32, 34 (Jan. 2000).

Without question, the dominant concern of Kales was securing the donor's obvious intent at the cost of consistency. Gray, on the other hand, was most committed to establishing consistent legal principles at the cost of defeating the grantor's intent.

Sidebar: W. Barton Leach on the Class Gift Rule

The application of the RAP to class gifts has created a most painful situation in that grandchildren who are alive at the time of the gift might be denied their bequest under the precedent of *Leake v. Robison*.[113] Unless the rule of convenience closes the class, the inclusion in the class of any member who would possibly violate the RAP eliminates the gift to the entire class, including those of the class who do not violate the rule.

This issue regarding a painful application of the RAP to class gifts drew the ire and piercing scholarship of W. Barton Leach.[114] The purpose of Leach's article on class gifts was explicitly stated.

> It is the thesis of this article that this rule is practically and analytically unsound; that no reason for the rule exists and that nothing which could be dignified by the name of a rationalization has ever been suggested; that the rule is anomalous in the light of analogies well established in English and American law; that, so far as it is a part of American law, it has become so through a mechanical citation of English authorities without independent examination of the problem involved; and that it is high time that American courts and legislatures began the process of expunging this doctrine from our law.[115]

Somewhat in the similar vein of Kales, Leach was asking, several decades later, for an independent American jurisprudence that would be more responsive to the settlor's unambiguous intent and less thoughtlessly subject to the hegemony of the "petrified rules" of the English authorities. Without a doubt, it was the outstanding scholarship of Leach that sparked the movement to revise the RAP in a way that was intended to reduce its quotient of irrationality; not, however, to make it more "rational." Leach and Gray were of two differ-

---

113. Leake v. Robinson, (1817) 2 Mer. 363.
114. *See* Leach, *supra* note 63.
115. *Id.* at 1329–30.

ent universes: Leach, a radical overseer of the pompous, illogical inconsistencies that are inherent aspects of this most revered rule of the common law; whereas Gray, a nineteenth-century scholar of exacting legal scholasticism, relied exclusively on the kernels of wisdom offered by the English judiciary. In this process, Gray's personal and professional predisposition found profound satisfaction in the imperial edicts formally issued by the common law decisions. These decisions deeply resonated with Gray and his need to deliver a standard of law that demanded strict accountability over all other considerations. He affirmed the English guillotine-like application of the RAP that needlessly eliminated the interest of innocent beneficiaries. Gray's generally intense support for a draconian application of *Leake* is stated with "dogmatic severity" and driven home by Gray's observation that "[i]t is immaterial that some persons are in esse who, should they reach twenty-five, would be entitled to share, for none of them may reach twenty-five, and the whole class may ultimately be composed of persons who are not born at the testator's death."[116] Gray's enforcement of a rather rigid rule emanating from *Leake*[117] moved Leach to question how Gray could support such a painful exorcism of the intended beneficiaries. Leach admonished: "It is hard to believe that Gray could have been very happy in writing [the aforementioned] sentence."[118]

Leach cited with approval the creative manner by which Chief Justice Doe of the New Hampshire Supreme Court avoided the painful and questionable results flowing from a blind application of *Leake.*[119] Doe, as previously noted, saved the devise by simply reducing the stated age for taking the distribution of the residuary bequest from the date when the youngest grandchild reaches forty years to the date when the youngest grandchild reaches twenty-one years.[120] Gray considered such inventive manipulation by Doe to be a "radical departure from the law as previously held."[121] It is interesting to note that Gray had

116. *Id.* at 1349 (citing John Chipman Gray, The Rule Against Perpetuities 394 (3d ed. 1915)).

117. *See* Perpetuities, *supra* note 3, at 394.

118. Leach, *supra* note 63, at 1349.

119. *Id.* at 1344, 1349.

120. *See* Edgerly v. Barker, 31 A. 900 (N.H. 1891); Morris & Leach, *supra* note 10, at 52 (noting that English authorities also adopted a similar solution to that of Chief Justice Doe by statute); Law of Real Property Act, 15 & 16 Geo. 5 1925, c. 20. §163(1) (Eng.). The English also codified relief for class gifts in the Perpetuities and Accumulations Act of 1964, s. 4. See also discussion of class gifts and the statutory modifications in D. J. Hayton, Hayton & Marshall, Commentary and Cases on the Law of Trusts and Equitable Remedies 199–200 (11th ed. 2001).

121. *See* Perpetuities, *supra* note 3, at 414–15.

separately excoriated this same judge for the absence of any legal authority regarding the same decision in a prior law review article that subsequently became Appendix G of his perpetuity treatise.[122] Despite the resulting defeat of the decedent's clearly defined intent, there was to be no deviation from the law of the English authorities as deciphered by Gray that somehow saved a bequest from the "peremptory command" of the RAP.

> The Rule against Perpetuities is not a rule of construction, but a peremptory command of law. It is not, like a rule of construction, a test, more or less artificial, to determine intention. Its object is to defeat intention. Therefore every provision in a will or settlement is to be construed as if the Rule did not exist, and then to the provision so construed the Rule is to be remorselessly applied.[123]

The issue of class gifts generated complex problems as it related to the application of the RAP. A series of rules and exceptions evolved over the last century by which some of the more egregious class gift problems were resolved by a combination of creative judicial engineering (rule of convenience)[124] and/or legislative repair.[125]

Endgame

Gray was the reigning chief oracle on the matter of future interests and the RAP until his death and for a extended period thereafter. During his life, there was no one in legal education that had attained his status or hegemony on the RAP. And, it is clear that all subsequent discussions of future interests, up to

---

122. *See* John Chipman Gray, *General and Particular Intent in Connection with the Rule Against Perpetuities*, 9 Harv. L. Rev. 242 (1899), *reprinted in* Perpetuities, *supra* note 3, at 752, app'x G.

123. Perpetuities, *supra* note 3, at 599 (footnote omitted).

124. *See* Morris & Leach, *supra* note 10, at 110 (describing the invention of the rule of convenience in connection with class gifts—the effect of this rule "is often to defeat the intention of the testator by excluding persons whom he meant to benefit. On the other hand, they sometimes have the effect of validating a gift which at first sight appears to be too remote") (footnote omitted); *see also* J.H. C. Morris, *The Rule Against Perpetuities and the Rule in* Andrews v. Partington, 70 L.Q.R. 61 (1954); E. H. Burn, Cheshire & Burn's Modern Law of Real Property 325 (16th ed. 2000) (explaining the similar impact of the class closing rule as possibly saving a portion of the designated class from the bite of the RAP).

125. *See, e.g.*, Perpetuities and Accumulation Act, 1964, c.55, §4 (Eng.). For an efficient discussion of class gifts and the RAP, see generally, Jesse Dukeminier, *A Modern Guide to Perpetuities*, 74 Cal. L. Rev. 1867, 1891–95 (1986).

the present time, one way or another, play through the prism of his scholarship. Quite an impressive achievement! Gray secured that which he desired: recognition, dominance, respect, status, power, a dedicated community of disciples, as well as an acclaimed position of lasting legal authority. The academy recognized and anointed a perpetual icon. His views on what the law of future interests should be, and the RAP in particular, became, in fact, the law enforced. In this respect, Gray, most likely, exceeded his most improbable dream.

Chapter 10

Americanization of the Rule Against Perpetuities

> Laws frequently continue in force long after the circumstances which first gave occasion to them, and which could alone render them reasonable, are no more.[1]

This chapter will demonstrate beyond per adventure the acclaim that Gray rightly secured in the international community as a common law scholar extraordinaire for his work on the scope and application of the Rule Against Perpetuities (RAP). Gray's dogmatic interpretation of the RAP as well as his exceptional scholarly achievement in becoming the lasting arbitrator of the history, purpose, scope, and application of the RAP must be fully acknowledged and celebrated. It was a supreme lifetime achievement. Moreover, the hegemony of his scholarship continues up to the present, though only the learned graduates of law school are fully apprised of the rule.

Among the various components of the RAP that Gray affirmed, emphasized, and insisted upon as constituting the essential ingredients of the rule are:

1. The purpose of the rule is concerned exclusively with remoteness of vesting in interest;
2. The rule is not about restraints on alienation;
3. The rule must be remorselessly applied;
4. The function of the rule is to defeat the intent of the grantor;
5. The rule has one simple and specific mathematical answer: in the matter of perpetuities questions, there is no room for judicial discretion;
6. One must consider, in applying the rule, any combination of possible events that preclude a determination that an interest will or will not vest within the prescribed period;

1. Adam Smith, An Inquiry into the Nature and Causes of the Wealth of Nations 166 (Encyclopedia Britannica, Inc. 1989) (1776).

7. The rule was invented to deal with indestructible executory interests and does not have any common law antecedent;
8. If executory interests were held to be destructible like contingent remainders, it is unlikely the RAP would have been invented;[2]
9. It is, as English case law has held, to be presumed in applying the RAP that women of any age are capable of having children.

These propositions are some of the more definitive views of Gray which through his scholarship became the binding guidance on all perpetuities questions. Over the years since the publication of *The Rule Against Perpetuities*, jurists and academics have been mesmerized, entranced, guided, and, more appropriately, dictated by his teachings on perpetuities issues. In short, Gray permanently branded his own personal mind-set on the rule. Notably, strict enforcement thereafter was demanded. This unique and lasting creation of Gray has been passed down to generations of successor academic disciples who passionately desire to preserve this ancient rule of law rule despite the fact that it suffers from the absence of any contemporary objective. It survives and continues as an inheritance of the past. There never has been an empirical study of the RAP's impact on society in modern times. The visual observations of the decadent large manors owned by way of primogeniture (owned in kind and not in trusts), which had become judicially observed, gave way to the modern and highly complex management of assets in trusts. The question now is whether the assumptions of some academics as to the presumed, theoretical social, economic, and political benefits of the RAP are a sufficient basis for continuance of the rule. Ultimately, we are captured by past beliefs embedded in modern minds; the continuation of the RAP is proof thereof.

Several scholars have been less impressed with the gospel of Gray, but one alone stopped the train in the last century. Although never calling for the repeal of the RAP, W. Barton Leach launched a fierce attack on imperfections of Gray's thesis; including, but certainly not limited to, the (1) all-or-nothing rule, (2) fertile octogenarian rule, (3) unborn widow rule, (4) dead hand, and (5) remorseless application. He alone lit the fires of discontent on the perfection of the perpetuities rule according to Gray.[3]

---

2. *See* John Chipman Gray, The Rule Against Perpetuities 153 (Roland Gray ed., 4th ed. 1942) (1886) [hereinafter Perpetuities] ("Had it been held that [executory] limitations could be destroyed like contingent remainders, the need of a rule against remoteness might never have been felt; even if some such rule had finally been evolved, it would probably have been in other than in its present form.").

3. Leach published a series of law review articles attacking the excesses of Gray's rule. *See infra* note 35; *see also* discussion of Leach's de novo review of Gray's RAP.

Another critic, legal historian A. W. Brian Simpson, questioned aspects of Gray's historical analysis.

> An older and more traditional attempt to get outside the professional culture has been the study of legal history, in particular the history of legal institutions, doctrines and procedures.... It hardly makes sense to study law without paying some attention to this rather obvious fact, and even the purest form of doctrinal exposition of the law—for example Gray's treatise on the rule against perpetuities—employs by way of justification accounts of the historical development of 'the rule', which, in a sense, Gray himself invented.[4]

Despite Gray's insistence that the RAP is concerned exclusively with the question of remoteness in vesting as opposed to the matter of alienation, one nevertheless could reasonably believe that the RAP is merely a logical extension of the evolving common law rules against perpetuities that precluded unbarrable estates.[5] These various forms of unbarrable estates directly and effectively restricted the alienation of property. Indeed, the history of future interests under the common law reveals a strong and consistent commitment to the preservation of the right of alienation. As each new device was spawned by the English conveyancers to impose limits on the consumption rights of each successor in interest, the English jurists closely monitored the extent to which such property interests effectively restrained the right of alienation. Yet, the increased potential for marketability of property as a result of alienability, along with the ease of convertibility into cash, provided the opportunity for the morally suspect successors in interest to consume and waste the family's resources.

If the RAP were not invented to deal with the impact of executory interests, the dominant norm and principal concern of the English—the ongoing preservation and active encouragement of the right of alienation—would have been equally inhibited. This would have been also true of the fee tail but for *Taltarum's Case* and of contingent remainders but for the Rule of Destructibility. Moreover, the invention of the Rule in *Shelly's Case* and the Doctrine of the Worthier Title greatly add to the enhancement of the right of alienation. Apart

---

4. *See* A. W. Brian Simpson, *Legal Education and Legal History*, 11 Oxford J. Legal Stud. 106, 109–10 (1991) (footnote omitted). Simpson explains in a footnote he is referring to Gray's historical invention of remorseless application and the corollary proposition that the rule is like a mathematical equation allowing for an objective determination. *Id.* at 110 n.12.

5. See Chapter 11 for discussion of the common law rules against perpetuities and their relation to alienation.

from the historic and mysterious function of *seisin* in the evolution of property interests, it would be exceedingly difficult to identify any more important criteria for the evaluation of property interests under the common law than the right of alienation.

With respect to the newly minted executory interest,[6] what limitation did such interest have on the right of alienability? Once such interest was declared indestructible,[7] was it not true that such interest essentially clogged the alienation of property in a manner quite comparable to earlier unbarrable interests of the common law? Albert Martin Kales and other scholars are mostly in agreement with Gray as to his assertion that the RAP was solely focused on the issue of remoteness in vesting as opposed to limiting the right of alienation.[8] By the nature of Gray's enduring hegemony on perpetuity implications, there was no room for injurious disagreement until a crack of lightning exploded at Cambridge again. In this case, it was the enlightening scholarship of Leach that forever broke the chalice from the palace; the RAP could never be fully repaired thereafter!

A subordinate question to the matters raised by Leach is whether the invention of the RAP is a purely legally spawned isotope in the nature of a deus ex machina formulation or merely, as suggested herein, a reformed rule based on the earlier common law rules against perpetuities. Equally important is the fact that the judicial evolution of the RAP, as Simpson points out, was not constructed in one day.[9] The RAP represents the evolving judicial responses as articulated over an extended period of time to the ongoing disputes over the authority of various parties to utilize, limit, or alienate property among and between the Crown, religious institutions, lords and barons as large landholders,[10] tenants, and then later, the emerging professional and business classes. Notwithstanding, it is the exceptional legal acceptance of Gray's scholarship on the RAP by the judiciary both in England and America that has generated a unique and faithful following of his gospel. The enormous deference attributed to Gray's doctrine of the RAP and its manifest internalization by the courts set his articulation as the *standard* and final word for more than a century. The aforementioned achievement is in addition to the hallowed reverence showered

---

6. Relatively "newly minted executory interests" were made enforceable at law by the enactment of the Statute of Uses in 1535. *See* Statutes of Uses, 1535, 27 Hen. 8, c. 10 (Eng.).

7. Pells v. Brown, (1620) Cro. Jac. 590.

8. *See, e.g.*, ALBERT M. KALES, ESTATES, FUTURE INTERESTS AND ILLEGAL CONDITIONS AND RESTRAINTS IN ILLINOIS 114–15 (2d ed. 1920) [hereinafter FUTURE INTERESTS].

9. *See* A.W. BRIAN SIMPSON, LEADING CASES IN THE COMMON LAW 96 (1995).

10. *See* SIR WILLIAM S. HOLDSWORTH, ESSAYS IN LAW AND HISTORY 103–04 (1995).

upon him by the academy. Gray's profound scholarly guidance and comprehension of the issues relating to the complex application of the rule have indeed become synonymous with the RAP. It is not an overstatement to say that Gray's teachings on the RAP became in fact the rule itself!

Legal Education and Student Indoctrination of the Modern RAP

In an analogous sense, there is nothing like the old-time religion as it provides security for the living and beatific repose for the dead. In many respects, the RAP fulfils the same function in legal education. Although the academic community does not require for admission a formal academic oath in support of the RAP, some professors of law nevertheless express or, more specifically, disclose a forthright political and ideological commitment to the preservation of the rule. The continuation of the RAP is or has been seen by some academics as an essential means to enhance both the equality of opportunity as well as reducing excessive differential in the allocation of wealth. Teaching of the doctrine adds a moral component to the pedagogical experience for some of the more passionate advocates of the RAP in that its enforcement is perceived as applying a measure of justice for the benefit of society, while its repeal represents a form of moral decadence.

Gray's theme song of the RAP has been absorbed as essential learning in law school for almost 125 years without any significant concern for the socioeconomic consequence of its application.[11] Generations of law professors have force-fed the challenging contingencies of the RAP to students without the slightest concern for the rule's actual impact. Yet, academics continue to express an unquestioned acceptance of the received traditional assertions of the purposes and consequences of the RAP, which is based on what only can be described as something akin to a cultural inheritance of the academy. In short, Gray's masterful scholarship on the RAP reified the alleged mathematical perfection of the rule to a religion while substantially reducing, if not otherwise completely eliminating, concern for its unknown consequences (discussed below).

Gray unequivocally ordained that there was one correct answer in resolving RAP puzzles regardless of the existence of unique facts, common sense, or unusual equities. There was to be no judicial discretion in its application under his doctrine. Notwithstanding that there were two prior nineteenth century

11. See discussion on the absence of economic analysis, *infra* notes 37–38.

treatises on the RAP by English authors,[12] Gray's treatise provided the definitive nineteenth century classical condensation of the RAP that was comparable, in effect, to the authority of an edict, *ius honorariurm*, issued by a Roman Praetor.[13] It was intended to be a binding statement of law for all subsequent scholars, judges, and law students alike. The academic discourse between Gray and his contemporary critics reveals a scholar completely engaged in a passionate defense of all that he asserts is absolutely "correct." For Gray, his articulation of the RAP was a definitive statement of law for the aforementioned members of the legal community to carefully study, digest, and apply. Consistent with Gray's precision and exactitude on the application of the RAP, scholars, lawyers, and judges would assuredly find comprehensive and dogmatic guidance whenever they faced the complex problem of properly resolving a perpetuities issue. Assuredly, the rule under Gray's tutelage and management provides to all who accept his assumptions the map to the esoterically "correct" answer. Gray crisply notes his scholarly intent in this respect in the preface to the first edition of his book:

> In many legal discussions there is, in the last resort, nothing to say but that one judge or writer thinks one way, and another writer or judge thinks another way. There is no exact standard to which an appeal can be made. In questions of remoteness this is not so; there is for them a definite recognized rule: if a decision agrees with it, it is right; if it does not agree with it, it is wrong. *In no part of the law is the reasoning so mathematical in its character; none has so small a human element.*[14]

Gray was never to equivocate about his assertion of *the* correct answer when it involved a perpetuities question. Not surprisingly, he never retreated from such a position throughout the many subsequent years of his scholarship.

From the publication of *Perpetuities* in 1886 to the present time, all successor scholars have been enormously influenced by his laconic, highly dogmatic, and formulaic rendition of the RAP. Most of the modest revisions to the RAP sponsored by the academic community during the middle period of the twentieth century were proposed, argued, and/or enacted from and through the

---

12. Both of these authors were cited by Gray in his book. *See* WILLIAM DAVIS LEWIS, A PRACTICAL TREATISE ON THE LAW OF PERPETUITY OR REMOTENESS IN LIMITATIONS OF ESTATES (1843); REGINALD G. MARSDEN, *Accumulations and Thellusion Act*, *in* THE RULE AGAINST PERPETUITIES: A TREATISE ON REMOTENESS IN LIMITATIONS, WITH A CHAPTER ON ACCUMULATION AND THE THELLUSON ACT (1883).

13. *See* BARRY NICHOLAS, AN INTRODUCTION TO ROMAN LAW 20–23 (1962).

14. *See* PERPETUITIES, *supra* note 2, at x.

permanent prism imposed on the rule by Gray. Some of the longtime academic supporters of Gray's edict on the RAP intuitively recognized that even minimal elimination or modification of the critical assumptions associated with the rule, particularly if engaged in by the American Law Institute, would jeopardize the entire authority of the rule. Such change, no matter how trifling, might reveal it to be less than a sacrosanct rule of property, possibly arbitrary, conceivably lacking a defined empirically validated purpose, and, perhaps, having no relevance to current socioeconomic conditions. In short, a complete anachronism delivered to law students over many centuries on the basis of faith.[15] Recall Adam Smith's astute statement quoted at the beginning of this chapter.

It is no exaggeration to assert that law students over the generations have been significantly stymied in their attempts to comprehend the contingencies and assumptions embedded by Gray in the application of this esoteric rule of law. Jesse Dukeminier Jr. noted the serious difficulty both for students and for judges to comprehend the ponderous complexities of the RAP.

> The Rule against Perpetuities has always seemed to be a modern labyrinth in need of a golden thread. To the student who first encounters it, the Rule appears terribly hard to understand. No matter how diligently studied, the way to solve perpetuities problems remains elusive: One minute you have it, the next minute you don't. Students are usually exhorted to keep trying—"soon you will see the light." They keep trying, but few see the light quickly, and some, groping through the intricate passages of the Rule, never do.[16]

With respect to a study of perpetuity decisions in a particular state, Dukeminier added:

> *The Rule against Perpetuities is essentially incomprehensible.* The conventional Rule can be stated with Delphic simplicity, but like oracles of old it has a reputation for being excessively resistant to understanding. The briefs and opinions in Kentucky perpetuities cases indicate this reputation is well-deserved. There have been 71 perpetuities case since 1900, an average of more than one a year. Of these

---

15. *See* Jeffrey Evans Stake, *The Uneasy Case for Adverse Possession*, 89 Geo. L.J. 2419, 2473 (2001) ("Property law moves very slowly. Rules can endure for centuries after losing all reason for being.").

16. *See* Jesse Dukeminier, *A Modern Guide to Perpetuties*, 74 Cal. L. Rev. 1867, 1867–68 (1986).

> 71 cases, 19 were wrongly decided according to orthodox doctrine and 16 are doubtful by the same standard. Only 36 (51%) of the perpetuities cases were clearly decided correctly—a surprising figure considering leading authorities are in large agreement on how the Rule applies. In practically all these "wrongly decided" cases the court maintained it was applying the common law Rule. Yet it serves no purpose to argue who is in error. That would get us into semantics. *The point is: there has been a breakdown in communications between the learned writers and the learned judges.*[17]

Thus, it appears that the science of applying the RAP in a correct fashion is beyond comprehension of a relatively high percentage of judges in one state and likely permanently incomprehensible to most law students. Dukeminier's observations are serious indictments either to the fact that the orthodox rule is incoherent or to the limitations of those trained to understand it by the masters of the RAP.

Students have received the doctrine of the RAP as passive consumers of academic truisms and obviously without the legal framework to question its purposes or function in contemporary society. Whatever the casebook states or the professor offers as the ultimate purpose or purposes of the RAP, such explanations and reiterations thereof become internalized as irrefutable fact for most law students. In short, law students are universally vulnerable to accepting law professors' narratives of and about the RAP and equally unconcerned by the illogical assumptions embedded in the rule's application. Obviously, most students desire a short circuit rule-of-thumb guide to its application.

A problematic aspect of Gray's formulaic contraction of the rule is the tendency of students to treat such abstraction as if it were a newborn statute delivered by the legislative process. Apart from a number of bricks thrown by Charles Sweet in his critical obituary of Gray in Chapter 9, Sweet added the following comment regarding the tendency of Americans in their treatment of the RAP:

> But in their systematic treatises on the English law of real property, *American lawyers seem to treat it as if it were a collection of rules drawn up by one legislator at one time, and therefore capable of being classified under leading principles.* In the attempt to subject the law of real property to this painful process, 'something has to break' (to use one of Gray's Americanisms), and any anomalies which suffer fracture are

17. *See* Jesse Dukeminier Jr., *Kentucky Perpetuities Law Restated and Reformed*, 49 Ky. L.J. 3, 54 (1960) (footnotes omitted) (second emphasis added).

> thrown away as useless. This brutal way of treating the English law of real property commends itself to our modern judges, for it saves a good deal of trouble, but it would have scandalized the conveyancers of the last generation.[18]

Part of this treatment is due to the enormous contraction of the evolution of future interests in many casebooks and the suspension of serious interest in the history of the common law. Thus considered, this conception of the rule being created on a certain day, conceals the long and tortuous process by which the English courts over the centuries fused together a series of rules relating to a variety of disparate conveyances showing either a so-called tendency to perpetuity or a sufficient muddling of the person or persons who are entitled to the exclusive use or control of the property. These conveyances were carefully designed in a manner in which they would possibly endure for indefinite periods. Simpson similarly noted the impact of Gray's contraction of numerous common law cases dealing with the matter of a so-called perpetuity.

> Unlike Langdell, whose only systematizing work was on his nutshell on contract law, Gray devoted his considerable talents to writing of legal treatises, works that lived off the theory of legal science. No such work ever expressed Langdell's theory of economy of principles more elegantly than Gray's *The Rule against Perpetuities* (1886). *He contrived to reduce the whole body of the doctrine, supposedly underlying hundreds of cases, many barely intelligible, to a mere thirty-two words; any cases which were not compatible with his rule were simply dismissed as wrong. Gray was fascinated with the idea that all perpetuity problems had a discoverable and incontrovertible answer.*[19]

One wonders whether Gray's laconic contraction of the rule unintentionally led to the slow, but steady, separation of the original common law rules against perpetuities from that which is referred to as the judicially invented "modern RAP" of 1681–82.[20] The failure to explain the common law rules against perpetu-

---

18. *See* Charles Sweet, *John Chipman Gray (*ob. *Feb. 25, 1915)*, 31 L.Q.R. 338, 339 (1915) (emphasis added).

19. Simpson, *supra* note 9, at 96 (emphasis added).

20. In Dukeminier's review of *The Modern Rule Against Perpetuities* by Robert J. Lynn, he noted the potential confusion as to which is the official "modern rule" of the RAP. Lynn then suggested that by reason of the English statutory reforms, "Gray's [explication] is the old Rule," whereas it was the view previously that the rule in *Whitby v. Mitchell*, (1889) 42 Ch.D. 494, was the old rule. By implication, Lynn is treating the reformed rule as the "new" modern rule. *See* Jesse Dukeminier, *Perpetuities: The New Empire—The Modern Rule Against*

ities (CLRAP) as an essential prerequisite to an understanding of the history of the RAP creates an unnecessary opacity as to the ancestry of the rule.[21]

Despite the American Revolution, the new nation absorbed the common law, via *Blackstone's Commentaries* and other treatises, along with most of its appendages and quirky assumptions, including the excessively complex RAP with all of its perplexing fictions. Gray's treatise of the late nineteenth century effectively affirmed the incorporation of the RAP as the critical rule of law of property law and, moreover, lessened the potential for any significant reconsideration of the RAP or its application to the emerging development of modern trusts. Despite the attacks of contemporaries such as Charles Sweet, Gray's scholarship was such that

> [b]y virtue of his erudition, his rigorous logic, his dogmatic style, and his position as the first great teacher of property law at Harvard, Gray became enthroned as not just the leading authority on the Rule but as *the* authority. He changed the republic into an empire ruled by himself.[22]

Indeed, the impact of his scholarship on the RAP raised the rule to greater importance and made the learning thereof, according to the dictates of Gray, essential training for all law students. The RAP, as one of the more complex rules of law confronted by first year law students, perfectly plays into the normal and natural intellectual assertion of power by law professors over law students. Gray's impressive scholarship on the RAP made the learning thereof an indelible experience of legal education. Comprehension of the intricacies of the RAP became something like a baptism requiring a total immersion by the legal neophytes who eagerly professed their acceptance of the new religion of Gray's law on the basis of faith alone. Gleefully, law students over the decades enjoyed opining the tortuous way of the RAP as a means of impressing and bewitching their non-law school imbibing companions.

Leach: De Novo Criticism of Gray's RAP

Gray canonized the RAP in a way to provide the definitive interpretation of the rule and thereby foreclose any differing thoughts as to the "correct" inter-

---

Perpetuities, 77 YALE L.J. 159, 162 n.10 (1967); ROBERT J. LYNN, THE MODERN RULE AGAINST PERPETUITIES 194 n.82 (1966).

21. For a further explanation of the CLRAP see Chapter 11.

22. Dukeminier, *supra* note 20, at 159.

pretation of the RAP. Most of the interminable discussions, law review articles, and proposed revisions of the RAP have been argued from and through the permanent prism imposed by Gray. The RAP, although born of English judicial invention and judicially modified as needed over time, was impregnated with aspects of Gray's persona[23]—it must be "remorselessly enforced" as its purpose is to "defeat the intention of the grantor," and if there is any mathematical possibility of violating the RAP (no matter how unlikely or technical) the affected future interest fails. There is no mercy or humanity under the cutting edge of Gray's guillotine-like interpretation of the RAP. In a real sense, Gray selected (in his abstraction of the rule) most all of the more negative and terse aspects of English judicial opinions. As a result, Gray created a legal juggernaut that subsumed the differing views of his contemporary scholars and was largely accepted by the judiciary as the final word on interpretative questions arising from the application of the RAP. The next succeeding generation of perpetuity scholars served largely as loyal acolytes to Gray's theological articulation of the RAP.[24]

By reason of Gray's choice to impose the most severe interpretation and also to demand strict adherence to his interpretation of this mysterious rule of law, he necessarily invited by implication one of equal skill and academic status to challenge the *ex cathedra* dictates incorporated into Gray's doctrine of the RAP. This surprising academic jousting took place decades after Gray's death when W. Barton Leach engaged in an extended analysis that pungently identified certain of the unnecessary, egregious burdens brought to bear under Gray's scientific articulation of the RAP. Recognition of Gray as master interpreter of the RAP had long been established prior to the penetrating attacks initiated by Leach in the 1930s. Among the many issues which he attacked was the rule of logical proof (an interest is void if it is not certain to vest or fail at the creation of the interest). Leach successfully led the charge to develop the wait-and-see reform as the antidote to the rule of logical proof.[25]

Distinguished perpetuities scholars, Dukeminier and Krier, accurately attributed the decline in support of the RAP to the academic scholarship of Leach.

---

23. See observations of Judge Noonan in the text in Chapter 12.

24. *See* W. Barton Leach, *Perpetuities Legislation: Hail Pennsylvania!*, 108 U. Pa. L. Rev. 1124 (1960). Leach suggested that Professors Percy Bordwell, Philip Mechem, Bertel Sparks, and, to some lesser extent, Lewis Simes, were all "brought up on the Gospel according to Gray and seem determined to die in the true faith, fundamentalist to the end." *Id.* at 1124–25 (footnote omitted).

25. *See, e.g.*, W. Barton Leach, *Perpetuities in Perspective: Ending the Rule's Reign of Terror*, 65 Harv. L. Rev. 721 (1952).

> In 1951 Professor W. Barton Leach paid homage to the Rule against Perpetuities, calling it "the *sanctum sanctorum* of the law." ... Its history implies a certain hardiness, which in fact the Rule enjoyed—until recently. Leach said it provided lawyers in the United States with "a blessed sheltering realization that lives-in-being-and-twenty-one years have the same validity after two world wars and four Democratic administrations that they had when Queen Victoria ascended the throne." Yet, only one year later, Leach attacked the Rule as a "technically-ridden legal nightmare" in urgent need of reform. Ever since Leach's assault, the Rule has been in decline, especially in the United States, where matters are now moving apace. In a growing number of jurisdictions, property owners are suddenly free to control the destiny of their estates with a cold dead hand, by way of perpetual trusts.[26]

The RAP has never been the same since Leach brought his unique skill and wit to demonstrate beyond per adventure the abhorrent and painful excesses generated by the application of Gray's stringent doctrine. After publishing numerous critical articles on the matter of perpetuities, Leach and coauthor J. H. C. Morris referred to the revered Gray as "the uncompromising exponent of the Rule against Perpetuities in all of its draconian rigor."[27]

Notwithstanding the pungent and thoughtful attacks by Leach, Gray's scholarship posthumously continued with vibrancy and greatly influenced subsequent judicial decisions and academic thought throughout the twentieth century. Indeed, Gray's scholarship was reiterated by the subsequent but slightly updated publication of his book on perpetuities in 1942. This last publication was edited by his son, Roland Gray. The ongoing authority of Gray and his articulation of the RAP seriously challenged future scholars to effect even a tepid revision of the rule without causing some loss of authority for this enigmatic and so-called sacrosanct rule of law. The consequence of Gray's scholarship on the RAP, while constituting a recognized academic achievement of the highest order, arguably foreshadowed in a most subtle sense the potential denouement of the rule itself. The excesses flowing from the rigid doctrine of Gray eventually became too troubling for some members of the academy as well as a few state legislative bodies by the middle of the twentieth century.

---

26. *See* Jesse Dukeminier & James E. Krier, *The Rise of the Perpetual Trust*, 50 UCLA L. Rev. 1303, 1304 (2003) (footnotes omitted).

27. *See* J.H.C. Morris & W. Barton Leach, The Rule Against Perpetuities 83 (2d ed. 1962) [hereinafter Morris & Leach].

Nevertheless, Gray's unique scholarly encryption of the RAP remained the universal standard on both sides of the Atlantic through the end of the twentieth century for this most complex rule of law—except for the reforms enacted or adopted and the numerous states that have repealed the RAP or made it optional. There are few, if any, efforts on the part of other American scholars that had an international impact or secured the level of acceptance as Gray's *Perpetuities*. It is also true that Gray was one of the major figures involved in the categorical ordering of different legal subject matters,[28] and his separation of the RAP from restraints on alienation was one of the more specific examples of this process. Oliver Wendell Holmes Jr., a lifelong friend of both Gray and his wife, Nina, explained in his eulogy the impact and importance of Gray's *Perpetuities* by the following: "He brought this scholarship to bear unobtrusively but powerfully when he came to write. His treatise on *Perpetuities* is a quiet masterpiece that stands on an equal footing with the most famous works of the great English writers upon property law."[29] Holmes Jr. added later, "It will be seen that I am trying to describe a master, who was listened to with equal respect by clients, by courts, and by all students of the law."[30]

These observations regarding the professional significance and lasting achievements of Gray by the distinguished Justice Holmes remain unusually enduring. One would not expect that their long friendship would have the slightest impact on the deliberate and exacting precision of judgment exercised by someone as acerbic as Holmes Jr. His inability to attend the proceeding of the Massachusetts Historical Society honoring their fallen member, although otherwise understandable, was, no doubt, personally disappointing to Nina Gray (who was a lifelong personal friend of Justice Holmes)[31] as well as the other members of the Gray family.

Nevertheless, the painful excesses flowing from Gray's RAP as brilliantly disclosed in a series of scholarly articles by the spirited and insightful criticisms of Leach eventually ignited the demand for a modest degree of academic reflection and debate. To question the authority of Gray on the RAP required

---

28. *See* Gregory S. Alexander, *The Transformation of Trusts as a Legal Category, 1800–1914*, 5 Law & Hist. Rev. 303, 308 (1987).

29. Roland Gray, John Chipman Gray Memoir 49 (Privately Printed 1918) [hereinafter Memoir] (eulogy of Associate Justice Oliver Wendell Holmes, as delivered by Charles Francis Adams, the President of the Massachusetts Historical Society, and recorded in its official proceedings on March 12, 1915).

30. *Id.* at 50.

31. See discussion of the personal relationship of Nina Gray and Oliver Wendell Holmes, *supra* Chapter 5.

a person of recognized academic standing and one who was an equal master craftsman of the many legal issues and mysteries encrypted in the historic development of that rule of law referred to as the Rule Against Perpetuities. Leach was by personality a provocateur of the first rank and by aptitude a distinguished student of the law, having clerked for Justice Holmes. Dukeminier aptly zeroed in on Leach as the protagonist of the first order.

> With an acid wit both legal and therapeutic, Leach heaped scorn on such hobgoblins of orthodoxy as the fertile octogenarian, the unborn widow, the magic gravel pit, the fertile decedent, and the precocious toddler (Leach joyfully supplied the names).... Leach has played Constantine to Gray's Augustus.[32]

The combination of legal talents and antagonistic inclinations made Leach the perfect candidate to attack the many excesses of the long revered rule of law whose birthing process can be seen germinating as early as the fifteenth century.

Leach focused exclusively on the rule as interpreted by Gray and over several decades identified the numerous excesses. Ironically, Leach had neither studied the matter of future interests while in law school nor was the subject matter a principal focus of his concern prior to joining the faculty of Harvard Law School in 1930.[33] Perhaps, it was because Leach was not academically indoctrinated into the perfection of the RAP that allowed him to freely identify and attack many of the ensconced superstitions associated with applications of Gray's RAP. After the enlightened scholarship and academic status of Leach, the RAP could no longer be sustained or contained simply on the basis of the dogmatic pronouncements by the distinguished Gray.

A rule of law cannot be indefinitely preserved simply on the basis of its historic resolution of past conflict. The test for the continuation of a rule of law must be based on an identifiable contemporaneous purpose. It should be understood that Leach was always an advocate for the continuation of the RAP and that he never called for its outright repeal. However, by his persistent demand for revision of Gray's formulation, Leach necessarily, *sub silento*, questioned the foundation for its continued existence. Dean Erwin N. Griswold accurately explained Leach's impact on the rule.

> But Bart's great work in the field of property, and his great distinction was in a special segment of that field, filled with history and intricacies, intertwining substance and technicality, the Rule Against

32. Dukeminier, *supra* note 20, at 161.
33. *See* A. James Casner, *In Memoriam: W. Barton Leach*, 85 HARV. L. REV. 717 (1972).

> Perpetuities. In carrying on this work, Leach was maintaining a tradition established by his great predecessor at the Harvard Law School, John Chipman Gray, whose book on the Rule Against Perpetuities was one of the notable scholarly productions from the School in the late nineteenth century. Gray had organized and systemized the field. But Leach redid it. I am sure that Gray himself would be the leader of those expressing admiration for Leach's achievement. Surely, *Perpetuities in a Nutshell*, which Leach wrote in 1938, is one of the classics of law and legal literature. He later published a book in the field, both in this country and in England, and his writings have led to extensive changes in the law. No one could deny that these changes go back almost entirely to the mind and energy of one man.[34]

Dean Griswold clearly described the devastating impact of Leach's analytical criticism of the RAP. As a result of his scholarship, the rule would never be the same.

Revision of Gray's RAP by the American Law Institute and Adoption of Modified USRAP

If, for example as asserted under Gray's thesis, it is really a rule against remoteness of vesting, why does it apply only to vesting in interest rather than in possession? Even Gray recognized the inconsistency of this distinction, but acknowledged it was too late to focus on a different approach. There is a major difference between vesting in interest and vesting in possession. Why should the rule be remorselessly applied? How is it that the purpose of the rule is to defeat the intent of the grantor? Why should it be presumed that all persons of any age are capable of bearing children? This latter question moved the charismatic Leach to invent the famed phrase of "the fertile octogenarian." That phrase became the source of great merriment for the male dominated law students of past generations. Separate from the infamous reference of Leach, most law students do not identify any other part of their study of the rule with any degree of merriment.

Apart from extended law review articles[35] on the subject of RAP throughout the early part of the twentieth century by Leach and other master-crafts-

---

34. Erwin N. Griswold, *Bart Leach*, 85 HARV. L. REV. 723–24 (1972).

35. *See, e.g.*, W. Barton Leach, *Perpetuities in a Nutshell*, 51 HARV. L. REV. 638 (1938); W. Baron Leach, *Powers of Sale in Trustees and the Rule Against Perpetuities*, 47 HARV. L. REV. 948 (1934); W. Barton Leach, *The Rule Against Perpetuities and Gifts to Classes*, 51 HARV. L. REV. 1329 (1938); Leach, *supra* note 25; W. Barton Leach, *Perpetuities: New Ab-*

men, the first serious sign of a modification to Gray's RAP occurred when several states like Pennsylvania began the process of amending the rule during the late forties and fifties. A number of diverse state legislative bodies enacted modifications aimed at reducing some of the interpretive excesses by allowing the courts to apply "wait and see" and "*cy pres*" reforms. Interestingly, there was no movement to repeal the rule as the underlying socioeconomic purposes for enforcement were consistently presumed to exist despite the absence of any attempt to review the actual impact of the rule. Indeed, did the RAP have an identifiable purpose, economic or otherwise, as distinguished from value preferences such as the very popular reference to dead hand control? The principal proponent of the dead hand reference, Sir Arthur Hobhouse, is frequently cited by contemporary scholars in support of limiting the extension of so-called dead hand control.[36] Most debates concerning the RAP start with the assumption that it does have a socioeconomic purpose and still fulfills a useful function. One searches for that socioeconomic function in the context of an advanced complex society wherein most assets held by trusts that are otherwise available for alienation.[37] In this respect, the original discussion of the actual consequences of RAP, as explained by the American Law Institute (ALI), remain as important today as when initially explained in 1944. As cited by Leach, the ALI report explains that the

> basis or justification for this assumption (that social welfare requires the imposition of restrictions upon the fettering of property) has never been adequately explored and has been seldom discussed. Insofar as this assumption lies at the root of the rule against perpetuities, some light as to its justification can be obtained by an examination of the purposes which are served by the rule.[38]

---

surdity, Judicial and Statutory Correctives, 73 Harv. L. Rev. 1318 (1960); W. Barton Leach, *Perpetuities: New Hampshire Defertilizes the Octogenarians*, 77 Harv. L. Rev. 279 (1963); W. Barton Leach, *Perpetuities: The Nutshell Revisited*, 78 Harv. L. Rev. 973 (1965).

36. *See* A. Hobhouse, The Dead Hand: Addresses on the Subject of Endowments and Settlements of Property (1880).

37. The economic rational frequently asserted for the invention of the RAP as a means to protect against enduring restrictions on the alienation of real property has always been assumed to exist. That assumption may indeed have been true in the feudal period when large estates were frequently the subject of fee tail transfers. *See* Leach, *supra* note 24, at 1135 (citing 4 Restatement of Property, pt. I, introductory cmt., at 2129 (1944)).

38. 4 Restatement of Property, pt. I, introductory cmt., at 2129 (1944). The introductory comments do suggest that there are other purposes for the RAP, such as limiting dead hand control, maximizing wealth utilization, and providing flexibility in the current management of property. *Id.* at 2129–33.

The absence of a defined social objective, however, is never a serious problem for the academy as there is always a wealth of purposes inventoried for use when others fail to meet the test of empirical reliability. Indeed, Jeffrey Stake notes the original purpose of the rule is no longer essential.

> Scholars often critique a rule by reference to the degree to which it accomplishes the purpose for which it was adopted. This Article avoids the historical question of why the Rule was adopted and, instead, identifies the beneficial consequences flowing from the Rule, regardless of whether they were intended. From this perspective, whether the Rule accomplishes its original purpose is unimportant.[39]

English legal scholars came close to conducting an economic study of the practical socio-economic impact of the RAP as recently as 1998. The Law Commission's Report (Report 251) on the question of empirical results is quite humorous in explaining the sudden decision not to conduct the study and the rational by which the question is no longer deemed relevant. Report 251 explains in part:

> We then considered the possibility of commissioning a full study of the economic implications of abolishing the rule. In the end, we were unable to proceed with this because it proved impossible to obtain sufficient data for the consultant to make such a task anything other than *guesswork*. In any event, as we have explained, in the light of the responses to consultation, we did not consider it appropriate to recommend abolition of the rule for a reason that was unconnected with its economic ramifications, namely the desirability of placing some restrictions on how far settlors could tie up property for the future. *Notwithstanding the absence of any economic assessment of the consequences of abolishing or retaining the rule, we consider that this reason for its retention is strong enough to outweigh any possible adverse economic effect.*[40]

Thus, we have no direct empirical data up to the present time to establish what the RAP achieves other than the academic desirability of placing some lim-

39. Jeffrey E. Stake, *Darwin, Donations, and the Illusion of Dead Hand Control*, 64 Tul. L. Rev. 705, 708 n.7 (1990); *see also id.* at 708 (quoting Professor Casner in his capacity as Reporter for the Restatement of Property as reaffirming the original observation of the ALI in its 1944 introductory comments).

40. Law Commission, The Rules Against Perpetuities and Excessive Accumulations, 1998, Report 251, at 20 (emphasis added).

its on the period in which such settlors can impose restrictions. In making the recommendation quoted above, Report 251 added in a footnote, "The economic consequences of dead hand control are not known."[41] As to the maximum period during which restrictions may be imposed, Report 251 recommended that the period be extended to 125 years.[42] Again, purposes are always easy to invent, justify, or assert as the essential objective to rationalize the continuation of the RAP, despite the fact that empirical consequences remain unknown and/or are deemed irrelevant. It appears it is always easier to simply extend the period of the RAP then to actually resolve the question of whether the rule should be continued.

To date, there appears to be no direct study of the extent to which the RAP has significantly carried out a defined socioeconomic purpose. The continuation of the RAP itself, and the passionate support by some members of the academy, may be more a product of our past legal education in which the rule is diligently consumed by law students as a most highly venerated rule of the common law. In view of the aforementioned, does the RAP survive mostly as a revered legal anachronism? There are, however, a number of inventoried purposes derived from one's institutional belief of what *ought* to be accomplished which are ready and available to be utilized by the academy whenever the question of the RAP moves into an open debate as to its socioeconomic functions. In short, there is never an absence of alleged purposes to justify its continuance as a primary rule of property law despite the apparent want of any definable, empirical objective. But, there are a few articles suggesting it may be the time for repeal.[43]

Over his lifetime, Leach's expository analysis of Gray's doctrine, that some interests could possibly fail to vest in interest within the now variable time period of the rule, permanently pierced the formidable cast of the RAP. The rule thereafter was seen as having considerably less authority and suffering from the absence of a clearly defined rational purpose. Leach's support for the proposed "wait and see" reform as a needed antidote to the painful mathematical possibility test eventually lead to a modest and deeply contested academic revision of the RAP during the second half of the twentieth century.[44] This modification in the 1970s by the ALI, in the context of the history of the RAP,

---

41. *Id.* at 20 n.55.

42. *Id.* at 7.

43. *See, e.g.*, Keith L. Butler, Comment, *Long Live the Dead Hand: A Case for Repeal of the Rule Against Perpetuities in Washington*, 75 WASH. L. REV. 1237 (2000); G. Graham Waite, *Let's Abolish the Rule Against Perpetuities*, 21 REAL EST. L.J. 93 (1992).

44. *See generally* Leach, *supra* note 24.

constituted a serious shattering of the illusory perfection of the rule. Once an essential element of Gray's RAP was publicly broken, the underlying sacred inscrutability historically assigned to the RAP was permanently exorcised. It should be recalled, as noted above, that a few of the states had started various limited steps toward statutory reform of the RAP a few decades prior to the academy gathering at the meetings of the ALI in the late 1970s.

Several academics opposed the views expressed by Leach, and others of a similar viewpoint were aggressively dedicated to preserving Gray's rendition of the RAP. Yet, Leach's scholarship was clearly the arrow that festered serious agitation in the academic community. The scholarly counterattack on Leach's criticism was such that he jocularly described himself as having been "gouged, kicked, and clawed."[45] Such feelings describe a fairly unusual experience for a scholar. Added to this is the fact that many of these scholars of an opposing viewpoint were long-time friends. Unfortunately, Leach died prior to subsequent modification of the RAP by the ALI in the late 1970s and the later adoption of the modified Uniform Statute of the Rule Against Perpetuities (USRAP) by The National Conference of Commissioners on Uniform State Laws (NCCUSL).

Prior to these developments, there was no identifiable movement for reform during Gray's lifetime or for many years thereafter. There were some contemporary scholars who quibbled with aspects of Gray's thesis and such conflict was discussed in Chapter 9. The casebooks and numerous law review articles, however, mostly reiterated the reified doctrine of Gray. Law schools rigorously enforced the propositions of Gray's scholarship on the perfection of the RAP as the definitive rendering. The rule and its name were something of a mantra for the novice law students; intriguing, rhythmic, and mysterious. Thus, there were generations of law students, some of which were future law professors, who diligently studied under the hegemony of Gray's teachings on the RAP.

The initial movement for reform undertaken during the middle to the later part of the twentieth century was limited exclusively to concerns for the lessening or, more properly, eliminating the excesses of Gray's RAP. There was no serious debate as to the outright repeal of the RAP as the usual litany of historically assumed purposes; namely, the desired antidynastic impact (limit the excessive accumulation of wealth by the few), elimination of the grasp of the dead hand (inordinately delaying the living of their rightful inheritance), enhancement of the right of alienation, and otherwise increase the flow of property in the capitalistic economy of the United States. Mary Louise Fellows provides an excellent and telling narrative of the movement for reform and

45. *Id.* at 1125 n.5.

the details of the debate at the ALI. "Interest [reform] was revived in 1979 when Professor Leach's colleague, Professor A. James Casner, led a rancorous, but successful, battle in the American Law Institute to accept wait-and-see as part of the Restatement (Second) of Property."[46]

Public Choice Theory and Repeal and/or Modification of the RAP

The more recent movement (1990 to present) to repeal the RAP outright has been effected by the highly energized political forces unleashed by the combined efforts of the state bar associations and banking institutions applying pressure at the respective state legislative level.[47] These changes were effected "formally" as a principal means to allow interested wealthy donors to fund family dynasty trusts that, allegedly, would be indefinitely exempt from the imposition of the generation-skipping tax. Other financial beneficiaries of these changes included, *inter alia,* the states wherein the trusts are administered, the banks as fiduciaries of such trusts, and the lawyers marketing the dynasty trust instruments. But the legal and social environment for this relatively sudden departure from the dominance of this sacrosanct rule of property law was considerably enhanced and supported by the milieu of revision and reform of the rule as conducted by the academic community, including the heralded debates on the "wait and see" proposal as adopted by the ALI and then, more importantly, the 1986 adoption of the USRAP allowing for an alternative specific period of ninety years[48] in the event the "modern" rule of Gray is otherwise violated.

There were prior thoughtful attempts undertaken during the middle period of the twentieth century by state legislative bodies[49] to alleviate some of the painful excesses generated in part by the permanent veneer that Gray encrypted

46. *See* Mary Louise Fellows, *Testing Perpetuity Reforms: A Study of Perpetuity Cases 1984–89*, 25 Real Prop. Prob. & Tr. J. 597, 605 (1991).

47. The author actively participated in the movement in the State of Ohio to make the application of the RAP optional for grantors of private trusts. For a current tabulation of legislative responses to the RAP, either extending the alternative vesting period (some up to 1,000 years), exempting private trusts, or repealing the rule, see Lynn Foster, *Fifty-one Flowers: Current Perpetuities Law in the States*, 22 Prob. & Prop. 30 (July/Aug. 2008).

48. The academic conflict on these developments was intensely debated by Dukeminier and Lawrence Waggoner in a series of law review articles. *See* Dukeminier et al., Property 265 n.32 (6th ed. 2006).

49. *See* Bregy, *A Defense of Pennsylvania's Statute on Perpetuities*, 23 Temp. L.Q. 313 (1950).

into the RAP. During the middle of the twentieth century, several states like Pennsylvania, California, and Kentucky engaged statutory attempts (utilizing wait and see and *cy pres* reforms) to rescue the RAP from its excessive complexity. On studying the effectiveness of these statutory reforms as eliminating the excesses of the RAP, Robert J. Lynn concluded that these enactments neither obviated nor rendered the enigmatic learning of the orthodox Rule "obsolete."[50] He prophesied there is no easy path to reform or exorcize mysteries of perpetuities issues.

> A mastery of the mechanics of the Rule will continue to be a prerequisite to solving a perpetuities question, irrespective of the form the Rule takes. As outworn niceties of the Rule are discarded, new facets of the Rule appear. There is little evidence that the lot of property lawyer has ever been an easy one. There is nothing in the perpetuities reform movement to suggest that it is about to become so.[51]

Those attempts of the early 1940s and 1950s, along with the subsequent reforms adopted by the ALI and NCCUSL, failed to resuscitate the rule from an apparent slow downward spiral from that of the premier sacrosanct rule of law in 1950 to that of *de facto* extinction by 2010. Some members of the academy, but far from all, believed that these prescriptions flowing from these protracted assizes of the academy during the extended debates at the ALI[52] in the late 1970s would secure continuation of the RAP for the indefinite future. That was not to be.

The attempted exorcisms or settlements of traditional perpetuity enigmas by the academy failed to secure the political foundation to preserve the rule[53] from public choice action.[54] Thus, the temporary expectation was soon dashed by a radical change in the political activities of the state bar associations, commercial interests of the banking industry, and the wetted appetites of clients who

50. *See* LYNN, *supra* note 20, at 13–14.

51. *Id.* at 5.

52. *See* Fellows, *supra* note 46.

53. *See* Joel C. Dobris, *Undoing Repeal of the Rule Against Perpetuities: Federal and State Tools for Breaking Dynasty Trusts*, 27 CARDOZO L. REV. 2537, 2538 n.3 (2006) ("Most but not all law professors want to keep the Rule.... We profs seem impotent in the face of this repeal movement of which we disapprove. Received university wisdom is being ignored. I'm shocked. I'm shocked.").

54. For discussion of the public choice theory and its relationship to the repeal of the RAP, see Peter A. Appel, *The Embarrassing Rule Against Perpetuities*, 54 J. LEGAL EDUC. 264, 277–79 (2004).

envision the fantasy of a material life after physical death in the form of a family dynasty trust. The subsequent marketing of dynasty trusts by: the banking industry, the large national law firms (having a large stable of very wealthy clients), boutique estate planning firms acting in part through the internet, and other more localized law firms, not surprisingly, generated a new fount of fees for the class of providers.[55] Indeed, the dreams of the elect creators of dynasty trusts also included the expectation that their newly created dynasty trust, adorned with spendthrift protections,[56] would be indefinitely exempt from the generation-skipping taxes (GST) as well as other legal forms of accountability.

The enduring dreams of property hanging from a sky hook and not otherwise accountable to the sovereign are not going to be realized. Such fantasies of a perpetual trust without accountability to the sovereign do not accord with political realities and will not be indefinitely continued. The sovereign must be paid and remain in control! At most, there is a temporary gap in congressional focus on this tax avoidance opportunity because of other pressing concerns of the country. The Joint Committee of Taxation is well aware the present revenue loss caused by the combination of a dynasty trust (the creation of a perpetual dynasty trust in those states which have repealed or modified the RAP) and the ongoing transfer tax benefits accruing from funding such a trust with an amount equal to the maximum GST exemption.[57] Also, the new Restatement (Third) of Trusts and the Uniform Trust Code provides increased authority for beneficiaries to call for termination of private trusts under certain conditions.[58] Eventually, these and other changes in the law, some of which may not yet be contemplated, will secure the same degree of accountability from the

---

55. *See* Joel C. Dobris, *The Death of the Rule Against Perpetuities, or RAP Has No Friends—An Essay* 35 REAL PROP., TR. & EST. L.J. 601, 651 (2000) ("The idea that people need perpetual trusts is fed by, among others things, the estate planning industry, the productization of trusts, and the specific peddling of dynasty trusts.").

56. A spendthrift provision generally limits the right of a creditor to attach the interest of the beneficiary as well as also prohibiting a beneficiary's right to assign her equitable interests. This creditor exemption has been extended by statute in several states to protect even grantors having a discretionary, beneficial interest in an irrevocable trust (i.e., asset protection trusts). *See, e.g.*, Adam J. Hirsch, *Fear Not the Asset Protection Trust*, 27 CARDOZO L. REV. 2685 (2006); Henry J. Lischer, Jr., *Professional Responsibility Issues Associated with Asset Protection Trusts*, 39 REAL PROP., PROB. & TR. J. 561 (2004).

57. *See* J. COMM. ON TAXATION, 108TH CONG., SUMMARY OF J. COMM. STAFF "OPTIONS TO IMPROVE TAX COMPLIANCE AND REFORM TAX EXPENDITURES" 392–95 (Comm. Print 2005).

58. *See* Ronald Chester, *Modification and Termination of Trusts in the 21st Century: The Uniform Trusts Code Leads to a Quiet Revolution* 35 REAL PROP. PROB. & TR. J. 729 (2001); JESSE DUKEMINIER, ROBERT SITKOFF & JAMES LINDGREN, WILLS, TRUSTS & ESTATES 655–58 (8th ed. 2009) (citing RESTATEMENT (THIRD) OF TRUSTS §65 (2003); UNIFORM TRUST CODE §41 (2004)).

modern wave of dynasty trusts as was true of Henry VIII when he seized the property of the monasteries and separately recovered lost revenue through the enactment (more properly referred to as the imposition of his will on Parliament) of the Statute of Uses.

With regard to the sudden decline for the continuation of an effective and vibrant RAP, there are a number of factors: first, the concomitant enormous complexity of its application, the cost of compliance; second, the mere act of redefinition of the RAP by the academy eliminated the mystique and authority of the RAP as a special preserve of the past law (if the period could be ninety years as established under the USRAP, why not 110 years certain for realty or completely repealed as to personal property as in Delaware or possibly 360 as in Florida);[59] and, finally, the waning emphasis placed on the study of the rule in the law school classroom.[60] Fellows observes a characteristic of human nature—the compulsion to control the use and enjoyment of property after one's death;[61] something like an instinctual drive to defeat mortality. It is the latter reality that has seriously caused the quick erosion of the rule—and as Joel Dobris cryptically observed, the forces to protect the castle have lost the passion and resources for the battle.[62]

Max M. Schanzenbach and Robert H. Sitkoff have made substantial studies on the forces leading to the movement to repeal the RAP. In one study they specify the flow of capital to those states who were leaders in the repeal of the

---

59. *See* Del. Code Ann. tit. 25, §503 (2009); Fla. Stat. §689.225 (2)(f) (2009). Dukeminier's concern about this possibility taking place was prescient. *See* Jesse Dukeminier, *The Uniform Statutory Rule Against Perpetuities: Ninety Years in Limbo*, 34 UCLA L. Rev. 1023, 1045–47 (1987). In fact, as predicted by Dukeminier, the State of Florida did exactly as he expected after having first enacted USRAP. Florida did this in three phases; first the modern rule was enacted, then USRAP was adopted in 1988, and finally Florida made a simple change in the number of years by substituting for the previous ninety year period a 360 year period. *See* Kyle B. Sill, *Is RAP Gone? How* Old Port Cove Holdings, Inc. *Still Leaves RAP Alive in Florida*, 10 Fla. Coastal L. Rev. 491, 492–93 (2009); Fla. Stat. §689.225 (2)(f).

60. For example, a casebook in 1931 covered the topic of the RAP in 102 pages with innumerable cases dealing with various aspects of its complex application. *See* 2 William F. Walsh, Cases on Property 243–345 (1931). Today the amount of casebook coverage on the RAP has been greatly reduced, while the study of the rule itself focuses mostly on a simplified method to apply Gray's formula. Noteworthy, a recent study sponsored by the American Bar Association recommends that less study be allocated to the matter of future interests. *See* Joanne Martin, *The Nature of the Property Curriculum in ABA-Approved Schools and Its Place in Real Estate Practice*, 44 Real Prop., Tr. & Est. L.J. 385, 425 (2009).

61. *See* Mary Louise Fellows, *Why the Generation-Skipping Transfer Tax Sparked Perpetual Trusts*, 27 Cardozo L. Rev. 2511, 2512 (2006).

62. *See supra* note 53 and quoted comments of Dobris.

RAP.[63] The study and data analysis reveal a close connection between the combination of a perpetuity free state and the absence of a state income tax as the dominant cause in attracting the flow of investment funds into that state. The authors note, in part, that "the only states that experienced an increase in trust business after abolishing the Rule were those that did not levy an income tax on trust funds attracted from out of state."[64] A second study follows up on the impact of the repeal of the RAP and the availability of the exemption of utilizing the exempt amount of the generation-skipping transfer tax. With respect to that relationship, the authors conclude that the increase in the utilization of dynasty trusts is "primarily a creature of the federal transfer taxes."[65]

Both of these studies are impressive, but neither directly addresses the empirical function of the RAP. The most interesting comment as it relates to the actual function of the RAP is the consistent observation that "Nonetheless, the prevailing academic view is that the Rule 'does, by and large, effectively prevent tying up property for an inordinate length of time.' "[66] This is an interesting comment which relies principally on the statement set forth in a book coauthored by proponents of the RAP.[67] There is a preceding sentence which has a tendency to be in opposition to the aforementioned quoted statement. It recognizes that most assets involving a future interest are held in trust in which most trustees possess the power of alienation and such assets are not removed from the market.

These latest developments will not likely be the last chapter of the RAP, and one expects the gathering of the academic and political community will reignite the rule and/or reign in the present opportunities to avoid generation-skipping transfer taxes. Remember, the forces of good are never fully overcome. The fantasy of preserving the RAP will never die in the minds of some academics. If federal transfer taxes can be modified in a way that does not require resuscitation of the RAP by indirection, it would be interesting to see if some still support an active RAP. It is a serious mistake to mix tax policy with the ancient Rule Against Perpetuities. In short, tax policy can be modified without the necessity of continuing the regime of the RAP.

---

63. Robert H. Sitkoff & Max M. Schanzenbach, *Jurisdictional Competition for Trust Funds: An Empirical Analysis of Perpetuities and Taxes*, 115 YALE L.J. 356 (2005).

64. *Id.* at 362.

65. Max M. Schanzenbach & Robert H. Sitkoff, *Perpetuities or Taxes? Explaining the Rise of the Perpetual Trust*, 27 CARDOZO L. REV. 2465, 2470 (2006).

66. Sitkoff & Schanzenbach, *supra* note 63, at 366; *see also* Schanzenbach & Sitkoff, *supra* note 65, at 2472 (both articles include the identical language quoted from JESSE DUKEMINIER, STANLEY M. JOHANSON, JAMES LINDGREN & ROBERT H. SITKOFF, WILLS, TRUSTS, AND ESTATES 675 (7th ed. 2005)).

67. DUKEMINIER, JOHANSON, LINDGREN & SITKOFF, *supra* note 66, at 675.

The Reigning Oracle of the RAP

All of the above events, occurring years after Gray's painstaking historic decoding of the RAP, fail to cast a shadow on the significance of his scholarly achievement. Indeed, in almost all of the articles for the last sixty years or more concerning the RAP, Gray's learning is elementary to understanding the application of the rule. There is no question that he has gained enduring fame and recognition as "the" final word on the scope and application of this most complex rule of the common law. Sir William Holdsworth, the distinguished English historian of the common law, accurately described Gray as "pre-eminently the historian of the modern rule against perpetuities."[68] Indeed, Holdsworth's observation regarding the impact of Gray's scholarship on the history of the RAP is noteworthy and retains full currency.

The Modern Rule Against Perpetuities

> The history of the rules against perpetuities has been more fully considered within the last half century than the history of any other branch of the land law. No doubt this is largely due to the fact that, as these rules are wholly judge-made, it is impossible to ascertain their relation to one another, and their application to the facts of concrete cases, without an enquiry into the various *rationies decidendi* of the many decisions and authoritative statements of various dates, upon which they depend. However that may be, there is no doubt that the searching historical scrutiny to which they have been constantly submitted considerably lightens the task of the legal historian. Of recent years the two men who have done more than any others to elucidate the history of these rules are Mr. Sweet and the late professor Gray. Mr. Sweet has elucidated the history of those older rules against perpetuities which has just been related; and my debt to his researches and acumen will be obvious to all those of my readers who are acquainted with his work. Professor Gray is pre-eminently the historian of the modern rule against perpetuities. Of the merits of his work, both as a history and as a statement of the modern law, it is hardly necessary to speak. It is sufficient to say that his book shares with Professor Dicey's book on the Conflict of Laws, the fame of being as nearly a book of authority in our courts as any modern book is ever allowed to be; and

---

68. *See* 7 William Holdsworth, A History of English Law 215 (2d ed., Fifth Impression 2003) (1925).

> that it is one of the few American law books which have attained this distinction. Hence my statement of the history of the modern rule in this section, though somewhat differently arranged, and told from a somewhat different point of view, must be largely a summary of Professor Gray's results.[69]

What more could possibly attest to the unique and honored status of Gray as the scholar of the modern RAP. No one can realistically quibble with that well deserved designation.

---

69. *Id.* (footnotes omitted).

Chapter 11

The Modern Rule Against Perpetuities: Direct Derivative of the Common Law Rules Against Perpetuities

The evolution of property law starts with the concept of seisin.

> Seisin was, in effect, a legal right to continue in a factual situation, which right was derived from previously having been in that factual situation. It was a right of possession independent both of ownership and of contract—a concept unknown either to Germanic law or to the older Roman law. This idea of "possessory right"—not possession but right of possession—has persisted in all Western legal systems to this day.[1]

Impact of Historical Context on the Creation, Application, and Comprehension of Property Rules

The ebb and flow of the various power bases engaged in conflict during the early feudal period is necessarily reflected in the evolution of the common law of property. To study the development of legal rules and their application without sufficient comprehension of the social and political context creates a form of philosophical schism. In this sense, the study of black letter law is a fiction based on another fiction. Simply stated, it is a distortion to separate specific judicial resolutions from their political or social context. In substance, a rule

1. Harold J. Berman, Law and Revolution: The Formation of the Western Legal Tradition 313 (1983) (footnote omitted).

of law is merely the abstraction of a particular factual narrative intentionally articulated by a court of law as its ultimate perception of the underlying factual reality in the context of the then existing norms of the community. This analysis is promptly followed by a crafty transposition of a particular factual narrative into an authoritative formulation of a rule of law, which conceals the human hand in constructing a newborn axiom of law.

Another truism is the older the birthing of a so-called rule of law, the greater the potential for the distortion of its unique historical context and original function. Law and religion share so much in the incessant search for consistency and exegesis of past sacred formulations. This is particularly true as each generation of authorized glossators apply their values to the narrative process. First, there is the separation of a rule of law from its original historical context and unique political implications. Second, the older the rule the more likely the current "established" historical narrative is suspect, particularly in view of the collective layers of nuanced interpretations applied by the succeeding glossators.

This is not to suggest that the original function of a rule of law is in some manner necessarily binding on future legal conflicts, as such determination of past usage and context, although relevant, provides only limited guidance to decision makers of the present. Generally, it is not effective to "manage" the rules of the ancient past, which are essentially norms of earlier societies, to resolve contemporary conflicts. But to comprehend the prior usage of a rule of law and its historical context can allow for a more nuanced appreciation of the differences and thereby lessen or eliminate the tyranny of ancient judicial pronouncements. Such a process, by which the past edicts serve only as limited guidance, would enhance the possibility of the judiciary to arrive at a new calculation that is both balanced with current norms and makes sense with respect to contemporary systems. It is both a virtue and an encumbrance that under our system of law we review the historical past in evaluating current legal issues. The virtue is consistency—the encumbrance is possible legal tyranny. But the study of history in the comprehension and application of ancient rules of law remains critical if we are to eliminate inefficiencies and curb potential judicial tyranny.

William F. Walsh noted years ago the importance of understanding history when it comes to the study of the law of property.

> In the law of property, real and personal, this knowledge [of history] is absolutely essential. A student not familiar with the way in which ownership either of lands or chattels has been made to depend upon possession from the early beginnings of the common law in the time of Henry II down to the present, has no fundamental grasp of the nature of ownership and title. He is to a very considerable extent illiter-

ate with reference to the principles which underlie nearly every branch of the subject.[2]

Today, most law students are far removed from the importance of history as it relates to the study of real property and other law school courses. This is because there is far too little time in which to cover the exponential increase in the modern legal issues that are now considered as the essential contemporary focus for first year law courses. Not only are we deleting allegedly modest concerns of history as related to property law, professors are intentionally limiting the time available to study the RAP[3] and future interests in favor of allotting more time to cover topics of a more pragmatic nature. Property casebooks of today reveal a steady and significant departure in the materials listed for extended coverage.[4] Recognizing the reality of editorial discretion regarding the subject matter to be covered in casebooks, authors are under constant conflicting pressure to maintain study of the important matters of the past while expanding coverage to include increased focus on contemporary material of a more pragmatic nature.

This dilemma fails to militate Walsh's sagacious advice that historical context is necessary if one is to engage in the study and application of the ancient rules of property. Although most property casebooks provide some modest historical context or summary of the major legal events regarding the development of property law, these succinct abstractions of legal history are far less than what is demanded if comprehension of the ancient rules of the common law remains an important pedagogical goal. But yet, these considerations are no longer important for an increasing number of law school professors.

The above observations are particularly relevant when focusing on the historic evolution of the RAP. In feudal times, there were many obvious legal and economic problems leading to the practice of wealthy English landowners utilizing various perpetuity devices by which real estate would be exempt from claims of creditors; avoid certain historic feudal obligations (taxation in the form of specifically designated services); protect the family title, while preserving real

---

2. William F. Walsh, *Legal History in Law School Courses*, 1 Ann. Rev. L. Sch. N.Y.U. 3 (1924).

3. *See, e.g.*, Posting of Ilya Somin to The Volokh Conspiracy, http://volokh.com/2007/08/11/should-we-teach-law-students-the-rule-against-perpetuities/ (Aug. 11, 2007, 14:32) ("[T]he RAP is virtually a byword for abstruse complexity.... Forcing law students to learn it is almost a form of hazing, much like making them learn the Blue Book.").

4. *See generally* Joanne Martin, *The Nature of the Property Curriculum an ABA-Approved Schools and Its Place in Real Estate Practice*, 44 Real Prop., Tr. & Est. L.J. 385 (2009).

estate for the benefit of each succeeding generation so as to secure and protect it as the principal source of familial security, power, and wealth. Some families were also rightly concerned about the possible *de facto* bankruptcy in the form of forfeiture of the family estate due to an act of treason (a tenant in fee simple participating in a losing confrontation or a failed conspiracy against the monarchy). These various perpetuity devices were designed in part to avoid the forfeiture of one's estate as a result of engaging in such treasonous activities against the crown. These were identifiable issues in which the judiciary was quite adept in either enhancing or eliminating the attempts to exempt property from the vicissitudes attendant to engaging in political struggles by the landed gentry. Other considerations might also apply to the judiciary; such as, a nascent predisposition for the flow of commerce as well as a confirmed policy favoring the right of alienation.

Other pressing concerns and values affected the legal process with respect to conveyances of in kind interests in estates and, subsequently, by way of executory devises. Some of these shifting values and political concerns were expressed in the form of statutes allowing for the creation of a future interest referred to as the fee tail; whereas other statutes allowed advancement of the freedom of alienation on the part of the tenants, and yet, other provisions addressed the potential excessive accumulation of real estate acquired by the dominant religious institution. All of these events reflected the constant power conflict between the competing parties; namely, the monarchy, lords and barons as large landholders, component members of the religious institution, and the emerging professional and business community.

The ambiguous and tentative transfer of the power to the judiciary to decide necessarily allocated a significant role in assessing the constantly vacillating power status of the participants; thus, giving birth to the details of the ever expanding common law. The judiciary, by and large, invented rules of law out of cloth, somewhat but not necessarily in direct proportion to its determination of the status of the litigants, as the principal technique for resolution of conflict. To survive and secure respect as a "partially independent" legal system, the judiciary was always keenly responsive to the expectations and wants of the most powerful institution at any particular time—in most instances the monarchy. Recall Edward Coke's untimely removal from the bench for refusing to give into the demands of James I, who was guided in part by the Machiavellian skills of Francis Bacon.[5] It is from this interactive judicial process that

5. *See* Catherine Drinker Bowen, The Lion *and* the Throne: The Life and Times of Sir Edward Coke (1552–1634), at 388 (4th Printing 1957); *accord* Catherine Drinker Bowen, Francis Bacon: The Temper of a Man 140 (1963).

the RAP was formally invented in the *Duke of Norfolk's Case* to limit the heretofore indestructible executory interests.[6] These unique executory interests were born of the Court of Chancery and eventually converted into legal interests following the enactment of the *Statute of Uses* in 1535.

It should be noted that, under the English common law, the RAP originally applied mostly to in kind conveyances of sequential future interests and to executory devises of property (situations in which no person possessed the right of alienation) rather than equitable interests in trusts. In modern times, the RAP has marginal impact, if any, with respect to transfers of real estate in kind. *For the most part, conveyances of future interests and executory interests are by way of equitable interests in modern trusts.* These modern trusts are most frequently funded with intangible assets in which the trustee possesses the power of alienation, whether acting alone or in concert with other individuals. Thus, there is a notable and major difference between the function of the RAP as utilized in the past compared to the contemporary application of such rule to equitable interests in a trust.

The RAP was developed in the context of limiting landowners' attempts to permanently immunize in kind conveyances of sequential future interests or in kind executory devises of land from various forms of legal exposure and accountability. These in kind estates or entailed interests were structurally subject to poor management as there was no person who possessed the power of alienation or could otherwise secure credit for capital investment. Thus, there was little reason for an individual holding merely a life estate to make investments in the operations, and there existed an inherent tendency to squeeze as much cash from the business as possible. As a result, some of these famous estates financially deteriorated.

The judges of the courts were visually observant of this decaying process. These decision makers of the feudal times saw the rapid failure of many large estates in the same vein as we see abandoned, blighted factories throughout large urban areas. These visual realities of the feudal age caused deep concern as these large landed estates were the exclusive source of wealth and power. The automatic assumption to apply the RAP, born of deteriorating landed estates and manors of the distant past, to equitable interests in modern trusts is somewhat problematic in view of these differences.[7] It is noteworthy that perpetuities scholars, J. H. C. Morris and W. Barton Leach, keenly observed that the decision to apply the RAP to trusts was made "without discussion or recogni-

6. Pells v. Brown, (1620) 79 Eng. Rep. 504 (K.B.).

7. J. H. C. Morris & W. Barton Leach, The Rule Against Perpetuities 12 (Stevens & Sons 2d ed. 1962).

tion of these differences."[8] They also note the obvious: the RAP "began life as a part of the land law designed to prevent tying up the soil of England in the hands of the great families."[9] These differences in the conditions are significant and all too often under appreciated.

John H. Langbein brilliantly clarified this reality when discussing an entirely different topic; namely, the process by which trust law became a product of statutory law in the United States.[10] He clarified the transition from using trusts in feudal times principally as a vehicle for the conveyance of real estate in which the trustees had little operational duties, to the modern utilization of trusts wherein the trustees are in need of extensive authority to effectively manage highly complex investment assets in an ever-changing economic environment.[11]

> What is new is that the characteristic trust asset *has ceased to be ancestral land and has become instead a portfolio of marketable securities.* Long into the nineteenth century, the trust was still primarily a branch of the law of conveyancing, that is, the law of real property. The early treatises on trusts, Gilbert (three editions from 1734 to 1811) and Sanders (five editions from 1791 to 1844) are exclusively devoted to land transfer and landed estates. The modern trust, by contrast, is primarily a management device for assembling and administering a portfolio of financial assets.... When, however, financial assets came to displace family land as the characteristic form of wealth held in trust, trustees had to be suitably empowered for the work of portfolio management. Because investing and managing financial assets require extensive discretion to respond to changing market forces, trust law had to make a 180-degree turn to accommodate the management trust.[12]

The RAP was applied to interests in real estate in which sequential future interests severely limited alienation. Thus, the RAP has little reference to the highly complex management trusts of today. The RAP is all about real estate interests in kind, not equitable interests in which trustees possess all of the necessary powers to develop and preserve the assets of the trust.

8. *Id.*

9. *Id.* at 11.

10. John H. Langbein, *Why Did Trust Law Become Statute Law in the United States?*, 58 ALA. L. REV. 1069 (2007).

11. *Id.* at 1072–73.

12. *Id.* (emphasis added).

Langbein, as quoted above, clearly shows the shift from the past utilization of trusts as essentially a means to convey interests in real estate to the management function of modern portfolio assets. The assets now held in most modern trusts are neither removed from commerce nor restricted from alienation. A question completely lacking from most academic analysis is whether there exists an economic purpose for the continuation of the RAP when most assets having future interests are now located in modern portfolio trusts. Oh yes, how long can the dead hand be allowed to prevent the living from the unfettered enjoyment and control over their inheritance? The aforementioned is the ultra incantation and the mantra of RAP's dedicated proponents.

For the above reasons, Lewis F. Simes, one of the great scholars on future interests and the enigmas of the RAP, explained that he would have concurred that the RAP has no rational application to modern trusts and should be abolished, but for the fact that there are other reasons to justify its continuance.

> In short, if, as judges have sometimes thought, alienability to secure productivity is the sole purpose of the Rule against Perpetuities, then we have reached a point where the Rule should be completely abolished.... I would not join them in this movement for reform. While the Rule against Perpetuities, for the reasons I have given, is not quite as significant from an economic standpoint as is sometimes supposed, there is still a policy to be conserved by it.[13]

Simes then moves into the exposition of the dead hand argument as the ultimate "justification" for the continuation of RAP; i.e., that there should be some limit on the period of "dead hand control." This is not unlike a bait and switch defense—there is always another reason for the continuance of the RAP. Apparently, an unconditional commitment to the RAP, for whatever reason, is and remains the endemic legacy of the academic community.

Common Law Rules against Perpetuity (CLRAP)

The employment of the term "modern RAP" necessarily suggests that there was at least a prior rule, or possibly a number of rules against perpetuities, that existed before the modern version. It has long been understood by some

13. Lewis M. Simes, *The Policy Against Perpetuities*, 103 U. Pa. L. Rev. 707, 721 (1955).

of the scholars of the common law, including A. W. B. Simpson, that there were a series of "so-called *old* rule against perpetuities."[14]

> There never was a single old rule, or a single body of doctrine, which was comparable to the new rule against remoteness of vesting; instead there were a number of interrelated rules and principles, some of them of uncertain scope, which together checked the excesses of settlors. Thus there was the principle which laid down that the entail was a barrable estate, the rules governing contingent remainder, the uncertain antecedents of the rule in *Whitby v. Mitchell*, the rule in *Purefoy v. Rogers*, the general principle that the fee simple was alienable and so forth—all this medley of doctrine added up to 'the old rule' against perpetuities.[15]

One of the more telling narratives of the relationship of the modern RAP to the CLRAP is set forth in Fearne's tenth edition on contingent remainders and executory interests.[16] Charles Butler's note of 1819, included in the tenth edition of Fearne's book, is of special relevance here. For that reason, the entire note of Butler is published as Appendix A. Butler explains in the critical portion of his commentary the nexus of the CLRAP to the modern RAP. It was the later modern RAP that was especially created and designed to eliminate the similar perpetuity problem created by an executory interest:

> After the introduction of executory uses, the question of perpetuity necessarily forced itself on the attention of the courts. The introduction of fines, and still more, the introduction of recoveries, which originated in an arbitrary decision of the Judges, in direct opposition to a positive statute [*De Donis Conditionalibus*], sufficiently shewed that such a modification of property, as rendered it perpetually inalienable, or postponed the power of alienating it to a period excessively remote, would not be endured. It was, therefore, incumbent on the courts to fix the boundary, beyond which executory limitations should not be permitted to operate. In fixing it, they proceeded by way of

14. *See* A. W. B. Simpson, A History of the Land Law 231 (2d ed. 1986).

15. *Id.*

16. *See* Charles Fearne, An Essay on the Learning of Contingent Remainders and Executory Devises 561–69 (Charles Butler & Josiah W. Smith eds., 10th ed. 1844). Reginald G. Marsden in his book on perpetuities also cited and quoted an extensive portion of Butler's note on the evolution of the RAP. Reginald G. Marsden, The Rule Against Perpetuities: A Treatise on Remoteness in Limitations, With a Chapter on Accumulation and the Thelluson Act 36–38 (1883).

> analogy to the legal effect of remainders at common law, in postponing the exercise of powers of alienation. The usual effect of such a settlement was to limit the lands to a person during his life, with an immediate remainder to his children or some of them in tail. In all such case, the tenant for life was in existence when the settlement began to operate; and it has been stated that the law did not allow such limitations of it as conferred a life estate on his children, with remainders in tail to their children.
>
> Thus the utmost restraint upon alienation, which the law, as it stood after the statute *de donis*, allowed in the settlement of real property, was the limitation of one or more life estates to persons in being, and a limitation of one or more estates tail in remainder expectant on the expiration of the preceding estate or estates for life.
>
> A power of alienation by fine or recovery was inseparably inherent to the seisin of an estate tail; but the exercise of it was necessarily suspended during the minority of a tenant in tail. Supposing, therefore, an estate to be limited in the usual manner to father for life, remainder to his sons successively in tail, and that the father died leaving an only son just born, or his wife enseint, *the land would be inalienable during the life of the tenant for life, and after his decease would remain inalienable during 21 years, (the term of the son's minority,) with a possible protraction of that term for a few months, to allow for the period of gestation. This was the utmost period to which the restraint on alienation could be protracted.* In reference to this obvious case, and without perplexing the general law on the subject by a further attempt at analogy, the courts, by a long series of determinations, fixed the actual boundary of executory limitation at an event so limited, that it must, from its nature, either take effect or become incapable of taking effect within the period of one or more life or lives in being, and a further term of 21 years, with an allowance of a few months, or at the immediate expiration of that period.[17]

Butler's observation clarifies the copycat design of the RAP and its nexus with the antecedent CLRAP. In this sense, the modern RAP is not a new species of law. It represents the well-known institution by which judges invent and expand the law by analogy. Judges and lawyers habitually apply known legal doctrines by analogy to resolve comparable problems arising in a slightly different context. Although the matter of *seisin* does not apply to the unique nature

17. Fearne, *supra* note 16, at 565–67 (emphasis added).

of an executory interest, the exact time differential applied to executory interests under the *modern RAP is practically identical to the established time differential previously determined to resolve the antecedent common law interests having a tendency to a perpetuity (fee tail) or creating an abhorred abeyance of* seisin *(contingent remainders).*

The Irish Law Reform Commission Report (2000) further confirmed the above relationship. The Report noted that the RAP is "the leading member of what could be called a family of rules" intending to make the ancient commitment to the right of alienation a reality for the English community (a direct derivative of *Quia Emptores* in 1290) and seeking to preclude any substantive limitation of such right by devices or conveyances tending to a perpetuity.[18] Principal components of the family of rules, as identified by the Report, include the: judicial invention of the means by which the tenant in tail could cut the fee tail as well as the remainder and the reversion, the rule against inalienability, the rule against trusts of undue duration, the contingent remainder rules and its extension by the rule of *Purefoy v. Rodgers*, the rule in *Whitby v. Mitchell*, and the rule against accumulations.[19] In view of this analysis of the RAP and other known problems, the Irish Law Commission, not surprisingly, recommended repeal of the RAP[20] and suggested as a simultaneous procedural offset to such repeal that certain courts be authorized to make whatever variations to a trust instrument that would provide a *benefit* to the applicant.[21] Although settlors would have an equal right to participate in the judicial proceedings, they would not have any special right of veto to modifications in the terms or conditions of the trust as the courts might decide are beneficial.[22]

---

18. *See* The Law Reform Commission, Report on the Rule Against Perpetuities and Cognate Rules 8, 2–8 (2000), *available at* http://www.lawreform.ie/publications/data/lrc111/lrc_111.pdf [hereinafter Irish Law Commission, RAP].

19. *Id.*

20. *Id.* at 58 ("Accordingly, we recommend that the rule against Perpetuities be statutorily abolished. We further recommend the introduction of Variation of Trusts legislation.").

21. *See* The Law Reform Commission, Report on the Variation of Trusts 2, 54 (2000), *available at* http://www.lawreform.ie/publications/data/lrc112/lrc_112.pdf [hereinafter Irish Law Commission, Trusts]; *see also* Jesse Dukeminier & James E. Krier, *The Rise of the Perpetual Trust*, 50 UCLA L. Rev. 1303, 1339–42 (2003) (expressing other methods by which perpetual trusts could be limited in a manner as proposed by the Irish Law Commission); *cf.* Joshua C. Tate, *Perpetual Trusts and the Settlor's Intent*, 53 U. Kan. L. Rev. 595 (2005).

22. Irish Law Commission, Trusts, *supra* note 21, at 54.

Another component that should be included in the antecedent family of rules against perpetuities (CLRAP) is the device by which grantors attempted to create, outside of the fee tail, a so-called perpetual freehold; i.e., either a series of successive life estates or imposition of forfeiture upon any attempt to alienate the estate. One might also add to this family of rules the statutory prohibition (*de Viris Religiosis*)[23] against transfers of property to religious bodies without license from the Crown. Such conveyances tended to create a *de facto* perpetuity in that religious institutions never died, married, or ever incurred the disability of minority. In a classic sense, such transfers were to the dead hands (*mortmain*). All of the aforementioned interests were equally subject to failure by judicial determination, other than mortmain transfers to religious bodies, as excessive legal restraints on alienation for indefinite periods or a violation of *seisin* (who is going to perform the feudal services to the lord?). The *mortmain* restriction, though not fully enforced by the crown, was somewhat rectified by the later dissolution of the monasteries and subsequent reallocation of their estates by Henry VIII in 1536.

Charles Sweet, arch critic of Gray's scholarship,[24] also supported the relationship of the CLRAP to the modern RAP. His scholarship reaffirmed, without conditions, the intimate relationship of the CLRAP to the RAP. Sweet also noted that the elimination of restraints on alienation by reason of *Taltarum's Case* sent landowners scurrying for other devices and means to curtail alienation.

> [T]o make their land inalienable [conveyancers] tried to prevent the barring of entails by annexing conditions of forfeiture, limitations over and other provisions; but all of these devices were held void because they were inconsistent with the liberty of alienation which the practice of barring entails had re-introduced. It is in connexion with these devices that the term "perpetuity" first occurs. Thus in *Corbet's Case* (1600), where a proviso (or "clause of perpetuity") restraining a tenant entail from attempting to bar the entail was held void.[25]

Finally, one cannot overlook William Holdsworth's discussion on the existence of the CLRAP. He has an extended discussion of these rules under the

23. Statutum de viris religiosis, 1279, 7 Edw. 1, c.13 (Eng.).

24. See discussion of Sweet's academic criticism of Gray, *infra* Chapter 9. Dukeminier considered Sweet one of the cadre English authorities on the law of property who were noticeably irritated by Gray's success and acclaim on questions relating to a perpetuity. They thought of him as an "usurper and resented the deference paid to him by English courts." *See* Jesse Dukeminier, *Perpetuities: The New Empire*, 77 Yale L.J. 159, 159 (1967).

25. Charles Sweet, *Perpetuities*, 15 L.Q.R. 71, 72 (1899) (footnotes omitted).

heading of *The Older Rules Against Perpetuities*.[26] Holdsworth's discussion replicates the general views expressed herein by Simpson, Charles Butler, Charles Sweet, and the Irish Law Reform Commission. However, the existence of the CLRAP are not universally accepted doctrine in the opinion of many other scholars, including Gray. In addition, there is no universal agreement about which of the ancient rules should be included within the category of the CLRAP. Assuming the case for the establishment of such family of rules concerning perpetuities is sufficiently sustainable for the reasons expressed herein, there is nothing radically new from this perspective in the invention of the modern RAP.

It is clear, beyond peradventure, that the modern RAP was chiseled out of the pre-existing framework applicable to common law conveyances having a tendency to a perpetuity. Such rules were then retooled by analogy so as to apply to the newly minted executory interests that were not otherwise subject to the aforementioned common law rules against perpetuity. The executory interests would have the same perpetual restraint on alienability, as did the aforementioned common law restraints. In view of the *Pells v. Brown*[27] decision, such executory interests would otherwise be immune to destruction but for the invention of the modern RAP. What law students need to understand is the time period of the modern RAP is the exact time differential established by the CLRAP!

Do students of the present and past realize that the modern RAP as first articulated by Lord Nottingham in the infamous *Duke of Norfolk's Case*[28] was neither a radical nor sudden departure from the established common law rules that generally applied to earlier conveyances having a tendency to a perpetuity? Nottingham simply decided that a condition or limitation which will necessarily occur within lives in being did not create an "Inconvenience"—i.e., no tendency to a perpetuity.

It is doubtful that law students possess this historical connection in view of the modest exposure to English legal history! English legal authorities, as noted above, were particularly concerned during the medieval period about the possible dangers that might occur if any conveyance caused an abeyance of *seisin*.[29]

---

26. *See* 7 Sir William Holdsworth, A History of English Law 197–214 (5th Impression 2003) (1925).

27. Pells v. Brown, (1620) 79 Eng. Rep. 504 (K.B.).

28. Duke of Norfolk's Case, (1682) 22 Eng. Rep. 931, 3 Ch. Cas. 1 (Ch.).

29. *See* quote of Professor Berman, *supra* note 1. He makes the important distinction between the *right* of possession as opposed to possession. The question as to the essential meaning of the legal term *seisin* as critically applied by the courts and utilized in the explanation of the English law of real property is not likely ever to be fully recovered intact from the mist of the legal past. *See* F. W. Maitland, *The Seisin of Chattels*, 1 L.Q.R. 324

"[T]here should always be some person capable of meeting adverse claims and preserving the seisin for successors ... there must never be an abeyance of seisin ... there must be an uninterrupted tenancy of the freehold."[30] Indeed, the transfer of *seisin* was seen as an essential part of the investiture in a freehold estate that secured status as a free person of good standing, entitled to greater recognition in communal affairs and a right to file a writ of *novel disseisin* in the King's court. "These rights gave him importance and dignity as a freeholder and a freeman."[31]

From this perspective, one's legal status under the common law was primarily dependent upon one's relationship to real property. After all, who would bear the burden of making good on the feudal obligations of service or securing payment of the relief (transfer cost for the oldest son to take as successor of their ancestor's estate)? If a successor to a prior freehold estate was granted a contingent remainder and failed to meet the condition precedent at or prior to the death or termination of the preceding estate life estate, such event would immediately cause an abeyance of *seisin*. It was for that reason validity of legal contingent remainders became subject to the Rule of Destructibility. George L. Haskins explained the basis for the Rule of Destructibility and the function of *seisin*:

> [I]t was not perceived how an owner could be seised of such a freehold interest if he were unknown or if a condition were attached to his taking it.... It became law that a contingent remainder in realty, unless in trusts and hence equitable, was subject to destruction.... [T]he common law refused to tolerate a gap in seisin. This reasoning required what has been referred to as natural destructibility.[32]

Thus, if there was no immediate successor entitled to take upon the natural termination of the preceding estate, the contingent remainder failed.

(1885); F. W. Maitland, *The Mystery of Seisin*, 2 L.Q.R. 481 (1886); F. W. Maitland, *The Beatitudes of Seisin*, 4 L.Q.R. 24 (1888). The English legal historian Kenneth Edward Digby noted the connection of status as a freeman as a product of one's relation to real property. *See* Kenneth Edward Digby, History of the Law of Real Property 135 (1892); *see also* 2 William Holdsworth, History of English Law 354 (5th Impression 2003) (1903).

30. E. H. Burn, Cheshire & Burn's Modern Law of Real Property 40 (16th ed. 2000) (1925).

31. James Kent, Commentaries on American Law 24 (14th ed. 1896).

32. George L. Haskins, *"Inconvenience" and the Rule for Perpetuities*, 48 Mo. L. Rev. 451, 462–63 (1983).

Simpson explained that every conveyance of a contingent remainder must also be preceded by a vested freehold estate in which *seisin* resided in a known person; otherwise no one would have *seisin*, and such attempted conveyance would necessarily fail.[33] The legal authorities of the past also tell us that the "common law abhorred an abeyance of seisin."[34] Although the law has no feelings, except by attribution, habitual anthropomorphism of the law remains nevertheless an indigenous practice of the profession. Unfortunately, it is a rhetorical device that catches most of us.

The early judicial review of contingent remainders presented a difficult conceptual question for the courts; they did not understand how an unknown potential grantee could acquire *seisin*. For this reason, the courts denied the recognition of such contingent interests. Accordingly, legal authorities expressed the view that contingent "legal remainders were subjected to inflexible rules largely based upon the sanctity of *seisin*."[35] Paraphrasing the great scholar of the common law, Edward Coke, *seisin* "was the golden met-wand and measure"[36] of the law of real property and the essential prism by which the English jurists invented the structure of future estates.

In a similar sense, the fee tail conveyance as authorized and expanded by judicial interpretation of the statute *De Donis Conditionalibus* allowed an indefinite line of descendents to take as successor tenants in tail. Upon an indefinite failure of issue, the property would either revert to the grantor or go to a designated beneficiary of a vested remainder. Approximately two hundred years after the enactment of *De Donis*, the courts authorized a legal procedure of common recovery, and then later by fine, that allowed a tenant in tail, at majority, to cut all other future interests including the potential successors in tail, reversion, and remainder.[37] Other than the later development of the technique of strict settlement,[38] a grantor could no longer be assured that a conveyance as a fee tail would be effective to protect the estate from the folly of his descendents. Subsequently, grantors still sought advice of their advisors, which led to the invention of cleverly constructed nuanced conveyances in the nature of unbarrable entails. The courts quickly rejected these techniques as a

---

33. *See* Simpson, *supra* note 14, at 213.

34. *See* Robert MeGarry & William Wade, The Law of Real Property 45 (Charles Harpum ed., 6th ed. 2000).

35. *See* R.E. MeGarry and H.W.R. Wade, The Law of Real Property 190 (1966).

36. Prohibitions del Roy, (1607) 77 Eng. Rep. 1342, 1343 (K.B.), 12 Co. Rep. 64, 65 (notes of Sir Edward Coke on his conference with James I).

37. Taltarum's Case, Y.B. 12 Edw. 4, pl. 25 (1472).

38. *See* Simpson, *supra* note 14, at 235–40.

means to do indirectly that which was no longer available in the form of a fee tail conveyance in the past.[39]

From the perspective of the Rule of Destructibility of Contingent Remainders and the ability to cut all future interests in a fee tail conveyance, we discern a simple maxim of the English legalist. We can now ask what is the maximum period during which a future estate may be delayed from vesting in interest under the CLRAP? First, what is the period during which a successor contingent remainder must vest in interest or fail under the Rule of Destructibility? The answer is simply *a life or lives in being*! Second, what is the corresponding maximum period during which a fee tail estate could be limited before the tenant in tail could convert his or her interest into a fee simple absolute with the right of alienation? As we know, the prior maximum period during which a fee tail estate could be restricted from alienation without the cooperation of the first tenant in tail, upon majority, was: *a life or lives in being plus twenty-one years—an extended period covering the possible minority of the first tenant in tail.* Is this descriptive duration for both the fee tail and contingent remainder reminiscent of the maximum period applicable to the RAP? Indeed, it is! *The time period is identical to the period applicable to fee tail interests and very comparable to the rule regarding contingent remainders*; except for limited additional time in the event of pregnancy (*en ventre sa mere*). Thus, do the rules otherwise applying to contingent remainders and fee tail interests under the common law provide direct guidance as to what Lord Nottingham deafly applied in the *Duke of Norfolk's Case*?[40] Definitely!

Nottingham applied the established legal doctrine that was otherwise applicable to the CLRAP to the nuanced executory interest. So long as the limitation or condition would happen during a life or lives in being, Nottingham held that "where the Limitation doth not tend to a Perpetuity, nor introduceth any visible Inconvenience, what should hinder that from being good,"[41] because after all "Perpetuities are abhorred, it is upon the Inconvenience, which hinders...."[42] It took the courts some one hundred and fifty years before resolving the exact time period for an executory interest to vest in interest. But for this resolution, such executory interests might have otherwise continued indefi-

---

39. English conveyancers invented the technique of "strict settlement" to avoid the application of the CLRAP introduced in *Taltarum's Case.* Such technique now allowed settlors to tie up estates through subsequent generations. Professor Simpson fully explains the technique. *See id.*

40. The Duke of Norfolk's Case, (1682) 22 Eng. Rep. 931, 3 Ch. Cas. 1 (Ch.).

41. *Id.* at 49.

42. *Id.* at 47.

nitely.[43] Nottingham's decision in the *Duke of Norfolk's Case* is in the minds of some experts a rule "for" perpetuities as opposed to "against."[44] Apart from that, RAP is a direct application of the internalized legal training that the English law students derived from their extended study of the CLRAP—as taught and learned, perhaps by rote and rule of thumb, at the various Inns of Court.

Therefore, the rules applicable to executory interests tending to a perpetuity are neither unique nor new. The RAP, as finally resolved, replicates the same time period during which it was determined the maximum period to clog a fee tail before the tenant in tail had the power to alienate and cut all future interests.[45] These pre-existing CLRAP constituted the principal matter of study for the English legal scholars and jurists during the late feudal period. These highly relevant considerations are seldom discussed in the indoctrination (i.e., the teaching of the rule) of the RAP as the *sanctum sanctorum* of property law.[46]

Contemporary Relevance of the RAP: Uncertain and Questionable

The dominant commitment of the academic community to the importance of continuing and enforcing the RAP, whether of the strict nature marketed by Gray or of the enlightened, so-called redesigned modern version of the late twentieth century, has been explained as applying a measure of justice for the benefit of society. The participants involved in the modification include the ALI, NCCUSL, state legislative bodies, and the courts by judicial inventions. As noted above, Gray's masterful scholarship on the RAP reified its exacting elements. Indeed, Haskins referred to Gray as the "high priest" of the RAP.[47] Conversely, the repeal of the RAP is seen by some members of the academic community as outright moral decadence and explained as another embar-

---

43. See explanation of *Pells v. Brown* by Professor Simpson, in SIMPSON, *supra* note 14, at 220–24.

44. Haskins, *supra* note 32, at 471 n.96.

45. *See* MORRIS & LEACH, *supra* note 7, at 9–11 (explaining the actual time period before the courts finally arrived at the identical duration as that established by the CLRAP). The final contours of the time period for the RAP were resolved when the House of Lords reached its decision in *Cadell* v. *Palmer*, (1833) 1 Cl. & F. 372.

46. *See* Dukeminier & Krier, *supra* note 21, at 1304 (citing W. BARTON LEACH, CASES AND TEXT ON THE LAW OF WILLS 203 (2d ed. 1951)).

47. George L. Haskins, *Extending the Grasp of the Dead Hand: Reflections of the Origins of the Rule Against Perpetuities*, 126 U. PA. L. REV. 19, 21 n.7 (1977).

rassing example of a "rush to the bottom." What is surprising or shocking is the fact that Gray's theme song of the RAP has been absorbed as essential learning in law school without any significant concern for its actual socioeconomic consequences,[48] other than standard reasons (assertions) for its enforcement.

Apparently, the important question for academic discussion during the twentieth century was simply the matter of how the RAP's excesses, as laid out by Gray, could be skillfully managed (eliminated) without causing a loss of support for its continued enforcement as a principal rule of property law. To excise a number of the fundamental tenets embedded in the RAP by Gray, called for an operation of a very technical nature that would also not endanger general support for its continuance.

Some of these excesses embedded in the RAP reflect aspects of Gray's extraordinary austere persona,[49] born of the milieu of the nineteenth century calling for accountability and remorseless enforcement of the law. The exorcism of Gray's remorseless enforcement of the RAP (e.g., Gray's comment that the purpose of the RAP is to defeat the settlor's intent) by the ALI and other institutions through the adoption of the "wait and see" reform had two principal objectives: first, to eliminate the inequitable results caused by a fierce enforcement of Gray's RAP; second, to retain broad-based support for the continued enforcement of the RAP. This operation is a difficult balance to achieve and was, perhaps, the catalyst for some to think of the *Impossible Dream*;[50] life without the RAP.

Again, the question of the RAP's beneficial impact or function in our society was never to become a serious focus of the academic inquiry.[51] In view of this record, it is not surprising to note that generations of law professors have been force-feeding the challenging contingencies of the rule to students without the slightest regard for the actual impact of the RAP. Like most indoctrination of ancient rules of law, the pedagogic objective simply becomes that of instilling a fealty-like acceptance of these received traditional assumptions and assertions regarding purposes associated with aggressive enforcement of the RAP.

The practice of accomplishment of purposes by authoritative assertion and reiteration is in contradistinction to focusing on the actual empirical consequences of the RAP. Nevertheless, such a pedagogic practice, particularly as it

---

48. 4 Restatement of Property, pt. I, introductory cmt., at 2129 (1944).

49. The direct relevance of one's personal value system to one's scholarship is succinctly explained by Judge Noonan in Chapter 12.

50. *The Impossible Dream*, *in* Man of La Mancha (Mitch Leigh & Joe Darion 1965).

51. *See* 4 Restatement of Property, *supra* note 48, at 2129–33.

relates to rules of law born of the ancient régime, continues to be a dominant institution in law school "training." In this sense, law school is more of a moderately concealed transfer of the deemed cultural values and historical narratives by the established centers of knowledge to vulnerable law students. As such, it becomes part of the students' objective truth. Collectively, the experience of legal education provides a base of established propositions of fact that are intended to constitute the essential framework for each graduating law student. This is not to deny that the more essential object of law school is to provide the student with analytical skills and the corresponding ability to construct arguments for or against any position; however, within these positive goals of developing analytical skills is the embedding of particular norms and factual narratives relating to the principles of law.

What are the principal asserted objectives of the RAP? There are the repetitive usual suspects: dead hand control, excessive concentration of wealth in the grasp of the few, limitation of the flow of goods in commerce, avoidance of taxation, and the concomitant dangerous establishment of family dynasties. In addition, how has the RAP limited any of the aforementioned alleged problems during the twentieth or twenty-first centuries? British legal scholars have deftly sidestepped both issues: first, by utilizing the technique of strict settlement during prior centuries and, more recently, by avoiding the dangerous question of the actual function of the RAP in their most recent study of the rule.

There has been both an enormous increase in wealth[52] as well as a significant increase in the percentage of assets owned by the Four Hundred. Indeed, one must ask whether the RAP has, at most, an imperceptible impact on modern society. Has the wealth of the few been significantly reduced or redistributed by and through the RAP, the national anti-trust doctrines, or even by the federal transfer tax system? Is the RAP a sacred rule of the past that has no effective function in the realities of the economy of today? The answer is most likely a product of your belief as to the degree that the RAP has been effective in this respect.

---

52. See a recent study conducted by a staff member of the Federal Reserve Board. Arthur B. Kennickell, Federal Reserve Board, *Ponds and Streams: Wealth and Income in the U.S., 1989 to 2007*, *in* Finance and Economics Discussion Series 2009–13, at 27, *available at* http://www.federalreserve.gov/pubs/feds/2009/200913/200913pap.pdf (discussing the construct of wealth, "changes in summary measures of its distribution over the 1989–2007 survey," and "clear[] indications of movement toward increased inequality").

Final Denouement of the RAP?

The academically constructed triage for the survival of the RAP has been thrashed in the last three decades, considering the reforms adopted by the ALI (1979); the adoption of USRAP by NCCUSL (1986, amended in 1990); and, its enactment by selective state legislative bodies. The desire of modern day barons to avoid aspects of the generation-skipping taxes, conjoined with the competition for trust business in respective states, as well as the marketing of dynasty trusts by lawyers, and other considerations has lead to either the outright repeal or the modification of the RAP in a way that makes the rule optional.[53] Approximately fifty percent of state legislative bodies have taken such action as a direct result of the intense advocacy applied by the respective state bar associations, the banking institutions, and serious concern for the loss of trust business to other more friendly state jurisdictions. Joel C. Dobris noted that law professors have had less impact when it comes to stopping the rash of movement to repeal the RAP.[54]

Despite the transformative modification of this sacrosanct rule of property law, the RAP has not yet been given an honorable burial. The RAP awaits a final, definitive closure and a well deserved release from purgatory. This formal release can only be delivered by the academic community. Currently, there is an increasing radical reduction of time allocated to teaching the Rule in law school; indeed, many professors have asked the simple question whether it should be taught at all. This evolving scholarly indifference is a product of the repeal or modification of the RAP by a number of states. As a result, the creation of the dynasty trust is now a simple option for those of significant wealth. Perforce, this development just might be the serendipitous manner by which the RAP finds its ultimate resting place. To paraphrase Douglas MacArthur's final address to Congress regarding the destiny of old soldiers: "old rules never die, they just fade away."[55] The current exponential practice of allocating less

53. Robert H. Sitkoff & Max M. Schanzenbach, *Jurisdictional Competition for Trust Funds: An Empirical Analysis of Perpetuities and Taxes*, 115 Yale L.J. 356 (2005).

54. *See* Joel C. Dobris, *Undoing Repeal of the Rule Against Perpetuities: Federal and State Tools for Breaking Dynasty Trusts*, 27 Cardozo L. Rev. 2537, 2538 n.3 (2006) ("Most but not all law professors want to keep the Rule.... We profs seem impotent in the face of this repeal movement of which we disapprove. Received university wisdom is being ignored. I'm shocked. I'm shocked.").

55. General Douglas MacArthur, Speech before the Joint Session of Congress (April 19, 1951). The speech concludes with the emotional peroration on his final separation from the military after some fifty-two years of service. His delivery of the speech and remarkable record of service to our country still resonates:

> The world has turned over many times since I took that oath on the plain at West

time to teaching the mysteries of the RAP, alone, might lead to its ultimate demise—even more exciting, perhaps within present lives in being!

> Point, and the hopes and dreams have long vanished, but I still remember the refrain of one of the most popular barrack ballads of that day which proclaim *old soldiers never die; they just fade away*. And like the old soldier of that ballad, I now close my military career and just fade away, an old soldier who tried to do his duty as God gave him the light to see that duty. Goodbye.

Id. (emphasis added).

Chapter 12

Conclusion

In asserting interpretations of Gray and his life, it is necessary to rely upon a review of his scholarship, professional life, letters, secondary sources, and to some extent, a more personal assessment of his character from the expressions and descriptions of his family and peers as mystically coded in a series of eulogies. The record as set forth herein is far too incomplete for a comprehensive biography,[1] but it is more than sufficient to provide a reasonable basis upon which to engage in responsible conjecture of his character and legal perspective. Hopefully, this essay provides a caring, and critical analysis of his life, perceptions, and *gestalt.*

These observations are not unique or specific to Gray, as it relates to the study of the interaction of culture with a person and how that person perceives and receives such interaction. This is a universal process that constitutes an inherent aspect attendant to one's existence in society. The impact of such broadly described processes affects all decision makers and plays a somewhat critical role in the development of their individual philosophy: that is, the process by which, over time, there occurs a simultaneous internalization and integration of one's professional values with one's personal values.[2] The rational element of our being plays a much less significant role in the formation of our individual framework. Its principal function is to justify, for a time certain, one's pre-existing commitment to particular legal and social facts. This

1. Andrew L. Kaufman spent forty years to complete an outstanding and comprehensive biography of Justice Benjamin N. Cardozo. *See* Andrew L. Kaufman, *Cardozo and the Art of Biography*, 20 Cardozo L. Rev. 1245, 1247 (1998). The extensive period during which Kaufman chooses to carefully reconstruct the nature and extent of Cardozo's law practice and the difficulty of that research in view of the very limited record available is inspiring. Kaufman observed the influence of Cardozo's law practice on his outlook as a judge. *Id.* at 1251.

2. On such an oblique but important observation, the internalization process is discussed in a prior article. *See* Gerald P. Moran, *A Radical Theory of Jurisprudence: The "Decisionmaker" as the Source of the Law—The Ohio Supreme Court's Adoption of the Spendthrift Trust Doctrine as a Model*, 30 Akron L. Rev. 393, 395–96 (1997).

individual framework is referred to as one's "idiosyncratic cognitive process." Such framework is not necessarily a comprehensive perception of reality that is frozen at any particular time; there is always room for modification. Yet, metamorphosis of one's socially constructed framework can and does occur. Justice Blackmun's radical change in judicial attitude represents a prime example of this ever remaining unique potential in human nature.[3]

Once the parameters of the framework are fixed and the internalization of the values are synthesized and/or connected, seldom are there perceptive differences between one's personal, external social stances and one's professional legal framework. Magically, in most of human existence, the personal and the professional values are identical. There are no two Justice Scalias; he speaks one language, and it is always of one conviction—"I am right, and if you disagree, you are wrong." There is no room for a schizophrenic decision maker. Finally, a decision maker, like other members of the species, tends to believe that what she believes on a personal-professional basis to be true *is* an empirically validated fact. There may be a further exception here for a decision maker who is conscious of this process and aggressively challenges her perceptions of facts by and through a radical commitment to active skepticism.[4]

Ultimately, John Chipman Gray is a man of mystery. From a *reflective and speculative* review of Gray and his work and life, one distills the picture of a man who is: very intelligent, well read, organized, dedicated, disciplined, charming (albeit somewhat taciturn[5]), concerned, supportive of students, friendly, while also being quietly ambitious, covertly competitive,[6] and one suspects, stealthily introverted, although disclosing a refined and practiced social, public persona.[7] As such, Gray was not one to take risks in personal relationships.

---

3. *See* Callins v. Collins, 510 U.S. 1141, 1153 (1994) (Blackmun, J., dissenting).

4. I would call the study of this process one of legal social psychoanalysis: the study of the impact of society in the construction and priority of a decision maker's values or norms, which are then applied to resolve legal controversies. In the vein of Eugen Ehrlich, the decision maker determines the living law according to her perception of critical norms and converts that determination into formal propositions of law. *See* EUGEN EHRLICH, FUNDAMENTAL PRINCIPLES OF THE SOCIOLOGY OF LAW (Transaction Publishers 2001) (1922).

5. Roland Gray described his father, in part, as "by nature reserved." *See* ROLAND GRAY, JOHN CHIPMAN GRAY, MEMOIR 38 (Privately Printed 1917) [hereinafter GRAY, MEMOIR].

6. Most sons can attest to the existence of or the absence of a temper on the part of their father; Roland saw his father as a person who had "a strong temper," albeit one that his father carefully managed to exercise admirable control over. *See id.* at 39.

7. See generally the comments of Mary Temple as quoted in, Stephen A. Siegel, *John Chipman Gray and the Moral Basis of Classical Legal Thought*, 86 IOWA L. REV. 1513, 1577 (2001) (quoting Letters from Mary Temple to John Chipman Gray (1869–1870) (on file at the Houghton Library, Harvard University, bMS Am. 1092.12)).

The most revealing aspects of his persona are caught by indirection from the observations and questions put forth in a series of Mary Temple's letters written to Gray and other biographies of Gray's friends, of the post-civil war period, when the mating selection dance was in high vogue in the Boston community. Mary was the very unusual and spirited young woman who caught the imagination of Oliver Wendell Holmes Jr., Henry James Jr., William James, and Gray, among others. Stephen A. Siegel, after having reviewed her correspondence, noted that her search for the explication of "Gray's fundamental beliefs was never satisfied."[8] Siegel concludes perceptively, "Our similar interest also may remain unrequited."[9] In view of Gray's finessed deception, this may be something of an understatement.

Gray was meticulous even in his last days; he prepared for death as few do. Gray organized his personal records as part of the process of accepting death (possibly destroying items of a very personal nature), while carefully seeing that his retained collection of letters from Mary were sent to Henry Jr. His manner was of the nineteenth century in so many ways.[10] One might also envision him as intentionally reserved while actively engaged in inventing his own personalized version of the English gentleman. In a basic sense, Gray was an American patrician: possessing a fine education, a formal and responsible commitment to family, and a quiet honor, certainly devoid of frivolity or exaggeration.

He was perpetually driven to secure a defined economic and social standing of the highest order in his rather special Brahmin community—*perhaps never forgetting the family social embarrassment engendered by his father's bankruptcy.* There can be no question that Gray was completely absorbed by the study and practice of law; he also sought to provide clarity and guidance, particularly as it related to teaching, from his perception and belief of the essential values of his life. Gray's drive for academic authority, scholarly recognition, and procuring universal acquiescence in the legal perfection of "his" progeny, the RAP. In some respects, Gray's scholarly pursuits were a personal search for inner meaning that the achievement of a successful practice and substantial remuneration alone could not, and did not, provide. He was a quiet man who also consciously desired recognition as a legal authority on both sides of the Atlantic. It was a personal mandate that he accepted and fulfilled with enduring results

---

8. *Id.*

9. *Id.*

10. This fact becomes somewhat palpable if one reads the preface to the second edition of his book on restraints. *See* John Chipman Gray, Restraints on the Alienation of Property iii–iv (2d ed., Rothman & Co. 1997) (1883).

derived from his enormous commitment to scholarship and discipline. Truly, the principal energies of Gray were consumed in fulfilling the extensive responsibilities of his life as a law teacher, scholar, practicing lawyer, and business manager.[11]

It is not infrequent that there are stories about a person that are most certainly apocryphal, but they are continued because they reveal an essential characteristic of the person as perceived by others. Students do have a way at conjuring up such fictional anecdotes regarding their professors that suit their occasional state of ill repair at a local distillery. One such story about Gray is particularly apropos.

> The most apocryphal story of all had it that in his younger days Gray was proctor of a dormitory, where midnight closing was strictly enforced. (*The impossibility of the tale is shown by the fact Gray never lived in a dormitory after he left college.*) A student who had been out till one o'clock with a sick friend banged on the dormitory door, trusting in Gray's knowledge of his excuse. Soon he heard Gray shuffling down the steps in slippers, murmuring to himself as he came, "The weight of authority is that I should keep this man out.—But reason urges me to let him in." And then with his hand on the knob, "I think I will let the weight of authority prevail." His footsteps died away up the stairs, leaving the luckless youth to seek lodging elsewhere.[12]

The law, the common law in particular, was "the magnificent opportunity" for Gray to ascertain the specific rules of a transcendent nature. Those rules, which were necessary for the universal good ordering of society, began with the most primitive verbal etchings or meanderings and expanded to extemporaneous offerings from the tongues of the English judges, as reflected in the resolution of hundreds of English cases.

---

11. While it is frequently noted that Gray only engaged in the practice for his firm on Fridays during the school semester, no one mentions or discusses his activities during the summer at the law firm or the time he spent in managing the business growth. Roland Gray noted that, after the death of John Codman Ropes, his father "continued until his death in active practice of law as *head* of the firm, which included, at that time, eight of his former students at Harvard Law School." *See* Gray, Memoir, *supra* note 5, at 21 (emphasis added). In the same sense, no one mentions the substantial additional income that Gray most likely earned as a partner in the firm or the actual time expended at the firm.

12. The Harvard Law School Ass'n, The Centennial History of the Harvard Law School 1817–1917, at 209–10 (1918) (emphasis added). This story appears to capture the legalistic mindset of the distinguished Gray. One might believe that he would have enjoyed this version himself.

Many of these common law cases involved complex and uncertain fact patterns. Indeed, these decisions were being forged in the rapidly changing conditions of a post-feudal society that was quickly followed by an emerging industrial economy.[13] These changing economic conditions, mostly observable in the political struggles against the monopoly of the Crown, eventually broke the chains of the tightly wrought interdependent social rules of the late feudal period. From this body of poorly reported opinions of the English judicial engines of centuries past,[14] Gray created, found, interpreted, or issued authoritative edicts (perhaps he did all four: created, found, interpreted, and issued edicts) of or about the law. In doing so, he arrived at the ultimate simplistic formulation of the RAP. Gray compressed this history of confusion and contradiction into the most simplistic legal propositions by recasting his interpretations in a talismanic way to conform to his "perception" of the existing community standards.[15] And finally, Gray would forcefully apply such deciphered rules or edicts in a most efficient and consistent manner, without the slightest allowance of any exception. In so many ways, Gray succeeded in his mission and no one can ever deny him that accomplishment! If law were a science, Gray's formula of the RAP would be its first rule.

Gray made a lasting impact on the Harvard Law School at its most vulnerable period of adjustment and national achievement. That he was a practitioner first, as was true of other members of the Harvard Law faculty, has been frequently understated in the transposition of the paradigm of the history of legal education. As previously noted, what was seeded as the principal and dominant achievement of Harvard Law School was the birth of a new teacher-scholar[16] in the form of James Barr Ames, a scholar of the law who had not sig-

---

13. *See generally* George L. Haskins, *Extending the Grasp of the Dead Hand: Reflections on the Origins of the Rule Against Perpetuities*, 126 U. Pa. L. Rev. 19, 22–27 (1977).

14. *See* Lord Rodger of Earlsferry, *The Form and Language of Judicial Opinions*, 118 L.Q.R. 226, 230 (2002) ("[A]n evolution [] is going on apace at the present time. Put briefly, the opinions are evolving from a form of communication that was normally oral to a form of communication that is normally written."). Lord Rodger was speaking in respect to the evolution of opinions beginning with the purely oral opinions of the eighteenth century judges through the present. *See id.* at 229.

15. Gray offered some insight about the philosophical aspects of the law. *See* John Chipman Gray, The Nature and Sources of the Law 216 (2d ed., Beacon Press 1963) (1909).

16. According to Alfred S. Konesfsky & John Henry Schlegel, *Mirror, Mirror on the Wall: Histories of American Law Schools*, 95 Harv. L. Rev. 833, 848 (1982), the articulated job description and justification for the then newly defined scholarly career of the academic-lawyer was most succinctly set forth in 1895 by Thayer. *See* James Bradley Thayer, *The Teaching of English Law at Universities*, 9 Harv. L. Rev. 169, 183–84 (1895).

nificantly experienced the innate chaos of a legal practice. This was, in a sense, the appointment of a surgeon of law who had never operated on a living patient. This caused a true institutional revolution in legal education; the positioning of a scholar, who otherwise did not include on their resume significant legal experience, as the enduring center and criteria of legal education. It was not immediately apparent as to how this development would influence the unfolding of legal education in America. Gray, with the support of Thayer, was resistant to empowerment of legal neophytes as the new center of legal education. It is clear that he found the attitudes of Langdell and Ames in questioning legal opinions of judges troubling and somewhat pretentious, if not outright arrogant.[17] However, in this disagreement, as well as in most other differences with Langdell and Eliot, Gray was not successful. Accordingly, Gray reluctantly accommodated himself to the radical change in the direction of Harvard Law School.

There were a number of identifiable formal factors that directly impacted on the construction of Gray's social stance: (1) the very critical drama and experience of his early years with his parents and siblings; (2) the enormous impact flowing from his relatively unreflective and stoic judicial authoritarianism of his half-brother, judge, and then associate justice, Horace Jr.; (3) the rather well-defined elements of the Boston community in which the status of individuals and their families were moderately fixed by the nature of their ancestors as well as the strength of their present economic position and the classification of their employment; (4) the context of the environment at Harvard Law School and the explosion of the Langdellian delivery of legal education; and (5) his enduring professional and personal romance with things British; that is, the deeply held perception as to the innate perfection of the common law as he interpreted it or projected it to exist.

These factors efficiently congeal into the character of Gray, the man, the teacher, the scholar, the lawyer, the brother, the father, and the husband. Gray saw the necessity of providing a pattern of strict rules of law that provided well-constructed and rational answers to a variety of complex social issues. He approached each legal issue with something of a necessary moral imperative; the law must be imposed on the members of society in a way that will make for a stronger and more balanced community. Gray's unique abilities, as well as his profound study of the common law, when combined with his attention to the details of the English cases, made him a formidable authority on the

---

17. See discussion of the conflict at Harvard Law School during the reign of Dean Langdell, *supra* Chapter 6.

structural perfection of the common law that few American legal scholars would ever achieve or choose to challenge. This is particularly true during the legal ascendancy and eventual hegemonic branding of the form of legal education by the Harvard Law School.

That Gray blended his unique sense of social morality within the interpretation of the common law has not been sufficiently recognized. The luster of his scholarship was also enhanced by his standing at the Cambridge "academy of law" during the apogee of its ascendancy to a position of unparalleled prestige in the nineteenth century. The confluence of these interacting transformations, when mixed with his personal and professional experience, balanced naturally in this quiet, taciturn, and reserved Brahmin. Gray was not a man of uncertainty; he was at the epicenter of exploding forms of knowledge during the nineteenth century—the period of an American renaissance.

Gray clearly found satisfaction in controlling most of the professional matters that he chose to confront and resolve. Although he may have been covertly shy in interpersonal social situations, that dimension never adversely affected him in a professional capacity when offering guidance or conclusions to the legal riddles of his time.

His personal ambition from the perspective of an outsider would seem to have been well-settled and fully realized. Yet, one doubts that Gray would fully concur in that assessment or find sufficient personal satisfaction with his achievements. Roland Gray noted his father's proclivity to wear the cloak of self-criticism:

> A man who undertook such heavy tasks in so many fields as did Mr. Gray could not lack confidence in his own powers; yet he was genuinely modest. What he took in hand he accomplished, but usually he was more apt than any one [sic] else to find ground for criticism in the results. He cared nothing for the praise of people in general. The personal respect and affection of his friends and of his past and present pupils he valued. But with regard to his work, he preached and practised the principle that the only good opinion worth having was that of those qualified to judge.[18]

Although mortality is not a matter on which we are consulted, Gray would most likely agree, with measured reluctance, that he did meet his self-described personal obligations and that he was satisfied with the measurable and sig-

18. Gray, Memoir, *supra* note 5, at 41. It is not unusual for one to be dissatisfied with one's achievements as most feel or believe that they could produce more.

nificant achievements of his professional life. From this it may be said that the RAP, as Gray interpreted it, was a natural intellectual dimension of the institutional manner in which he viewed the function of law as a concrete rule that was a necessary prerequisite to the preservation of the well ordering of the community. While the RAP existed as an abstract intellectual progeny of Gray's will or intention, it nevertheless was based and had an empirical existence in the history of the common law. He made the RAP the centerpiece of his scholarly efforts and considered such rule and its draconian application as a fundamental guarantee to the delivery of a free and secure society. The benefits of the Rule were either a necessary ingredient or coincident to the delivery of liberty.

In the preface to *The Nature and Sources of the Law*, Gray stated, "[I]t seemed desirable to show how, in approaching the Law from different points of view, the same truths emerge as fundamental."[19] It is as if he believed that the law, properly considered, contained within it the needed and consistent prescription for the appropriate safeguard and evaluation of social action. It provided not only the fair and correct legal answer; it was in a sense, the source of principles[20] of morality for society. Thus, his life as a lawyer and scholar had underlying social and personal significance so long as he was searching for the ultimate pragmatic goodness of society. It is as if he had discovered a secular natural law system flowing from his keenly defined perception of the metaphysical nature of man in society, which propelled his personal vision regarding the appropriate balance of power that must be achieved. This quest also allowed him to identify and apply the values of society that he thought were necessary for its preservation. Thus, he believed the consequences of legal decisions were certain, measurable, and integral to the preservation of the essential morals of the community. These views are clearly found in his two major works: *Restraints on the Alienation of Property* and *The Rule Against Perpetuities*. These factors also appear by implication in his philo-

---

19. GRAY, *supra* note 15, at viii.

20. There is no question that Gray was potentially influenced, and if not, certainly he was fully exposed to the early germination of what was to become the American philosophical school of pragmatism. *See* LOUIS MENAND, THE METAPHYSICAL CLUB: A STORY OF IDEAS IN AMERICA 215–16 (2001) (noting that Gray was an active member of the Club with, among others, Holmes, John Ropes, Henry James, Henry Adams, and Arthur Sedgwick). The Club met on the second of each month and discussed philosophical matters. *Id.* Menand describes the social and intellectual milieu in which the theory of pragmatism evolves from this unique group interaction. And, oh yes, Horace Gray Jr., was also a member of one of the earlier elite dinner groups and, not surprisingly, the younger brother followed in Horace's shadow.

sophical tome. He was never to abandon these criteria as to the interrelationship of law and secular morality as he found it and the *role of man in society as he described it.*

Apart from legalistic criticism from the perch of the twentieth and twenty-first centuries as it relates to the application of the modern RAP to future interests in a trust, another of the essential themes flowing from this essay of Gray concerns the potential impact that the internal dynamics of his cultural environment, personal values, and unique personality had on his scholarly interpretation of the RAP. These interactive elements are inextricably projected into his scholarship on the RAP. He is truly the avatar of the RAP. There is a pattern of dogmatic and moralistic ideologies that relate to the personhood of Gray and are either imposed and/or highly emphasized as the *sine qua non* of the modern RAP. Gray was insistent in requiring a "remorseless" application of the RAP and equally resolute that the intent of the RAP was to "defeat the intent of the settlor."[21] These edicts are all part of Gray's moralistic interpretation of the RAP. Indeed, if there was any conceivable manner by which a gift might fail to vest within the prescribed time period—no matter how unlikely, impracticable, or inequitable—Gray would gladly apply the rule ruthlessly![22] For him, the RAP was a test of legal accountability and certainty. Consider him the executioner and RAP the guillotine for legal accountability. The merger of the man and his values with the Rule became inseparable. Students of the RAP do not simply study the rule; they also study the pre-existing values and perceptions of Gray the man—a refined gentlemen of the rarified Cambridge culture of the nineteenth century. He is truly the epitome of the RAP.

---

21. Professor Gray was very upset with a decision by Chief Justice Charles Doe of the New Hampshire Supreme Court in which a gift held in trust to be distributed when the youngest such grandchild reached age forty was held to be valid on the alleged distinction between a devise of general intent and particular intent; the first type valid and the second invalid under the application of the RAP. *See* John Chipman Gray, *General and Particular Intent in Connection with the Rule Against Perpetuities*, 9 Harv. L. Rev. 242, 250–51 (1895) ("This piece of legal history is full of instructions. The Rule in Shelly's Case is not a rule for interpretation, it is a Rule the object of which is to defeat intention.... The Rule against Perpetuities is, in like manner, a positive rule intended to defeat intention."). It is to be noted as a matter of some limited irony that the same Chief Justice Doe died shortly after the critical commentary of Gray was published. Chief Justice Doe received a very favorable eulogy published in the Harvard Law Review recognizing the importance of his role in scholarship. *See id.* at 535.

22. Recall the anecdotal and apocryphal story that the students of Harvard Law School conjured up regarding Gray's sense of mercy and the importance of strict application of the law. *See supra* note 12 and accompanying text.

The relationship of the person to his or her historical interpretation of the law is an emerging realization of our times. John T. Noonan Jr. explained the relationship of *interpreter* of the law to the law by the following:

> As I reached what seemed to me the heart of law's dependency on history, however, I became increasingly conscious of the central place of the human person in any account of the law. I also became increasingly conscious of the neglect of the person by legal casebooks, legal histories, and treatises of jurisprudence. Only in the response of the person to the person, so it seemed to me, did history have a significance to law. *Neglect of persons, it appeared, had led to the worst sins for which American lawyers were accountable.*[23]

Judge Noonan rightly admonished us to recognize that when one studies the history of law; one cannot omit consideration of the interpreter. It is doubtful that one could find a better example of this insightful observation than that of Gray.

To effectively repeal the RAP, the ideological components born of Gray's personality as applied to his RAP must be identified, uncovered, and confronted. In some respects, the revisions of the Rule in the late 1970s constituted an attempt to accomplish that objective without focusing on Gray. Most likely the RAP will be repealed within lives in being. What is uncertain is whether the academy will attend the burial.

One necessarily tends to become invested in that which is the focus of one's energies and in the product of one's intellectual creation. Not surprisingly, this intellectual creation becomes an extension of one's being. Thus, the intensity of focus produces within and without the oneness of being—the person and the rule are one. John Chipman Gray *is* the Rule Against Perpetuity.

---

23. *See* John T. Noonan Jr., Persons and the Masks of the Law: Cardozo, Holmes, Jefferson and Wythe as Makers of the Masks, at xv (First California Paperback 2002) (1976) (emphasis added).

Appendix A

Butler's Note

At the end of this Work it may not be improper to present the reader with a succinct account of the rise, progress, and actual state of the Law of England, respecting the settlement of entail of Real and Personal Property. With this view, an attempt will be made to give,—1st. A general outline of the variations of the English law respecting the settlement of real estate,—2dly. A short statement of the original principle of the law of perpetuity,—3dly. Its application to the entail of real and personal estate, and its ultimate result;—and 4thly. Mention will then be made of the laws of some other nations respecting the entail of landed property, and some miscellaneous observations offered on the general tendency and effect of the English law of entail.

I. Under the feudal polity, as it stood in its original simplicity, when land was granted to a man and his heirs, the lord was entitled to the services of his tenant, and to the reverter of the land, if the tenant died without heirs; the tenant was entitled to the actual enjoyment of the land, and its warranty and acquittal by the lord; and the heir was entitled to the inheritance, on the decease of the tenant; but the heir derived his title, under the terms of the grant, and was therefore said to claim the fee above, not under his ancestor. Thus, land was then subject to the three distinct rights of the lord, the tenant, and the heir. And though the lord and the tenant might join in the disposition of the inheritance, yet, the concurrence of the heir in such disposition not being to be had, as in the view of the law he did not exist in the lifetime of the ancestor, it was, therefore, *wholly inalienable, and consequently could not be modified into any form of settlement.* The feudal incidents of dower and curtsey were attached by law to estates of inheritance, and were the only provisions that could be claimed against the lord or the heir.

By degrees, the rights of the lord and the heir, so far as they restrained the tenant's alienation of the land, ceased to be considered: it is supposed that, as early as the reign of Henry the Third, a free alienation of land was allowed.

2. This general power of alienation introduced *Conditional Fees*; one species of them was formed by a grant of land to a person and the heirs of his body. This mode of limitation operated as a settlement of the land, so far, that till the done had issue inheritable under it, he could not alien or charge the land;

but after he had issue, the condition was supposed to be performed, and he might dispose of it at his pleasure: if he made no such disposition, the land descended to the heirs, of the body of the grantee; and, on a failure of such heirs, it reverted to the lord. This was the first attempt in our law, at a settlement of real property; and Bracton, 2 lib. c. 6. fol. 18. b., mentions that these limitations might be so far multiplied, that, on failure of heirs of the body of the first done, the land might be successively limited to others and the heirs of their bodies.

3. But, after the grantee had issue, he and every person, who came into possession of the land, under such a grant, might dispose of it, and thus neither the heir nor the donor had any security for its devolving to him. Therefore, the statute of the 13 Edw. I., commonly called the statute *de donis conditionalibus*, was passed: it made the alienation of such property unlawful, and thus secured it to the heirs, while there were heirs to succeed, and on failure of heirs, to the lord. This gave rise to the settlement of real property by way of *Estates tail and Remainders.*

Thus a considerable restraint arose on the alienation of property, and a large proportion of the land of the kingdom was taken out of commerce. To evade this restraint, Fines and Recoveries were introduced; by the former, the issue in tail, by the latter, both the issue in tail and the persons in remainder and reversion, might be barred of their estates, and the tenant in tail might acquire the fee simple of the land.

4. Estates tail and remainders over being thus completely subjected to the power of the tenant in tail, a further extension and security of settlement was made, by limiting the land to a person for his life, and *entailing it, after his decease, on his children.* But this was found to leave the children too much at the parent's mercy; for, while there was no such child in existence, the tenant for life might destroy the limitations to the children; and, if the inheritance was vested in him, might by his own act, and if not vested in him, then with the concurrence of the person in whom it was vested in remainder or reversion, acquire the absolute ownership of the fee.

5. To remedy this, *the limitation to trustees for preserving contingent remainders*, was introduced about the time of the Commonwealth. That limitation supports the remainders to the children, and all other remainders in contingency, against the acts of the tenant for life. On this footing, the settlement of real property, by way of remainder, continues at this day.

6. A new mode of settlement of real property gradually found its way into the jurisprudence of England, by the introduction of Executory Uses. By these, on a given event, land, which had been limited or permitted to descend to a person, might be divested from him and vested in another. Such limitations might

take effect either on an event specified in the instrument prescribing it, or by a future direction of the party himself, or of some person appointed by him. When they were limited in the latter mode, they were termed Powers. Such are the powers of jointuring, of charging with portions, or leasing, of making exchanges and sales, now generally inserted in settlements.

Thus, a settlement of real property, as it is now usually framed, either by deed or will, operates partly by way of remainder, and partly by way of executory use. So far as the limitations created estates for years, for life, in tail, or in fee simple, to take effect after the regular expiration of previous estates, the settlement operates by way of remainder; so far as the limitations create estates for years, for life, in tail, or in fee simple, which determine estates previously created, the settlement operates by way of executory use.

II. The reception of executory uses into the law of England gave rise to that important part of its jurisprudence which respects the *doctrine of perpetuity, or excessive restraint on alienation.* No question of perpetuity could arise at the common law, or under the statute *de donis.* It has been shown, that, after the statute *de donis,* and before the introduction of executory uses, future estates could only be created by way of remainder. The remoteness of a remainder, however great, was no objection to it, on its creation. If the event, upon which it was to vest, took place during the continuance of the preceding estate, or at the instant of its determination, the remainder would vest in possession immediately on the determination of the preceding estate; if the event did not take place during the continuance of the preceding estate, or at the instant of its determination, the remainder would wholly fail of effect: during this period, therefore, of our law, all inquiry respecting perpetuity was out of question.

The cases of a possibility upon a possibility, (see *ante* page 251,) may be considered as exceptions from the rule. They proceeded on a different ground, and gave rise to this important rule, that if land is limited to an unborn person during his life, a remainder cannot be limited, so as to confer an estate by purchase on that person's issue.

After the introduction of executory uses, the question of perpetuity necessarily forced itself on the attention of the courts. The introduction of fines, and still more, the introduction of recoveries, which originated in an arbitrary decision of the Judges, in direct opposition to a positive statute, sufficiently shewed that such a modification of property, as rendered it perpetually inalienable, or postponed the power of alienating it to a period excessively remote, would not be endured. It was, therefore, incumbent on the courts to fix the boundary, beyond which executory limitations should not be permitted to operate. In fixing it, they proceeded by way of analogy to the legal effect of remainders at common law, in postponing the exercise of powers of alienation.

The usual effect of such a settlement was to limit the lands to a person during his life, with an immediate remainder to his children or some of them in tail. In all such cases, the tenant for life was in existence when the settlement began to operate; and it has been stated that the law did not allow such limitations of it as conferred a life estate on his children, with remainders in tail to their children.

Thus the utmost restraint upon alienation, which the law, as it stood after the statute *de donis*, allowed in the settlement of real property, was the limitation of one or more life estates to persons in being, and a limitation of one or more estates tail in remainder expectant on the expiration of the preceding estate or estates for life.

A power of alienation by fine or recovery was inseparably inherent to the seisin of an estate tail; but the exercise of it was necessarily suspended during the minority of a tenant in tail. Supposing, therefore, an estate to be limited in the usual manner to the father for life, remainder to his sons successively in tail, and that the father died leaving an only son just born, or his wife enseint, the land would be inalienable during the life of the tenant for life, and after his decease would remain inalienable during 21 years, (the term of the son's minority,) with a possible protraction of that term for a few months, to allow for the period of gestation. This was the utmost period to which the restraint on alienation could be protracted. In reference to this obvious case, and without perplexing the general law on the subject by a further attempt at analogy, the courts, by a long series of determinations, fixed the actual boundary of executory limitation at an event so limited, that it must, from its nature, either take effect or become incapable of taking effect within the period of one or more life or lives in being, and a further term of 21 years, with an allowance of a few months, or at the immediate expiration of that period.

But, as it was understood that an executory use ingrafted on an estate tail was liable to be defeated by the recovery of the tenant in tail, it was obvious that the danger of perpetuity did not arise on such limitations. Leaving, therefore, at large, those executory limitations which were ingrafted on estates tail, the courts required that those executory limitations should be confined within the boundary assigned, which were ingrafted on estates in fee simple, permitted to descend or actually limited.

III. It has been mentioned, that our law never allowed of limitations of *Personal Estate* by way of remainder, in the proper sense of that word. It is observable, that, while the civil law, in respect to heirship and alienation, and the other general rights of property, makes little perceptible distinction between real and personal estate, except in the term of prescription, the nature of them is the English law is wholly dissimilar, and scarcely any rule of law which applies to the one is applicable to the other. This is owing to the universality which prevails in England, of the law of tenure, in which personal estate is of no account.

Hence probably it proceeded, that, till a late period of our law, personal property was not considered to be susceptible of modification. When, at length, it attracted the attention of the courts, it was held, that it could only be settled by way of executory bequest or executory trust, and that executory bequests and executory trusts of it should be confined within the period assigned for the boundary of executory limitations ingrafted on estates in fee simple.

Thus the general result of the English system of the modification of property is, that both real and personal estate may be so far fixed in settlement as to be confined in a particular course of devolution, and rendered absolutely inalienable, during one life, or any given number of lives in being at the same time, and a further period of 21 years and a few months; but that, at the end of this period, the property again becomes open to alienation, with this difference, that, at the end of the period, the real estate must either vest in some person for an absolute estate in fee simple, which includes a general power of alienation, or must vest in some person for an estate tail: in which latter case, by a fine or common recovery, he may acquire the absolute fee; but at the end of the same period, personal estate must vest absolutely.

IV. *The law of other countries* is different. In Scotland a tailzie of simple destination limits the estate in a particular line of devolution, subject to a full power of alienation in each successive possessor; a tailzie with prohibitory clauses, limits the estate in the same manner, but it may be disposed of or charged for a valuable consideration, and it is attachable by creditors, unless the substitutes or persona in remainder, by a process, which is called an inhibition, secure their rights against future debts or contracts; a tailzie with irritant and resolutive clauses, is a strict entail which cannot be opened.

In the civil law, entail finally rested on the 159th Novel, by which it was stopped at the fourth degree, including the party himself who instituted the substitution. The Ordonnance of 1747, fixed the French law of entail to two degrees: the Code Napoleon, Art. 896, prohibits all substitutions, with an exception (Art. 1048,) in favour of parents, who are authorized to give life estates to their children, and to limit over the property absolutely to the children of those children; and a further exception (Art. 1049) which authorizes persons who die without issue, to give life estates to their brothers and sisters, or any of them, and to limit over the property absolutely to the children of those brothers and sisters.

Whatever may be the merit of those laws, it seems clear, that, whether it be considered in reference to the general polity of the country, or in reference to the objects of individuals, the English system of the settlement of property has a wise and salutary tendency. The limits, within which it confines the restraints on alienation, prevent the subtraction from commerce of an undue proportion of the national wealth, and leave as much of it for circulation as is sufficient to answer the wants of those who wish to purchase; and while a perpetual entail is avoided, such an entail may be framed as will effect all those provisions, which it is consistent with the limited reach of human prudence to design; and, when the entail is discharged, it most frequently happens that the rights or views of the parties interested in the property, lead wholly or partially to a renewal of the entail; and thus, while individuals have the means of effecting reasonable arrangements, that succession of respectable proprietors is preserved, which conduces so much to public and private happiness.

Appendix B

Students' Letter to Gray

Dear Professor Gray,

We were all very much surprised to learn that you could not teach us any longer in Property III and very much disappointed. This part of the law has become so closely associated with your name that we have looked forward all through the School course to studying it with you. We are very glad indeed that we could have you for the first half of the year. It has meant a great deal to us. We could not tell you at the time how much we thought of you, but these hours with you have been something to remember all our lives. It is not only the solid legal reasoning that we shall recall, but the insight you have given us into the minds of testators and judges and your whole attitude toward the law. We hope that the gift we are sending may express some of our gratitude and appreciation. We wish that we may often meet you in the School during the spring, while you are working on the new book, to whose publication we are all looking forward.

James B. Waller, Jr.
George S. Raup.
Leonard C. Bigelow
Joseph H. Henderson
J.W. Eckelberry
Samuel Spring
Joseph B. Keenan.
George Swift Brengle.
Maxwell Barus.
Allen T. Klots.
Z. Chafee Jr.
R. C. Brewster
Walter S. Bartlett
Harris H. Gilman
Louis A. Susdorff, Jr.
Oscar R. Ewing
W. M. Spencer, Jr.
J. C. Spicer
Earle T. Fiddler
H. S. Cragin
F. S. Wyner
LeRoy P. Perry
Roger Sherman
Walter S. Logan

George S. Harrison.
Richard K. Hawes
W. H. Hoover
Horace Guild.
Stephen H. Phillips.
Richard S. Fellows
Alexander Wheeler
Robert A. Haven.
Ruthven A. Wodell.
Edwin Merrick Dodd Jr
Richard S. Holmes
John Fine
Stafford F. Johnson
Donald G. Lamont.
Frank B. Ober
Alan C. Van Fleet.
Frank W. Sullivan
Thomas Amory Lee
Max Thorp
Warren H. Pillsbury
M. P. Mackenzie
H. Ralph Cover
R. W. Perkins, Jr.
W H Butler

J. W. Foster
H F Bruning
R. M. Page
H. P. Fowler
H. W. Ampaul
Robert A. Taff
S. A. Leventall
Charles W. Hatch
Silas Williams
George W. Ryley

and all other members of the class in Property III.

Appendix C

Gray's Appreciation of Students' Letter

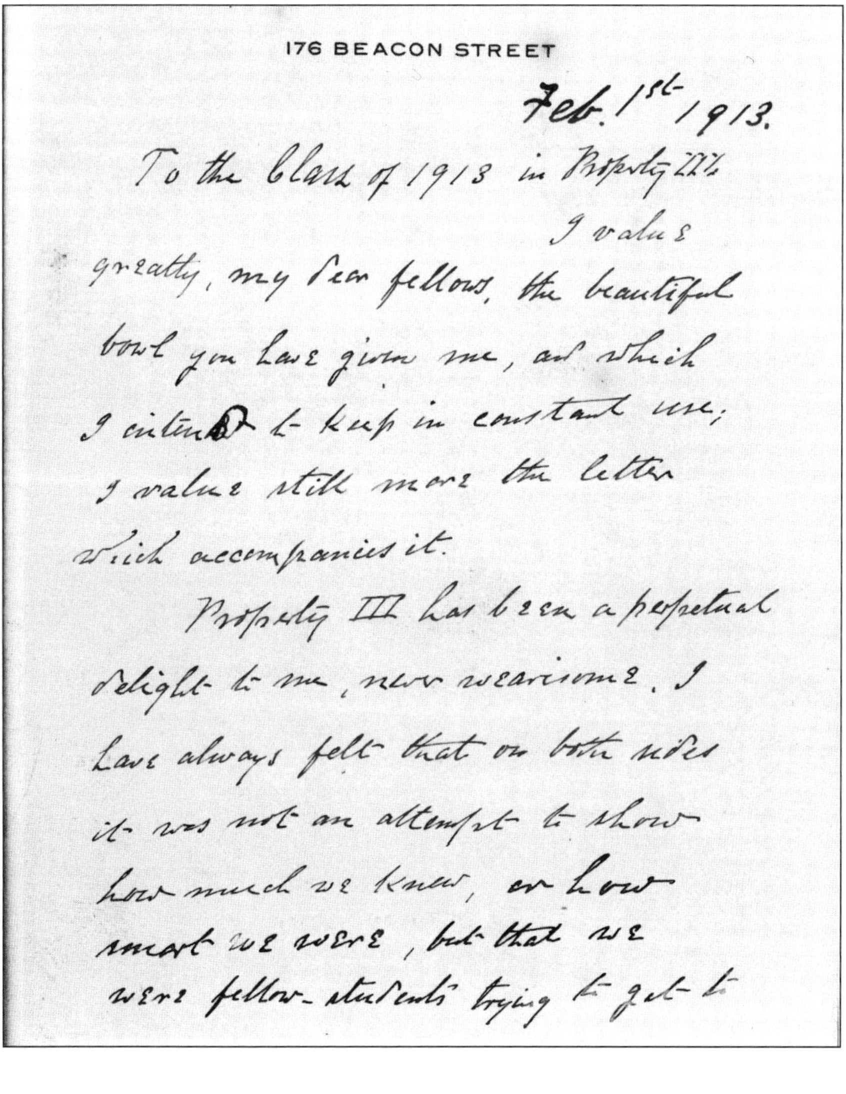

176 BEACON STREET

Feb. 1st 1913.

To the Class of 1913 in Property III.

I value greatly, my dear fellows, the beautiful bowl you have given me, and which I intend to keep in constant use; I value still more the letter which accompanies it.

Property III has been a perpetual delight to me, never wearisome. I have always felt that on both sides it was not an attempt to show how much we knew, or how smart we were, but that we were fellow-students trying to get to the bottom of a difficult subject.

I made up my mind some time ago that you would be my last class, and I determined that my swan song should be my best; I was much disappointed that it seemed wisest for me to stop now.

I want to bespeak your good will to my successor for the rest of the year. He is a better lawyer than I am.

With my best wishes for your success and happiness, I am

Yours most sincerely,

John Chipman Gray.

Bibliography

Cases and Statutes

13 Edw. I, c. 1 (1285) *De Donis Conditionalabis*
Broadway Nat'l Bank v. Adams, 133 Mass. 170 (1882)
Brooks v. Codman, 162 U.S. 439 (1896)
Cadell v. Palmer, (1833) 1 Cl. & F. 372
Callins v. Collins, 510 U.S. 1141 (1994)
Catskill Bank v. Gray,14 Barb. 471, (N.Y. Sup. Ct. 1851)
Codman v. Brooks, 34 N.E. 689 (Mass. 1893)
Conro v. Gray, 4 How. Pr. 166 (N.Y. Gen. Term 1852)
Del. Code Ann. tit. 25, §503 (2009)
Dred Scott v. Sandford, 60 U.S. 393 (1856)
The Duke of Norfolk's Case, (1682) 22 Eng. Rep. 931, 3 Ch.Cas.1 (Ch.)
Edgerly v. Barker, 31 A. 900 (1891)
Fla. Stat. §689.225 (2)(f) (2009)
Fitchie v. Brown, 211 U.S. 321 (1908)
Fisher v. Minot, 76 Mass. (10 Gray) 260 (Mass. 1857)
Frost, (1890) 43 Ch.D. 246
Gray v. Coffin, 63 Mass. (9 Cush.) 192 (Mass. 1852)
Gray v. United States, 21 Ct. Cl. 340 (1886)
Herring v. Boston Iron Co., 67 Mass (1 Gray) 1345 (Mass. 1854)
Julliard v. Greeman, 110 U.S. 421 (1884)
Kevern v. Williams, (1832) 5 Sim. 171
Kuhn v. Fairmont Coal Co., 215 U.S. 349, 370 (1910)
Law of Real Property Act, 15 & 16 Geo. 5 1925, c. 20. §161 (Eng.)
Leake v. Robinson, (1817) 2 Mer. 363
Lochner v. New York, 198 U.S. 45 (1905)
Mass. Gen. Laws ch. 184, §3 (2009)
Melledge v. Boston Iron Co., 59 Mass. 158 (Mass. 1849)
Merchants' Loan & Trust Co. v. Smietanka, 255 U.S. 509 (1921)
Nebbia v. New York, 291 U.S. 502 (1934)

Nichols v. Eaton, 91 U.S. 716 (1876)
Odell v. Odell, 92 Mass. (10 Allen) 1 (1865)
OHIO REV. CODE ANN. §2131.09(B) (West 2009)
Pac. Nat'l Bank v. Windram, 133 Mass. 175 (1882)
Pells v. Brown, (1620) 79 Eng. Rep. 504 (K.B.)
Plessy v. Ferguson, 163 U.S. 537, 552 (1896)
Re Powell's Trusts, (1869) 39 L.J. Ch. 188
Proceedings of Horace Gray, Jr., Memorial, 182 Mass. 613 (1903)
Prohibitions del Roy, (1607) 77 Eng. Rep. 1342 (K.B.), 12 Co. Rep. 64
Rous v. Jackson, (1885) 29 Ch.D. 521
Scott v. Bank One Trust Co., 577 N.E.2d 1077 (Ohio 1991)
Statutum de viris religiosis, 1279, 7 Edw. 1, c.13 (Eng.)
Statutes of Uses, 1535, 27 Hen. 8, c. 10 (Eng.)
Taltarum's Case, (1472) Y. B. 12 Edw. 4, pl. 25
Thomas v. Minot, 76 Mass. (10 Gray) 263 (1857)
Tremlett v. Hooper, 76 Mass. (10 Gray) 254 (1857)
Whitby v. Mitchell, (1890) 42 Ch.D. 494

Books and Articles

CHARLES FRANCIS ADAMS, PROCEEDINGS FROM MASSACHUSETTS HISTORICAL SOCIETY Vol. XVI 1903)
GREGORY S. ALEXANDER, COMMODITY & PROPRIETY: COMPETING VISIONS OF PROPERTY IN AMERICAN THOUGHT 1776–1970 (1997)
Gregory S. Alexander, *The Transformation of Trusts as a Legal Category, 1800–1914,* 5 LAW & HIST. REV. 303 (1987)
A MEMOIR OF THE LIFE OF JOHN CODMAN ROPES, LL.D. (Privately Published 1900)
James Barr Ames, *Professor Langdell—His Services to Legal Education,* 20 HARV. L. REV. 12 (1906)
Peter A. Appel, *The Embarrassing Rule Against Perpetuities,* 54 J. LEGAL EDUC. 264 (2004)
Hamilton Vaughn Bail, *Harvard's Commemoration Day July 21, 1865,* 15 NEW ENGLAND Q. 256 (July 1942)
J. H. BAKER, AN INTRODUCTION TO ENGLISH LEGAL HISTORY (1971)
LIVA BAKER, THE JUSTICE FROM BEACON HILL (1991)
Joseph H. Beale, *John Chipman Gray,* 28 HARV. L. REV. 548 (1915)
Joseph H. Beale, *Langdell, Gray, Thayer, and Ames—Their Contributions to the Study and Teaching of Law,* 8 N.Y.U. L.Q. 385 (1930–1931)

Joseph H. Beale, Jr., *Professor Langdell—His Later Teaching Days*, 20 HARV. L. REV. 9 (1907)

Michael R. Belknap, *From Pound to Harley: The Founding of AJS*, 72 JUDICATURE 78, (1988)

HAROLD J. BERMAN, LAW AND REVOLUTION: THE FORMATION OF THE WESTERN LEGAL TRADITION (1983)

Wayne R. Bettner, *The Rule Against Perpetuities As Applied To Powers Of Appointment*, 27 VA. L. REV. 149 (1940)

FRANCIS BIDDLE, MR. JUSTICE HOLMES (1942)

Robert Bloom, Deputy Administrative Assistant to the Supreme Judicial Court Justices, *The Origin of the Supreme Judicial Court Law Clerk System*, http://sjclawclerks.socialaw.com/history.htm

Book Notices, 14 AM. L. REV. 233 (1880)

CATHERINE DRINKER BOWEN, FRANCIS BACON: THE TEMPER OF A MAN 140 (1963)

Catherine Drinker Bowen, The Lion *and* The Throne: The Life and Times of Sir Edward Coke (1552–1634) (4th Printing 1957)

ALBERT BOYDEN, ROPES-GRAY 1865–1940 (Privately Printed by Lincoln & Smith Press of Boston 1942)

Louis D. Brandeis, *The Harvard Law School*, 1 GREEN BAG 10 (1889)

CARL M. BRAUER, ROPES & GRAY (1991)

Bregy, *A Defense of Pennsylvania's Statute on Perpetuities*, 23 TEMP. L.Q. 313 (1950)

GEORGE A. BRUCE, THE TWENTIETH REGIMENT OF MASSACHUSETTS VOLUNTEER INFANTRY 1861–1865 (Houghton, Mifflin & Co. 1906)

E. H. BURN, CHESHIRE & BURN'S MODERN LAW OF REAL PROPERTY (16th ed. 2000) (1925)

Keith L. Butler, Comment, *Long Live the Dead Hand: A Case for Repeal of the Rule Against Perpetuities in Washington*, 75 WASH. L. REV. 1237 (2000)

WILLIAM SEAL CARPENTER, FOUNDATIONS OF MODERN JURISPRUDENCE (1958)

Paul D. Carrington, *A Tale of Two Lawyers*, 91 NW. U. L. REV. 615 (1997)

Paul D. Carrington, *The Revolutionary Idea of University Legal Education*, 31 WM. & MARY L. REV. 527 (1990)

2 HAMPTON L. CARSON, THE SUPREME COURT OF THE UNITED STATES: ITS HISTORY AND ITS CENTENNIAL CELEBRATION (1891)

James Casner, *In Memoriam: W. Barton Leach*, 85 HARV. L. REV. 717 (1972)

H.W. Challis, *Determinable Fees*, 3 L.Q.R. 403 (1887)

RON CHERNOW, THE HOUSE OF MORGAN; AN AMERICAN BANKING DYNASTY AND THE RISE OF MODERN FINANCE (Grove Press 2001) (1990)

Ronald Chester, *Modification and Termination of Trusts in the 21st Century: The Uniform Trusts Code Leads to a Quiet Revolution* 35 REAL PROP. PROB. & TR. J. 729 (2001)

George C. Christie & Patrick H. Martin, Jurisprudence (2008)

1 GILBERT J. CLARK, LIFE SKETCHES OF EMINENT LAWYERS (Fred B. Rothman & Co. 1983)

CHARLES HORTON COOLEY, HUMAN NATURE AND THE SOCIAL ORDER (1902)

BURKE DAVIS, THE CIVIL WAR: STRANGE & FASCINATING FACTS (1988)

Elbridge B. Davis & Harold A. Davis, *Mr. Justice Horace Gray: Some Aspects of His Judicial Career*, 41 A.B.A. J. 421 (1955)

KENNETH EDWARD DIGBY, HISTORY OF THE LAW OF REAL PROPERTY (1892)

JOHN PATRICK DIGGINS, THE PROMISE OF PRAGMATISM: MODERNISM AND THE CRISIS OF KNOWLEDGE AND AUTHORITY (1994)

Joel C. Dobris, *The Death of the Rule Against Perpetuities, or RAP Has No Friends—An Essay* 35 REAL PROP., TR. & EST. L.J. 601 (2000)

Joel C. Dobris, *Undoing Repeal of the Rule Against Perpetuities: Federal and State Tools for Breaking Dynasty Trusts*, 27 CARDOZO L. REV. 2537 (2006)

JOHN H. DRYFHOUT, THE WORKS OF AUGUSTUS SAINT-GAUDENS (1982)

Jesse Dukeminier, *A Modern Guide to Perpetuties*,74 CAL. L. REV. 1867 (1986)

Jesse Dukeminier, Jr., *Kentucky Perpetuities Law Restated and Reformed*, 49 KY. L.J. 3 (1960)

Jesse Dukeminier, *Perpetuities: Measuring Years* 85 COLUM. L. REV. 1648 (1985)

Jesse Dukeminier, *Perpetuities: The New Empire-The Modern Rule Against Perpetuities*, 77 YALE L.J. 159 (1967)

JESSE DUKEMINIER, ET AL., PROPERTY (6th ed. 2006)

Jesse Dukeminier, *The Uniform Statutory Rule Against Perpetuities: Ninety Years in Limbo*, 34 UCLA L. REV. 1023 (1987)

JESSE DUKEMINIER & JAMES KRIER, PROPERTY (5th ed. 2002)

Jesse Dukeminier & James E. Krier, *The Rise of The Perpetual Trust*, 50 UCLA L. REV. 1303 (2003)

JESSE DUKEMINIER, ROBERT H. SITKOFF & JAMES LINDGREN, WILLS, TRUSTS, AND ESTATES (8th ed. 2009)

H.W.E., *Review of The Rule Against Perpetuities*, 2 L.Q.R. 394 (1886)

Editorials, 5 YALE L.J. 143 (1895)

EUGEN EHRLICH, FUNDAMENTAL PRINCIPLES OF THE SOCIOLOGY OF LAW (Transaction Publishers 2001) (1922)

Charles W. Eliot, *Langdell and the Law School*, 33 HARV. L. REV. 518 (1920)

HOWARD W. ELPHINSTONE & FREDERICK T. MAW, THE MODERN LAW OF REAL PROPERTY (5th ed. Sweet & Maxwell 1906)

BETTY G. FARRELL, ELITE FAMILIES CLASS AND POWER IN NINETEENTH CENTURY BOSTON (1993)

DREW GILPIN FAUST, THIS REPUBLIC OF SUFFERING: DEATH AND THE AMERICAN CIVIL WAR (2008)

Charles Fearne, An Essay on the Learning of Contingent Remainders and Executory Devises (Charles Butler & Josiah W. Smith eds., 10th ed. 1844)

Mary Louise Fellows, *Testing Perpetuity Reforms: A Study of Perpetuity Cases 1984–89*, 25 Real Prop. Prob. & Tr. J. 597 (1991)

Mary Louise Fellows, *Why the Generation-Skipping Transfer Tax Sparked Perpetual Trusts*, 27 Cardozo L. Rev. 2511 (2006)

Franklin G. Fessenden, *The Rebirth of Harvard Law School* 33 Harv. L. Rev. 493 (1920)

3 Shelby Foote, The Civil War A Narrative: Red River to Appomattox (1974)

War Letters 1862–1865: John Chipman Gray *Major, Judge Advocate* and John Codman Ropes *Historian of the War* (Worthington Chauncey Ford ed., 1927)

Jabez Fox, *The Criticism Of Cases*, 6 Harv. L. Rev. 195 (1892)

Jerome Frank, Law and the Modern Man (Coward-McCann 1970) (1930)

Felix Frankfurter, *Samuel Williston: An Inadequate Tribute to A Beloved Teacher*, 76 Harv. L. Rev. 1321 (1963)

Felix Frankfurter, *Some Reflections on the Reading of Statutes*, 47 Colum. L. Rev. 527 (1947)

Lawrence M. Friedman, History of the American Law (1985)

Lawrence M. Friedman, *The Dynastic Trust*, 73 Yale L.J. 547 (1964)

3 The Justices of the United States Supreme Court, Their Lives and Opinions (Leon Friedman & Fred Israel eds., 1997)

Thomas P. Gallanis, *The Future of Future Interests*, 60 Wash. & Lee L. Rev. 513 (2003)

Joseph Gold, *General Testamentary Powers and the Rule against Perpetuities*, 58 L.Q. R. 400 (1942)

Paul Goodman, *Ethics and Enterprise: The Values of a Boston Elite, 1800–1860*, 18 Am. Q. 437 (1966)

Lyndall Gordon, A Private Life of Henry James: Two Women and His Art (1998)

Anna Lyman Gray, Along the Road (1930)

Anna Lyman Gray, The Magi Brought From Foreign Parts (1918)

Edward Gray, William Gray of Salem (1914)

Horace Gray, *Notes*, 36 Amer. L. Rev. 886 (1902)

Horace Gray & John Lowell, *The Case of Dred Scott*, 10 Monthly L. Rep. 10 (1857)

J.C. Gray, *Cases and Treatises*, 22 Am. L. Rev. 756 (1888)

J.C. Gray, *Determinable Fees*, 3 L.Q.R. 399 (1887)

John Chipman Gray, *General and Particular Intent in Connection with the Rule Against Perpetuities*, 9 Harv. L. Rev. 242 (1895)

John Chipman Gray, *General Testamentary Powers and the Rule Against Perpetuities*, 26 Harv. L. Rev. 720 (1913)

John Chipman Gray, Restraints on the Alienation of Property (2d ed., Rothman & Co. 1997) (1883)

1 John Chipman Gray, Select Cases and Other Authorities on the Law of Property (2d ed. 1905)

John C. Gray, *Some Definitions and Questions in Jurisprudence*, 6 Harv. L. Rev. 21 (1892)

John Chipman Gray, The Nature and Sources of the Law (1909)

John Chipman Gray, The Nature and Sources of the Law (2d ed., Beacon Press 1963) (1909)

John Chipman Gray, *Remoteness of Charitable Gifts*, 7 Harv. L. Rev. 406 (1894)

John Chipman Gray, Restraints on The Alienation of Property (2d ed., Rothman & Co. 1997) (1883)

John Chipman Gray, The Rule Against Perpetuities (1886)

John Chipman Gray, The Rule Against Perpetuities (2d ed. 1906) (1886)

John Chipman Gray, The Rule Against Perpetuities (3d ed. 1915) (1886)

John Chipman Gray, The Rule Against Perpetuities (Roland Gray ed., 4th ed. 1942) (1886)

John Chipman Gray, Whitby v. Mitchell *Once More*, 29 L.Q.R. 26 (1913)

John Chipman Gray & John Codman Ropes, War Letters 1862–1865 (Riverside Press 1927).

Robert Gray, Amy Heard: Letters from the Gilded Age (2005)

Roland Gray, John Chipman Gray, Memoir (Privately Printed 1917)

Michael Steven Green, *Legal Realism as Theory of Law*, 46 Wm. & Mary L. Rev. 1915 (2005)

Thomas C. Grey, *Judicial Review and Legal Pragmatism*, 38 Wake Forest L. Rev. 473 (2003)

Thomas C. Grey, *Langdell's Orthodoxy*, 45 Pitt. L. Rev. 1 (1983)

Erwin N. Griswold, *Bart Leach*, 85 Harv. L. Rev. 723 (1972)

35 Halsbury's Laws of England (4th ed. 1981)

Charles Harpum (Robert Megarry & William Wade), The Law of Real Property (6th ed. 2000)

Harvard Memorial Biographies Vol. 1 (1867)

George L. Haskins, *Extending the Grasp of the Dead Hand: Reflections on the Origins of the Rule Against Perpetuities*, 126 Univ. Pa. L. Rev. 19 (1977)

George L. Haskins, *"Inconvenience" and the Rule for Perpetuities*, 48 Mo. L. Rev. 451 (1983)

Davis J. Hayton, Hayton and Marshall Commentaries and Cases on the Law of Trusts and Equitable Remedies (11th ed. 2001)

MARY THACHER HIGGINSON, THOMAS WENTWORTH HIGGINSON: THE STORY OF HIS LIFE (1914)

THOMAS WENTWORTH HIGGINSON, ARMY LIFE IN A BLACK REGIMENT (Riverside 1900) (1869)

George F. Hoar, *Memoir of Horace Gray*, Vol. XVIII Proceedings of the Massachusetts Historical Society (Vol. XVIII 1904)

A. HOBHOUSE, THE DEAD HAND: ADDRESSES ON THE SUBJECT OF ENDOWMENTS AND SETTLEMENTS OF PROPERTY (1880)

SIR WILLIAM HOLDSWORTH, A HISTORY OF ENGLISH LAW (1922)

2 SIR WILLIAM HOLDSWORTH, A HISTORY OF ENGLISH LAW (5th Impression 2003) (1903)

3 SIR WILLIAM HOLDSWORTH, A HISTORY OF ENGLISH LAW (5th ed. 1991)

7 SIR WILLIAM HOLDSWORTH, A HISTORY OF ENGLISH LAW (2d ed., 5th Impression 2003) (1925)

SIR WILLIAM S. HOLDSWORTH, ESSAYS IN LAW AND HISTORY (Oxford University Press 1946)

SIR WILLIAM S. HOLDSWORTH, ESSAYS IN LAW AND HISTORY (A.L. Goodhart & H.G. Hanbury eds., LawBook Exchange, Ltd. 1995) (1946)

Oliver Wendell Holmes, Jr., *A Selection of Cases on the Law of Contracts, with a Summary of the Topics Covered by the Cases by C.C. Langdell*, 14 AM L. REV. 233 (1880)

OLIVER WENDELL HOLMES, JR., THE COMMON LAW (1991) (1881)

Oliver Wendell Holmes, Jr., Speech at the Quarter-Millennial Celebration of Harvard College (Nov. 5, 1886), *in* 3 L.Q.R. 118, 122 (1887)

OLIVER WENDELL HOLMES, SR., ELSIE VENNER: A ROMANCE OF DESTINY (1861)

Oliver Wendell Holmes, Sr., *The Professor's Story*, V ATLANTIC MONTHLY NO. XXVII, 88, Jan. 1860

MORTON J. HORWITZ, THE TRANSFORMATION OF AMERICAN LAW 1870–1960: THE CRISIS OF LEGAL ORTHODOXY (1992)

MARK DEWOLFE HOWE, JUSTICE OLIVER WENDELL HOLMES: THE PROVING YEARS (1963)

MARK DEWOLFE HOWE, JUSTICE OLIVER WENDELL HOLMES: THE SHAPING YEARS, 1841–1870 (1957)

JAMES WILLARD HURST, THE GROWTH OF AMERICAN LAW (1950)

Insolvents in Massachusetts, 10 MONTHLY L. REP. 431 (1847)

Jeffrey D. Jackson, *The Selection of Judges in Kansas: A Comparison of Systems*, 69 J. KAN. B. ASS'N 32 (Jan. 2000)

HENRY JAMES, NOTES OF A SON AND BROTHER (1914)

J. COMM. ON TAXATION, 108TH CONG., SUMMARY OF J. COMM. STAFF "OPTIONS TO IMPROVE TAX COMPLIANCE AND REFORM TAX EXPENDITURES"

CHARLES C. JONES, JR., THE SIEGE OF SAVANNAH IN DECEMBER, 1864, AND THE CONFEDERATE OPERATIONS IN GEORGIA: THE THIRD MILITARY DISTRICT OF SOUTH CAROLINA DURING GENERAL SHERMAN'S MARCH FROM ATLANTA TO THE SEA (1875)

Francis R. Jones, *Horace Gray-An Encomium*, 14 THE GREEN BAG 403 (1902)

Albert Martin Kales, *A Modern Dialogue Between Doctor and Student on the Distinction Between Vested and Contingent Remainders*, 24 L.Q.R. 301 (1908)

Albert Martin Kales, *Contingent Future Interests After A Particular Estate Of Freehold*, 21 L.Q.R. 118 (1905)

Albert Martin Kales, Correspondence on the Rule Against Perpetuities, 1904–1913: Finding Aid (Feb. 2006), http://oasis.lib.harvard.edu/oasis/deliver/~law00184.

ALBERT M. KALES, ESTATES, FUTURE INTERESTS AND ILLEGAL CONDITIONS AND RESTRAINTS IN ILLINOIS (2d ed. 1920)

Albert Martin Kales, *General Powers and The Rule Against Perpetuities*, 26 HARV. L. REV. 64 (1912)

A.M. Kales, *Several Problems Of Gray's Rule Against Perpetuities, Second Edition*, 20 HARV. L. REV. 192 (1906)

Albert Martin Kales, *Should The Law Teacher Practice Law?* 25 HARV. L. REV. 253 (1911)

Albert Martin Kales, *The Next Step in the Evolution of the Case-Book*, 21 HARV. L. REV. 92 (1907)

Albert Martin Kales, *Vested And Contingent Remainders*, 8 COLUM. L. REV. 245 (1908)

Albert Martin Kales, *Vested Gifts to a Class and the Rule Against Perpetuities*, 19 HARV. L. REV. 598 (1906)

Laura Kalman, Legal Realism at Yale 1927–1960 (1986)

Andrew L. Kaufman, *Cardozo and the Art of Biography*, 20 CARDOZO L. REV. 1245 (1998)

William A. Keener, *Methods of Legal Education*, 1 YALE L.J. 143 (1893)

William A. Keener, *The Inductive Method in Legal Education*, 28 AM. L. REV. 709 (1894)

Arthur B. Kennickell, Federal Reserve Board, *Ponds and Streams: Wealth and Income in the U.S., 1989 to 2007*, *in* Finance and Economics Discussion Series 2009–13, at 27

JAMES KENT, COMMENTARIES ON AMERICAN LAW (14th ed. 1896)

Bruce A. Kimball, *Langdell on Contracts and Legal Reasoning: Correcting the Holmesian Caricature*, 25 LAW & HIST. REV. 345 (2007)

Bruce A. Kimball, *The Langdell Problem: Historicizing the Century of Historiography, 1906–2000s*, 22 LAW & HIST. REV. 277 (2004)

Bruce A. Kimball, *Young Christopher Langdell, 1826–1854: The Formation of an Educational Reformer*, 52 J. Legal Educ. 189 (2002)

Alfred S. Konesfsky & John Henry Schlegel, *Mirror, Mirror on the Wall: Histories of American Law Schools*, 95 Harv. L. Rev. 833 (1982)

Peter Krass, Carnegie (2002)

John H. Langbein, *Why Did Trust Law Become Statute Law in the United States?*, 58 Ala. L. Rev. 1069 (2007)

C.C. Langdell, *Teaching Law as Science*, 21 Am. L. Rev. 123 (1887)

C.C. Langdell, A Selection on the Law of Contracts (1871)

William P. LaPiana, Logic and Experience: The Origin of Modern American Legal Education (1994)

Law Commission, The Rules Against Perpetuities and Excessive Accumulations, 1998, Report 251

Alexander A. Lawrence, Present for Mr. Lincoln (1997)

W. Barton Leach, Cases and Text on the Law of Wills (2d ed. 1951)

W. Barton Leach, *Perpetuities in a Nutshell*, 51 Harv. L. Rev. 638 (1938)

W. Barton Leach, *Perpetuities in Perspective: Ending the Rule's Reign of Terror*, 65 Harv. L. Rev. 721 (1952)

W. Barton Leach, *Perpetuities Legislation: Hail Pennsylvania!*, 108 U. Pa. L. Rev. 1124 (1960)

W. Barton Leach, *Perpetuities: New Absurdity, Judicial and Statutory Correctives*, 73 Harv. L. Rev. 1318 (1960)

W. Barton Leach, *Perpetuities: New Hampshire Defertilizes the Octogenarians*, 77 Harv. L. Rev. 279 (1963)

W. Barton Leach, *Powers of Sale in Trustees and the Rule Against Perpetuities*, 47 Harv. L. Rev. 948 (1934)

W. Barton Leach, *Perpetuities: The Nutshell Revisited*, 78 Harv. L. Rev. 973 (1965)

W. Barton Leach, *The Rule Against Perpetuities and Gifts To Classes*, 51 Harv. L. Rev. 1329 (1938)

A. H. F. Lefroy, *The Basis of Case-Law*, 22 L.Q.R. 293 (1906)

William David Lewis, A Practical Treatise on the Law of Perpetuity or Remoteness in Limitations of Estates (1843)

Karl Llewellyn, *Some Realism About Realism—Responding to Dean Pound*, 44 Harv. L. Rev. 1222 (1931)

Karl Llewellyn, The Common Law Tradition: Deciding Appeals (1960)

Francis C. Lowell, *Horace Gray*, Proceedings of the American Academy of Arts and Science (Vol. XXXIX 1904)

Robert J. Lynn, The Modern Rule Against Perpetuities (1966)

F.W. Maitland, *The Beatitudes of Seisin*, 4 L.Q.R. 24 (1888)

F.W. Maitland, *The Mystery of Seisin*, 2 L.Q.R. 481 (1886)

F.W. Maitland, *The Seisin of Chattels*, 1 L.Q.R. 324 (1885)

Dr. William P. Marchione, *Horace Gray: Father of the Boston Public Garden*, *available at* http://www.bahistory.org/HoraceGray.html

Reginald G. Marsden, The Rule Against Perpetuities: A Treatise on Remoteness in Limitations, With a Chapter on Accumulation and the Thelluson Act (1883)

Joanne Martin, *The Nature of the property Curriculum in ABA-Approved Schools and Its Place in Real Estate Practice*, 44 Real Prop., Tr. & Est. L.J. 385 (2009)

Alpheus Thomas Mason, Harlan Fisk Stone: Pillar of Law (1956)

Emlin McClain, *The Uses of Cases in Teaching Law*, 3 Yale L.J. 17 (1893)

James M. McPherson, Battle Cry of Freedom (1988)

R.E MeGarry & H.W.R. Wade, The Law of Real Property (1966)

Robert MeGarry & William Wade, The Law of Real Property (Charles Harpum ed., 6th ed. 2000)

Louis Menand, The Metaphysical Club: A Story of Ideas in America (2001)

Richard Miller, Harvard's Civil War: The History of the Twentieth Massachusetts Volunteer Infantry (2005)

Stephen Robert Mitchell, Mr. Justice Horace Gray (1961)

Reid Mitchell, The Vacant Chair (1993)

Gerald P. Moran, *A Radical Theory of Jurisprudence: The "Decisionmaker" as the Source of the Law–The Ohio Supreme Court's Adoption of the Spendthrift Trust Doctrine as a Model*, 30 Akron L. Rev. 393 (1997)

Gerald P. Moran & Craig F. Frederickson, *The Rule Against Perpetuity: The Case for the Exemption or Repeal of the Rule*, 6 Prob. L.J. Ohio 10 (1996)

J.H. C. Morris & W. Barton Leach, The Rule Against Perpetuities (Stevens & Sons 2d ed. 1962)

J.H. C. Morris, *The Rule against Perpetuities and the Rule in* Andrews v. Partington, 70 L.Q.R. 61 (1954)

Gustavus Myers, History of The Supreme Court of The United States (1968)

National Register of Historic Places Inventory—Nomination Form, Boston Public Garden, *available at* http://pdfhost.focus.nps.gov/docs/NHLS/Text/87000761.pdf

Allan Nevis, The War for the Union, Volume One: The Improvised War, 1861–1862 (1959)

Barry Nicholas, An Introduction to Roman Law (1962)

John T. Noonan, Jr., Persons and the Masks of the Law: Cardozo, Holmes, Jefferson and Wythe as Makers of the Masks (First California Paperback 2002) (1976)

Sheldon M. Novick, The Young Master Henry James (1996)

David M. O'Brien, Storm Center (2005)

Patricia O' Toole, The Five of Hearts: An Intimate Portrait of Henry Adams and his Friends, 1880–1918 (1990)

Joel Francis Paschal, Mr. Justice Sutherland: A Man Against The State (1951)

David W. Peck, Decisions at Law (1961)

Edward Pessen, Riches, Class, and Power Before the Civil War (1973)

Plato's Mexnexenus, §9, *reprinted in* Harvard Memorial Biographies ii (Thomas Wentworth Higginson, ed., vol. 1, 1867)

Frederick Pollock, *English Law Reports*, 37 A.L.R. 684 (1903)

1 Sir Frederick Pollock & Frederic William Maitland, The History of English Law: Before the Time of Edward I (2d ed. Cambridge University Press 1968) (1895)

2 Sir Frederick Pollock & Frederic William Maitland, The History of English Law: Before the Time of Edward I (2d ed. Cambridge University Press 1968) (1895)

Roscoe Pound, *Do We Need a Philosophy of Law*, 5 Colum. L. Rev. 339 (1905)

Roscoe Pound, *Fifty Years of Jurisprudence*, 51 Harv. L. Rev. 777 (1938)

Roscoe Pound, *Joseph Henry Beale*, 56 Harv. L. Rev. 695 (1943)

Roscoe Pound, *Mechanical Jurisprudence*, 8 Colum. L. Rev. 605 (1908)

Roscoe Pound, *The Call for Realist Jurisprudence*, 44 Harv. L. Rev. 697 (1931)

Roscoe Pound, *The Need for Sociological Jurisprudence*, 19 Green Bag 607 (1907)

John Phillip Reid, Chief Justice The Judicial World of Charles Doe (1967)

Report of the Thirtieth Annual Meeting of the Am. Bar Ass'n (Lord Baltimore Press 1907)

Robert D. Richardson, William James In The Maelstrom of American Modernism (2006)

Lord Rodger of Earlsferry, *The Form and Language of Judicial Opinions*, 118 L.Q.R. 226 (2002)

John Codman Ropes, The Army Under Pope (1901)

John C. Ropes, *The Campaign of Waterloo*, Scribner's Mag., vol. 3, issue 4, April 1888

Ellen Rothman, Hands and Hearts (1984)

Edward Rubin, *What's Wrong with Langdell's Method, and What to do About It*, 60 Vand. L. Rev. 609 (2007)

C. S., *Limitations of Land to Unborn Generations*, 29 L.Q.R. 304 (1913)

Albert Sacks, *Remembering Austin Scott*, 33 Harv. L. Sch. Bull. 27 (Fall 1981)

FRANCIS W. SANDERS, AN ESSAY ON USES AND TRUSTS (5th ed. 1824)

Max M. Schanzenbach & Robert H. Sitkoff, *Perpetuities or Taxes? Explaining the Rise of the Perpetual Trust*, 27 CARDOZO L. REV. 2465 (2006)

Frederick Schauer, *Formalism*, 97 YALE L.J. 509 (1988)

David J. Seipp, *125th Anniversary Essay of Holmes's Path*, 77 B.U. L. REV. 515 (1997)

JOHN E. SEMONCHE, OXFORD COMPANION TO THE SUPREME COURT OF THE UNITED STATES (Kermit L. Hall, ed. 1992)

Steve Sheppard, *Casebooks, Commentaries, and Curmudgeons: An Introductory History of Law in the Lecture Hall*, 82 IOWA L. REV. 547 (1997)

Stephen A. Siegel, *John Chipman Gray and the Moral Basis of Classical Legal Thought*, 86 IOWA L. REV. 1513 (2001)

Stephen A. Siegel, *John Chipman Gray, Legal Formalism, and the Transformation of Perpetuities Law*, 36 U. MIAMI L. REV. 439 (1982)

LEWIS M. SIMES, HANDBOOK OF THE LAW OF FUTURE INTERESTS (2d ed. 1966)

Lewis M. Simes, *The Policy Against Perpetuities*, 103 U. PA. L. REV. 707 (1955)

LEWIS M. SIMES & ALLAN F. SMITH, THE LAW OF FUTURE INTERESTS (1956)

A.W.B. SIMPSON, A HISTORY OF THE LAND LAW (2d ed. 1986)

A.W. B. SIMPSON, BIOGRAPHICAL DICTIONARY OF THE COMMON LAW (1984)

2 A.W.B. SIMPSON, ENGLISH COMMON LAW, THE NEW PALGRAVE DICTIONARY OF ECONOMICS AND THE LAW (1998)

A. W. BRIAN SIMPSON, LEADING CASES IN THE COMMON LAW, LEGAL SCIENCE AND LEGAL ABSURDITY (Clarendon Press Oxford 1996) (1995)

A. W. Brian Simpson, *Legal Education and Legal History*, 11 OXFORD J. LEGAL STUD. (1991)

A.W. B. SIMPSON, LEGAL THEORY AND LEGAL History: Essays on the Common Law (1987)

Robert H. Sitkoff & Max M. Schanzenbach, *Jurisdictional Competition for Trust Funds: An Empirical Analysis of Perpetuities and Taxes*, 115 YALE L.J. 356 (2005)

ADAM SMITH, AN INQUIRY INTO THE NATURE AND CAUSES OF THE WEALTH OF NATIONS (Encyclopedia Britannica, Inc. 1989) (1776)

John Malcolm Smith, *Mr. Justice Horace Gray of the United States Supreme Court*, 6 S.D. L. REV. 221 (1961)

Robert M. Spector, *Legal Historian on the United States Supreme Court: Horace Gray, Jr., and the Historical Method*, 12 AM. J. LEGAL HIST. 181 (1968)

STAFF OF THE FOUNDATION FOR RESEARCH IN LEGAL HISTORY UNDER THE DIRECTION OF JULIUS GOBEL, JR., A HISTORY OF THE SCHOOL OF LAW COLUMBIA UNIVERSITY (1955)

Jeffrey E. Stake, *Darwin, Donations, and the Illusion of Dead Hand Control*, 64 TUL. L. REV. 705 (1990)

Jeffrey Evans Stake, *The Uneasy Case for Adverse Possession,* 89 GEO. L. J. 2419 (2001)

Stewart E. Sterk, *Jurisdictional Competition to Abolish the Rule Against Perpetuities: RIP For the RAP*, 24 CARDOZO L. REV. 2097 (2003)

Ronald Story, *Harvard and the Boston Brahmins: A Study in Institutional and Class Development,* 8 J. SOC. HIST. 94 (1975)

WILLIAM W. STORY, THE LIFE AND LETTERS OF JOSEPH STORY LAW BOOK EXCHANGE, LTD. (2000) (1851)

Summary of Events, 5 AM. LAW REV. 177 (1870)

Arthur E. Sutherland, Jr., *One Man In His Time*, 78 HARV. L. REV. 7 (1964)

ARTHUR E. SUTHERLAND, THE LAW AT HARVARD (1967)

Charles Sweet, *Contingent Remainders and Other Possibilities*, 27 YALE L.J. 977 (1918)

Charles Sweet, *John Chipman Gray* (ob. *Feb. 25 1915)*, 31 L.Q.R. 338 (1915)

Charles Sweet, *Perpetuities*, 15 L.Q.R. 71 (1899)

Charles Sweet, *Restraints on Alienation II*, 33 L.Q.R. 342 (1917)

Charles Sweet, *The Monstrous Regiment of the Rule Against Perpetuities*, 18 JURID. REV. 132 (1906)

Charles Sweet, *The Rule in* Whitby v. Mitchell, 12 COLUM. L. REV. 199 (1912)

Joshua C. Tate, *Perpetual Trusts and the Settlor's Intent*, 53 U. KAN. L. REV. 595 (2005)

ARLINE BOUCHER TEHAN, HENRY ADAMS IN LOVE: THE PURSUIT OF ELIZABETH SHERMAN CAMERON (1983)

LOUISE HALL THARP, MRS. JACK: A BIOGRAPHY OF ISABELLA STEWART GARDNER (1968)

EZRA R. THAYER, TRIBUTE TO HORACE GRAY, PROCEEDINGS OF THE AMERICAN ACADEMY OF ARTS AND SCIENCES (1904)

Ezra Ripley Thayer, *John Chipman Gray*, 28 HARV. L. REV. 539 (1915)

James Bradley Thayer, *The Teaching of English Law at Universities*, 9 HARV. L. REV. 169 (1895)

THE HARVARD LAW SCHOOL ASS'N, THE CENTENNIAL HISTORY OF THE HARVARD LAW SCHOOL, 1817–1917 (1918)

The Impossible Dream, in MAN OF LA MANCHA (Mitch Leigh & Joe Darion 1965)

The Insolvent Law of Massachusetts, 10 MONTHLY L. REP. 33 (1848)

THE LAW REFORM COMMISSION, REPORT ON THE RULE AGAINST PERPETUITIES AND COGNATE RULES (2000)

THE LAW REFORM COMMISSION, REPORT ON THE VARIATION OF TRUSTS (2000)

THE OXFORD COMPANION TO THE SUPREME COURT OF THE UNITED STATES (Kermit L. Hall et al. eds., 1992)

J.L. Thorndike, *General Powers and Perpetuities*, 27 HARV. L. REV. 705 (1914)

3 HERBERT T. TIFFANY & BASIL JONES, TIFFANY REAL PROPERTY (2009) (1939)

COLM TOIBIN, THE MASTER (Paperback ed. Scribner 2005) (2004)

2 LAWRENCE H. TRIBE, AMERICAN CONSTITUTIONAL LAW (1988)

NOAH ANDRE TRUDEAU, LIKE MEN OF WAR, BLACK TROOPS IN THE CIVIL WAR 1862–1865 (1998)

NOAH ANDRE TRUDEAU, SOUTHERN STORM: SHERMAN'S MARCH TO THE SEA (1st ed. 2008)

MARK TWAIN & CHARLES DUDLEY WARNER, THE GILDED AGE (Library of America 2002) (1873)

WILLIAM L. TWINING, KARL LLEWELLYN AND THE REALIST MOVEMENT (1973)

UNITED STATES DEPARTMENT OF VETERAN AFFAIRS, FACT SHEET: AMERICA'S WARS, NOVEMBER 2008, http://www1.va.gov/opa/fact/amwars.asp

William R. Vance, *Rights of Reverter and the Statue of Quia Emptores*, 36 YALE L.J. 593 (1927)

Lawrence W. Waggoner, *A Perspective of Wait and See*, 85 COLUM. L. REV. 1714 (1985)

Lawrence W. Waggoner, *Perpetuity Reform*, 81 MICH. L. REV. 1718 (1983)

Lawrence W. Waggoner, *The Uniform Statutory Rule Against Perpetuities: The Rationale of the 90-Year Waiting Period*, 73 CORNELL L. REV. 157 (1988)

William F. Walsh, *Legal History in Law School Courses*, 1 ANN. REV. L. SCH. N.Y.U. 3 (1924)

Eugene Wambaugh, *Professor Langdell—A View of His Career*, 20 HARV. L. REV. 1 (1906)

G. Graham Waite, *Let's Abolish the Rule Against Perpetuities*, 21 REAL EST. L.J. 93 (1992)

2 CHARLES WARREN, HISTORY OF THE HARVARD LAW SCHOOL (1909)

Peter D. Webster, *Selection and Retention of Judges*, 23 FLA. ST. U. L. REV. 1 (1995)

Ernest J. Weinrib, *Legal Formalism: On the Immanent Rationality of Law*, 97 YALE L.J. 949 (1988)

G. EDWARD WHITE, JUSTICE OLIVER WENDELL HOLMES—LAW AND THE INNER SELF (1993)

JOSHUA WILLIAMS, PRINCIPLES OF THE LAW OF REAL PROPERTY (T. Cyprian Williams ed.,17th ed. Sweet & Maxwell 1892)

T. Cyprian Williams, *Contingent Remainders and the Rule Against Perpetuities—A Criticism of the Case of* Whitby v. Mitchell, 14 L.Q.R. 234 (1898)

Samuel Williston, *John Chipman Gray*, 28 HARV. L. REV. 544 (1915)

SAMUEL WILLISTON, LIFE AND LAW: AN AUTOBIOGRAPHY 97 (Boston Little Brown 1941)

Thomas L. V. Wilson, Aristocracy of Boston; Who They Are, and What They Were: Being a History of Business and Businessmen of Boston (1848)

Gordon S. Wood, The Purpose of the Past (2009)

John Maxcy Zane, The Story of The Law (The Liberty Fund, Inc. 1998) (1927)

Letters

Letter from Henry Adams, Historian-Scholar Extraordinaire, to John Chipman Gray, Professor, Harvard Law School (Jan. 25, 1885) (on file with the Houghton Library of Harvard College, in the John Chipman Gray Correspondence File, MS Am. 2152 (3), folder ([4]p.)

Letter from John Albien Andrews, Governor, State of Massachusetts, to E. M. Stanton, Secretary of War, (Sept. 5, 1862) (on file with the Houghton Library of the Harvard College, in the John Chipman Gray Correspondence File MS Am. 2152, (8), folder ([2] p.)

Letter from Franklin Bartlett, to Anna Lyman Gray (Apr. 17, 1894) (on file with the Houghton Library of the Harvard College, in the John Chipman Gray Correspondence File, MS Am. 2152, folder 31)

Letter from George Austen Fox, to Mrs. Eleanor [Gray] Tudor (Dec. 26, 1832) (Houghton Library of Harvard College, in the John Chipman Gray Correspondence File, Call No. 2152, folder ([4]p.) (45–47)

Letter from John Chipman Gray, Professor, Harvard Law School, to Charles W. Eliot, President, Harvard College (Jan. 3, 1883) (on file with Harvard University Archives, Box 71, Folder 1883 (G-L))

Letter from Ephraim Gurney, Dean of Faculty, Harvard College, to Charles W. Eliot, President, Harvard College (on file with Harvard University Archives, Presidential Papers, Box 71, folder 1883 G-L)

Index